Walker Percy's Search for Community

JOHN F. DESMOND

Walker Percy's Search for Community

THE UNIVERSITY OF GEORGIA PRESS
Athens & London

© 2004 by the University of Georgia Press
Athens, Georgia 30602
All rights reserved
Designed by Walton Harris
Set in 10.2/13 Minion by Bookcomp, Inc.
Printed and bound by Thomson-Shore
The paper in this book meets the guidelines for permanence
and durability of the Committee on Production Guidelines
for Book Longevity of the Council on Library Resources.
Printed in the United States of America
08   07   06   05   04   C   5   4   3   2   1

Library of Congress Cataloging-in-Publication Data
Desmond, John F.
Walker Percy's search for community / John F. Desmond.
    p. cm.
Includes bibliographical references and index.
ISBN 0-8203-2588-0 (alk. paper)
1. Percy, Walker, 1916– —Criticism and interpretation.
2. Community in literature.   3. Peirce, Charles S. (Charles Sanders),
1839–1914—Influence.   4. Semiotics and literature.   I. Title.
PS3566.E6912 Z655 2004
813'.54—dc22
2003021380

British Library Cataloging-in-Publication Data available

CONTENTS

Acknowledgments ix

List of Abbreviations xi

Introduction 1

ONE   The Footprint on the Beach: *The Moviegoer* 41

TWO   Ground Zero and the Iron Horsehead:
       The Last Gentleman 81

THREE The Thread in the Labyrinth: *Love in the Ruins* 118

FOUR   The Worm of Interest: *Lancelot* 144

FIVE   The Gift of the Word: *The Second Coming* 179

SIX   Community, History, and the Word:
       The Thanatos Syndrome 215

       Epilogue 249

       Notes 259

       Works Consulted 265

       Index 269

ACKNOWLEDGMENTS

A book about community owes its life to a community of scholars, readers, and supporters whose interest inspires and guides the work. I am grateful to the many who have made up this community and have generously supported this project. In particular, I wish to thank Gary Ciuba, Edward Dupuy, Jan Gretlund, Lewis A. Lawson, John R. May, Lewis P. Simpson, and Karl-Heinz Westarp. Each of them in ways spoken and unspoken has directed and shaped my efforts to come to terms with the complex question of community in Percy's writings. Patrick Samway, S.J. has been an invaluable resource and a loyal supporter of my research for longer than I can remember. In addition, I owe a special debt of gratitude to Richard Giannone, who read portions of the book in manuscript and offered astute and stimulating comments that improved it immeasurably.

I wish to thank the National Endowment for the Humanities for awarding me a grant to pursue this project in its early stages. I also want to thank Whitman College and the Faculty Development Committee for their support of this project and for their generous and continuing support of my scholarly efforts. I would also like to thank Nancy Grayson of the University of Georgia Press for her support and commitment to my work, and Sarah McKee for her genial help as project editor. Jeanée Ledoux's copyediting improved the manuscript considerably, and for this I am very grateful.

Finally, I want to thank my wife, Linda, for her steadfast encouragement through the years while I worked on this project, as well as that of our children, Matthew and Monica. Together, they constitute my community *sine qua non*.

ABBREVIATIONS

CP   *Collected Papers of Charles Sanders Peirce*

Con.   *Conversations with Walker Percy*

LL   *Lancelot*

LG   *The Last Gentleman*

LC   *Lost in the Cosmos*

LR   *Love in the Ruins*

MB   *The Message in the Bottle*

More Con.   *More Conversations with Walker Percy*

MG   *The Moviegoer*

SC   *The Second Coming*

SSL   *Signposts in a Strange Land*

TS   *The Thanatos Syndrome*

TP   *A Thief of Peirce*

Walker Percy's Search for Community

Introduction

Sometime during 1976, Walker Percy wrote a poem celebrating his companionship with a small group of friends with whom he shared a weekly lunch at Bechacs restaurant in his hometown of Covington, Louisiana. The poem is titled "Community."

Now comes the artist to his life's surprise—
A fond, abstract middle-aged public man is he,
Come to a place in his time when he thought he knew something.
What?
Namely, that on the short lovely Louisiana afternoons,
The winter sunlight making spaces, pale gold above
And in the live oaks, a shafted gloom like rooms
Of moss and leaf and tenant squirrels and jeweled birds—
He trafficked in loneliness, little brother, cellmate
And friend to him, and even turned it to good use,
A commodity, a good business man selling solitariness
Like GM selling Chevrolets or Burns furniture.
A strange success, this selling to other selves the very
Sealed-offness of self from selves.

Now comes the surprise—
What?
That in the very things he had denied and done so well
Denying—

Friendship, laughter, good red wine (well, anyhow, Early Times)
Marichal [*sic*] merriness, Lyn loveliness—
All the good things we Catholics used to stand for
Until something went wrong—
Did I help them go wrong?
I hope not—I only named the wrongness
Which in a way is to make it right and turn it around.
But what a surprise!
Twenty years of solitariness and success at solitariness,
Solitary with his family like the Swiss family on their island,
Then all at once community.
Community? What, friends out there in the world?
Yes. (Samway, *Walker Percy*, 327–28)

As this little poem suggests, solitariness and community were defining axis points in Walker Percy's life and work. The poem's emphasis on solitude and solitariness certainly reflects Percy's temperamental disposition to be a detached observer of the world. This disposition was reinforced by the difficult circumstances of his early life, by his illness from tuberculosis and the sedentary routine it enforced, by his renouncing an originally chosen profession of medical doctor, and by his vocation as a writer. At the same time, Percy's emphasis on solitariness in the poem reflects his awareness of the tension between solitude and community inherent in the human condition, a tension exacerbated by the increased self-consciousness he perceived in post-Enlightenment Western society. Most of Percy's fictional characters are "loners" in a radical existential sense; for Percy the human community is a "paradoxical" one "whose members are both alone and yet not alone" (SSL, 151). In fact, solitariness as a path to self-scrutiny and self-knowledge is an abiding precondition for community.

Nevertheless, Percy's sense of himself as a solitary being was counterbalanced by the fact that he lived in a web of communities both visible and invisible. By the time he came to write this poem in 1976, Percy had been a Covingtonian for many years, and he enjoyed the company of a close circle of family and friends. Moreover, as his biographers Patrick Samway and Jay Tolson have shown, Percy played an active role within his community—as husband, father, church member, and public citizen. Beyond his hometown, he belonged to an extended community of fellow writers and scholars, as well as a worldwide audience of readers and admirers of his work. An active member of the Catholic

Church since his conversion in 1947, including service on the Pontifical Council for Culture, Percy, along with his wife, Mary Bernice ("Bunt"), joined the religious community of the Third Order of St. Benedict, a community that emphasized the call to solitude within community, shortly before his death. This commitment was a visible sign of his belief in the Catholic community of saints in the mystical body of Christ (Samway, *Walker Percy*, 412). Nevertheless, his lifelong sense of solitariness remained unallayed. It was both personal and, he believed, symptomatic of the general condition of life in modern culture. Hence Percy's "surprise" in the poem at "all at once" discovering community and "friends out there in the world."

Yet if we see Percy's little poem, as I wish to see it, as the expression of a representative American in the latter half of the twentieth century, we can see that it expresses that sense both of personal solitariness and of the tenuousness of community all too familiar as one of the characteristic signs of modern life. But the poem also conveys Percy's joy in the sudden discovery of community. Moreover, it affirms the real possibility and hope of finding some community with others, however fragile, in the face of our radical separateness as humans. With increasing insistence and directness, Percy's novels record this search for community. Both sides of the issue—alienation and separateness, hope and the possibility for communion—reflect the spirit of Percy's obsession (I don't think the word is too strong) with community throughout his career as a writer. Much of his life's work was devoted to examining the fractured state of our actual communities, and to probing our very capacity as humans *for* community. But equally important, his writings were devoted to exploring the ground of genuine community and possible ways to recover it, without which we remain locked within ourselves like the alienated selves Percy depicted in *Lost in the Cosmos.*

The landscapes of Percy's fictions are littered with the rubble of broken, decadent, and pseudo-communities. We see the fading Old South world of noblesse oblige and stoic values represented by Emily Cutrer and her set in *The Moviegoer,* as well as by the elder Barretts and Lamars in *The Last Gentleman, The Second Coming,* and *Lancelot.* Specious and perverse forms of community abound as well: the New South exurbia of the Vaught family; Tom More's Paradise Estates; Lance Lamar's mad, gnostic dream of a utopian community in Virginia; and the Fedville scientists' demonic dream of a pharmacologically "purified" society in *The Thanatos Syndrome.* At the same time, there are small, resilient signs of genuine community, and therefore hope, in Percy's writings: Val Vaught's community among the Tyree children in *The*

Last Gentleman; the senior citizens' community planned by Will Barrett and Allison Huger in *The Second Coming;* the Lost Cove remnant at the end of *Lost in the Cosmos;* and Father Rinaldo Smith's community of the dying in *The Thanatos Syndrome.* All of Percy's fictions show a movement toward some genuine community as the novel ends, even if only between two people, a *solitude à deux,* which is for Percy the bedrock of all human community. Such movements came to be portrayed more explicitly in his later fiction. Moreover, the search for community is implicit throughout his essays as well. And most significantly, in his last public address, the 1989 Jefferson Lecture at the National Endowment for the Humanities, Percy proposed a way to begin to reconcile the scientific and religious communities through the development of a "new anthropology" based on the semiotic concepts of Charles Sanders Peirce. Percy's proposal, as we shall see, offered the hope for reuniting forms of knowledge and experience that have followed divergent paths at least since the late Middle Ages.

My study is an attempt to elucidate Percy's search for community as it unfolds in his novels, principally, and in his other writings. Initially, I want to make two points about my title. First, I use the word "search" in order to emphasize the evolutionary character of Percy's thinking about and representation of the idea of community, partly but not wholly in response to changing conditions in the culture. The theological basis of Percy's beliefs about community and history remained essentially unchanged throughout his writing career. Ontologically, humans are fallen creatures, separated from God; their history can be seen as the record of their attempts to find some redemption from this state. Nevertheless, Percy was constantly examining and "testing" those religious beliefs within the context of a changing society, a generally antipathetic intellectual milieu, and his own periods of personal trial and doubt. Percy's thought evolved in important ways over the course of his career. His deep, existential sense of his own historical moment and of the mystery of things left his searching open ended. Many philosophical, religious, and personal questions remained unanswered, shrouded in mystery, yet open to further exploration. This "openness" is especially true of his ideas on language and his engagement with the thought of Charles Sanders Peirce and its implications. Percy's realistic semiotic is grounded in the dynamic open-endedness of sign relations. Percy struggled to understand Peirce's triadic theory of signs and assimilate it, insofar as was possible, with his Catholic beliefs. In short, I do not subscribe to the view that Percy's thought was "fixed" by the influences of traditionalist Catholic philosophers and theologians or by his reading of Søren Kierkegaard around the time of his conversion in the mid-1940s, or that his subsequent development was simply that of a reactionary religious conservative.[1] Such views of Percy are much too simplistic. Even in his last days, he was still searching for new clues and breakthroughs that might help answer his own restless searching, as well as help a society that he believed had gone adrift. Rather than think of him as a reactionary, I believe it is more accurate to think of Percy as a progressive thinker who searched for ways to unite the best of traditional and contemporary knowledge toward developing a future society that would help humans recover a true sense of being.

Second, my use of the term "community" could well be pluralized, for important reasons. Percy's vision of community was complex and multifaceted. At its root is a theological conception of community, of a mystical community of spiritual beings existing both within and beyond time, under God. For Percy, the historical axis of this community was the Christian Incarnation, the entry of the divine Logos into history, or what he referred to more broadly as the "Jewish-Christian Event." This event and its sacramental dimension—in particular the sacrament of the Eucharist—defined his sense of history and of historical evolution. The Eucharist is the essential sign of mystical community made real in human history. Belief in the Incarnation and in the real presence of God-in-Christ in the Eucharist, with all its reticular implications, was the core belief that informed his theology, his philosophy, his theories of language and of fiction writing (the community of art), and his own practice as a novelist. Belief in the divine Word made flesh, for Percy, is the central truth of community.

Percy's theological vision of community was interwoven throughout his thought and writing with his belief in philosophical realism. Patrick Samway describes how Percy said, during Samway's last visit shortly before the writer's death in 1990, that he felt it crucial to believe in a "realistic" philosophy and theology that could lead to absolute certainty, such as the certainty that the Eucharist was not a symbol but a reality, and that God was genuinely present as a person in the consecrated bread and wine. Samway regards this, as I do, as "the central intellectual intuition" of Percy's life.[2] Percy's remark indicates that the vision of community presented in his fictions and essays was grounded in his attempt to synthesize his theological beliefs with the realist philosophical tradition as it had developed from the Scholastics and through the triadic semiotic developed by Charles Sanders Peirce. (The precise term for Peirce's epistemological method is "semeiotic," not "semiotic." However, throughout his writings Percy used the more familiar "semiotic," a practice I follow in this study.) A committed realist, Percy was well aware of the permutations in scholastic realism that had occurred over time. Adopting a rigid scholastic-realist stance on language would have incurred the danger of being trapped in an essentialist position that had been undermined by progress in the sciences, especially linguistics, and in the history of ideas. He wished to fashion a more nuanced approach that would take into account the "fall" in language, and the general drift into linguistic relativism, and yet still preserve the core truth of realism.[3] In this search he enlisted the help of Peirce, whose semiotic method, by focusing on the mystery of human language exchanges, enabled Percy to develop a pragmatic realism—a phenomenological approach—that would avoid the latent dualism of a strict scholastic position.

Human language—the possibilities of communication between humans, and between humans and God, through signs—thus became the focal point of his search for community, explicitly and implicitly. Both his novels and philosophical essays explore the nature of semiotic community, the web of sign relations that constitute the real, though invisible, relationships between beings. Percy's theological, philosophical, and linguistic realism set him in radical opposition to the traditions of nominalism and skepticism, especially their modern manifestations in the social sciences. Strict nominalism in particular, with its denial of objective knowledge and of the possibility of general truths, signaled the death of community, since the ultimate consequence of such nominalism is that no *real*, shared bond of meaning is possible. In a paradoxical way, it was precisely Percy's opposition to prevailing philosophical views on language that made him a progressive thinker, as he strove to find a way out of an epistemological predicament that would ultimately lead to solipsism. Percy's novels, especially *Love in the Ruins* and *The Thanatos Syndrome*, record the dire consequences brought about by the ascendancy of linguistic nominalism in modern culture.

As befitting one deeply interested in diagnosing the immediate state of things, Percy focused his search on America and its various forms of social community. In his novels he explored and satirized what he saw as the debilitated state of modern American culture, trapped in its self-absorbed individualism, consumerism, violence, racism, and a general spiritual anomie. With characteristic probity, he saw this debilitated state as a sign of the death throes of the collapse of a Western culture dominated by scientific humanism. Like Romano Guardini and other thinkers, Percy saw this collapse as "the what it means to be human, as Percy elucidated in his essay "The Loss of the Creature" (MB, 46–63). Scientism's hegemony, for Percy, produces a radical "incoherence," a reductive ontology fundamentally at odds with the nature and experience of humans as humans. Hence he observed in modern society a profound sense of dislocation—from self, from world, and from God. In his fictions, Percy aimed his satire at exposing the contradictory and incoherent anthropological, philosophical, and linguistic assumptions underlying scientism. In the Jefferson Lecture he emphasized this incoherence and proposed the realism of Charles Sanders Peirce as a way to recover a genuinely human scientific perspective and to return science to its true concerns.

Percy also argued in several essays and interviews for the power of art to create a genuine, although temporary, community of meaning between writer and audience (MB, 83–100). His belief in the power of art to form community was coextensive with his belief in the possibility of a genuine scientific community. Art and science, properly understood, are complementary forms of knowledge, two legitimate modes of understanding reality. Art is cognitive, Percy insisted, and therefore as "scientific" in its own way as pure science. Hence he spoke of novel writing as a "new science," a mode of knowledge by which to diagnose humanity in all of its longings and searching (SSL, 139–53). His novels themselves, in both form and idea, can be seen as a working out of his notions of community through art. Regarding form, Percy insisted that his approach to novel writing was phenomenological, meaning that he began with a character "in a predicament" and then traced that character's journey through trials, recoveries, and changes in consciousness. This approach allowed for a certain "looseness" of form. But Percy's novels are also shaped by a firm sense of the ultimate purpose of the journey, that it is a journey toward meaning. The search for meaning is governed by Percy's sense of the importance of the concrete and of time itself, a sense of the absolute significance of the moment. This sense of the importance of the concrete and of time, a gift to Percy of his southern heritage, was everywhere deepened and expanded by his Catholic faith. That faith's confirmation of the value of concrete detail, of the particular, was for Percy the true source of both genuine science and of novel writing in Western culture (SSL, 352–68, 368–73). Percy saw the capacities of science and art to form a genuine community of meaning to be rooted ultimately in the Christian Incarnation and in the spiritual community that the Jewish-Christian Event embodied in the ordinary human world, here and now. Consequently, his hope for a recovery of genuine community ultimately meant a "return" to humanity's true being as knowing creatures under God—as "sovereign wayfarers" journeying toward salvation.

As we begin a new millennium, we are all aware that terms like "community," "intersubjectivity," and "reconciliation" and phrases such as "the need for understanding" have become numbing clichés in our current parlance. No one was more aware than Percy himself of the devaluation of such terms. He recognized that signs evolve over time and eventually lose their power to communicate. He understood the artist's need to revitalize the signs, to "make it new." More important, he understood that we are living in the midst of a great spiritual crisis, of which language is the supreme manifestation—the crisis of the meaning of meaning itself—or what George Steiner has called the radical separation of "word from world" (*Real Presences*, 93). Percy's novels, with their lacerating satiric attacks on dead language and the "white noise" of meaningless babble, dramatically confront this crisis. At times in his novels, community seems impossible, and, echoing Guardini, Percy foresees the need for a wholesale collapse of regnant social forms and the materialist ethos shaped by scientism. Catastrophe seems preferable to spiritual dry rot. Moreover, Percy believed that human community is not the ultimate community. Union with God is the final goal of the search. Still, for Percy there is always a resilient hope and possibility for renewal in the world, one that affirms his belief in the human spirit. This hope was the ground of his search for community in his novels and essays, and my aim in this study is to track the development of that search across his six novels. I begin by sketching some philosophical and theological foundations for Percy's notions of community. As I noted, Percy's philosophical ideas about community are rooted in the realism of Aristotle, Aquinas, Duns Scotus, John Poinsot, and other scholastics—realism as "updated" by the semiotic theories of Charles Sanders Peirce, whose writings Percy studied for at least forty years. I make no attempt to be exhaustive in this review of Percy's theological and philosophical underpinnings in realism. Such would be a book unto itself, and others have already approached the subject.[4] My concern is to elucidate those key ideas that help to shape the visions of community Percy created in his fictions.

Analyzing Percy's oeuvre presents special challenges to the reader-critic. Unlike most other major modern novelists—one thinks perhaps of Umberto Eco as a notable exception—Percy was a serious writer in two genres: the novel and the philosophical essay, especially essays on language. The challenge this presents is formidable indeed: to understand the integral relationship between the ideas Percy developed in his essays and fictions, and still give each its due as a distinct literary form. But the challenge points to an even deeper, more complex issue, one that may also provide a clue. Undoubtedly Percy's philosophical ideas and language theories are profoundly implicated in his novel writing. In this respect, his writings can be seen as "all of a piece." Yet as George Steiner has argued persuasively, as modes of discourse, the novel and the philosophical essay are ontologically incompatible (*Real Presences,* 82–83). Philosophical writings and language theories aim at general truths. They are intellectual explorations whose purpose is to uncover the principles or laws that govern cases in general. Novels represent the particular, the individual, the concrete, albeit that through symbolic language they aim to depict the universal in the particular. Still, Steiner's point is well taken. No theory—be it philosophical, theological, linguistic, psychological—can explain the mysterious essence of a single work of art. Theory is inherently abstractive. It views the individual case as an exemplary model, hence abstractly and in some degree reductively. Steiner's point speaks to the danger of viewing Percy's novels as *only* expositions of philosophical ideas, as narrative enactments of ideas. In examining the novels, it is important to insist on their unique mystery, or what Henry James called "the alchemy of art." This sense of mystery was reinforced by Percy's semiotic realism, which affirms the open-endedness of the sign, and by his Catholic belief, which affirms the ever-present possibility of grace and conversion. However, it is well to recognize that, at times, some of Percy's plot actions and characters do seem "staged" in order to exhibit certain ideas. When this occurs, the problem may well point to Percy's own inner struggle over his "two-mindedness"—his desire on the one hand for objective, empirical certitude, and on the other, his belief in the power of imaginative narrative as a way to fathom the mysterious truth of ordinary existence. At the root of his struggle, in whatever form it found expression, we can see Percy's wrestling with the ontological status of the word, and with the question of the meaning of meaning itself.

Many different reasons might be suggested for why Percy chose novel writing as a vocation. These include his natural gift for storytelling, his genius for humor and satire, plus his practical sense that writing philosophical essays or cultural commentaries alone would provide neither sufficient income nor a large audience for his work. While there is a measure of truth in all of these reasons, my own view is that Percy's turn to novel writing was a deeply religious choice, a direct consequence of his conversion. That is to say, if we understand the term "religious" (as Percy did) etymologically as a "binding together" or fastening, I think we can see that for Percy the novel was the medium par excellence for discovering and uncovering, through language, the truth of being itself, and sharing it with a larger community of readers. In his essay "Why Are

You a Catholic?" Percy argued that in the "theorist-consumer" age of scientism, language has become devalued and emptied of meaning. Only two signs, he argued, retain essential meaning—the "self" and "the Jews"—neither of which can be explained by theory. Thus Percy implied that his conversion to Catholicism was, in part, a decision stemming from a semiotic insight. Judeo-Christianity's respect for the absolute value of the concrete and the uniquely individual coalesced with Percy's sense of the importance of novel writing as a vehicle for the search for meaning (ssL, 139–67, 304–16). Seen from a semiotic perspective, Percy's conversion to Catholicism and to novel writing coalesced with his interest in Peirce and realism. As Michael L. Raposa has noted, Peirce's theological semiotic affirmed that God can be known through His signs within creation, which is His "great poem," a view that Percy also shared (*Peirce's Philosophy of Religion,* 137).

For Percy, the novel afforded the best means to "bind together" the mysterious truths of concrete experience, unable to be represented by theory, with the ramifying extensions of meaning and significance encoded in particular signs. Stated differently, novel writing was the mode through which Percy could best conduct his own personal search for meaning and community. It was a test of his faith in the power of the word, and not just an intellectual challenge or an aesthetic exercise.

The root of this faith in fiction was Percy's belief in the doctrines of Christ's Incarnation and the Eucharist. The divine Logos, as Steiner argues, is the ultimate ground or "Author-ity" for meaning in language. If, as the nominalist deconstructionists contend, the word signifies only itself, such an argument constitutes "a denial of the theological possibility and of the *Logos* concept which is pivotal to the possibility" (*Real Presences* 99, 100–16, 119–20). For Percy, as I have said, that divine Logos entered history and thereby transformed meaning, bringing to mankind the "good news" of possible redemption from its predicament. The real presence of the Logos, signified preeminently in the Eucharist and the sacraments, is the living sign of abiding relation or community between God and mankind. Like Flannery O'Connor, Percy believed that the Catholic sacramental view of reality verified the absolute spiritual integrity of the particular, of *things,* allowing them to be what they are, no more and no less.[5] Consequently, belief in the incarnate Logos and the eucharistic community are the core of his vision of history, human nature, language, science, and art as well as of his practice of novel writing. They are the visible and invisible realities, expressed in concrete signs and actions, against which all of his created images of community are to be measured.

Another major challenge Percy's writings pose for the reader-critic concerns the vocabulary with which to discuss Percy's fundamental philosophical and theological views. The language of Percy's philosophical essays, especially those on language, is often abstract, dense, and technical. Such is also the case with Charles Sanders Peirce, whose writings often seem so abstract as to be almost impenetrable, especially because of the dearth of specific examples to illustrate concepts. Percy himself complained of this problem as he struggled to understand Peirce; however, he also assimilated some of Peirce's terminology, as well as that of other philosophers and theorists of language, into his own writing. To compound the problem, many of the traditional terms used in philosophical and theological discourse—words such as "redemption," "being," "essence," "self," "alienation," "intersubjectivity"—have suffered linguistic devaluation, as Percy well recognized. Many of our words, he argued, and the realities and values they once signified in common understanding, have been "evacuated" of meaning. We now live, as Steiner notes, in the time of the "after-Word," when the bases of consensus about meaning in the community of language have eroded. In fact, one important aspect of Percy's search for community in his novels was to uncover and name the demonic source of this devaluation, particularly in *Love in the Ruins* and *The Thanatos Syndrome,* as I have noted. Consequently, in a reflexive way, the very problems of language inherent in the discourse become the reader-critic's own as he attempts to create an analytic community of meaning with readers. Indeed, it would be a consummate irony to write a book about community that is so laden with abstract, technical, and abstruse terminology as to make it unreadable except by specialists.

My attempt, then, in my overview of some major philosophical and theological ideas in Percy, is to render them as intelligible as possible for the general reader. Conceptual language is, at times, unavoidable, though my goal is to make it lucid without resorting unduly to academic jargon or the technical obscurities of the professions, yet hopefully without oversimplification. I presume a knowledge of Percy's essays on the part of the reader. I quote excerpts from these as well as from Peirce's writings where relevant to my argument, and I cite references for further explanation. My goal is to keep the focus on my main subject—community in Percy's fictions—yet situate that subject in the larger context of his thought.

Following my initial discussion of the intellectual ground of Percy's ideas of community, I take up each of his novels in turn, using his essays and interviews to shed light on my analyses. I discuss how the idea of community both shapes and is manifested in each work, and how Percy's representation of this idea developed over time. Finally, I discuss Percy's crucial Jefferson Lecture, "The Fateful Rift: The San Andreas Fault in the Modern Mind," to show his prophetic hope for the reestablishment of grounds for a human community—in history—yet with an openness to the mystery and reality of God.

Walker Percy's search for community began at home—"home" in this case being the America of the latter half of the twentieth century. What he witnessed and felt as a person and as an observer was a society lacking any genuinely coherent sense of community, yet one always longing to achieve it, and embracing one factitious version after another only to discover its inadequacy. In typical fashion, Percy came to analyze the historical, philosophical, and theological roots of this predicament and longing. This search led him to the belief that the root of the immediate problem lay in the modern, post-Enlightenment Western world's lack of a coherent theory of man, much of the blame for which rested, in Percy's view, with Descartes and his followers. In a letter to philosopher Vincent Colapietro (February 23, 1990), Percy said: "the difficulty is the mind-set of the entire Western world, beginning with Descartes, which is supposed to be based on the scientific revolution but is not. Descartes is the villain in my book. . . . The mind-set of an era is all-powerful and all-construing" (TP, 193).

Percy saw America as afflicted with a particularly virulent strain of this Cartesian malady. In a 1989 interview with Scott Walter, he said: "Tocqueville—an amazing fellow—said it 150 years ago: All the Americans I know are Cartesians without having read a word of Descartes. He meant that an educated American believes that everything can be explained 'scientifically,' can be reduced to the cause and effect of electrons, neurons, and so forth. But at the same time, each person exempts his own mind from this, as do scientists. I see this endemic Cartesianism, and my criticism is that it leaves us without a coherent theory of man. Consequently, modern man is deranged" (More Con., 232–33).

Tocqueville also saw the loss of community to be a major consequence of this Cartesianism. Remarking on American individualism, he said: "in ages of equality every man seeks his opinions within himself . . . all his feelings are turned toward himself alone" (*Democracy in America,* 104). For Percy, as for Tocqueville, the Cartesian spirit was the source of that radical individualism so embedded as an idol in the American psyche—at once self-assertive, given to role playing and sociopathic impersonation, and yet haunted by a ghostly sense of solitariness. Its archetypal figure was the loner, typified for Percy in his essay "Decline of the Western" by the frontier hero, from Daniel Boone to Shane.[6]

Although the South in which Percy grew up and lived his adult life was, and to some extent still is, lauded for its sense of community, he saw the region as equally afflicted with this Cartesian spirit and its stepchild, individualism. In the old South it took the form of a stoicism that, in spite of the region's nominal Christianity, shaped much of the South's value system. Speaking of this stoic culture, Percy noted its inherent solipsism and despair: "Its most characteristic mood was a poetic pessimism which took a grim satisfaction in the dissolution of its values—because social decay confirmed one in his original choice of the wintery kingdom of the self" (SSL, 83–89). Reading his fictions, one can see Percy making a similar argument about the prosperous modern South. The poetic pessimism that confirmed the "wintery kingdom of the self" in the old South has been transformed into a progressive consumerism like the rest of America, further undermining whatever vestige of genuine community the South once possessed. From Percy's philosophical perspective, the stoic individualism that shaped southern society was as quintessentially American as that which shaped life in Oshkosh, Wisconsin, or the south Bronx.

Such a doctrine of individualism, as both Percy and Peirce recognized, is both theologically and semiotically antithetical to genuine community. Rene Girard argues that excessive individualism "presupposes the total autonomy of individuals, that is, *the autonomy of their desires*" (*I See Satan*, 8). Such a view inevitably causes a rivalry and competition that undermines community. Autonomy leads to self-idolatry and the ever-intensifying assertion of personal will, a delusion of "independence" that causes spiritual isolation and despair. Girard's countermodel to the autonomous self is Christ, the "one for others" who subjected personal desire to the will of the Father (13). So also, as creatures made in the image of God, we are constituted by our relations to others, to God and fellow humans, and not as autonomous individuals (137). In a similar vein, Peirce regarded the rampant individualism of nineteenth-century America as antithetical to the goal of genuine community. Peirce saw the doctrine of individualism as metaphysically rooted in nominalism, at odds with the fundamental truth of *relation*. As a social ethic, individualism was a force promoting selfishness and greed, hence destructive of the ideal of Christian community based on love and charity (Raposa, *Peirce's Philosophy of Religion*, 72–87). As we shall see, Percy followed Peirce in affirming humans as constituted also by sign relations in the semiotic community, contrary to the notion of an autonomous self. Percy argued that human consciousness and signs are inherently social and noted: "What Descartes did not know: no such isolated individual as he described can be conscious" (LC, 105).

Percy's starting point for understanding modern man's "derangement"— a person's separation from his own true being and from others, hence from community—was his belief in philosophical realism. When asked in a 1983 interview with Robin Leary if he thought "the distinction between Idealist versus Materialist is a meaningful one," Percy replied: "Not as meaningful as the issue of Realism versus Nominalism. That is, the belief that there is a real world out there which we can to a degree know (including God) versus the belief that there is nothing really knowable or scientifically lawful or meaningful but a bunch of sensory impressions which we give names to."[7] The "real world out there," which Percy affirms "we can to a degree know (including God,)" is a nonmaterial yet true reality, a world of sign relations, a semiotic community of meaning. Here, a crucial distinction between the "real" and "existence" must be noted. In helping Percy to understand Peirce, Professor Ken Ketner pointed out in a letter that some realities, such as "your constitutional rights," are real but nonexistent. "The real is that which has the properties it has independently of any single person or group of persons who wish or hope or dream that it have those properties" (TP, 77–79). Signs themselves are realities, as is mind itself. In contrast, strict nominalism claims that the properties of the real are only arbitrary signs or designations of meaning; they are not independent, true realities. Following Peirce, Percy's affirmation of realism formed the basis of his idea of community and his effort to create a "new anthropology" of man, as we shall see. How, then, to understand these concepts as they developed in Percy's thought and came to shape his writings?

Percy's realist conception of the self and community had a theological and philosophical foundation. Although many thinkers contributed to Percy's understanding of semiotics, clearly the most important influence was Peirce, the American philosopher generally regarded as the father of the modern science of semiotics. As I have noted, Percy studied and absorbed Peirce's writings throughout his adult life, eventually making Peirce's realism the centerpiece of most of his own thinking on language. Nevertheless, there were crucial differences between Peirce's and Percy's thought, differences shaped by Percy's religious beliefs, as we shall see later. Percy's serious and continuous attraction to Peirce obviously stemmed from his own scientific interests, particularly his desire to find a coherent philosophical view. In addition, as Raposa has shown, Peirce's semiotic theories can to a considerable degree be assimilated to Christian theology. Although he was not a practicing Christian believer, and though he tended to view Christ as an ideal figure rather than as a unique savior, Peirce found great support for his philosophical ideas in the Scriptures. Peirce's commingling of aspects of Christian theology, ethics, logic, and semiotics would have had strong appeal for Percy. But unlike for Peirce, Percy's belief in the Christian Incarnation and the sacraments gave a crucial added dimension—a historical ground—to his own scientific and linguistic perspectives.

From 1984 until his death in 1990 Percy carried on an extensive correspondence with Kenneth Laine Ketner, professor of philosophy at Texas Tech University and an authority on the writings of Peirce. Pursuing the study of Peirce's semiotic that had occupied him for several decades, Percy asked Ketner to help clarify certain elements of Peirce's thought, especially his triadic theory of language. The correspondence developed into an epistolary friendship based on their mutual interest in Peirce and was subsequently published as *A Thief of Peirce: The Letters of Kenneth Laine Ketner and Walker Percy,* edited by Patrick Samway, S.J. The title of the volume refers to an important and revealing remark Percy made in a letter dated February 27, 1989, in response to Ketner's announcement that he wanted to dedicate a new volume on Peirce he was editing, *Reasoning and the Logic of Things,* to Percy. Percy replied:

> As you well know, I am not a student of Peirce. I am a thief of Peirce. I take from him what I want and let the rest go, most of it. I am only interested in CSP insofar as I understand his attack on nominalism and his rehabilitation of Scholastic realism. . . .
>
> But this is not the worst of it. What would set CSP spinning in his grave is the use I intend to put him to. As you probably already know, and if you don't, let us keep the secret between us, I intend to use CSP as one of the pillars of a Christian apologetic. . . .
>
> So if you want to dedicate this book to me, please do so with the understanding that I admire at the most one per cent (two pages) with the understanding to [*sic*] that it would spin CSP in his grave. Naturally I love the idea—using CSP as the foundation of a Catholic apologetic, which I have tentatively entitled (after Aquinas) *Contra Gentiles.* (130)

Percy died a little more than a year later without fulfilling his dream to write a Peircean-based Catholic apologetic. Nevertheless, the basic argument for such a work is spelled out in the Jefferson Lecture he delivered at the National

Endowment for the Humanities on May 3, 1989 (less than three months after his letter to Ketner), titled "The Fateful Rift: The San Andreas Fault in
the Modern Mind." More important, Percy's stated plan to use elements of
Peirce's semiotic to support a Catholic apologetic not only pointed to a future project but also, I believe, revealed much of what he had been doing all
along in his novels and essays. Percy's statement was in this respect as much a
confirmation of his accomplished work as it was a prospectus for future writings. Percy gleaned a central truth from his study of Peirce's semiotic and,
more broadly, from the tradition of philosophical realism. This truth is that
human beings are constituted *by nature* as relational beings. We are structured to fulfill our natures not individualistically, but through relationships,
through community. This truth reinforced and was reinforced by the belief in
the mystical community in Percy's Catholic faith. For both Peirce and Percy,
as I have argued, any notion of Cartesian-based individualism runs counter
to the very nature of being and leads to what Percy referred to as our modern
"derangement." Signs are the means by which we know and participate in the
community of meaning. Language enables us as humans to discover, name,
and affirm the Real. Shared knowledge (i.e., knowing with another *[con-scio]*)
creates the community of meaning.

The plan Percy disclosed to Ketner can be elucidated in part by examining
the central ideas about language he shared with Peirce, as well as the broader
implications for community that derive from linguistic realism. Nevertheless,
several caveats are in order when considering this intellectual kinship between
Percy and Peirce.

First of all, both thinkers' ideas on realism and the triadic semiotic evolved
throughout their respective careers, gaining in clarity, nuance, and implication. Consequently, a static or all-inclusive perspective cannot be ascribed to
either man. In fact, given the dynamic nature of sign relations, the very notion of a closed system of thought is completely antithetical to Peirce's semiotic. Second, Peirce's enormous canon of disparate writings, estimated at more
than two million words, is still in the process of being assimilated. His volumi-
nous writings are extremely diffuse, dense, abstract, and often recapitulative
in thought. Furthermore, the exact chronology and depth of Percy's study of
Peirce has yet to be firmly established. Evidence suggests that he was probably introduced to Peirce's thought in 1947 when he moved into a house in
New Orleans owned by Julius Friend, editor of the *Double Dealer,* a literary
journal. Friend gave Percy an inscribed copy of *The Unlimited Community:
A Study of the Possibility of Social Science,* written with Professor James K.

Feibleman, an officer of the Charles Peirce Society. As the title suggests, the work focused on the open-ended possibilities for a broad-gauge anthropological study of human society. Among other ideas, *The Unlimited Community* contains a vigorous attack on nominalism and nominalistic-based social science (Samway, *Walker Percy,* 148–49). Percy may also at this time have become acquainted with Feibleman's seminal work, *An Introduction to Peirce's Philosophy: Interpreted as a System.* In addition, probably from the time of his hospitalization at Trudeau Sanitarium, Percy was also closely studying the writings of St. Thomas Aquinas, which gave him a foundation in basic principles of philosophical realism, especially its relation to nominalism, within a tradition reaching back to Aristotle and within a specifically Catholic context.

Percy's essay "Semiotic and a Theory of Knowledge" (1957) reveals his familiarity with Peirce's triadic theory of meaning early in his career (MB, 243–64). In a 1976 interview with Marcus Smith, Percy cited Peirce's theory of language authoritatively while attacking Cartesian behaviorism for its materialist view of man and language (Con., 129–45). Throughout subsequent essays and interviews and of course in his fictions, Percy's incorporation of Peircean semiotic into his thought can be readily seen. For example, in his essay "The Symbolic Structure of Interpersonal Process" (1961), although he does not cite Peirce directly, Percy's analysis of the semiotic triad of relations and the intersubjective community that derives from those relations is clearly Peircean (MB, 189–214). The distinction between dyadic and triadic events so central to Peirce's idea of semiotic community receives major emphasis in Percy's 1972 essay "Toward a Triadic Theory of Meaning," as well as in his essays "The Delta Factor" (1975) and "A Theory of Language" (MB, 159–88, 3–45, 298–330). Thereafter, Percy's use of Peircean semiotic, especially to analyze the predicament of the individual in a Cartesian-dominated culture and to explore the possibilities of community, became increasingly explicit. In *Lost in the Cosmos* (1983), his "Semiotic Primer of the Self" extrapolates from Peirce's triadic theory to affirm the possibility of a "secular redemption" of man through a shared community of meaning. Near the end of his career, Percy turned more and more to his plan to write the Peirce-based "Catholic apologetic" he mentioned to Ketner, a plan sketched in the Jefferson Lecture but never completed. Percy also mentioned his plans for more extensive work on Peirce in earlier interviews with Zoltan Abadi-Nagy (1986) and Phil Mc-Combs (1988) (Con., 72–86; More Con., 189–207). However, exactly how, and how extensively, Peirce's concepts helped shape Percy's fiction—in the mystery of the creative process, rather than in the analytic process—is probably impossible to elucidate fully. But as I hope to demonstrate, Peirce's semiotic and its larger social, philosophical, and theological implications melded with Percy's Catholic faith to form the basis of Percy's search for community in his fictions.

A second difficulty in studying the Peirce-Percy connection involves Percy's interpretation and use of Peirce's concepts. Do his writings accurately reflect Peirce's main ideas? According to Patrick Samway, the noted Peirce scholar Thomas A. Sebeok felt that Percy "had a narrow conception of semiotics and worried about certain issues that were not mainstream" (*Walker Percy,* 351). Even very late in his life, as we shall see, Percy had trouble understanding and accepting Peirce's formulation of the central idea of the "interpretant" or "coupler" in the triadic exchange of meaning. In his letters to Ketner, Percy argued that Peirce had failed to adequately explain the nature of the coupler at the heart of triadic intersubjective communication. Therefore, Percy questioned whether Peirce had a "coherent anthropology." This crucial issue, as we shall see, was a fundamental point of difference between the two thinkers. At the same time, one can also question how selective Percy was in his use of Peirce's ideas. What special application or modification did these ideas receive in Percy's writings? How did his thinking about and use of Peirce evolve over the almost fifty years of his career as a writer? Most important, what elements in Percy's personal life—especially his Catholic faith and his deep involvement in his daughter Ann's hearing impairment problems—helped to shape his use of Peirce's ideas? And finally, how much of Peirce's wide-ranging thinking about ethics, religion, science, art, aesthetics, and social community might Percy have absorbed and adopted as his own thought? Mindful of these caveats and questions, I want to examine some fundamental philosophical correspondences between the two thinkers.

In his seminal essay "The Fixation of Belief," Peirce defined the Real as follows: "There are Real things, whose characters are entirely independent of our opinions about them; those realities affect our senses according to regular laws, and, though our sensations are as different as our relations to the objects, yet, by taking advantage of the laws of perception, we can ascertain by reasoning how things really are, and any man, if he have sufficient experience and he reason enough about it, will be led to the one true conclusion. The new conception involved here is that of reality."[8] Peirce's definition of the real affirms the existence of objective truth, which can be discovered by humans both independently and in a collective striving for knowledge. Robert S. Corrington classifies Peirce as a realist in two senses and points to the antinominalist basis of Peirce's thought: "In the first sense, he is a realist because he insists that truth exists in what is the case regardless of what any individual may believe. Fact and objective reality are independently real. In the second sense, he is a realist because he insists that general categories and classes exist independently of our nomenclature. That is, classes are real in themselves and are not mere products of human language and its internal classificatory schemes. Peirce's pragmaticism is antinominalist throughout and always seeks general and universals in the semiotic realm outside of language" (*Introduction to C. S. Peirce*, 53). If truth and general categories are independently real, then a community of knowledge and of knowers is also objectively real. Peirce recognized the profound social implications of the realism-nominalism debate for community in his 1871 review of Alexander Campbell Frazier's edition of the works of George Berkeley:

> But though the question of realism and nominalism has its roots in the technicalities of logic, its branches reach about our life. The question whether the *genus homo* has any existence except as individuals, is the question whether there is anything of more dignity, worth, and importance than individual happiness, individual aspirations, and individual life. Whether men really have anything in common, so that the *community* is to be considered an end in itself, and if so, what the relative value of the two factors is, is the most fundamental practical question in regard to every public institution the constitution of which we have it in our power to influence. (Hoopes, *Peirce on Signs*, 140)

Elsewhere, Peirce argued that "the very origin of the conception of reality shows that this conception involves the notion of COMMUNITY, without definite limits, and capable of a definite increase of knowledge" (82). Joel Weinsheimer has underscored the importance of this view: "The idea that the real creates and depends on communities, that it is what is common to many men, and thereby makes of many one—this idea is central to Peirce's realism."[9] Peirce therefore understood the semiotic community to be a nonmaterial web of intelligible sign relations that is open ended, unlimited, and evolving in meaning as the human race grows in knowledge throughout history.

Peirce and Percy's central thesis about humans as creatures living in a semiotic community of relations is that those relations are fundamentally triadic in nature. As is well known, Peirce and Percy distinguished between two fundamental types of events in the world—dyadic and triadic. Dyadic events are cause-effect exchanges, as between physical forces. Triadic events, by contrast, are a semiosis, a relation of meaning. Percy cited Peirce's distinction in his essay "Toward a Triadic Theory of Meaning": "All dynamical action, or action of brute force, physical or psychical, either takes place between two subjects . . . or at any rate is a resultant of such action between pairs. But by "semiosis" I mean, on the contrary, an action, or influence, which is, or involves, a cooperation of *three* subjects, such as a sign, its object, and its interpretant, this tri-relative influence not being in any way resolvable into actions between pairs" (MB, 161). All triadic events, Percy argued, "characteristically involve symbols and symbol-users" and "cannot be reduced to a series of dyadic relations" (162). In triadic exchanges of meaning the interpretant or coupler acts as mediator between the object and the sign. The basic unit in triadic language exchange is the sentence, and, Percy argued, every "sentence is uttered in a *community*" (172). Triadic relations make possible an "inter-subjective community," an I-Thou relationship between persons. Thus triadic relations and man's uniqueness as a symbol maker are the semiotic ground for Percy's entire concept of community.

Peirce's realism and his triadic theory of human relations derive from his fundamental ontology. Peirce affirmed three irreducible yet independent ontological categories of being—Firstness, Secondness, and Thirdness. Peirce defined the three categories, albeit quite abstractly, in an October 12, 1904, letter to Lady Welby:

> Firstness is the mode of being of that which is such as it is, positively and without reference to anything else.
>
> Secondness is the mode of being of that which is such as it is, with respect to a second but regardless of any third.
>
> Thirdness is the mode of being of that which is such as it is, in bringing a second and a third in relation to each other.
>
> I call these three ideas the cenopythagorean categories.[10]

Peirce explained Firstness as "what the world was to Adam on the day he opened his eyes to it, before he had drawn any distinctions, or had become conscious of his own existence"(CP, 1.357). Robert S. Corrington interprets the cosmological significance of Peirce's explanation as follows: "Adam came upon a world that he had not made but that as yet had no name or shape. Religious myths of a primal garden or of a golden age are imaginative ways of pointing toward pure Firstness. The flight from the garden is equivalent to the emergence of Secondness, with all of its distresses. Hence, sin brings Secondness into the world. It is important to note that Peirce's Adam does not even have self-consciousness at this stage. He is pure awareness, moving through the world without guile or any sense of its underlying structures and powers (126–27). Secondness refers to dyadic interactions between two elements," that is, cause and effect relations (Corrington, *Introduction to C. S. Peirce*, 127). However, Peirce as well as Percy argued that it "is impossible to resolve everything in our thoughts into those two elements (Firstness and Secondness) . . . the idea of meaning is irreducible to those of quality (Firstness) and reaction (Secondness). Another category is needed—Thirdness." Peirce thus affirms that "every genuine triadic relation involves meaning, as meaning is obviously a triadic relation," and that "a triadic relation is inexpressible by means of dyadic relations alone" (CP, 1.343, 345–47). Triadic relations of meaning are expressed by means of signs. Viewed in a theological perspective, Peirce's triadicity is a semiotic version of the divine Trinity. In his last Lowell lecture, as Raposa points out, he "identified the Creator of the world as an 'infinite symbol,' its interpretant and ground being identical with it." Peirce then correlated triadicity with the Trinity. "The interpretant is evidently the Divine Logos or word . . . the Son of God. The *ground,* being that partaking of which is requisite to any communication with the Symbol, corresponds in its function to the Holy Spirit" (*Peirce's Philosophy of Religion*, 167).

Peirce's correlation of triadicity with the Trinity formed the basis of what Raposa has termed his "theosemiotic." Theosemiotic denotes the semiotic process by which a person becomes "attuned to the traces of the divine sign maker in the world" (Corrington, *Introduction to C. S. Peirce*, 206). As Raposa explains: "Universal semiosis is the mechanics, the dynamics of objective mind. In religious terms, then, it is the means by which God relates to and communicates with lesser minds. Moreover, given the fact of continuity, in one sense, semiotic is always already theosemiotic. If all of reality is continu-ous, then everything is potentially a sign of God's presence" (146). Corrington further argues that theosemiotic is at the heart of all semiotic exchange. Like Raposa (and Percy), he believes that "signs become open at both ends. In addition to their correlation with objects and interpretants, signs represent the body of God in nature. The universe of signs is also the universe of divine action and growth. . . . Theosemiotic is the culmination of semiotics precisely because of the spiritual core at the heart of each sign" (207).

Understanding Peirce's categories is important for establishing the ontological basis of his notion of community, and also for seeing the particular attitude Percy took toward this aspect of Peirce's philosophy. Percy showed little interest in Peirce's categories of Firstness and Secondness. In a letter to

Ketner dated February 27, 1989, he said: "I have not the slightest interest in his formal logic, existential graphs and such like. I use his 'logic of relatives' for my own purposes, that is, as a foundation for my own categories. This means that I expropriate his two categories, Firstness and Secondness, as the ground of an ontology, setting aside 'Firstness' since it, Firstness, is an idealized notion and is not to be exemplified in 'reality.' As CSP put it, 'It is the mode in which anything would exist in itself, irrespective of anything else.' But, of course, nothing exists like that but only in relation to something else" (TP, 130). But Peirce's category of Thirdness was crucial to Percy's semiotic and to his concept of community. In particular, Peirce's view of the open-ended, unlimited nature of genuine community reinforced from a philosophical perspective Percy's religious belief in the human community evolving through history and time toward some form of redemption. As well, Peirce's semiotic community reinforced the belief in the mystical community proclaimed in Percy's Catholic faith. Percy thus wished to attempt a synthesis of Peircean semiotic and basic doctrines of the Catholic faith. As he remarked in a letter to Ketner, he hoped to use Peirce to construct "a new anthropology . . . a theory of man by virtue of which he is understood by his very nature open to the *kerygma and news*" (131) (italics mine).

Percy's stated intention to use Peirce to define a new anthropology, one that affirms man as by nature open to "the *kerygma* and news," reveals one of his principal goals as a writer. He hoped to use Peircean triadicity to expose the inherent contradictions of the reigning ideology of scientism and thereby to establish the basis for a new community of knowledge that would reopen the path to the divine Word. Percy held to the fundamental compatibility of Peirce's realist philosophy and his own Catholic beliefs. He always insisted on the importance of his philosophical writings. What he hoped to develop, in fact, was no less than an anthropological basis for the creation of a revitalized organon of truth.

According to Peirce, every triadic relation of meaning both presupposes another triadic relation and itself forms the basis for another triad. Thus Peirce affirms that a real continuity of sign relations exists, which includes both actualities and "possibilities beyond all multitude" (Raposa, *Peirce's Philosophy of Religion*, 19). Peirce likewise affirmed the doctrine of evolution (purposive continuity) energized by love (agapism). In discussing evolution he alluded to the Christian doctrine of God as the Alpha and Omega and explicitly linked it to his ontological categories (Raposa, *Peirce's Philosophy of Religion*, 66; CP, 6.429). "The starting point of the universe, God the creator, is the Absolute

First; the terminus of the universe, God completely revealed, is the Absolute Second; every state of the universe at a measurable point of time is the third" (CP, 1.362; 6.581). The "third," as Peirce described it, is equivalent to the "delta factor" Percy described in his seminal essay of the same name. Moreover, as Corrington points out, Peirce's notion of continuity denies any break between mind and matter or between the personal and social self, and so emphatically rejects Cartesian dualism (102).

Yet in spite of the strong sense of compatibility he felt with Peirce's semiotic, Percy disagreed with Peirce on a central point. Percy's disagreement was rooted in his understanding of a key Catholic doctrine, one that deeply affected his understanding of and search for community. This disagreement concerned Peirce's emphasis on mind as, ultimately, the basic reality, and the notion that "individuals" are relative.[11] Peirce's philosophy contained a strong idealist element that inclined him to affirm that ultimately "mind is all" and that matter is, as he called it, "effete mind." Percy felt that such an emphasis on mind disabled Peirce from truly resolving the Cartesian mind-body split. Their differences on this issue emerged in an important exchange of letters with Professor Ketner. Ketner explained to Percy that for Peirce, "the basic stuff of the cosmos is relation," and then continued: "Such a doctrine that the basic stuff is relation is a form of philosophical idealism. CSP is an idealist—an objective idealist. Idealism can solve [Descartes's] old mind/body problem with no mention of the pineal gland or any other wiggling organ. It does it basically by saying that there is no body—it's all mind. As CSP said, matter is just effete mind, too weak, too hide-bound with habit to be vigorously interpreting mind. Matter, in other words, is just a certain kind of relational pattern or system (as is everything, says the Cenopythagorean)" (TP, 32–33). Corollary to Peirce's idealistic view of matter is that "individuals are not basic. They are derivative." An "individual" is merely a "hypostatic abstraction"; the term "individual" merely denotes a being who is essentially a particular unity of signs (33). Ketner elaborated this point in the same letter: "The usual strategy in everyday speech is to take individuals as fundamental and to explain things in terms of individuals. Thus our culture thinks of a society as a collection of individuals—individuals are basic, and then they explain the nature of the group. In CSP's approach, an individual is a convenient abbreviation for something that is more basic, a particular web of semeioses, a rather complicated one, actually, and one that is changing all the time. . . . This is the meaning of [Peirce's] remark that 'man is a sign,' which could be understood as 'human beings are, ontologically speaking, semeoises'" (33; CP, 7.583).

Percy found this explanation to be not entirely convincing, particularly its implicit claim to have resolved the Cartesian mind-body problem. Percy might well have asked himself what humans are a sign of and how the community of meaning relates to a community of actual persons living in the ordinary world. In a subsequent letter to Ketner dated November 5, 1987, he raised the issue again in connection with a question that continued to trouble him in his efforts to understand Peirce's triadic theory—the role of the interpretant or coupler in the act of communication. He asked, in effect, What actually occurs in the sign exchange? How is the community of meaning between humans really established? He wrote:

> Okay. But what I want CSP to tell me or draw for me is not an existential graph or a trivalent node, but a picture of the sort of thing which is happening in the brain of the speaker. And I am not talking about the latest in neurology and electrochemistry of the synapses. I am talking about this sort of thing. Of course, I believe that there is no escaping some sort of non-chemical, non-electrical agent, call it mind, soul, whatever you like.
>
> Our problem, of course, is whether this lands us back in Descartes' old dualism, the mind-body split, the only progress being that instead of locating the mind in the pineal gland, now we locate it in the Brodmann language area. (25)

For Percy, to view matter as only "effete mind" seemed to dissolve the mystery of the mind-body relationship by simply idealizing matter. Such a solution, he believed, could not be demonstrated scientifically; as well, it was at odds with his Catholic belief in the uniqueness of the human person, rooted in the incarnate person of the God-man, Jesus, and in the Holy Spirit. Ketner's explanation of Peirce's view of matter and the person seemed to Percy to involve a gnosis that avoided the central problem of the nature of the interpretant: "*Re:* the Nag Hammadi stuff: Interesting, but I cannot but express mild surprise. Which is to say, I don't see how a Peircean scholar can go for this ancient gnosis which seems not to require a semeiosis, that is to say, a transaction in signs between people, an intersubjectivity, a realism to the degree that the transaction is taken to be about something which, to some degree, can be known and talked about. Whereas all this gnosis requires is oneself" (33). Percy objected on both scientific and theological grounds to the idea that matter can be reduced to "effete mind" and the individual to a "bundle of semioses." His objections reveal a deep tension within his own mind, I believe, the tension between reason and faith, which he had addressed in his essay "The Message in the Bottle." On the one hand, from a scientific viewpoint Percy searched for a natural explanation for the role of the interpretant in the act of communication, one that was empirically demonstrable, even while he believed that "there is no escaping some sort of *non-chemical, non-electrical agent,* call it mind, soul, whatever you like" (25) (italics mine). On the other hand, from a Christian metaphysical and theological viewpoint, rooted in the Incarnation, Percy affirmed the absolute uniqueness of the person as a hypostatic mystery. As early as 1976, Percy pinpointed the tension created by these dual perspectives in his interview with Marcus Smith. Speaking of "The Message in the Bottle," he said:

> What I was interested in doing was beginning with a behavioral approach, the phenomenon of language which everyone accepts and about which there is no dispute, and then seeing how far an analysis of language would take us toward an understanding of these other equally unique human traits.
>
> There is one sense in which I plead guilty to the imputation of the word "metaphysical" if it is used loosely, which it usually is. And that is that the prime element of the theory of language which I propose is, at least for me, a mystery. That is to say, in the explanatory model for linguistic behavior, it is more or less obvious that there is such a thing as a "coupler," an agent which couples, just as in Descartes' *Cogito,* there is an "I" which thinks. If subject and predicate or name and thing are coupled, there is a coupler. I do not presume to say what it is. . . . I leave that completely undefined. And in that sense you could say my theory is consonant with Christian belief. *There is the ultimate mystery of who or what is the coupler.* I think this is superior to Descartes' *Cogito ergo sum* because you can't see Descartes thinking, and so you can't prove his self. But I can see and hear you uttering a sentence. I say if there are elements of a sentence and if they are coupled, therefore there is a coupler. So I stop there. I say: "There is a coupler." (Con., 130–31) (Italics mine)

Nevertheless, in a 1988 interview with Sr. Bernadette Prochaska, Percy affirmed the mysterious coupler to be God. Speaking of Will Barrett's recovery of being in *The Second Coming,* he said, "it's Catholic that the discovery of one's being does not occur in a solitary enterprise. It involves at least two people, one being another person, and the second, the third member of the community of course is God, which the novelist has no business mentioning."[12] Here Percy stated his belief that the primary relation in self-discovery is a triadic community composed of the self, another person, and God. Implicit in his remark is the belief that the Trinity—God the Father, Son, and Holy Spirit— is God's self-communication to humans, and ultimately the ground for all human relations and community. For Percy, the coupler is specified in history in the real presence of Christ and the Holy Spirit.

Obviously, Percy was not content to let the mystery of the coupler/interpretant alone, as his letters to Ketner almost a decade later reveal. While maintaining the "mystery" of the interpretant as a key to the mystery of the human self, Percy also wanted a clearer scientific description of its nature and role in human communication. But of course a clear scientific explanation, even if theoretically possible, runs counter to the Christian view of the mystery of the Incarnation and of the human person as a unique mystery to whom the "good news" is personally addressed, both staple beliefs in Percy's Catholicism. His struggle was to find a way to integrate the science of semiotics with his religious belief, to unite human knowledge and faith. While believing that God was the coupler, Percy as a natural scientist could not "name" God as a demonstrable element in a semiotic diagram. Yet in rejecting Peirce's reduction of matter to "effete mind" as an "ancient gnosis," Percy did so in his response to Ketner precisely in terms of his religious beliefs: "I guess I find myself on the side of the Apostle and my friend, Flannery O'Connor. Paul said (to fuse two passages): If Christ is not God himself entered into history and if He did not in fact die and was resurrected from the dead, then our teaching is in vain and we're back in our sins.

"Flannery (answering an Anglican): If the Eucharist (the bread and the wine) is nothing more than a symbol of Christ, I say to hell with it" (25–26).

The crucial point here, of course, is Percy's identification of God with the Christ of history, the Word made flesh. It is crucial because that belief centered the philosophical notion of semiotic community in the concrete historical event of the Incarnation. The importance of this belief for Percy can be seen in an early draft of the Jefferson Lecture, entitled "Science, Religion, and the Tertium Quid" (printed in TP, 81–116). In this draft, Percy spelled out his argument about science, religion, and Peirce's triadic theory and repeatedly named the Christian Incarnation as the key element of his proposed "tertium quid." He affirmed the notion of a God who "has in fact entered history as a man" and "allowed himself to be executed as a criminal for the salvation of other men"; one who also instituted a church and "provided a means of worshipping God and receiving certain gifts from him, for example, the Eucharist which, though having the appearance of bread and wine, is believed to be in a real, not a symbolic sense, the body and blood of the man-God himself." Such propositions are, Percy said, "scandalous from a certain scientific perspective" because they cannot be categorized or explained as just another datum of human experience or culture (87–89). Their truth claim, Percy argued in "The Message in the Bottle," is of a different order; it is knowledge as "news" rather than merely knowledge *sub species aeternitatis.* To attempt to categorize it as just another datum of human experience and culture is to use the word "true" only in an analogous sense. Such a move evades the central issue of the truth or falsity of the Jewish-Christian claim in *all of its scandalous uniqueness.*

While Percy insisted that, historically, science's attention to the particular is rooted in the Incarnation, he also noted how the Incarnation's radical affirmation of the particular is offensive to science's impulse to generalize (93). This abstractive, categorizing impulse was, he argued, both ancient and modern. He pointed out that "Julian, a Platonist of the Fourth Century, was offended to the point of apostasy by the Jewish and Christian claim that God entered history at a particular time and place, by entering into a covenant with a particular people, with them and no other, and as a single man, he and no other" (94).

Against this abstractive impulse Percy set a realistic ontology grounded in Catholic doctrine and a Peircean semiotic. Again, in the "Tertium Quid" draft, he focused particularly on the point of intersection between mind and matter: human language, specifically man's triadic symbol-making power. But his discussion of Peirce's triadic theory in this draft version again brought him up against the problem of defining the coupler. After affirming that the interpretant-actor-agent is a nonmaterial reality, Percy described the role of the interpretant as "the dark dipole where the spark jumps—or rather . . . it is not that the spark jumps as it jumps across the million synapses in the brain. *It is rather that the spark is jumped. There is a jumper*" (114–15).

And what, or who, is the jumper? Clearly, it is a nonmaterial agent acting within the sign, within the act of communication. In his letters to Ketner, as I have noted, Percy questioned Peirce's reported claim that individuals are not basic and that matter is only "effete mind," which for him did not solve Cartesian dualism. Here, even though he does not say so explicitly, it seems clear that for Percy the "jumper" within the human triadic relation—the interpretant that makes possible the relation—is a person, God the divine Logos, Jesus the incarnate Word who entered history, and whose presence, for Percy the Catholic, continues in the real sign of the Eucharist and the sacraments as the workings of the Holy Spirit. The "jumper" is the one who verifies the absolute uniqueness of the individual whole person, body and spirit. Thus Percy ended this draft of the Jefferson Lecture by affirming man "as a person in a mystery, a predicament, a person moreover who is open to news appropriate to his predicament" (116).

Percy's implication of Jesus the incarnate Word as the interpretant and his invoking of the mystery of the Eucharist—the sacrament of real presence—are decisive for understanding his view of the human person and community in history. Peirce's view of matter suggests that the material elements of the sacrament—the bread and wine—are the particular instances (or existents) of the sign relation. That is, they signify the relation of community between God and the individual believer *and* between all believers (i.e., a semiotic community). The Eucharist signifies the ideal of a community of faith, hope, and charity made possible to mankind through the Incarnation. However, if as Ketner argued Peirce believed that matter is only "effete mind," then the bread and wine are finally reducible to "a bundle of semioses." Percy could well accept the idea of the Eucharist as a sign relation or semiotic event, but like Flannery O'Connor, as a believer he would not dissolve the mystery of the relation between the actual bread and wine, the real presence of Christ, and the sign action. To elucidate the dimensions of that mystery, I want to explore briefly a semiotic approach to the theology of Jesus as sign, focused on the Eucharist. Although this exploration is technical and difficult, it is essential for understanding Percy's synthesis of semiotics and Christology.

To begin, it is important to recall that for Percy and Peirce as realists, sign activity or symbolizing is an *action,* not a thing. That is, it denotes a *relation,* a relation of meaning, between humans and the "world," including the transcendent order. The nonmaterial real, as Peirce insisted, truly exists as an objective reality. Its meaning is independent of the human mind and therefore not assigned by humans. Human sign acts express this basic relation to the objective real and are also a personal act of self-communication that establishes an intersubjective relation between persons, as Percy explained in his essay "Semiotic and a Theory of Knowledge" (MB, 243–64). This personal act of self-communication denotes a giving, a gift of self, one that for humans is tangibly expressed through the material, through the body of the world. For example, the lover's gift of a diamond ring to the beloved involves both the physical object and, more important, the gift of self in the intersubjective relation between the two persons symbolized by the ring. The "meaning" of the ring lies not simply in its physical reality but in the nonmaterial relation it signifies. Scientism, by contrast, tends to "objectify" reality by ignoring the personal intersubjective dimension of the sign, ignoring the fact that the real is not physical in its essence.

This basic understanding of sign activity or symbolizing under realism is crucial for discovering the uniqueness of the Eucharist as a sign-event. Historically, much of the theological discussion of the Eucharist as a sign and of the real presence of Christ has centered on the idea of transubstantiation, the changing of the bread and wine into the body and blood of Christ. Jesus' words at the Last Supper—"This is my Body. . . . This is my Blood"—have often been the focus of debates over the meaning of His presence in the "substance," the objects of bread and wine involved in transubstantiation, rather than on the meaning of the sign action that occurs. More recent approaches to Eucharistic theology, as Joseph Powers has shown, emphasize the phenomenological and semiotic dimensions of the event and speak of "transsignification."[13] This perspective focuses on the meaning of the symbolic sign action by which Christ is present in the Eucharist. It includes the fact of transubstantiation, but rather than focus on questions of material "substance," it emphasizes the unique relation between God and the human world established in the event viewed as a sign exchange.

What is unique about the Eucharist is that it signifies Christ the incarnate Son of God's gift of Himself to humanity, a gift in the signs of transubstantiated bread and wine. The Eucharist is not essentially an object; it is an act of self-communication. This gift giving of Christ is the essence of the meaning of real presence. (We recall that gift giving was Peirce's quintessential example of triadicity.) The Eucharistic act really and actually incarnates the divine triadic reality of God the Father, Son, and Holy Spirit and offers that relation to humanity as a new triad: God, Christ and Holy Spirit (the "coupler"), and mankind. Moreover, the action of transubstantiation that occurs in the consecration is an action done *by Christ* through His words, and not by the celebrant who repeats them. As Joseph M. Powers states, "Christ is truly, really and objectively present in the Eucharist" (*Eucharistic Theology,* 120). It is Christ who affects the ontological change of the bread and wine into His body and blood, offering Himself in sacrifice to God on behalf of humanity and to the world for salvation. The phenomenal reality of bread and wine remains, but the intrinsic *meaning* of those concrete things is transformed by Christ's action. There is an interior transformation of the sign affected by Christ's words that is absolutely unique.

Since Christ's action is one of sacrificial gift giving, it signifies a new relation between God and humans; hence, a new semiosis. Christ's transforming action defines the ultimate meaning of all created reality, all signs, centering their concrete meaning and value in the transcendent reality beyond space and time. Powers notes that "in transubstantiation the bread comes to the full potential of its meaning in being taken up into the eternal action of Christ" (133). The same is true of all created things, both extensively and semiotically. All created things are "taken up" in the eternal action of the risen Christ so that they may realize their full potential meaning, beyond space and time. Thus the Eucharist as sign-event points to the ultimate fulfillment of relation and community—union between God and humanity.

Yet as Percy well recognized, the Eucharist as sign-act is ultimately a mystery that cannot be fully explained. Still, it can be considered by analogy to human sign-acts, the semiotic relations between persons. The similarities and differences in this regard also point to the absolute uniqueness of the Christ event. As was stated, for Percy the realist the human sign-act or act of symbolizing has two dimensions. It is objectively real, meaning that it denotes the nonmaterial relation expressed through the material signs of the world. At the same time, it expresses an intersubjective relationship, a communion between persons who are "present" to each other as persons. This personal presence is objective and real, yet dependent for its full realization on the intersubjective communion of the persons involved. As Powers states, "genuine personal presence is basically a 'spiritual' reality; it consists in the confrontation of free consciousnesses." Personal presence is "necessarily mediated by bodily presence, but is more than that" (160).

In the case of the Eucharist, Christ is really and objectively present, but his presence is spiritual. That is, His presence is not dependent on the ordinary bodily conditions of earthly existence. His presence is in the bodily form of the *risen* Christ, which is radically and mysteriously different from earthly bodily form. To explain this difference, Powers elaborates on the distinction between "objectivity" and "objectifiable." In the Eucharist, as I have noted, the risen Christ is really, objectively present. His presence is a given, a gift offered, and not simply created by the faith of believers. His presence is personal as well (as a sign-act) and is "aimed at subjectivity, the appropriation in faith of the gift of Christ" (161). But Christ's presence in the Eucharist is not "objectifiable." Because He is the risen bodily Christ, he is no longer subject to the ordinary conditions of human existence. Powers makes the distinction clear:

> Christ's presence is not simply a material fact . . . his presence demands a religious response from the believer for its full inter-personal reality . . . the fact that the Risen Christ is not an objectifiable reality brings out the transcendent difference between his condition and the earthly human condition, bound as

it is to the limits of a spatio-temporal existence. In the human condition, real objective personal presence only comes about as the foundation for genuine personal relations to the extent that the bodily reality of one personal subject confronts that of another. . . . The exact opposite is true of the Risen Jesus. He does not live subject to time and space. It is the sovereign freedom of His gift of Himself which makes Him present in the manifestation which occurs after the resurrection. . . . His gift of Himself is His presence. (161–62)

The risen Christ's presence in the Eucharist—real and objective, transcendent yet incarnated in the material signs of bread and wine—is a mystery, a semiotic mystery, which cannot be reduced to the dimensions of human knowledge. But its real implications are ontologically revolutionary, for in the mystery of the Eucharist Christ manifests Himself as the sign of all signs, the source and verifier of the meaning of meaning. At the same time, the mystery of Christ's presence in the Eucharist validates the open-endedness of all signs, since their ultimate meaning is to be fulfilled in the transcendent freedom of the risen Christ and the meaning of His redemptive action in history. Stated differently, the Eucharist as sign-act denotes the openness in possibility to a spiritual reality that transcends the human condition. This is the ever-present reality and action of the Holy Spirit, the coupler in all human sign relations of meaning. As Powers says, "the personal reality and the personal function of the Spirit is precisely that of being the bond between persons" (169). Because of the ongoing presence of the Holy Spirit in the human semiotic community, the transsignifying action performed by Christ at the Last Supper is both a historical event and a "timeless actuality."

This semiotic of the Eucharist, in all its full phenomenological and anthropological significance, is the basis for Percy's vision of community, though he was well aware that the meaning of the eucharistic sign has largely been lost to a modern audience. Still, the mystery of the Spirit incarnated in the sign-action, centered in the Eucharist, is the precise "scandal" of Christianity, a scandal especially to philosophers, as St. Paul said. Why? As Powers argues, from an ontological viewpoint the Eucharist initiates a radical transformation in the possibilities of being and consequently of the meaning of all signs. George Steiner has pointed to the significance of this event in Western culture: "At every significant point, Western philosophies of art and Western poetics draw their secular idiom from the substratum of Christological debate. Like no other event in our mental history, the postulate of God's *kenosis* through Jesus and of the never-ending availability of the Savior in the wafer and wine of the Eucharist, conditions not only the development of Western art and rhetoric itself, but at a much deeper level, that of our understanding and reception of the truth of art—a truth antithetical to the condemnation of the fictive in Plato" (*Grammars of Creation*, 67).

For Percy, then, the meaning of history is centered in relation to the pivotal event of the Incarnation and the Eucharist. Matter, the physical world, attains its ultimate significance in relation to this event. As a sign of the indwelling presence of the God-man, the Eucharist incarnates the mystical community in the actual here and now, as well as the real possibility of its ultimate fulfillment. The words of consecration, the verbal signs—"*This* is my Body, and *this* is my Blood"—instantiate the *kerygma* or "good news." As signs, they point to the ultimate meaning and goal of human history—community with God.

Percy understood that since the Eucharist is a semiotic event like no other, its full meaning cannot be subsumed like other signs under a theory of language. If bread as substance were reducible merely to "effete mind" or a "bundle of semioses," then bread is "nothing" in itself, and neither is any other substance. If bread cannot be bread (a unique metaphysical entity), then, as Percy saw, the unique person is reducible to a mental abstraction, and one can murder Jews, or the elderly, or "defective" children or the unborn.[14] Conversely, through the Incarnation and the Eucharist, the sacramental dimension of all creation is confirmed. Percy's commitment to the mystery of the Eucharist points to the scandal of Christianity in history. As Father Smith says in *The Thanatos Syndrome*, the "Jews" are a sign that cannot be evacuated of meaning. As the sign of all signs, the Eucharist and the Holy Spirit exist as the agent of meaning and grace for both individual and communal salvation.

Given his understanding of the Eucharist, Percy continued to maintain in another letter to Ketner that Peirce had not fully explained the sign exchange between humans. Hence, by extension, he felt that Peirce had not adequately defined man *qua* man. Percy wrote, "My difficulty with CSP is that he did not have an anthropology, which God knows he should have. I am not talking about something vaguely Christian or Unitarian or Eastern or what. I am talking about a scientific, i.e., rational, theory of man. He has, God knows, a theory of everything else, from language to metaphysics, but he is seriously disappointing here" (158). Writing a few weeks later, Percy reiterated his complaint: "*Re:* 'philosophical anthropology'; an awkward term meaning no more than a scientific theory of man, *without* theological presuppositions. . . . I was hopeful that CSP, having it on triadicity as a beginning, would develop one. He didn't, aside from that vast goings-on about "interpretant," which in the

end is so ambiguous as to be meaningless" (159). Percy's dilemma over the
interpretant is apparent, and his complaint against Peirce actually reflected
the struggle over this linguistic problem that had engaged him for decades.
Percy's obsession with the coupler was crucial to his own attempt to formulate an anthropology—a model of the self—and thus important for his understanding of community. Without some intelligible grasp of the meaning
of the coupler, any definition of the self he might wish to affirm ran the risk
of repeating a Cartesian dualism or a strictly behaviorist-functionalist view.
As I noted, if such were to occur, no *real* community, no *real* bond of shared
meaning between humans could be affirmed. Percy's study of language, then,
led him back to theological mystery, yet mystery that he believed to be in some
sense intelligible.

In "The Message in the Bottle," Percy described key elements of his own
anthropology and man's predicament vis-à-vis community by focusing on
the relation of knowledge and belief. Percy began by distinguishing between
"knowledge" and "news," a distinction he developed from Kierkegaard, which
was important in his own conversion to Catholicism. The former is "knowledge *sub species aeternitatis* . . . which can be arrived at anywhere by anyone
at any time" (MB, 125). "News" is knowledge of a different kind. He defined it
as "a synthetic sentence expressing a contingent and non-recurring event or
state of affairs which event or state of affairs is peculiarly relevant to the concrete predicament of the hearer of the news" (126). News can take the form
of knowledge of the world or knowledge of the transcendent (i.e., religious
knowledge). Percy insists that the Christian message, the "good news," not be
taken as knowledge *sub species aeternitatis*. Its object is "not the teaching but
a teacher," a single person (Jesus Christ), and it is addressed to the unique
predicament of the hearer. To see the Christian message only as knowledge
sub species aeternitatis is to ignore its fundamental claim: that it is based on
an absolutely unique event, God's entrance into history in the person of Jesus
Christ, a historical event existing *here and now*.

Since the "Jewish-Christian Event," as Percy called it, exists here and now, it
exists as part of the semiotic web of relations, part of the community of meaning that is capable of being heard, understood to some degree, and acted on.
For Percy, human beings are free to accept or reject the message as "news" pertinent to our specific predicament, which is that of "castaways" who are aware
of our fundamental "homelessness" in this world. Accepting the message requires an act of faith, but unlike Kierkegaard, Percy does not see faith and
reason as antinomies. While he accepts Kierkegaard's notion that "faith is the

organ of the historical," Percy follows St. Thomas Aquinas in distinguishing between scientific knowledge and knowledge of faith and then argues that in the knowledge of faith, "scientific knowledge and assent are *undertaken simultaneously*" (MB, 145) (italics mine). In this view, knowledge of the transcendent ("news") is both scientific knowledge, confirmable to anyone anywhere, and knowledge of faith or assent, unique to the hearer. Since it includes scientific knowledge, it is knowable in some degree by reason; in other words, it can be known *as* mystery, though it is finally irreducible to mind alone. Stated differently, the "good news" speaks to the unique predicament of the hearer in the here and now, offers a way to understand the deepest truth of the predicament, and offers a means of recovery from it.

Yet while affirming the possibility of receiving the "good news," Percy recognized the formidable challenge presented by the domination of modern culture by the scientistic viewpoint. Scientism undermines the possibility of genuine community at all levels. Percy astutely identified the crux of the problem as being within "the individual consciousness of postmodern man." As he explained:

> The wrong questions are being asked. The proper question is not whether God has died or been superceded by the urban-political complex. The question is not whether the Good News is no longer relevant, but rather whether it is possible that man is presently undergoing a tempestuous restructuring of his consciousness which does not presently allow him to take account of the Good News. For what has happened is not merely the technological transformation of the world but something psychologically even more portentous. It is the absorption by the layman not of the scientific method but rather of the magical aura of science, whose credentials he accepts for all sectors of reality. Thus in the lay culture of a scientific society nothing is easier than to fall prey to a kind of seduction which sunders one's very self from itself into an all-transcending "objective" consciousness and a consumer-self with a list of "needs" to be satisfied. It is this monstrous bifurcation of man into angelic and bestial components against which old theologies must be weighed before new theologies are erected. Such a man could not take account of God, the devil, and the angels if they were standing before him, because he has already peopled the universe with his own hierarchies. (MB, 113)

At the heart of the predicament of the modern scientistic consciousness, Percy saw, is the problem of language. Signs undergo a natural process of transformation, decay, and—possibly—rejuvenation. But beyond this natural evolution, Percy saw the deeper theological crisis in modern consciousness over the threatened collapse of meaning itself—the *meaning* of meaning. As Steiner has noted, the "very concept of *meaning-fulness*, of a congruence, even problematic, between the signifier and the signified, is theological. . . . . The archetypal paradigm of all affirmations of sense and of significant plentitude—the fullness of meaning in the word—is a *Logos*-model" (*Real Presences*, 119).

Both Peirce and Percy traced the source of this epistemological crisis to nominalism. Its modern stepchild is deconstruction, a manifestation of the scientistic spirit in the field of linguistics. In *Lost in the Cosmos*, Percy identified deconstruction as a derivative form of French structuralism and nominalism (87). Steiner pinpoints the radical antinomy: "The issue is, quite simply, that of the meaning of meaning as it is re-insured by the postulate of the existence of God. 'In the beginning was the Word.' There was no such beginning, says deconstruction; only the play of sounds and markers amid the mutations of time" (*Real Presences*, 120). In contrast to deconstruction's play of language markers, the foundation of Percy's and Peirce's realism is ultimately theological. Both recognized that attacks on the power and authority of the word to establish real meaning and community were ultimately attacks on the divine Word.

In *The Second Coming*, Will Barrett names Satan as the ultimate source of this deprivation of meaning. So also does Father Rinaldo Smith in *The Thanatos Syndrome*. In *Love in the Ruins*, Percy again, through Father Smith, links the corruption and collapse of the social community to the ascendancy of satanic "principalities and powers," manifested particularly in the confusions over language. Again like Flannery O'Connor, Percy wished to clearly identify the Adversary, the "depriver of meaning," as the source of modern evil. In *The Death of Satan: How Americans Have Lost the Sense of Evil*, Andrew Delbanco has argued that a "gulf has opened up in our culture between the visibility of evil and the intellectual resources available for coping with it" (3). Percy clearly saw this "gap" and depicted its moral and social consequences for the human community throughout his novels. Paradoxically, hope for his protagonists lay in "catastrophe," the collapse of the fraudulent "world" erected by scientism, and a possible reawakening of the word as communion in truth.

Percy's search for community and meaning, then, led him to attempt to synthesize his Catholic belief in the incarnate Word with Peirce's semiotic realism. Using this perspective, Percy began to explore in his essays and novels the possibilities for a recovery of community with God and fellow humans through the triadic use of language. In a 1984 interview with Linda Whitney

Hobson, Percy insisted that language, especially the language of art, creates community, and that this community is a form of "secular redemption" (More Con., 84–102; see also LC, 88–94). Speaking of the three levels of consciousness he named as C1, C2, and C3 in *Lost in the Cosmos*, Percy equated them in theological terms with "the unfallen state," "the fallen state," and the "redeemed state," respectively. He then equated the C3 level of consciousness with the breakthrough into the triadic use of language that makes genuine human community possible. On the secular level, Percy argued, the triadic breakthrough makes possible a way to temporarily transcend the alienation and isolation humans inevitably experience upon achieving self-consciousness, the semiotic "fall." It also makes possible the discovery of communion with God. C3 consciousness and language are what make the self truly human and enable one to achieve communion with another in knowing and naming reality together. This "recovery" of community or "secular redemption" through language, especially through the language of art, was the subject of Percy's seminal essay "The Man on the Train" (MB, 83–100).

Since Percy frames the relationship between language and consciousness in "theological terms," the direction of his thought is clear. Although he claimed to Marcus Smith that his concerns with language were strictly scientific and that he was not concerned with metaphysics, Percy nevertheless based his investigations on a particular metaphysical viewpoint. His notion of a "fall," though framed in semiotic terms, reveals this (LC, 105–12). Likewise, his claim to Ketner that he wished to formulate a "new anthropology" that would stand the test of science without "theological presuppositions" is also only partly true. Given his religious beliefs in the fall, the Incarnation, and the redemption by Christ and the sacraments, Percy clearly presupposed a certain theological view and had already, in a sense, accepted a Christian anthropology for man. Thus when he argued to Ketner that triadicity makes it possible for mankind to hear the "good news" of salvation and experience the *kerygma,* he implicitly linked the idea of community and "secular redemption" to the theological belief in redemption in history, through the "Jewish-Christian Event." The link is also evident in his preoccupation in his fiction with the meaning of the Jews, as we shall see. The incarnating of the word among the Jews established their uniqueness as a sign within the human community. They became the sign of the way history could move toward redemption under God (a sign by which all might unite into one community, as St. Paul affirmed). In Percy's view, the destiny of the Jews and the destiny of the human community are inextricably wedded, as his fictions increasingly make explicit. Likewise, for Percy, they are wedded to the condition of language, the evolution and devolution of words within the human community, as *The Thanatos Syndrome* makes especially clear.

Percy's attempted synthesis of Peirce's triadic semiotic and his own religious belief also became the basis of his attempt to bridge the gap between science and art. Triadicity offered a possible way to reintegrate the intellectual community, to promote the search for Peirce's ideal of a community of knowers. Peirce saw a consonance between the activity of the scientist and the artist: "The work of the poet or novelist is not so utterly different from that of the scientific man. The artist introduces a fiction; but it is not an arbitrary one; it exhibits affinities to which the mind accords a certain approval in pronouncing them beautiful, which if it is not exactly the same as saying that the synthesis is true, is something of the same general kind" (CP, 1.383; 5.535). Joel Weinsheimer emphasizes the larger significance of Peirce's view: "Peirce called into question the antithesis of the true and the beautiful, as well as that of truth and fiction. By definition, no fiction represents the actual, but that does not preclude fiction from being true, for the true represents the real, and the real is a category more comprehensive than the actual since it includes real possibilities and real generals. Such possibilities and generalities are precisely the object of science as well as art insofar as science is not the intuition of the thing itself but rather the search for general laws by means of hypotheses, the (potentially true) fictions of science" ("Realism of C. S. Peirce," 256).

In a similar vein, Percy affirmed the relationship between literature and science and their role in the larger community of knowledge. In "The State of the Novel: Dying Art or New Science?" Percy argued that art is cognitive, "as cognitive and affirmable in its own way as science" (SSL, 150). Both art and science share the power to know and express truths about reality. However, Percy maintained that the truths they express are different because the object of science is general truth, whereas the object of the novelist is the truth of individual existence. As he said in a well-known statement: "The great gap in human knowledge to which science cannot address itself is, to paraphrase Kierkegaard, nothing less than this: What it is like to be an individual, to be born, live, and die in the twentieth century" (151). However, while expressing the truth of individual existence, the novelist must also capture the general condition in the particular, else it would be impossible to communicate (i.e., form a community of shared meaning) with the reader. This is what the best novelists do, Percy insisted. As he affirmed in "The Man on the Train," art possesses the special power to overcome alienation, a condition he believed was exacerbated by the misplaced faith in scientism as the sole definer of reality. For Percy, modern allegiance to scientism threatened to subsume the individual. But the writer stands on the side of the individual, expressing the truth of his situation: "It is the artist who at his best reverses the alienating process by the very act of seeing it clearly for what it is and naming it, and who in this same act establishes a kind of community. It is a paradoxical community whose members are both alone and yet not alone, who strive to become themselves and discover that there are others who, however tentatively, have undertaken the same quest" (SSL, 151). Percy again reinforced this view of art's power to create community when he equated the c3 level of consciousness, the breakthrough into the triadic use of language, with community and the "redeemed state":

> when [the reader] picks up a novel by Marquand and reads about another alienated commuter, a very strange redemption occurs. He recognizes himself and a social interaction takes place. . . . That, in a way, is a redemption. . . . That's what happens in almost any artistic transaction, whether we're talking about poetry or fiction or art or music. . . . And fiction, of course, helps because it actually tells how the self is. That, in a way, is a secular form of redemption. Art establishes community, even if you're reading a book alone. If it's a great book, there is community established between you, the writer, and the words he is using. This is a double triadic relationship, with two triangles placed base to base, with the writer and the reader the opposing points. (More Con., 90–91)

Percy's essays on writing and his interviews show clearly his sense of the relationship between the vocation of writing and the semiotic view of community. Essays such as "The Man on the Train" affirm the power of art to establish a community. His essays on novel writing, symbolism, and art in general are hopeful statements in the sense that they were part of his attempt to heal the generally fractured community of meaning. His views are particularly relevant given the current balkanized nature of the disciplines of linguistics, literary theory, and literary criticism.

Much of the focus of Percy's analysis of the collapse of the community of meaning was on the corruption of genuine scientific community (especially the social sciences) by scientism. Percy's critique of scientism was all of a piece with his view of semiotic, artistic, and religious community. The culmination of this critique of scientism—and his hope for the redemption of genuine science and its reintegration into the larger community—came in the Jefferson Lecture, in which he envisioned a reunion of the arts and sciences based on recognition of their mutual goal of understanding the true nature of being. Together they might shape a "new science" of man based on a "new anthropology." As he said in closing the Jefferson Lecture, with the "new anthropology . . . one might even explore its openness to such traditional Judeo-Christian notions as man falling prey to the worldliness of the world, and man as pilgrim seeking his salvation" (SSL, 291).

In this brief overview I have tried to suggest the multifaceted nature of Percy's vision of community, as well as the theological and philosophical roots of that vision. However, Percy was well aware that, because he wrote within a generally secular culture, one in which language had become devalued, direct appeal for his vision would have fallen on deaf ears. Moreover, although so inclined, he acknowledged that he lacked the "authority" to preach directly of such matters. However, novel writing was a way to explore that vision of community indirectly, through representation of the shattered and deformed state of society and the searching of his protagonists, and through suggesting possibilities for healing their riven state. Percy the novelist became a searcher for the "hidden" divine presence in the word and sign, a parable writer who cryptically veils and unveils the meaning of the times.

CHAPTER ONE

The Footprint on the Beach

The Moviegoer

During the first private conversation between Binx Bolling, the protagonist of *The Moviegoer,* and his cousin Kate Cutrer, she asks Binx, "How do you make your way in the world?" Binx answers with characteristic evasiveness: "Is that what you call it? I don't really know. Last month I made three thousand dollars—less capital gains" (43). Kate's question expresses the central theme in the novel: Binx Bolling's search for himself in relation to community. Her question is Percy's formulation of the classic dilemma for the religious seeker posed by St. Paul: how to be *in* the world but not *of* it, or as Percy once phrased it, how to live without "falling prey to the worldliness of the world" (SSL, 291). The dilemma is further complicated by the essential solitariness of each individual person, a condition that can never be fully meliorated in this life. The challenge Binx faces is formidable, and the stakes are the highest—the very meaning of his existence. Stated differently, the key question Binx faces is, What does it mean to be a self in the world?—a question that is of course inseparable from his relation to God and others.

Beneath the wry humor of narrator Binx, there is an existential terror at the heart of *The Moviegoer* that is often overlooked. The terror lies in the danger of "falling prey" so readily and completely to the world's distractions, and to personal delusions, desires, and self-deceptions, that the mystery of one's uniqueness as a creature and one's place in creation is lost. Instead, the self capitulates to the ready-made attractions of the reigning culture, such as wealth and pleasure. The culture that dominates Binx's society is a deformed semiosis; that is, it is a community governed largely by a scientistic perspective. Hence it looks on the world and human interactions as causal and dyadic rather than as relational and triadic. Its citizens suffer a displacement from being. Binx senses this fundamental displacement in himself and in those around him. Percy grasped this terror as the dark underside of American individualism, and like Tocqueville, he saw it as the stepchild of Cartesian dualism. Binx Bolling, whom Percy once described as a "victim of Descartes," is particularly susceptible to the world's allurements (More Con., 160). Yet he is also a highly self-conscious young man who is intuitively aware of the danger, though he resists facing it. But just as there is terror, for Percy there is also hope, and by the end of the novel Binx will have found a way to "stick himself" into the world; that is, to locate himself in community with others and still continue his search, which ultimately signifies a search for relation to God.

Percy's complex treatment of Binx's search for community in *The Moviegoer* is intricately bound up with the manner of narration and the structure of the novel. As a victim of Descartes, the highly self-conscious Binx suffers many of the afflictions of Cartesian dualism. He is prone to taking a detached observer's stance toward the world, to formulating experience reductively, and to abstracting and categorizing others—a form of alienation—though Percy constantly undercuts Binx's postures with wry humor. As with most citizens of his culture, Binx's mind, sensibility, and heart have been deformed to some degree by scientism. His role playing, his often callow sarcasm and irony, his evasions and his deviousness all attest to a detached consciousness that would shape the world to its own narcissistic ends. But as with many of Percy's dualists, desire—especially sexual desire—becomes the real stumbling block Binx cannot circumvent by "objective" detachment or rationalizations. Like St. Augustine, after whose *Confessions* much of the novel is modeled, Binx experiences desire as the two-edged sword that both ties him to the world and impels his search for relation to some transcendent being who is the source of meaning and purpose. In his deepest self Binx intuits that there exists a real, invisible world of spiritual relations, signs of which can be glimpsed and known, and which are clues to his longing for meaning and communion. Binx's narrative then, in itself, records the conflict in consciousness Percy sees besetting all those inhabitants of a world where real spiritual relations have been occluded by scientism (MB, 113).

Just as Binx's conflicted consciousness is a sign of the mind of the times, so also on the narrative level is the elliptical structure of the novel. With its many shifts and breaks in the story line and its movement between action, memory, and reflection, the novel's form suggests the fragmented state of modern culture and the difficulties of finding identity and community in such a shattered world. Percy himself admitted to Shelby Foote an inability to write a well-structured, "architectonic" novel. He preferred to situate a character "in a predicament" and follow his progress through random, yet significant, happenstances (Tolson, *Correspondence,* 168–223). Yet on a deeper level, the novel's "loose" form re-creates the real semiotic community that Peirce described in his concept of triadicity, with asynchronic overlapping of signs from past, present, and anticipated future, and a flow of triadic interactions between these signs. This semiotic world is not structured according to the simple laws of causality affirmed by scientism and behaviorism. Rather, it represents the real, dynamic community of sign relations by which we mysteriously participate in being. Through this underlying web of sign relations Percy constructs the novel's inner meaning. Its disjunctive surface engages the reader in an interpretive search to understand the novel's signs, just as Binx searches to understand his world. This process, as Percy claimed, creates a community of meaning between reader and author (MB, 83–102). As I have suggested elsewhere, the form of *The Moviegoer* strongly resembles the activity of musement described by Peirce as the phenomenological way in which the relational mind searches for God.[1] Peirce also argued that the practice of musement, which he regarded as a form of prayer, had become difficult if not impossible in modern culture (see Raposa, *Peirce's Philosophy of Religion,* 137–38). Finally, underlying the semiotic structure of the novel, and informing it at every turn, is what I will call the community of real presence. This is the reality of the presence of God in the "here-and-now," manifested especially in Percy's use of sacramental signs. Binx is a muser who intuits this true invisible community in his heart and longs for it, but he is constantly distracted from it. There is a terror in this presence as well, since it threatens to break the closed heart open into love. The community of real presence is the human community into which the divine Logos has come, and where He is always present. Yet that true reality, as Percy well understood, has been largely submerged in a culture too preoccupied with its own distractions to take account of such "good news." Nevertheless, Binx's persistent fascination with the mystery and wonder of the here-and-now is an indelible sign of the reality of that community and of the spirit guiding his search.

As a beleaguered victim of Descartes, Binx vacillates between different possible identities and roles for "making his way" in the world. Two possibilities seem to be offered by the prevailing culture of scientism—that of consumer immersed in the material world and that of "objective" theorist of experience, seduced by abstraction. Both postures are antithetical to mystery and wonder; both dehumanize the self; yet Binx adopts both at various times in his journey. A third possible role is that of the searcher, a way that speaks to Binx's deepest desires and need, but which he has trouble remembering in a world glutted with distractions. Part of his difficulty is personal. Desire for pleasure and a defective will make it difficult for him to follow his deepest intuitions. But part of it is the culture's indifference or hostility to the idea of mystery and a search for God. In *The Confessions* St. Augustine could name the true source and goal of his longing. Binx says he "cannot make head or tails" of God, even though he claims to be "onto Him." While he is often distracted, he senses the elusive presence of the divine in the world.

One such distraction is moviegoing, the central motif in the novel. Percy's use of this motif is complex and multivalent, as the many critical discussions of it have suggested.[2] At times Binx's moviegoing seems the refuge of the romantic, the escapes Percy named in his essay "The Man on the Train" as "rotations from the human nest, the family familiar, Sartre's category of the viscous" (MB, 93). Binx recognizes this behavior in the romantic young man he sees on the bus from New Orleans, who is a moviegoer though he doesn't go to movies. Movies and moviegoing can provide a temporary escape from the anxiety of living over the "abyss," an "aesthetic solution" to the terrors of alienation (93–95). More important, movies can create a sense of heightened reality, a world in which the "pure possibility" of being and actuality seem to meet, as in the case of the western hero who acts with "gestural perfection" (94). Insofar as the film creates this sense of heightened reality, it represents the search for self-fulfillment that all seekers desire to undertake and fulfill. Thus the film is serious and to be taken seriously. As Binx says, movies are "on to the search," though they "screw it up" by closing off the openness of the search and returning the protagonist to the quotidian despair of everydayness. In a significant comment, Binx cites a study reporting that "a large percentage of solitary moviegoers are Jews" (89). Binx identifies with the solitary Jews as a people of exile, which is to say, paradoxically, that he feels a sense of community with the loners. Given what we learn of Binx's "connection" to the Jews, and their importance as a theosemiotic sign of the divine Logos in the world, Percy seems to suggest that, on this level, movies can represent something of the deepest spiritual longings for a transcendent reality in which the "possible" is fully actualized. But the movie in and of itself cannot realize that ideal.

As Percy argued, the "aesthetic solution" provided in art is not an "existential solution" to living in the everyday world (MB, 93–94). To attempt such a translation in the world is a kind of self-deception, shown repeatedly in Binx's vain attempts to emulate the "gestural perfection" of movie stars like Gregory Peck or Rory Calhoun. Such attempts, and their inevitable failure, only intensify alienation and despair. They lure Binx into false role playing as an exalted hero, an escape from the burden of undertaking the search with another person in the actual here-and-now. Apropos this truth, in two extended descriptions of moviegoing in the novel, Percy focuses not on the content of the films but on the movie experience as part of a larger semiotic context. In one episode Binx and Kate visit a favorite theater, nicknamed "The Pit." Binx attempts to "overcome" time by repetition of an earlier moviegoing experience and fails miserably, as we shall see. In the second episode, Binx's watching a western at the drive-in serves as a catalyst for a communion of love between him and his half-brother, Lonnie Smith. In sum, in his complex handling of the moviegoing motif Percy acknowledges the transfiguring power of film in the semiotic web of modern culture—as diversion, as sign of the times, or as clue to the search. But like Binx and Lonnie at the Moonlite Drive-In, the moviegoer must be "on to" the illusory nature of film as sign, enjoying its satisfactions while recognizing that the truer reality is to be found not as a solitary moviegoer but in the suffering community of the world.

One way that Percy dramatizes Binx the moviegoer's predicament is by examining his alienation from the various pseudo or deformed communities in the novel. Binx has only two genuine relationships in the novel: with Kate and Lonnie. Only with them does he have a truthful communion of words—a triadic, intersubjective relation—one that touches the depth of his being, through love. His other relationships—with his great-aunt Emily and her set, with his secretary Sharon, with college friends and business associates, even with his mother—are marked by misunderstanding and miscommunication, attempts at manipulation, and sometimes by Binx's deliberate evasiveness and deceit. In these exchanges "talk" proceeds by formula, a simulacrum of genuine community. Sometimes Binx responds in kind, assuming a "role." At other times, Binx falls silent, withdrawn into himself, or else he retreats solitarily to Gentilly. Percy's satiric depiction of the pervasive spiritual malaise in these pseudocommunities—"where everyone becomes an anyone" and people are "dead, dead, dead . . ."—sharply focuses the radical force of Kate's question to Binx: "How do you make your way in the world?" By pressure or allurement these pseudocommunities seek to incorporate the individual at a terrible price—relinquishing one's unique mysterious self. To "fit in" one must acquiesce in prefabricated roles, conventions, and speech, like a masked member of a Mardi Gras krewe. Conformity undermines authentic freedom and openness to mystery, to the signs of real presence in the world.

All of the pseudocommunities Binx engages in his search foster reductively "objective" views of the self. Binx's relation to his great-aunt Emily is a prime example of such a pseudocommunity. A grand lady of the old South, Emily is determined to shape Binx into her own image of what he should be. Many critics have pointed out that she is the voice of stoicism in the novel.[3] As we have already seen, Percy saw stoicism as the governing ethos in southern culture, in spite of the South's avowed allegiance to Jewish-Christianity. Stoicism affirms the "wintery kingdom of the self" and so is a logical derivative of the Cartesian spirit that Percy, following Tocqueville, saw as endemic in American culture (MB, 83–89). Although as a member of the southern gentry Emily Cutrer professes an elitism that sets her above "common" people, in her philosophical stoicism she is as American as those citizens Tocqueville identified two hundred years ago. Her stoicism is rooted in despair; it counsels dignified resignation to a doomed humanity in a doomed culture. Its vaunted indifference to pain and adversity reveals a lack of compassion. Its notion of community is of a closed world, without access to any transcendent order of being, a view certainly antithetical to the Christian belief in the risen Christ and resurrection of the body. Consequently, it commands allegiance to an ethic that is truly outmoded and retrogressive. It is radically anti-Christian in that it denies the in-break of the divine Word into history, and Jesus' command to love others in humility and charity. Emily has no use for commoners. Moreover, her stoicism precludes the possibility of real community. Binx instinctively recognizes this fact. He knows that his great-aunt's counsels are "dead" words, and so he ignores them for the most part as irrelevant to his predicament. For her part, she cannot fathom the nature of his search.

Emily's call for allegiance to her philosophy is sounded in the opening of the novel when Binx remembers the day his older brother, Scott, died. Walking with him near the hospital, she says: "Scotty is dead. Now it's all up to you. It's going to be difficult for you but I know you're going to *act like a soldier*." Recalling her remark now, he thinks: "This was true. I could easily act like a soldier. Was that all I had to do?" (4) (italics mine). Binx sees that she has already typecast him in a prescribed role, that of the "honorable" southern gentleman upholding stoic values in a chaotic, dissolute world. Binx's question to himself—"Was that all I had to do?"—reveals his sense of the deadly inadequacy of such a role, deadly precisely because it denies the mystery of living in the here-and-now, where the real clues to finding an authentic self lie. Ironically, Binx did "act like a soldier" in Korea, but not heroically or stoically. In fact, his close brush with death in the war awakened him to his predicament in the here-and-now and initiated his true search.

As Binx recognizes the fatalism of Emily Cutrer's philosophy, he also sees that the formulaic cultural Catholicism of her husband, Jules, is another simulacrum of genuine community. Binx wryly remarks:

> Uncle Jules is the only man I know whose victory in the world is total and unqualified. He has made a great deal of money, he has a great many friends, he was Rex of Mardi Gras, he gives freely of himself and of his money. He is an exemplary Catholic, but it is hard to know why he takes the trouble. For the world he lives in, the City of Man, is so pleasant that the City of God must hold little in store for him. I see his world plainly through his eyes and I see why he loves it and would keep it as it is: a friendly easy-going place of old-world charm and new-world business methods where kind white folks and carefree darkies have the good sense to behave pleasantly toward each other. No shadow ever crosses his face, except when someone raises the subject of last year's Tulane-L.S.U. game. (31)

In the elder Cutrers, then, Percy represents two deadening responses to the personal terror and the challenge of being a searcher for the real, for genuine community with others and with the divine presence in the world. Adjunct to the Cutrer world is Walter Wade, once the "arbiter of taste" as a fraternity man and friend to Binx in college. Walter has evolved smoothly from college life into a successful businessman and leader of "the best all-around krewe in Carnival" (34). Now he would initiate Binx into the community of conformist-consumers just as he guided him into his college fraternity. But even while in college Binx was alienated, "bemused and dreaming . . . lost in the mystery of finding myself alive at such a time and place" (38). He feels "slightly embarrassed" in Wade's company because of the role expectations; he feels "the stretch of the old tightrope, the necessity of living up to the friendship of friendships, of cultivating an intimacy beyond words" (40). So Binx resigns from the group he had initially joined, along with Wade and others, to purchase a houseboat for weekend parties, just as he earlier abandoned the two friends he went hiking with on the Appalachian Trail. Binx knows that such contrived attempts at intimacy in community, at finding "the real thing," are

literally *self*-defeating. They are diversions from the wonder, the mystery, of
being in the world, and as Binx says, "Not for five minutes will I be distracted
from the wonder" (42). Yet his statement is not entirely true. He is often distracted from the "wonder" while living as a solitary observer in Gentilly and
while pursuing the diversions of money making and romance. But desire—
"longing"—will drive him in search of genuine communion.

Percy makes clear that the pseudocommunities represented by the Cutrer-
Wade world are not atypical. Rather, they exemplify the standard of conformity seen, for example, in Binx's street encounter with Eddie Lovell, a fellow
businessman married to Binx's cousin Nell. While chatting with Eddie, Binx
has the clear impression that "everyone is dead," including himself, and that
their conversations are "spoken by automatons who have no choice in what
they say." As he listens to Eddie and Nell prate about their comfortable adjust-
ment to the world and their "enduring" values ("To make a contribution, however small, and leave the world just a little better off"), Binx reflects, "beyond a
doubt this is death. . . . We part laughing and dead" (99–100). Through Binx's
sense of their death-in-life existence, Percy probes beyond the conventional
criticism of 1950s American conformist culture to suggest its deeper metaphysical and theological roots. The "death" Binx intuits is their displacement
from the mystery and wonder of being, signified by the corruption of language
into exchanges of deadly clichés. When Nell talks to Binx of "making a contribution" to society, she is thinking in conventional ethical terms of the "good"
citizen's obligation. Percy does not deny the value of such commitments to the
social community, but for him the social world is not the whole community.
In fact, at the end of the novel Binx will begin to assume a constructive role in
the community as a physician, but on quite different terms. What will differ-
entiate Binx's commitment from that of the conformist Lovells is his insight
and his interior disposition. Binx knows that the mundane world is not his
true "home," but that he is nonetheless called to live and serve within the ordinary community, "for good and selfish reasons" (i.e., for his own salvation).
He knows there is the good of the spirit beyond the social good.

For Binx to live like the Lovells, notwithstanding their good deeds, would
be to narrow his vision to only the mundane world and turn away from the
mystery of the meaning of his existence within the semiotic-mystical community. To live like Nell and Eddie, or his aunt Emily Cutrer prefers, would mean
becoming a dispenser-consumer of good works and "honorable" deeds and
refusing the deeper challenge of the religious search. Here Percy shows a close
link between the stoicism of Emily Cutrer and the "positive" conformity of the

Lovells. Both typify the conformist's attitude of closure to the mystery encoded in the signs of the times. Binx senses this threat, and his silent foreboding accounts paradoxically for much of his easygoing posture toward others in the novel. Conformity, as Rene Girard has shown, is a theological and not merely a social issue. To do the will of the crowd is to reject the personal freedom that God wills for the self, as well as the command to search for and attune the human will with the divine will (*I See Satan*, 191).

Through Binx's predicament Percy also examines the limitations of the scientific viewpoint and of the scientific community when it presumes to explain existence totally according to abstract principles or postulates an all-embracing ideology. Such an ideology ignores divine agency and mystery and reduces creatures to dyadic organisms, as Percy argued later in *Lost in the Cosmos*. Binx calls the deductive method of this inflated scientism "the vertical search." Like the young engineer Will Barrett in *The Last Gentleman*, Binx tries for a time to "master" reality by adopting the role of objective, "scientific" theorist, but his efforts only aggravate his feeling of alienation:

> During those years I stood outside the universe and sought to understand it. I lived in my room as an Anyone living Anywhere and only for diversion took walks around the neighborhood and saw an occasional movie. Certainly it did not matter to me where I was when I read a book such as *The Expanding Universe*. The greatest success of this enterprise, which I call my vertical search, came one night when I sat in a hotel room in Birmingham and read a book called *The Chemistry of Life*. When I finished it, it seemed to me that the main goals of my search were reached or were in principle reachable, whereupon I went out and saw a movie called *It Happened One Night* which was itself very good. The only difficulty was that though the universe had been disposed of, I myself was left over. There I lay in my hotel room with my search over yet still obliged to draw one breath and then the next. (69–70)

Binx's experience of alienation is the inevitable result of adopting such a theoretical approach. He finally abandons his "vertical search" as well as a career in scientific research when he is overcome by the mystery of the here-and-now. The pivotal insight comes while he is working in the laboratory, doing research one summer on renal calculi with a fellow student named Harry Stern:

> I became extraordinarily affected by the summer afternoons in the laboratory. The August sunlight came streaming in the great dusty fanlights and lay in

yellow bars across the room. The old building ticked and creaked in the heat. Outside we could hear the cries of summer students playing touch football. In the course of an afternoon the yellow sunlight moved across old group pictures of the biology faculty. I became bewitched by the presence of the building; for minutes at a stretch I sat on the floor and watched the motes rise and fall in the sunlight. I called Harry's attention to the presence but he shrugged and went on with his work. He was absolutely unaffected by the singularities of time and place. His abode was anywhere . . . he is no more aware of the mystery which surrounds him than a fish is aware of the water it swims in. . . . By the middle of August I could not see what difference it made whether the pigs got kidney stones or not (they didn't, incidentally), compared to the mystery of those summer afternoons. . . . I moved down to the Quarter where I spend the rest of the vacation in quest of the spirit of summer and in the company of an attractive yet confused girl from Bennington who fancied herself a poet. (51–52)

Binx here experiences the world as a sign of the mystery of his own being, which is irreducible to "objective" formulation. He senses his "place" within the larger semiotic-mystical community, suggested by "the presence" he experiences. But mystery is elusive and always in danger of being romanticized, as when Binx leaves the laboratory and sets off "in quest of the spirit of summer." Still, such a discovery of mystery can inspire a genuine search for being and for communion with others. By rejecting the reduction of scientism here, Binx keeps himself open to such a search.

Binx's personal inclination to be the detached observer is balanced against his deeper desire for community and love, signified by the search that led him away from the laboratory and by his many flirtations with his secretaries. Early in the novel, his sudden memory of "the search" disrupted his peaceful life in Gentilly. When he recalled the first time the possibility of a search occurred to him, during the Korean War, he sensed that he was "onto something" and vowed to pursue the search later, but then soon forgot. Now the possibility of a search returns to him as he rides the bus to his great-aunt's house. Binx describes the search obliquely, since it cannot be defined directly. The search is Percy's mysterious sign for the heart's desire for union with God.

What is the nature of the search? you ask.

The search is what anyone would undertake if he were not sunk in the everydayness of his own life. This morning, for example, I felt as if I had come to myself on a strange island. And what does a castaway do? Why, he pokes around the neighborhood and he doesn't miss a trick.

To become aware of the possibility of the search is to be onto something. Not to be onto something is to be in despair. (13)

Binx then raises the question of the ultimate goal of the search: "What do you seek—God? you ask with a smile?" But he avoids trying to answer it, aware that the very attempt to define the mystery of the search is reductive, particularly in a culture given to abstract formulations of experience. Moreover, since he is a victim of Descartes, Binx's own excessive self-consciousness exacerbates the separation he feels between his felt experience, the world, and the "dead" language so often used to describe the search. Given this cultural and personal predicament, Binx knows that *talk* of God is well-nigh impossible. So Binx declares honestly, "On my honor, I do not know the answer" (14). The idea of a "search for God" has become a hollow, abstract formulation—empty words. Yet through Binx's evasiveness Percy infers that the search to be undertaken is not for the transcendent "God," but for the signs of the divine presence in the ordinary, concrete world. As Peirce noted, God's communication to the world is indirect and mysterious (Raposa, *Peirce's Philosophy of Religion*, 142–54). For Percy, those communications come through the Holy Spirit of God's presence, the incarnate Word of truth in the world. Binx's oblique but real commitment to this truth is evident in his response to the "wonder" and mystery of presence in the laboratory and his desire to pursue it. All Binx *does* know now is his desire to know, and that "answers" to his unique predicament are somehow bound up with his relations to others, especially his dead father. As the novel unfolds, Percy develops the meaning of Binx's search within this larger semiotic community.

Binx senses that there is a deep connection between his own predicament of how to "stick himself" into the world and that faced by his father years ago. Early in the novel, while examining a picture of his father and the two brothers, Dr. Will and Judge Anse, a picture he says he never tires of looking at, Binx notices that while the others are "serene in their identities" and that each "coincides with himself," his father seems out of place. He searches his father's eyes and concludes, "Beyond a doubt they are ironical." In his father's eyes Binx sees the same desire and "longing" and sense of displacement that he feels. Understanding his father's predicament and fate will be a key to his own self-discoveries. As he says later, "Any doings of my father, even his signature, is in the nature of a clue in my search" (71).

Binx's father was never able to accept the mystery of his place within the or-
dinary world, with its extensions into the semiotic-mystical community. Like
Binx, the elder Bolling was a romantic, alienated from the world he inhabited.
(There is a logical connection between the Cartesian spirit and romanticism.
Both infer a "flight" or dissociation from the incarnate real—flesh and spirit—
a flight from real presence as grounded in the Incarnation of God-in-Christ.
The romantic, sentimental flight from the real is "suicidal" to the genuine
self.) In the end, Binx's father was defeated by his predicament. Like Binx, he
tried various diversions to placate his restlessness. He built a duck club, "Roar-
ing Camp," for recreation and camaraderie, like Binx's houseboat venture. He
bought a telescope to study the universe and so assumed the "objective" observer role in the manner of Binx's failed vertical search. Both father and son
tried travel as a cure for restlessness; both have a strong desire for women; both
are insomniacs. Sleeplessness drove Mr. Bolling to "long walks" on the levee, as
it drives Binx to wander the streets of Gentilly at early morn, fascinated by the
wonder of place. Both are deeply misunderstood by those close to them; Binx
by his great-aunt Emily, and his father by his wife. As Binx says of his mother,
"She had a way of summing up his doings in a phrase that took the heart out of
him" (85). Mrs. Smith reduced her husband's mystery to the deadly formulae
of behavioral psychology. She labeled him as "overwrought" because of "his
psychological make-up," believed that he was temperamentally unsuited for
the life of an ordinary doctor, and that "he really should have been in research"
(154). (Eventually, Binx will also reject a career in medical research for the life
of an ordinary doctor, presumably with happier results.) Binx's mother fears
mystery and works to "manage" the "uncanny shocks of life," as when her
oldest child, Duval, died. She cannot understand her disabled son Lonnie's
penitential fasting in his weakened physical condition. Neither could she understand her husband's (or Binx's) restless searching, nor her own probable
complicity, given her attempts to "manage" life, in her husband's predicament.
In the end, when Binx's father cannot solve his restlessness, he escapes through
the ultimate stoic gesture, a "heroic" death in war.

Although both Binx and his father are romantics, Binx realizes the toll
this living by grand ideas took on his father and his generation. "Somewhere
it, the English soul, received an injection of romanticism that nearly killed
it. That's what killed my father, English romanticism, that and 1930 science"
(88). Whether Binx's statement is completely true—it smacks ironically of the
kind of "summing up" he accuses his mother of—it does give him a clue to
his own predicament. Immediately after describing what "killed" his father,

Binx cites a line from his own notebook: "Explore the connection between romanticism and scientific objectivity. Does a scientifically minded person become a romantic because he is a left-over from his own science?" (88). Binx is also a romantic "leftover" from the science of his vertical search. Knowing what defeated his father helps, but knowledge alone is not enough to cure his longing.

While Binx's search to know himself by understanding his father provides him with important clues, the crucial element propelling his search is his sense of his relation to the Jews. Binx's connection to the exilic search of the Jews in their covenant with God underlies Percy's exploration of community in *The Moviegoer*. Percy introduces the matter of the Jews immediately following Binx's talk of his father's fatal despair. Binx notices that "since Wednesday," the day he recalled the search, "I have become acutely conscious of Jews. There is a clue here, but of what I cannot say" (88). Binx remembers how once all of his friends were Jews and that he is "Jewish by instinct. We share the same exile. The fact is, however, I am more Jewish than the Jews I know. They are more at home than I am. I accept my exile." Binx then concludes, "Jews are my first real clue" (89).

Percy situates Binx's reflections on the Jews strategically between his thoughts of his father's fate and his encounter with Lonnie Smith, the most tangible living sign of eucharistic presence in the novel. This triadic relation— Binx and his father, the Jews, Lonnie Smith—constitutes the heart of Binx's search. By "the Jews," as stated earlier, Percy means the whole Jewish-Christian tradition, with the Incarnation as its axis point. The Jews are the semiotic link between God and humankind, the sign of covenant and mystical community in history. God's covenant with the Hebrews is established in prophetic scripture. In Christianity, the divine Word becomes human in a specific time and place as God's gift of Himself in His Son, an event that radically redefines the meaning and direction of history. The Jews, as Owen Barfield argued, are history's memory (*Saving the Appearances*, 155–66). Percy developed the implications of this triadic relation in various ways throughout his writings, most forcefully in *The Thanatos Syndrome*, as we shall see later. Here, Binx's sense of his link to the Jews as a clue to his predicament gives his horizontal search a specific historical and ontological axis. It implicitly links his search to the presence of the Word in history as the root of mysterious sign relations between humans. Hence, it is the focal point of semiotic community. Binx's search to "stick himself" into the world stands as a sign of the journey to recover that lost relation to true being, signified by the mysterious presence of the divine Word made flesh in concrete signs, which is threatened by the culture of scientism.

Percy never states this directly, of course, but the clues in Binx's narrative are unmistakable. Speaking of his connection to the Jews, he says: "When a man is in despair and does not in his heart of hearts allow that a search is possible and when such a man passes a Jew in the street, he notices nothing. When a man becomes a scientist or an artist, he is open to a different kind of despair. When such a man passes a Jew in the street, he may notice something but it is not a remarkable encounter. To him the Jew can only appear as a scientist or artist like himself or as a specimen to be studied. But when a man awakes to the possibility of a search and when such a man passes a Jew in the street for the first time, he is like Robinson Crusoe seeing the footprint on the beach" (89).

Percy's choice of terms in this pivotal passage is crucial. When Binx says that his relation to the Jews is a clue that makes a search *possible,* he is affirming Peirce's notion that sign relations include all that *could* occur in a real semiotic relation, as well as whatever *actual* relation exists. Stated differently, for Binx a sign relation to the Jews of history in the here-and-now is the existential opening to hope, the antithesis to that closure to being implicit in the stoic despair of his great-aunt Emily and his father. When Binx ties his search to the Jews and then compares it to "Robinson Crusoe seeing the footprint on the beach," he is affirming the possibility of a community of searchers who are open to such a sign as the "good news" of revelation, the divine Logos come into history through the Jews (MB, 119–50). Thus unlike the romantic quest, Binx's search for community is both existential and historical.

Binx's reawakening to the possibility of the search, his probing of his father's life as a clue to his predicament, and his thoughts about the Jews come at a critical turning point in the novel, namely, during his visit with his secretary Sharon Kincaid to the Smith's fishing camp on Bayou des Allemands. As I stated, Percy triangulates the key elements in this episode to suggest its full meaning. On the one hand are the clues to Binx's father's life that he gleans from talking to his mother. On the other hand are his reflections on his sense of identity with the Jews. The third in this semiosis is his relation to his crippled half-brother, Lonnie, the person of deep faith. Lonnie is a living sign of the reality of the Word in the world, linked to the Eucharist, the sacrament of community. As many commentators have noted, with Lonnie Binx speaks openly and honestly; together they establish an intimate bond of communion.[4] As he did earlier with Kate Cutrer, Binx immediately drops his role of wry, "objective" observer. Lonnie is a mystery who cannot be "formulated" cleverly as Binx did with the Lovells. Binx's initial comments about his half-brother reveal both their unique bond and Lonnie's deep spirituality: "He is my favorite, to tell the truth. Like me, he is a moviegoer. He will go see anything. But we are good friends because he knows I do not feel sorry for him. For one thing, he has the gift of believing that he can offer his sufferings in reparation for men's indifference to the pierced heart of Jesus Christ. For another thing, I would not mind so much trading places with him. His life is a serene business" (137). Binx is compassionate, but not sentimental, about Lonnie's illness; more important, he stands in awe of his half-brother's gift of faith. Lonnie's offering of his suffering in reparation for men's indifference to Jesus' suffering reveals the youth's belief in the reality of the mystical community and the communion of saints. His expiatory action—a *real* semiotic event— emulates the action of Christ in His sacrifice and spiritual gift giving. Near the end of the novel, when Lonnie dies, Binx will also affirm this community and the belief in the resurrection of the body.

Lonnie's life is marked by intense faith in that resurrection, yet he is also fully rooted in the here-and-now. He desperately wants to win first prize—a Zenith Trans-World radio—in a subscription drive contest, partly to compensate for having given up television for Lent. Moreover, he is ecstatic when Binx and Sharon take him to see a western, *Fort Dobbs,* at the Moonlite Drive-In, where, in one of the fine communal scenes of love in the novel, Lonnie and Binx intuitively share their "secret" joy and humor in watching hero Clint Walker triumph. Their unspoken bond of mutual love and joy shines through translucently in this scene.

Percy emphasizes Lonnie's importance as a sign of indwelling mystical community by focusing on the sacraments, especially the Eucharist. During his recent illness, Lonnie received the sacrament of the sick—Extreme Unction—to "strengthen him physically as well as spiritually" (142). Moreover, he now wants to fast and abstain during Lent, acts of self-denial and reparation that his mother cannot understand, though Binx does. More important, Lonnie's spiritual life is centered in the Eucharist, which becomes the topic of his and Binx's key colloquy in the novel. In their conversation Percy links the power of true words to form community—a *solitude à deux*—to the communal significance of the bread and wine. As they discuss renewing Binx's magazine subscription, Binx notes the integrity of Lonnie's speech: "his words are not worn out. It is like a code tapped through a wall. Sometimes he asks me straight out: do you love me? and it is possible to tap back: yes, I love you" (162). Binx advises Lonnie not to fast because of his poor health, but he insists on fasting to counteract "an habitual disposition" to envy his dead brother, Duval. Lonnie then accuses himself of having taken "joy at another's misfortune" by being glad that his brother is dead. Now acting as spiritual adviser-friend, Binx reminds him that he has already confessed this sin and received absolution. Binx invokes the mystical community when he reminds Lonnie that Duval now "sees God face to face." Moreover, he advises Lonnie to "concentrate on the Eucharist," a "more positive thing to do" because the "Eucharist is the sacrament of the living" (164). After their talk, Binx takes Lonnie for a ride along the boardwalk, then "wrestles" with him, playfully imitating Akim Tamiroff. But just before Binx and Sharon leave, Lonnie calls him back for a few final words.

> "Wait."
> "What?"
> He searches the swamp, smiling.
> "Do you think that Eucharist—"
> "Yes?"
> He forgets and is obliged to say, straight out: "I am still offering my communion for you."
> "I know you are."
> "Wait."
> "What?"
> "Do you love me?"
> "Yes."
> "How much?"
> "Quite a bit."
> "I love you too." But already he has the transistor in the crook of his wrist and is working at it furiously. (165)

Lonnie's abbreviated half-question—"Do you think that Eucharist—" is followed by his statement that he is still offering his communion for Binx, revealing his belief in the power of the Eucharist to bring grace to Binx. Percy also suggests that Lonnie may be offering his communion for Binx specifically as one of those "indifferent to the pierced heart of Jesus Christ" (137). If so, his expiatory gift of love to Binx may also suggest that the real clue to "sticking" oneself into the world is personified in Christ, the God-man, who, paradoxically, empties "the self" out of love for others. Perhaps this is also a clue to Binx's final commitment to Kate Cutrer and his vocation of healer at the end of the novel. Here, Percy's "answer" to individualism and the solipsism of the age is encoded in the mystical sign of the Eucharist and in the real communion of love between Binx and Lonnie. Such a *solitude à deux* becomes the ground of all genuine community in Percy's fictions, the hope of all solitary wayfarers. Yet Binx should not be interpreted as a covert "believer" who has the same faith as his half-brother. Percy's art is more subtle than this, of course. In the episodes at the Smiths' fishing camp, he offers clues to Binx's search so as to suggest its spiritual mystery, but it is mystery that Binx must live out, a possibility he must realize by his own choices and actions.

A clear indication of this mystery is Binx's inner crisis while at the fishing camp. He awakens in the middle of the night (like his father) to find himself "once again in the grip of everydayness. Everydayness is the enemy. No search is possible" (145). Angry, he vows not to be defeated by everydayness. For Binx, his sense of isolation from almost everyone around him is at the crux of his oppression by everydayness. "Neither my mother's family nor my father's family understand my search," he says (145). His great-aunt Emily misreads his restlessness stereotypically as a youthful need for a "fling" or *wanderjahr,* and while wishing to cast him in the role of stoic hero, she thinks he's best suited for a career in research. Similarly, his mother and step-father believe his vocation is to scientific research. On matters religious, the Smiths also misunderstand Binx. In typical self-deprecating fashion, Binx says: "My mother's family thinks I have lost my faith and they pray for me to recover it. I don't know what they're talking about. Other people, so I have read, are pious as children and later become skeptical. . . . Not I. My unbelief was invincible from the beginning. I could never make head or tail of God. The proofs of God's existence may have been true for all I know, but it didn't make the slightest difference. If God himself had appeared to me, it would have changed nothing. In fact, I have only to hear the word God and a curtain comes down in my head" (145). Binx's apparent agnosticism is another of the masks he wears before the world. Like the young St. Augustine, Binx is profoundly self-divided, since he admitted elsewhere that in his search he is "onto" the God of mystery and presence. His focus here is on the deadening attempts by those around him to formulate "God" in conventional language or propose rational proofs. Binx rejects "God talk," but he does not deny the *possibility* of a search for God. At the same time, his so-called "invincible" unbelief reveals his deformed Cartesian consciousness, which makes it nearly impossible for him to hear the "good news" as a personal revelation. As for his father's family, Binx says they "think that the world makes sense without God and that anybody but an idiot knows what the good life is and anyone but a scoundrel can lead it" (146). Their worldview is fashioned on a humanistic ethic that precludes mystery and the possibility of a God who issues a personal call to the individual.

Yet notwithstanding these two crippling "parental" influences, Binx refuses to abandon his search, vowing "Not to move a muscle until I advance another inch in my search." His advance comes in the form of a fresh insight, recorded in his notebook:

REMEMBER TOMORROW.
Starting point for the search:
It no longer avails to start with creatures and prove God.
Yet it is impossible to rule God out.
The only possible starting point: the strange fact of one's own invincible apathy—that if the proofs were proved and God presented himself, nothing would be changed. Here is the strangest fact of all.
Abraham saw signs of God and believed. Now the only sign is that all the signs in the world make no difference. Is this God's ironic revenge? *But I am onto him.*
(146) (Italics mine)

Binx's question—"Is this God's ironic revenge?"—is crucial for understanding the modern predicament of the religious searcher as Percy presents the dilemma here. Binx suggests that the collapse of signs and the devaluation of language may be a logical consequence of the rejection of the divine Word and that God in his gift of freedom to humanity has allowed this collapse, perhaps even as part of some mysterious design. Percy pursued this implication further in the "silence" of Father John in *Lancelot,* and in his various meditations on language in *The Thanatos Syndrome.* As he once said, the devaluation of language "is the pathology of the twentieth century" (Con., 230). Nevertheless, Binx does affirm here the possibility of God as integral to his search. What is missing, however, is some specific connection between Binx the searcher and the "possibility" of God, though his intuition that he is a Jew suggests the semiotic and historical link to the incarnate Word. That connection will emerge in the reciprocal love Binx finds with Kate Cutrer and the *solitude à deux* community they create. Like Lonnie, Kate is linked symbolically to the Jews. She becomes the living sign for Binx of the real possibility of community in the world. His present apathy is indeed a sign of his egotism and his "indifference to the pierced heart of Jesus Christ." But through his relation with Kate, Binx will begin to develop genuine love and care for others, without which talk of God becomes dead words and "love" degenerates into lustful desire.

Binx's relationship to Kate Cutrer is the most important, complicated, and controversial element in the novel. Some critics have emphasized Kate's fragile, unstable personality; her erratic behavior; and her psychological dependence on Binx even after they are married.[5] Though she is vulnerable, Kate also has a resilient spirit. Part of her vulnerability comes from her acute awareness of the terror and pitfalls of trying to live as an honest person in a deformed culture. The "abyss" she so keenly recognizes is the threatening loss of her true self. She too is searching for community with another, and as I noted, Kate is the only person besides Lonnie with whom Binx can talk honestly. Kate pierces the facade of Binx's role playing; Binx in turn shares with her his ideas of the search (and apparently with no one else). In the end, their mutual love and care enables them to join in a genuine *solitude à deux* so that they can live a life together in hope and as truthful searchers.

Binx's first meeting with Kate occurs when he is called to his great-aunt Emily's house to help Kate through another of her crises. When he arrives, she is withdrawn from the group—Emily, Uncle Jules, her fiancé Walter Wade— silent and watchful as Binx role-plays for his great-aunt as the feckless young scion of the family. When Kate and Binx finally meet alone in the ground-level basement, Kate asks the probing question: "How do you make your way in the world?" Binx tries to deflect the question, but she persists:

> "And how do you appear so reasonable to mother?"
> "I feel reasonable with her."
> "She thinks you're one of her kind."
> "What kind is that?"
> "A proper Bolling. Jules thinks you're a go-getter. But you don't fool me."
> "You know."
> "Yes."
> "What kind?"
> "You're like me, but worse. Much worse." (43)

Kate knows they are both searchers, alienated from the factitious social communities around them. But unlike the hypocritical and more accommodating Binx, she refuses to play a role at the cost of her integrity. Instead, alone and desperate, she walks a spiritual "tightrope," conscious of the "abyss" beneath them. She tries honestly to face the catastrophe of alienation that has overtaken them in their world. She searches for some way to span the abyss but is disabled by her own penchant for "objectifying" reality.

Emily Cutrer's way of dealing with Kate's crises is to deny their seriousness, assign superficial causes to them, or call on Binx to cajole her back into a "normal" social role. But Binx understands something of the depth of Kate's predicament, since it mirrors *in extremis* his own. Both are inclined to assume "objective" theorist stances toward the world, Kate to more detrimental effect because she is more serious minded than Binx and less able to resist the tendency to objectify. Intense and self-absorbed, she lacks Binx's shield of humor and self-deprecating irony, as well as his nascent faith. Listening to her describe a case she handled as a social worker, Binx feels "the sense of our new camaraderie, the camaraderie of a science which is not too objective to pity the folly and ignorance of the world" (45). In her "objective" mode, Kate is as much a victim of Descartes as is Binx. Like the scientist, and like Binx when he pursued the vertical search, Kate sets herself "outside" the world and attempts to construe it causally and dyadically. In so doing she "loses" herself as an incarnate creature living within mystery. But when her flight into objectivity falters, Kate comes crashing down to ordinary life and is sunk deeper in her predicament. She needs Binx to help, as it were, "reincarnate" her and help her survive these crises by guiding her through simple concrete decisions in the here-and-now. Kate's predicament is one Percy often pointed to: how to live through the next minute, hour, day—a four-o'clock Wednesday afternoon—without succumbing to despair?

What binds Kate and Binx deeply is their mutual awareness of the "abyss" of inauthenticity that surrounds them. They share this "secret" because both have experienced disasters that paradoxically gave them back their lives (i.e., the knowledge of themselves as alienated creatures living in mystery, as well as clues to the possibility of a search). Binx discovered this when he was wounded in the Korean War; Kate when she survived the car wreck that killed her first fiancé, Lyell. But as Percy's Lancelot Lamar will ask later, "What do survivors *do?*" Now Kate cannot deal with ordinary experience. In her excessive objectivity she is in danger of becoming an "Anyone from Anywhere," as Binx said of himself. Even when she breaks her engagement to Walter Wade and exults in her "freedom," she cannot ease the threat of breakdown and the "abyss." Because he realizes her predicament, Binx can help her, though there is the risk that their close relationship may degenerate into manipulation. Binx senses this after they watch the movie *Panic in the Street:* "She sounds better but she is not. She is trapping herself, this time by being my buddy, best of all buddies and most privy to my little researches. In spite of everything she finds herself, even now, playing out the role. In her long nightmare, this our old friendship now itself falls victim to the grisly transmogrification by which she unfailingly turns everything she touches to horror" (63).

Kate is "trapping herself" too often, Binx sees, so he tries to help her by creating diversions from her crises, especially by moviegoing. He takes her to see a western at a movie house nicknamed "The Armpit," a theater Binx frequented years ago. With his familiar Cartesian habit of objectifying, Binx claims that nothing has changed at the theater since those earlier days. He calls the evening's diversion a "successful repetition." He thinks to himself, "What is a repetition? A repetition is a re-enactment of past experience toward the end of isolating the time segment which has elapsed in order that it, the lapsed time, can be savored of itself and without the usual adulteration of events that clog time like peanuts in brittle" (79–80). The intervening twenty years, Binx says, "were neutralized, the thirty million deaths, the countless torturings, up-rootings and wanderings to and fro. . . . There remained only time itself, like a yard of smooth peanut brittle" (80). Binx tries to abstract and "purify" time of its contingency, but his claim to have neutralized history and canceled out the mystery of time and place is a hollow one, as he quickly realizes: "How, then, tasted my own fourteen years since *The Oxbow Incident?* As usual it eluded me. There was this: a mockery about the old seats, their plywood split, their bottoms slashed, but enduring nevertheless as if they had waited to see what I had done with my fourteen years. There was this also: a secret sense of wonder about the enduring, about all the nights, the rainy summer nights at twelve and one and two o'clock when the seats endured alone in the empty theater. The enduring is something which must be accounted for. One cannot simply shrug it off" (80). Binx's adaptation of Kierkegaard's concept of repetition here leads him to an important revelation.[6] It is an incarnational moment—one that requires a measure of faith to grasp. The "mockery" of the "enduring" old seats calls Binx to account for "what I had done with my fourteen years." The "secret sense of wonder" Binx feels in the here-and-now is a semiotic link to the wonder and mystery of the search. The "enduring" of the seats "which must be accounted for" is a sign of the real yet invisible semiotic web of relations between past and present Binx inhabits. He intuits this real-ity, this mystery of real presence, though he does not link this intuition to the incarnate God-in-Christ who sanctifies time and place and lives in the signs of the ordinary world. Though Binx misses this ultimate relation, his sense of the mystery of presence works to undermine his attempt to isolate—and thereby "neutralize"—the reality of history's thirty million dead and count-less tortures. Binx is forced to see that he is *in* history, *in* time, in a web of sign relations that *mean* and that call him to account for his life. He cannot abstract himself from it.

Percy immediately follows Binx and Kate's diversionary moviegoing with their pivotal discussion of the search. The scene also registers the depth of their growing bond. As they wander through the college campus together, Kate asks Binx, "What is this place?" He replies, "I spent every afternoon for four years in one of those laboratories up there" (81). Kate questions him, trying to identify with him in his search:

> "Is this part of the repetition?"
>
> "No."
>
> "Part of the search?"
>
> I do not answer. She can only believe I am serious in her own fashion of being serious: as an antic sort of seriousness, which is not seriousness at all but despair masking as seriousness. I would as soon not speak to her of such things, since she is bound to understand it as a cultivated eccentricity. . . .
>
> "Why don't you sit down?" I ask her irritably.
>
> "Now the vertical search is when—"
>
> "If you walk in the front door of the laboratory, you undertake the vertical search. You have a specimen, a cubic centimeter of water or a frog or a pinch of salt or a star."
>
> "One learns general things."
>
> "And there is excitement to the search."
>
> "Why?" she asks.
>
> "Because you get deeper into the search, you unify. You understand more and more specimens by fewer and fewer formulae. There is the excitement. Of course you are always after the big one, the new key, the secret leverage point, and that is the best of it." (82)

Kate understands how the vertical search nullifies the person as a searcher:

> "And it doesn't matter where you are or who you are."
>
> "No."
>
> "And the danger is of becoming no one nowhere."
>
> "Never mind."

Binx tries to break off the conversation, aware that Kate's attempt to for-mulate and explain the search runs the risk of reducing its mystery to another datum of empirical knowledge. Such an approach only exacerbates alienation. The search, as mystery, cannot be categorized, defined, or spoken of directly. Binx sees how "Kate parses it out with the keen male bent of her mind and yet with her woman's despair. Therefore I take care to be no more serious than she" (83). Binx is deliberately evasive, but Kate persists:

> "On the one hand, if you sit back here and take a little carcass out of the garbage can, a specimen which has been used and discarded, there remains something left over, a clue?"
>
> "Yes, but let's go."
>
> "You're a cold one, dear."
>
> "As cold as you?"
>
> "Colder. Cold as the grave." She walks about tearing shreds of flesh from her thumb. I say nothing. It would take very little to set her off on an attack on me, one of her "frank" appraisals.
>
> "It is possible, you know, that you are overlooking something, the most obvious thing of all. And you would not know it if you fell over it."
>
> "What?"
>
> She will not tell me. Instead, in the streetcar, she becomes gay and affectionate toward me. She locks her arms around my waist and gives me a kiss on the mouth and watches me with brown eyes gone to disks. (83)

Binx is rightly perplexed. Percy couples Kate's accusation that Binx is "cold as the grave" with her "tearing shreds of flesh from her thumb." Both have "missed" a clue to their relation. Binx retreats into aloofness, while Kate reverts to distracted self-abuse of her body. Is the clue Kate tells Binx he is overlooking a true revelation of her affection for him, or is it just another "move" in her attempt to objectify reality? Does Kate herself even know? Yet although she will not tell him what she has in mind, Kate answers with a frank kiss. Perhaps the clue, the "something left over" from their talk of the search, is her unspoken love for him. Hence, she insists that in his vertical searching he is "cold as the grave." Both are maimed and self-isolated creatures, yet both are searchers. As Kate is drawn to Binx, so also is he drawn to her as the one who knows him best, one with whom he can share his deepest longings. This fact is soon made clear by Binx's unconventional proposal of marriage to Kate. Eventually, such a union and all the risks it entails will propel them from detachment and self-absorption into the mystery of love.

Binx's marriage proposal to Kate comes during his own "crisis," when his comfortably isolated life in Gentilly is disrupted by his uncle Jules. Although

Binx claims to be in love with his secretary Sharon Kincaid, it is merely another of his flirtations, signified by his role playing as "Gregory Peck" or "Rory Calhoun." Such flirtations leave him sick with unfulfilled desire, as restless as the young St. Augustine. Then suddenly his uncle Jules orders him to attend a business conference in Chicago, that "great beast" of a "noplace" where, years before, Binx's father attempted to form an intimate bond with his son and failed miserably. Now Binx awakens in the middle of the night and contemplates another possible career, building and managing a service station. When Kate appears, she is overly ecstatic at a new discovery of her "freedom," made during a conversation with her analyst Merle. She believes "a person does not have to *be* this or *be* that or anything, not even oneself. One is free" (114). But Binx recognizes this as another of her "objective" orbits: "[she] is nowhere; she is in the realm of her idea" (113). When he sees her flight of transcendence begin to falter as she sinks back into the concrete present, Binx proposes a life for them together:

> "We could stay on here at Mrs. Schexnaydre's. It is very comfortable. I may even run the station myself. You could come sit with me at night, if you liked. Did you know you can net over fifteen thousand a year on a good station?"
>
> "You sweet old Binx! Are you asking me to marry you?"
>
> "Sure." I watch her uneasily.
>
> "Not a bad life, you say. It would be the best of all possible lives!"
>
> She speaks in a rapture—something like my aunt. My heart sinks. It is too late. She has already overtaken herself. (116)

Kate's brief flight of "freedom" collapses again into paralyzing terror. "I'm so afraid," she groans. "What am I going to do?" Binx assures her that "everything is going to be all right" and takes her to the French Market for coffee. Here Binx is willing to assume a role of authority and show Kate what to do. This direction comes from his loving concern for her and his sense of what she needs most—a way to live and act within the ordinary world and the here-and-now, without balancing precariously over the abyss.

Percy triangulates the individual crises of Binx and Kate with Binx's marriage proposal to develop their movement toward a *solitude à deux*. But their solidarity is again threatened with the arrival of Sam Yerger, a writer-lecturer and cultural guru. Sam is a romantic wanderer, and his search for the "ultimate" experience is one of the many parody versions of the search in Percy's fictions. Yerger's search is egoistic and sentimental, not religious. His quest for the transcendent, self-fulfilling experience is a flight from the mystery of incarnate presence that signifies the genuine search. Such a romantic quest is symptomatic of the loner-individualist's deep alienation from real community; hence, it is driven by despair. Sam has arranged for Kate to receive counseling in New York from Etienne Sue, a therapist said to be one of those "continental geniuses," and to live with "The Princess," a seventy-five-year-old doyen who wants a "nice Southern girl" as companion. Secretly, Yerger has other motives; that night he proposes marriage to Kate. With Yerger's and Emily's connivings, and Binx's commanded trip to Chicago, Percy compounds the mutual crises Kate and Binx now face.

To underscore this development as a crucial turning point, Percy juxtaposes Binx and Kate's conversation about her latest crisis and his marriage proposal with the dinner conversation of Emily, Yerger, and others. Binx and Kate meet in the "dark little mezzanine" adjacent to but hidden from the dining room. As a narrative strategy, Percy creates this triangular vantage point from which to mediate the action and meaning of the two interwoven scenes. While Yerger spiels on in the background, Kate tells Binx of her night of crisis, how she felt as if she "were coming to the end of [her] rope" after several hours of heady "talk" with Sam and her aunt. Against Sam's conversational "flight," Kate sets Binx's modest marriage proposal. "I thought about your proposal and it seems to be that it might be possible after all. If only I did not ruin everything" (178). Kate is afraid to embrace the quotidian life, of living in the here-and-now, as she is terrified of her own flights into "objectivity," knowing of the inevitable crash. She insists to Binx that she did not intend suicide when she overdosed on sleeping pills, but that she wanted only to "break out, or off, off dead center," because everything "seemed so—no 'count somehow, you know?" (181). While they speak, they overhear in the background Emily and Sam talk of their "messianic hopes," of "the new messiah, the scientist-philosopher-mystic who would come striding through the ruins with the *Gita* in one hand and a Geiger-counter in the other" (181–82). (Of course neither Emily nor Sam would recognize the possibility that the Messiah has already come and is present.) Hearing her aunt and Yerger talk, and aware of their manipulations, Kate suddenly decides to "break off" dead center by going to Chicago on the train with Binx, even wondering if they can flee "out West" afterward. Binx answers cagily: "It is possible."

In presenting the train ride to Chicago, Percy satirically depicts Binx and Kate's fellow passengers as other representative victims of Descartes. Each of them suffers from the Cartesian split: abstraction and theorizing on the one hand, and entrapment in desacralized flesh on the other. For example, as Binx and Kate approach the crisis of their own sexual intimacy, Binx recalls attending a book signing by Dr. and Mrs. Bob Dean, coauthors of *Technique in Marriage*. Percy parodies their "scientific" approach to sexual foreplay, the dyadic, causal approach of behaviorism, using its own jargon: " 'Now with a tender regard for your partner remove your hand from the nipple and gently manipulate—' It is impossible not to imagine them at their researches, as solemn as a pair of brontosauruses, their heavy old freckled limbs twined about each other, hands probing skillfully for sensitive zones, pigmented areolas, out-of-the-way mucous glands, dormant vascular nexuses" (190). At the same time, Binx observes a passenger from St. Louis reading an article headlined "Scientist Predicts Future If Nuclear Energy Is Not Misused" (190). This pseudoprophetic writing with hubristic optimism forecasts "the gradual convergence of physical and social science," a prediction that to Binx "howls through the Ponchitoula Swamp, the very sound and soul of despair" (191).

Yet despite Binx's recognitions, he and Kate are also victims of this dualistic ethos. Both are free floating and dislocated throughout the train ride, suffering "the peculiar gnosis of trains." Binx says, "as the train rocks along on its unique voyage through space-time, thousands of tiny thing-events bombard us like cosmic particles" (190). Percy suggests that their dislocation is symptomatic of a culture that has lost its relation to the definitive space-time event, the Incarnation, the heart of semiotic mystical community. Kate is especially disturbed, afraid of what their actions might forebode for a future together. "You're nuttier than I am. One look at you and I have to laugh. Do you think that is sufficient grounds for marriage?" she asks. Binx replies, "As good as any. Better than love" (192). Binx realizes that mutual awareness of their predicament is a better starting point than the vagaries of romantic "love" and yearning. But Kate is terrified that marriage to Binx might trap her again in the abyss of falseness. She mistrusts Binx's clever verbal obliquity and so again tries to "parse it out" objectively. Kate argues:

> "The only way you could carry it off is as another of your ingenious little researches. Admit it."
> "Then why not do it?"
> "You remind me of a prisoner in the death house who takes a wry pleasure in doing things like registering to vote. Come to think of it, all your gaiety and good spirits have the same death house quality. No thanks. I've had enough of your death house pranks."

"What is there to lose?"

"Can't you see that after what happened last night, it is no use. I can't play games now. . . . Losing hope is not so bad. There's something worse: losing hope and hiding it from yourself."

"Very well. Lose hope or not. Be afraid or not. But marry me anyhow, and we can still walk abroad on a summer night, hope or no hope, shivering or not, and see a show and eat some oysters down on Magazine." (193–94)

Binx senses that Kate has reached a crisis point over his offer of marriage and is again in danger of "transcending" herself and then crashing. When the train stops in Jackson she waxes romantically over the "beauty of the city in moonlight," but Binx insists that "Beauty, the quest for beauty alone, is a whoredom" (196). Binx is wise enough to know that the idea of a romantic quest for aesthetic fulfillment is inadequate to the heart's deepest longings. Against this aesthetic desire Percy subtly poses the idea of the religious seeker.[7] In another of her revelations, Kate claims that she has now discovered who she is and a way to live—by Binx "telling [her] what to do." When Binx asks "What are you?" she exclaims:

"I am a religious person. . . . What I want is to believe in someone completely and then do what he wants me to do. If God were to tell me: Kate, here is what I want you to do; you get off this train right now and go over there to that corner by the Southern Life and Accident Insurance Company and stand there for the rest of your life and speak kindly to people—you think I would not do it? You think I would not be the happiest girl in Jackson, Mississippi? I would." (197)

On the surface it may seem that Kate's remark is another of her erratically "transcendent" epiphanies and therefore self-defeating. But on a deeper level it reveals her desire to find someone she can believe in as an authority, someone whose words will tell her how to live. Kate intuits that somehow this need is a key to her spiritual well-being, a relation that could begin to heal her riven self, providing she does not exchange her crippling gnostic "flights" for crippling dependence. Kate is indeed a religious person who longs for God, the ultimate Authority. But as another victim of Descartes living in what Steiner calls the time of the "after-Word," she cannot "locate" that divine presence in the here-and-now. But she does see Binx as one who might help her by directing her steps in the ordinary world where she must find her way.

For Percy, Kate's spiritual predicament reflects that of the age. It is the predicament Percy observed in "Notes for a Novel about the End of the World," when he described the modern mind as so infected with Cartesian scientism that hearing the "good news" of the *kerygma* becomes nearly impossible (MB, 113). The divine semiosis—God, Jesus the Word, mankind—has been occluded or distorted. Moreover, in Kate's wished-for relation with Binx, Percy alludes indirectly to Kierkegaard's essay "On the Difference between a Genius and an Apostle," an influential essay in his conversion to Catholicism. The genius, Kierkegaard argues, can convey truths *sub species aeternitatis,* confirmable by anyone, anywhere, anytime. But only the apostle can convey truths on his own authority as a news bearer, as one who utters truths ("news") specific to the unique predicament of the individual hearer.[8] Binx clearly lacks such authority. He is not an apostle to bring Kate the "good news" of Christian redemption. But he can serve as an "authority" insofar as he helps her to act in the concrete world. Binx eventually assumes this burden as part of his vocation to help others, even though he is also a victim of the times. Here, Kate is willing to put her faith in Binx because she believes he is not "religious" in any conventional sense:

> "You can do it because you are not religious. God is not religious. You are the unmoved mover. You don't need God or anyone else—no credit to you, unless it is a credit to be the most self-centered person alive. I don't know whether I love you, but I believe in you and will do what you tell me. . . . Will you?"
>
> "Sure." (197)

Kate's belief that Binx doesn't "need God or anyone else" is wrong, of course. Binx's search, which he admitted is linked to the God he is "onto," is intimately bound up with finding communion with another person. The two strands of his search—for God and for loving *caritas* with another—signify his desire to find his true place, understood as the real, mystical community. But Kate's charge that he is self-centered is two edged, as Percy intends. On the one hand, it points to his selfish use of others to try to gratify his desire and longing. On the other hand, it conveys Percy's idea that becoming an integral human person, such as Lonnie Smith, is an essential part of any genuine religious search. Both Kate and Binx find that self-integration difficult to achieve at this point. Kate is in danger of transfiguring Binx into her own image of him, and thereby manipulating him for her own ends. He is not the "unmoved mover," of course, but neither is he a diffident or stoic dilettante. While he can be a human voice of authority for her to help her out of her paralyzing, self-destructive flights of "objectivity" and reorient her to the ordinary world, that role also has its terrors, particularly because of Binx's lust. Thus when Kate, out of her desperate anxiety to "prove" her fleshly womanhood, entices him into "a little fling," Binx again falls prey to sexual desire, his constant nemesis, and to romantic role playing as the lover and accommodating southern "gentleman."

Binx and Kate attempt a communion of flesh to experience "the real thing" and appease their solitude and longing. Significantly, it takes place in a "no place," the train Binx named as saturated with gnosis. Percy's choice of the phrase "the real thing" is deadly accurate. While it echoes Henry James, it more importantly points to the semiotic real, the spiritual bond signified in and through the physical. But the real thing eludes Binx and Kate, as he acknowledges in speaking to his role model and alter ego "Rory Calhoun":

> We did very badly and almost did not do at all. Flesh poor flesh failed us. The burden was too great and flesh poor flesh, *neither hallowed by sacrament nor despised by spirit* (for despising is not the worst fate to overtake the flesh), but until this moment seen through and canceled, rendered null by the cold and fishy eye of the malaise—flesh poor flesh now at this moment summoned all at once to be the all and everything, end all and be all, the last and only hope— quails and fails. The truth is I was frightened half to death by her bold (not really bold, not whorish bold but theorish bold) carrying on. I reckon I am used to my blushing little Lindas from Gentilly. Kate too was scared. We shook like leaves. Kate was scared because it seemed now that even Tillie the Toiler must fail her. I never worked so hard in my life, Rory. I had no choice: the alternative was unspeakable. Christians talk about the horror of sin, but they have overlooked something. They keep talking as if everyone were a great sinner, when the truth is that nowadays one is hardly up to it. There is very little sin in the depths of the malaise. The highest moment in a malaisian's life can be that moment when he manages to sin like a proper human. (Look at us, Binx—my vagabond friends as good as cried out to me—we're sinning! We're succeeding! We're human after all!). (200–201) (Italics mine)

In this important passage, Percy sets the failure of Binx and Kate's sexual escapade precisely in the context of a Cartesian-deformed world in which the mystery of spirit-in-flesh signified by the Incarnation and the sacrament of the Eucharist has been subverted by scientism. Consequently, in the age of the after-Word, language's power to name and judge true reality is also subverted. "Sin" as a spiritual reality is "canceled" out or vaporized; as Hawthorne's Young Goodman Brown said, sin has become but a "name." The attenuations of scientism have undermined the authority of the Word. Yet the victims of

Descartes strain to affirm their real humanity through sex. Percy's sense of the dilemma of the modern self not centered in sacramental mystery is acute. "Flesh" as sign is neither "hallowed" by Christian sacrament nor "despised by spirit" (as in dualism). Binx recognizes his world as both "post-Christian" *and* post-romantic idealist. In this malaise, "flesh," the incarnated human self, is reduced to an object for manipulation, no more than an organism with "needs" to fulfill. Binx and Kate's attempted union, in which everything is staked on the physical bond alone, terrifies both of them. Their sexual act becomes another "performance" doomed to failure, a desperate parody of the losing-oneself-to-find-oneself in a real communion of intimacy and love with another. Instead, Binx and Kate ironically act out a failed demonstration of the Deans' sex manual, *Technique in Marriage*. Only later, with Will Barrett and Allie Huger in *The Second Coming*, would Percy describe a successful word-in-flesh sexual union, a coming together of lovers that is a gift giving in language and deed.

Later, Binx also recognizes their sexual failure as a symptom of the general cultural malaise. In this desacralized world, human sexuality has lost its ontological and ethical ground as a mystery that points to the ultimate source of being. The physical union that once possessed spiritual meaning has now been reduced to a mechanistic exchange. Consequently, Binx intuits at the heart of despair a separation of human sexual desire from the true source and goal of human longing—union with God:

> What an experience, Rory, to be free of it for once. Rassled out. What a sickness it is, Rory, this latter-day post-Christian sex. To be pagan it would be one thing, an easement taken easily in the rosy old pagan world; to be Christian it would be another thing, fornication forbidden and not even to be thought of in the new life, and I can see that it need not be thought of if there were such a life. But to be neither pagan nor Christian but this: oh this is a sickness, Rory. For it to be longed after and dreamed of the first twenty years of one's life, not practiced but not quite prohibited; simply longed after, longed after as a fruit not really forbidden but mock-forbidden and therefore secretly prized, prized first last and always by the cult of the naughty nice wherein everyone is nicer than Christians and naughtier than pagans, wherein there are dreamed not one but two American dreams: of Ozzie and Harriet, nicer-than-Christian folks, and of Tillie and Mac and belly to back. (207)

The "two American Dreams," of course, point to the regnant Cartesian spirit and the dilemma it poses for Kate and Binx. Lancelot Lamar will express the same dilemma more angrily later, when he condemns God for creating human sexuality and desire in the first place. But Binx, riding the train to Chicago, does not reach the depth of sexual despair that Lancelot will during his search later.

After their sexual misalliance on the train, Binx's trip to Chicago continues to be a "catastrophe," but a beneficent catastrophe that eventually brings him to a decisive turning point in his search. Binx feels dislocated in Chicago, threatened by anonymity and the strange "genie-soul"—the palpable spirit— of the city. As is so often the case in Percy's fiction, the possible loss of identity Binx feels threatened with is signified by a sense of dislocation from space and time. Binx stands on street corners "blinking and bemused," literally disoriented. Kate, by contrast, seems "at home" in the free-floating anonymity of the big city, taking charge while Binx stands paralyzed by the "five million personal rays of Chicagoans" (203–4). To compound his spatial-temporal dislocation, Binx is deeply afflicted by the awakened memories of earlier trips to Chicago with his father.

A crucial event in the search for community by Percy's male protagonists is their encounter with the father figure, as William Rodney Allen and several other critics have shown.[9] The father is a decisive presence in the semiotic world of the searcher. The encounter often takes the form of a recovered memory of a key event in the protagonist's earlier life. The father figure is a "voice" of authority, for good or ill, in the protagonist's mind. His influential words and presence, even when long dead, command attention and respect; they create an intimate and indissoluble bond between father and son. Percy subtly links the "crisis" of Binx's recollection of earlier trips to Chicago with his father to the broader malaise in America, romantic individualism and scientism's belief in progress, both of which proved fatal to the elder Bolling. On their first trip, his father took Binx and his brother Scott to see the *Century of Progress* exhibit; later, they went to the World Series. Recalling that trip now, Binx explains how every place has a "genie-soul" that must be met and mastered, at the risk of losing one's sense of specific locus in space-time. He then admits his own failure to master the genie-soul of a place—in San Francisco, "the sadness of coming at last to the sea, the coming to the end of America" (202). Binx's association of his father as a victim of romantic restlessness and "1930 science" with the celebration of the "Century of Progress," and then with the "end of America" in San Francisco, suggests the larger fate of the solitary restless self in America that Tocqueville and Percy saw as the inevitable consequence of the prevailing Cartesian spirit. The loneliness Binx's father felt is symptomatic of the national condition. His alienation from genuine community, from place and a sense of "home," typifies the national ethos. As Binx says, "This Midwestern sky is the nakedest loneliest sky in America" (203).

The "Century of Progress" in America, Percy suggests, is in fact a romantic retrogression within the culture, a flight from the terror of solitude and the hard demands of real community. During their Chicago trips Binx's father also took him "underground" (a foreshadowing of Percy's solitary protagonists' attraction to caves, dark and secret places) "to see the pool where Tarzan-Johnnie-Weissmuller used to swim," the aquatic "home" of the American athlete-hero-primitive *cum* movie star. Some years later, he takes Binx to another monumentalized symbol of "progress," the Field Museum, where they "stood before a tableau of Stone Age Man, father mother and child crouched around an artificial ember in postures of minatory quiet" (204). This emblem of a prehistoric family ironically mocks the romantic ideal of primitive community so engrained in the American psyche. As well, it serves as a backdrop and semiotic counterpoint to the failure of intimacy and love between father and son, as Binx now recalls: "feeling my father's eye on me, I turned and saw what he required of me—very special father and son we were that summer, he staking his everything this time on a perfect comradeship—and I, seeing in his eyes the terrible request, requiring from me his very life; I, through a child's cool perversity or some atavistic recoil from an intimacy too intimate, turned him down, turned away, refused him what I knew I could not give" (204). Binx's refusal of "an intimacy too intimate" with his father touches the paradoxical heart of his predicament. Initially it seems to reveal his measured selfishness, the emotional "coldness" Kate sees in him and which the grown Will Barrett in *The Second Coming* recognizes in himself after a similar failed attempt to bond with his father. But it also suggests the radical solitariness of all creatures. Young Binx cannot verify his father's being ("requiring from me his very life"); he cannot appease his father's desire by assuming the role his father hopes Binx will fulfill for him. His father's deep, insatiable need and their failed intimacy are signs of the dead end of romantic longing, a longing that Binx too feels. As a grown man now, and knowing what he already knows about the life and death of his father, Binx understands the hopeless solipsism of such a life.

Percy introduces a possible alternative to the elder Bolling's despair when Binx attends the business conference, held in the "blue cave" of a hotel ballroom. Here, Binx hobnobs with other salesmen, "very decent fellows," and remarks, "What good people they are. It is not at all bad being a businessman. There is a spirit of trust and cooperation here" (205). But in light of Binx's earlier conversation with fellow businessman Eddie Lovell, when he sensed that they were all "dead," his reaction here seems a sentimental delusion. For him to join the ranks of "decent" fellow salesmen would be to succumb to the comfortable role of successful businessman mapped out for him by Uncle Jules. And as we recall, Kate was "not fooled" by Binx's playing the bondsman's role; she saw how it masked his alienation and deep longings. Kate has a strong sense of the seriousness of their predicament and is more honest in being willing to face it. Therefore, Percy makes clear that, in Binx's mind, Kate is linked to the origin of his search: "There I see her plain, see plain *for the first time since I lay wounded in a ditch* and watched an Oriental finch scratching around in the leaves—a quiet little body she is, a tough little city Celt; no, more of a Rachel really, a dark little Rachel bound home to Brooklyn on the IRT" (206) (italics mine).

It might be argued that Binx is trying to "transfigure" her here, again objectifying her. But the triad of signs—from "wounded in a ditch" to "tough little city Celt" to "Rachel"—is unmistakable. Kate is a mysterious sign of the *possibility* of grace for Binx in his ongoing search, a clue to how to make his way in the world. Binx's naming of Kate as a "dark little Rachel" links her symbolically to the spiritual mother of the Jews, hence to Binx's belief that his relation to the Jews is a primary clue to his search. Percy thus relates Binx's searching and Kate to the meaning of the Jews in history and, inferentially, to the meaning of community informed by the Incarnation of the Word. Through these linked signs, Percy suggests that Binx's future openness to the search is linked to his loving yet difficult relationship to Kate in the here-and-now present. Not for him the romantic wanderlust of his father or the life of contented bond salesman, the archetypal consumer-profiteer. But despite Binx's intuition of his vocation, he and Kate are presently threatened by the "great beast" of anonymity in Chicago, and to escape it they "dive into the mother and Ur-womb of all moviehouses—an Aztec mortuary of funeral urns and glyphs"—the last visit to the death-house escape of moviegoing Binx mentions in the novel. Their escape is short lived, however, and when they emerge into "the wind . . . from the terrible wastes of the north," Kate is again frightened and senses that "Something is going to happen" (211).

The "something" that is going to happen, of course, is their inevitable return to New Orleans (not a trip West), where Binx will face the wrath of his great-aunt Emily. More important, Binx and Kate must resolve the question of their marriage and his choice of a way to "stick himself" into the world. Percy will situate their eventual coming together within a web of signs that point to the mystery of divine Presence—the living Word in the human community. This community offers the chance for a life bound within the transforming power of love and charity, the antidote to Cartesian dualism. And in the ending, the signs of this community will extend from the here-and-now to the mystical eternal. Percy carefully orchestrates his "ending," in reality an open-ended beginning—a continuation of the search—by showing a variety of alternative ways "to be" in the world, all of which are self-defeating.

Two such ways are represented by fellow passengers Binx meets on their bus ride back to New Orleans, who signify opposite sides of the posture of Cartesian dualism. One passenger is a young man, a romantic, who sits reading *The Charterhouse of Parma*. Binx sees him as one who is in the world yet who "finds himself under the necessity of sticking himself into the world in a certain fashion, of slumping in an acceptable slump, of reading an acceptable book on an acceptable bus. . . . He is romantic" (214–15). Binx says the young man is a "moviegoer" (though he doesn't go to movies) and muses about his fate: "The poor fellow. He has just begun to suffer from it, this miserable trick the romantic plays upon himself: of setting just beyond his reach the very thing he prizes" (215). Binx intuits that the young man "hopes to find himself a girl . . . and live the life of Rudolpho on the balcony, sitting around on the floor and experiencing soul-communions." But "he will defeat himself, jump ten miles ahead of himself, scare the wits out of some girl with his great choking silences . . . or having her, jump another ten miles beyond both of them and end by fleeing to the islands where, propped at the rail of his ship in some rancid port, he will ponder his own loneliness" (216). The romantic is the abstracted gnostic, isolated by self-consciousness from the concrete present, unable to "stick himself" into the world in any real way as he longs hopelessly for the transfiguring "real thing" experience. Binx surely sees elements of himself, and his father, in the young man on the bus. The encounter is both sign and warning about his potential fate as a moviegoer.

The opposite extreme, the life of immanence, is represented by a salesman from Murfreesboro, who unlike the romantic has no trouble sticking himself into the world. Binx says that like "many businessmen, he is a better metaphysician than the romantic" (216). He is a "better metaphysician" because he has a keener grasp of the hard actualities of existence and is not beset by vague romantic longing. To Binx he extols the virtues of his product, a two-edged blade, demonstrating its heft and balance. "The hand knows the blade, practices its own metaphysics of the goodness of the steel," Binx says. (Later, Binx will heft another blade connected to a defective way to be in the world—Emily Cutrer's bent letter opener.) The salesman is happy and self-assured in his immanent world, but he has no clue to his human predicament, of the need for a search for meaning, or any sense of how his mundane family life and consumerism might connect to any larger invisible community beyond the material world. As Binx observes, "Businessmen are our only metaphysicians, but the trouble is, they are one-track metaphysicians" (217). Such would be the fate of Binx were he to abandon his search and become the successful salesman-consumer like his uncle Jules, a "one-track metaphysician" who is contented being both in the world *and* of it. As we shall see, Percy's answer to the Cartesian extremes represented by the romantic and the salesman is the incarnational way, in the world and yet open to signs and the possibility of its transformation by grace.

Binx and Kate return to New Orleans at the beginning of Lent, the penitential season that anticipates the glorious resurrection of the Word and Christ's ongoing presence in the world, especially in the sacraments. Percy's liturgical setting implicitly affirms the reality of the mystical community. In this final setting Percy reveals the fractured condition of the twentieth-century American community and the bankruptcy of its intellectual foundations, as well as the real possibilities of a recovery of genuine communion between individuals, however difficult.

Binx's last conversation with his great-aunt Emily, when she summons him to answer for his behavior with Kate in Chicago, is a failure of words, a *miscommunication*, a broken semiosis. Throughout their meeting, Binx remains mostly silent, respectful but nevertheless aware that Emily has "nothing to say" to his predicament. As many critics have pointed out, Emily's inquisition of Binx and her condemnation of modern American democratic life are governed by her aristocratic elitism and philosophical stoicism.[10] Emily's social elitism implies that her view of community is essentially anti-Christian. As she says, "The charge is that people belonging to my class think they're better than other people. You're damned right we're better" (223). As Binx sees, throughout his life his great-aunt has tried to "transfigure" him within the code of stoicism as a young knight of honor. Naturally, to Emily his behavior with Kate is an unforgivable reproach to her value system. Speaking from a judgmental position of "ominous objectivity," she assumes the role of last defender of the stoic values—honor, nobility, decency, and a fateful acceptance of the inevitable doom of a present civilization whose "moral fiber" is rotten.

As such, Emily is a spokeswoman for the "wintery kingdom of the self" Percy attacked in "Stoicism in the South," the code that governed the southern *aristos* in spite of their nominal Christianity. Percy gives her viewpoint and its heroic standard of ethical values its due here. Although elsewhere he paid tribute to this code as an honorable one—a legacy from his "uncle" Will Percy—what is important to see here is both its pagan ethos and its antagonism to the open-ended hope for the resurrected community-to-come signified by the Easter season. The fatal isolation of "the wintery kingdom of the self" is radically at odds with that hope and possibility. Percy does not say this explicitly, but Binx's silence in the face of his great-aunt's charges, while he fiddles with her bent letter-opener, reveals his awareness that the vision and way of life she planned and expected for him is an anachronistic and dangerously dark vision that counsels despair and the death of the search and mystery itself. Indeed, it is a regressive vision, as the voice of the chimney sweep in the background, proclaiming that the Cutrer hearth needs to be cleaned from top to bottom, pointedly signifies.

Against the three possible ways to "stick himself" into the world that seem available to Binx—as romantic, as consumer-salesman, and as stoic "Black Prince"—Percy offers a fourth alternative. Emily totally misconstrues Binx and Kate and their complex relationship, but she does ask Binx three critical questions: "What do you love? What do you live by?" and "What do you think is the purpose of life—to go to the movies and dally with every girl that comes along?" (226). Although Binx is evasive with Emily, his meeting with Kate after being dismissed by his great-aunt reveals Percy's "answer" to those questions, as well as a way to transform human desire. Now at the crisis point in his life, Binx is again tempted to succumb to the world, to lust, and return to the role of seducer, without love or community. Any further idea of a search seems futile. He ponders the crisis:

Now in the thirty-first year of my dark pilgrimage on this earth and knowing less than I ever knew before, having only to recognize merde when I see it, having inherited no more from my father than a good nose for merde, for every species of shit that flies—my only talent—smelling merde from every quarter, living in fact in the very century of merde, the great shithouse of scientific humanism where needs are satisfied, everyone becomes an anyone, a warm and creative person, and prospers like a dung beetle, and one hundred percent of people are humanists and ninety-eight percent believe in God, and men are dead, dead, dead; and the malaise has settled like a fall-out and what people really fear is not that the bomb will fall but that the bomb will not fall—on this my thirtieth birthday, I know nothing and there is nothing to do but fall prey to desire.

Nothing remains but desire, and desire comes howling down Elysian Fields like a mistral. My search has been abandoned; it is no match for my aunt, her rightness and her despair, her despairing of me and her despairing of herself. Whenever I take leave of my aunt after one of her serious talks, I have to find a girl. (228)

Binx does "find a girl," but it is not his secretary Sharon or her roommate Joyce, immediate objects that might temporarily appease his "Rory-ish" lust. Sitting near the "ocean wave" playground ride, a sign that echoes the "sad end of America" Binx associated earlier with the ocean at San Francisco and the westward movement, Binx contemplates the end of his own world. His personal apocalypse and sense of an ending synchronizes with the dead end of the world shaped by scientific humanism, the legacy of Descartes. "Elysian Fields glistens like a vat of sulphur; the playground looks as if it alone had survived the end of the world," he observes (231). But in the ruins of this world Binx honestly faces his own despair and death wish—*and* the possibility of a discovery of a genuine self: "Is it possible that— For a long time I have secretly hoped for the end of the world and believed with Kate and my aunt and Sam Yerger and many other people that only after the end could the few who survive creep out of their holes and discover themselves to be themselves and live as merrily as children among the viney ruins. Is it possible that—it is not too late?" (231). That possibility of such recovery on this Ash Wednesday is real and comes to Binx as a grace when Kate appears in the "watery sunlight" that breaks through the sulfurous smoke. Binx sees himself in her—"she could be I myself, sooty-eyed and nowhere"—sees Kate as the fellow maimed searcher with whom he can try to build a life together in the ruins. In his marriage commitment to Kate, Binx will discover how to "stick himself" into the world:

> There is only one thing I can do: listen to people, see how they stick themselves into the world, hand them along a ways in their dark journey and be handed along, for good and selfish reasons. It only remains to decide whether this vocation is best pursued in a service station or—
>   "Are you going to medical school?"
>   "If she wants me to." (233)

Is Binx's discovery of mutual commitment with Kate and a vocation of helping others a sign of grace linked to Lonnie Smith's offering of his commu-

nion for Binx and for all those "indifferent to the pierced heart of Jesus Christ"?
Does Binx's anticipated "new life" signify a kind of conversion? Percy establishes this, semiotically, as a *possibility*. Certainly Binx's earlier life of romantic
role playing suggests a self-indulgent indifference to the ideal of love, of suffering with others, and of a life lived in charity with another within the human
community. Now he forsakes that "old life." As well, his chosen vocation of
medicine (a "listener" psychiatrist?) suggests a new care for others and a sense
of their communal destiny, a turn away from the egoistic consumerism of the
culture at large. But Percy does not "say" this explicitly, and so remains faithful
to the mystery.

Mystery nonetheless is imaged forth in concrete signs. Binx's discovery of
marriage and a vocation, and the possibility of divine presence, is signified
here by the graceful "sunlight" of Kate's presence. Moreover, Percy suggests
Binx's chosen vocation as listener and healer is a way to combat the alienation caused by the Cartesian split, a "way to be" that counters the false transcendence of the romantic-objectivist and the capitulation to "the world" of
the immanentist-consumer. Percy reinforces this mysterious possibility when
Binx wonders about the meaning of a Negro businessman he sees coming out
of church: "The Negro has already come outside. His forehead is an ambiguous sienna color and pied: it is impossible to be sure that he received ashes. . . .
I watch him closely in the rear-view mirror. It is impossible to say why he is
here. Is it part and parcel of the complex business of coming up in the world?
Or is it because he believes that God is present here at the corner of Elysian
Fields and Bons Enfants? Or is he here for both reasons: through some dim
dazzling trick of grace, coming for the one and receiving the other as God's
own importunate bonus?

"It is impossible to say" (234–35). It may be impossible *to say*, especially in
a culture hostile to mystery and suffering the deformed perspective of viewing
all things causally, but in the mystery of the real, it is wholly possible. Having
Binx claim earlier that he is "onto" God, Percy follows Peirce here in suggesting
how perhaps God "works" in the world, in and through the ordinary signs of
experience. In the mystical semiosis, the ultimate reaches of community—
extending from this New Orleans street corner to the cross at Jerusalem and
to the reigning Father of the Word—is affirmed as real and "possible."

Binx's discovery of a way to "stick himself" into the world by helping others
and by being helped along, and his commitment to Kate in marriage, herald
his new life in communion with others. Reconciled to his great-aunt Emily,
who now accepts him as "not one of her heroes but a very ordinary fellow," he

follows her wishes that he study medicine, knowing that the external form of his caring—as physician or as service station manager—is secondary to the inner disposition of charity toward others. As for his search, Binx refuses to speak on the matter. As he says in the epilogue, there is no way in the present culture to speak openly of such matters without the falseness of being "edifying" (linguistic merde), since the language of belief has been almost completely devalued in the culture of scientific humanism. But Binx has not abandoned his search, as the signs of mystery in the novel's final pages make clear.

The ending of *The Moviegoer,* then, is open, and fittingly so, since the very nature of our existence within an evolving community of signs is one of openness. Thus, in the epilogue, Percy focuses on two interrelated actions that signify this mysterious vision—Binx's loving relation to his fragile wife on the one hand, and his relation to the dying Lonnie Smith and his sisters and brothers on the other. Binx's once restless desire is now transformed into compassion for others as a way to challenge the malaise and alienation. Stated differently, the predicament of the solitary self under Descartes is countered here by the model of *kenosis*—"self-emptying"—instantiated in Christ as "the man for others." Kate is still subject to the terrors of the moment, of trying to find a way to be in the world without constant "objectifying," and to her Binx offers care and guidance in the ordinary matter of doing an errand and riding the streetcar. By assuring Kate that he will be "thinking of her" during the whole of her streetcar ride downtown, Binx affirms the invisible bond between them, signified by the emblematic cape jasmine he gives her to hold as she rides (241).

Percy enfolds this action within the final hours of Lonnie Smith's life on earth, and in so doing he expands the dimensions of the immediate action to the ultimate hope and possibility of any search—union with God. Now dying, the anointed Lonnie, the apostle of eucharistic presence, informs Binx that he has conquered a "habitual disposition" to envy his dead brother, Duval. For his part, Binx affirms their relation beyond the grave with a vision of mystical community in the resurrection of the body—Christ's promise—at the end of time. When Donice asks, "When Our Lord raises us up on the last day, will Lonnie still be in a wheelchair or will he be like us?" Binx answers, "He'll be like you" (240). Percy suggests the possibility of the transformation of human desire and its fulfillment in the "new body" in Christ—the risen, fully realized person.

Thus in Binx's answer, Percy affirms the mystical community as a real possibility within the mystery of the semiotic community we inhabit as humans.

It is the ultimate "home" and goal of all displaced journeyers in the world. Such a possibility is not an ephemeral gnostic ideal, however. It is grounded in history by the Incarnation, by the mysterious presence of the Word within the signs of the world, in the here-and-now. In the real semiotic drama of *The Moviegoer,* Binx and Kate are free to struggle with shortcomings—with their inner divisions and failings, with their mutual misunderstandings and lapses—yet also with the possibility of growth in love and charity. The ending is *really* open ended and mysterious. We don't know how their story will "turn out," particularly in light of the temptations within the deformed general culture. Binx and Kate are still subject to the terrors of alienation, to the possibility of despair, and to the challenge of "everydayness," but their bond of love, their *solitude à deux* amid the ruins, strengthens them as they go forth as wayfarers, still searching.

CHAPTER TWO

Ground Zero
and the Iron Horsehead

The Last Gentleman

In the bond of communion between Binx Bolling and Kate Cutrer at the end of *The Moviegoer,* Percy offered a modest but firm sign of hope for locating oneself in "the world," in spite of its fractured community. His second novel, *The Last Gentleman,* is less optimistic. Its more somber tone is keynoted by Percy's use of a prefatory quotation from Guardini's *The End of the Modern World,* cited in my introduction, which prophesizes the collapse of forms of community that have existed in the West since the late Middle Ages: "We know that the modern world is coming to an end . . . at the same time, the unbeliever will emerge from the fogs of secularism. He will cease to reap benefits from the values and forces developed by the very Revelation he denies. . . . Loneliness in faith will be terrible. Love will disappear from the face of the public world, but the more precious will be that love which flows from one lonely person to another . . . the world to come will be filled with animosity and danger, but it will be a world open and clean" (132). Yet the novel's somber diagnosis of the communal malaise is filtered through a comic vision in which the threatened social upheaval is counterbalanced by signs of the real divine presence in the world—the mystical-semiotic community signified by sacrament—a possibility for those whose hearts and wills are open to it.

In his second novel Percy examines the signs of collapsing community in 1960s America through the experiences of Will Barrett, another victim of Descartes, an addled young southern engineer wandering in search of himself and a home in the world. Will's own physical and psychological symptoms are signs of the disjointed times writ small. Often he is dislocated from time and space; he suffers spells of amnesia and déjà vu; his knee jerks uncontrollably; he sometimes lapses into fugue states. In contrast to Binx, Will feels bewilderment rather than wonder as his dominant mental state.[1] Yet as always, Percy's fictional sword is two edged. Though somewhat disabled, Will is gifted with a prescience, a fine-tuned "radar" that enables him to penetrate the sham of superficial social relations and the masks of other characters. He is another searcher, more desperate and confused than Binx Bolling, yet also attuned to the mystery he inhabits but cannot clearly fathom. Like Binx, he has a good nose for merde, though he cannot name it as such. So also is he plagued by desire, the world of the flesh, and by the devastating loss of the father as a credible guide and figure of authority. As a true heir of St. Augustine, Percy is concerned in *The Last Gentleman* with the problem of the will, with desire, and with how to live and act in a world of dissolving or incoherent norms. But Will is younger and more disoriented than Binx. He lacks any present family structure, and his hyperacute sense of dislocation seems to only intensify his estrangement. Finding a way to stick himself into the world and descend from the realm of "pure possibility" is much more precarious and painful than it was for Binx. Will does not find a *solitude à deux* bond of love with another by the end of the novel. Even though he is technically engaged to Kitty Vaught, no marriage occurs. And from what we know of Kitty, she seems incapable of any intimate relation, bent instead on fulfilling the stereotypical roles of sorority girl–cheerleader and middle-class suburban housewife. Marriage to Kitty, should it occur, portends disastrous spiritual consequences for Will.

In *The Last Gentleman*, Percy undertook the more ambitious and darkly serious task of mapping a landscape of spiritual malaise broader than in *The Moviegoer*, anticipating the general social collapse shown in his third novel, *Love in the Ruins*. No doubt this was partly Percy's response to the times. Will Barrett's picaresque journey across America—from New York City to the Deep South and then to the West—is dramatized within the context of the social rebellions and tragedies of the 1960s: the revolt of the youth against the establishment, racism and the civil rights movement, the sexual revolution, and the assassination of John F. Kennedy. In the intricate semiotic narrative web of signs that Percy creates, these events are ever "present." Sometimes their presence is explicit, as when Will gets caught up in a campus riot over the enrollment of a Negro student in a southern university. Sometimes they are implicit, as when Percy triangulates in Will's consciousness the "shot" of Will's father's suicide with the shots that killed John F. Kennedy, and with those of a riot in nearby Harlem.[2] All are part of the invisible but real community of signs that shape the broader meaning of the novel's action.

But with his characteristic probity, Percy was not content simply to write a satirical social critique of the American 1960s. He was concerned with revealing the ontological roots—the disorder in being—of which the social upheavals were a manifestation. For Percy, as I have argued, that disorder is largely a result of a rejection by "advanced" Western society of the divine Logos who entered history and offered the real possibility of a redeemed human community under God. As in *The Moviegoer,* the world in which Will must make his way is mainly the world of the after-Word, where as Tom More says later, "the center did not hold." The dissolving social fabric in *The Last Gentleman*—the fragmentation and polarization of groups, the individuals' psychic and spiritual confusions, the intense animosities and violence, the devaluation of language—bears witness to a society reaping the effects of a post-Cartesian rejection of a realist ontology that, for Percy, is rooted in the Christian Incarnation and its communal forms, the sacraments.

Apropos Percy's broader and more ambitious thematic concerns, the fictional strategies of *The Last Gentleman* are far more complex than those of *The Moviegoer.* Instead of a first-person narrative, Percy creates a subtle, ironically humorous third-person voice as a perspective from which to record the struggles of Will Barrett. This allows the reader to both "see" into and stand apart from the confusing interplay of thoughts, memories, fugues, and imaginings in Will's consciousness as he tries to comprehend and act in the world. This inside/outside narrative perspective creates a dynamic semiosis in which a welter of evolving signs is complexly triangulated to give structure and meaning to the novel, as Simone Vautier has suggested.[3] The interplay between narrative voice and Will's mind both mirrors the fragmentations and *con-fusion* of signs in the consciousness of the age (making Will typical in that respect) and provides a way for Percy to render that fragmentation coherent. In the time of the after-Word, the center of consciousness, lacking some ordering belief or authoritative principle, also did not hold. The almost diffuse structure and the Babel-like contention of voices and viewpoints in Will Barrett's world suggest the centrifugal "coming apart" of the American community.

To further complicate the narrative, Percy developed a third perspective— Dr. Sutter Vaught's philosophical notebooks—as a way to examine and emphasize the metaphysical and religious roots of the disorders of the culture, of which both Sutter and Will are victims. Percy was ever inclined toward the analytic, prophetic posture, as he admitted in a letter to Caroline Gordon

when he said that as a writer he wanted to tell people what to do and how to
live their lives (Samway, *Walker Percy,* 223–24). Later, he would examine the
demonic aspects of that inclination with withering self-scrutiny in his fourth
novel, *Lancelot.* Here, Percy uses Sutter's voice to link Will's story and the general cultural malaise to the ontological heart of the problem. As Percy suggests,
that problem is the catastrophic loss of belief in the Word, the centering sign
in human reality. On the train ride to Chicago, after his sexual failure with
Kate, Binx Bolling ruminated on the sexual "sickness" of the post-Christian,
post-Cartesian age. In *The Last Gentleman,* using Sutter's perspective allowed
Percy to develop an extended meditation on modern sexual malaise as the
principal sign of the age's ontological incoherence, a "sickness" that Sutter
links explicitly to the collapse of belief in the Eucharist and the sacraments in
general. Although Sutter tacitly refuses to be the figure of authority and tell
Will how to "live his life," he nevertheless knows, as Will intuits, the principal
clues to the culture's derangements. Those derangements are so profound and
dispiriting, and so disastrous in their consequences, that the predicament of
the modern self in search of community seems ridiculous, even absurd. But
the generous humor of Percy's narrator and the sympathetic portrayal of Will
counterbalance the despairing voice of Sutter. Like Kierkegaard, Percy associated humor and comedy with the religious sense. And so it is that the comic
spirit of the narrator is a sign of hope that the predicament can be named truly,
that truth in the Word does "hold," and that with divine grace the situation
can be meliorated.

Percy's emphasis in *The Last Gentleman* on sexual malaise in
America as the principal sign of ontological disorder bears careful scrutiny
if we are to understand the inner core of Will Barrett's searching. Human
love, the analogue of divine love, is the intersection of personal desire and
the possibility of real community, of the *solitude à deux.* At the intersection
of divine and human love—historically and ontologically—is the living sign
of the Father's loving gift to and covenant with humankind, the Word made
flesh in Christ. This center is what Will's age has largely abandoned in the
aftermath of Descartes. But Cartesian dualism cannot "account for" the mystery of human desire. Longing, especially sexual longing, defies abstraction
and rational definition. Sutter Vaught recognizes the sexual malaise caused
by dualism and its dire effect on communal relations. Thus he is "onto" the
problem, as Binx might say, but his vision is limited because he too suffers
the effects of the "split" in being. Percy shows this in the very fact that Sutter's

important philosophical observations on the contemporary malaise are cast in the form of abstract journal entries. Thus Sutter functions as both one-eyed prophet and victim of the times. Riven by dualism, he is both "objective" observer and flagrantly promiscuous seducer. At the same time, however, the journal entries are a key to Percy's philosophical analysis of the age. They serve as the thematic spine that semiotically links Will's relation to Kitty; to her brother Jamie; to Sutter's ex-wife, Rita; to his suicided father, Ed Barrett; and to Sutter and Val Vaught.

Will discovers Sutter's notebook while searching for a clue to the where-abouts of Sutter and Jamie after they have departed for New Mexico. After reading several entries about various autopsy findings, Will begins to read Sutter's speculations on sexual behavior. One passage reads: "Lewdness = sole concrete metaphysic of layman in age of science = sacrament of the dispos-sessed. Things, persons, relations, emptied out, not by theory but by lay read-ing of theory. There remains only relation of skin to skin and hand under dress. Thus layman now believes that entire spectrum of relations between persons (e.g., a man and a woman who seem to be connected by old complexus of relations, fondness, fidelity, and the like, understanding, the comic, etc.) is based on "real" substratum of genital sex. The latter is "real," the former is not (cf. Whitehead's displacement of the Real)" (279–80). Sutter's notebook entry is an abstract formulation of the predicament Percy wishes to drama-tize in the novel. Lewdness as the "sole concrete metaphysic of layman in age of science" points to the dominance of a scientistic ideology that reduces the triadic mystery of signs—the real ground of community—to a mechanical ex-change of impulses. Scientism reinforces the "displacement of the Real." Phys-ical relations are taken to be the sole realities, not signs of spiritual relations. In a reductive move, "Things, persons, relations" are "emptied out," emptied of metaphysical content (as Binx remarked of the blade salesman he met on the train). Thus lewdness becomes "the sacrament of the dispossessed," an attempt to "relate" to another through desacralized flesh as a way to affirm a "real" self.

In contrast, true sacraments, in Percy's Catholic belief, are real signs cre-ated by Christ as gifts of spiritual life (grace) to believers. Sacraments are the signs of spirit-in-matter, Word-in-flesh, since the mysterious action of grace is signified through material objects.[4] The Eucharist, as I have argued, is for Percy the manifest sign of community between God and mankind. Yet when these sacraments of the real are disbelieved, that is, when the "possibility" of sacralized reality is rejected, the human longing for both transcendence and for a way "to live" in the world does not evaporate. Rather, as Sutter sees, a displacement occurs, a perversion of true sacrament. The real "possibility" of God's presence in the sign is exempted; mystery is rejected. Instead, humans elevate matter and physical relations to an absolute (as Lance Lamar will later) and become idolaters, "dispossessed" votaries of sexual technique *(techne)* as the means to arrive at a mock "salvation."

Sutter believes that the modern scientist, as a proponent of the "objective," antimetaphysical view of the world, is especially vulnerable to the reduction of mysterious being that leads to lewdness. He writes, "Scientist not himself pornographer in the practice of his science, but the price of the beauty and the elegance of the method of science = the dispossession of the layman. Lewdness = the climate of the anteroom of science. Pornography stands in a mutual relation to science and Christianity and is reinforced by both" (280). Both science and Christianity emphasize the significance of the discreet concrete thing, though for different reasons. Christianity sees the individual concrete as a sign of God's mysterious presence; science sees it as a sign from which universal laws of nature can be abstracted. Pornography debases both perspectives, absolutizing flesh as flesh at the same time that it renders it an "object" for manipulation. Sutter understands the displacement this effects in the popular mind:[5] "Science, which (in layman's view) dissolves concrete things and relations, leaves intact touch of skin to skin. Relation of genital sexuality reinforced twice: once because it is touch, therefore physical, therefore 'real'; again because it corresponds with theoretical (i.e., sexual) substrata of all other relations. Therefore genital sexuality = twice 'real' " (280). Thus Sutter concludes that the "perfect pornographer" would be a technician living in the "twilight of Christianity," perhaps a lapsed Christian southerner who lives in a "no place" like Berkeley or Ann Arbor and seduces total strangers "in the service of both the theoretical 'real' and the physical 'real' " (281).

Many of Sutter's notebook entries, as Will discovers, are addressed to his sister Val (Sister Johnette Mary Vianney) as part of their ongoing debate about the spiritual disorder in the culture and possible responses to it. Their debate centers on the fundamental predicament Will faces—how to discover some meaning and purpose in his life, and how to live in the world. In this debate Percy represents the opposing views of scientism and sacramentalism, which eventually come to focus on the pivotal question of the Eucharist as the real substance of God. Sutter the "scientist," himself riven between flesh and mind, argues that the sacramental vision and experience is now defunct: "I do not deny, Val, that a revival of your sacramental system is an alternative to lewdness (the only other alternative is a forgetting of the old sacrament), for lewdness itself is a kind of sacrament (devilish, if you like). The difference is that my sacrament is operational and yours is not" (281). Sutter's use of the term "operational" suggests how the spirit of scientism has infected him, for his own indulgence in the decadent "sacrament" of sexual promiscuity only leaves him spiritually depleted and suicidal. Still, he tries to defend the "honesty" of his behavior in the face of American society's moral hypocrisy: "But I am not a pornographer, Val, like the optician, now a corpse, i.e., an ostensible liver of a "decent" life, a family man, who fancies conventions with smokers and call girls. I accept the current genital condition of all human relations and try to go beyond it. . . . I am a sincere, humble, and even moral pornographer. I cultivate pornography in order to set it at naught" (281). Despite Sutter's claimed "honesty," he does not acknowledge that his reduction of human relations to sexual manipulation is the same as that of the dead optician/covert pornographer. Both are dualists ridden with despair. Given his perverse view of human sexual relations, there is no "going beyond it." Nevertheless, Sutter does grant the truth of Val's argument that belief in the Eucharist as the living mysterious sign of divine presence and grace in the world counters dualism and reductivism. "The only difference between me and you is that you think that purity and life can only come from eating the body and drinking the blood of Christ. I don't know where it comes from," he writes (282). Later, Will reads an entry in which Sutter sees little hope of recovery in the present culture: "Christ should leave us. He is too much with us and I don't like his friends. We have no hope of receiving Christ until Christ leaves us. There is after all something worse than being God-forsaken. It is when God overstays his welcome and takes up with the wrong people" (372).

As Percy intends, there is a measure of truth in Sutter's observation here, as it echoes Guardini's view of the depleted state of Christendom quoted in the novel's epigraph. Sutter calls for the collapse of bankrupt forms of Christendom that, under scientism, have domesticated belief, devalued religious language, and either reduced sacramental life to ceremonial observance or displaced it into profane "sacraments." Only with the collapse of this formulaic Christianity is there any hope for a recovery of Christ, Percy suggests. Barring that, Sutter is stranded in his transcendent mode, with fornication as "the sole channel to the real," the practice of which leaves him in despair. What Sutter cannot see or accept is the mysterious possibility of God's presence in the here-and-now of the hypocritical, tawdry world, the possibility of faith and grace Binx saw in the Negro man leaving church. Thus Sutter accuses Val of betraying her principles by dealing with local businessmen, taking gifts from them. For Val, this involvement in the community is of the essence of her witness to Christ in the present world; for her, the kingdom of God has come and *is*, here and now. Sutter's moral elitism echoes that of Emily Cutrer in *The Moviegoer* and is equally self-defeating.

Will is intrigued and disturbed when he reads Sutter's notebook, but he insists "there were no clues here" (283). Initially Will cannot find any personal clues to help solve his predicament, but the notebooks do offer clues for the reader to understand Percy's religious and metaphysical perspective in the novel. The opposing views expressed by Sutter and Val establish the semiotic context within which Percy focuses the meaning of Will's journey. This triadic relation—Will, Sutter, Val—creates the community of signs that link immediate events in Will's quest to their larger metaphysical and theological context.

Like Binx Bolling, the addled Will seeks a way to stick himself into the world. Unlike Binx, he has "lived in a state of pure possibility, not knowing what sort of man he was or what he must do, and supposing therefore that he must be all men and do everything" (4). A paralyzing objectivity characterizes his "transcendent" state; "he had to know everything before he could do anything" (4). His occupation—engineer—signifies his condition, as does his talismanic telescope, as Lewis Lawson has shown.[6] The invention of the telescope, as poet John Donne noted in "An Anatomy of the World," heralded the beginning of the modern scientific objectivist viewpoint, and in Donne's view, the concomitant erosion of a coherent vision of cosmic order.[7] Yet Will yearns for genuine community, an intimate relationship with someone to answer his heart's longing. In the opening scene he "falls in love" via the telescope with an unknown woman spied in Central Park, someone in whom he thinks he sees "himself" and "his better half." She is Kitty Vaught. In Will's instant romantic reaction, Percy humorously reveals Will's naïveté and delusion by ironizing the idea of the search. As a young man who wants some "sign" to reveal to him how to live, Will's falling in love "at a distance of two thousand feet" parodies the intimate encounter of a *solitude à deux*.

Percy's opening characterization of Will shows him to be a victim of almost all of the spiritually disabling forces Percy sees afflicting post-Cartesian man. Will's southern legacy of *noblesse oblige* and stoicism proves crippling in the fragmented, volatile 1960s. Once his ancestors knew how to act with honor and acted quickly and decisively. But now "his family had turned ironical and lost its gift for action" (9). That southern world of elite *commutatis* is now gone, its underlying despair to be revealed later in Will's discovery of his father's suicide. As the narrator remarks, in the end Will's father "was killed by his own irony and sadness and by the strain of living out an ordinary day in a perfect dance of honor" (10). Now unsure of how to act, Will has become "a watcher and listener and wanderer" who has trouble either ruling out or moving beyond the purely "possible." Being "onto" the possible in the Peircean sense is good, since it signifies an awareness of the semiotic mystery of life. But Will has trouble connecting it to the immediate world of concrete action.

Will's detachment, his extreme dualism as a victim of Descartes, is manifested comically in the split between his intuitive acuity as an interpreter of signs—his "radar"—and his body. The delusions, déjà vu, disjointed memories (real and imagined), fugues, and spells of amnesia that bombard him reveal his disordered consciousness. His bouts of amnesia are especially significant, since Percy linked them to Jewish-Christianity's sense of time and history. Following Eric Voegelin's distinction between "the unhistorical cyclical time of the Greeks and Orientals . . . and the historical linear time of Israel," Percy claimed, "Barrett's amnesia suggests a post-Christian shakiness about historical time" (Con., 13). Moreover, Will's body refuses to act in tune with his spirit. In addition to his uncontrollable knee jerking, he suffers from hay fever and wacky spurts of kinetic energy that he discharges by throwing boxing "combinations" at the air. In good theorist fashion, he tries to "fit into" various communities through education and cultural enrichment and by "cultivating rewarding interpersonal relations with people" (12). The society he inhabits, saturated with scientism, endorses these popular modes of "self-realization." But such maneuvers cannot solve the "gaps" in experience; that is, the sense of alienation from being. Thus Will is doubly alienated—from himself and from others.

"His trouble came from groups," the narrator explains, meaning the accepted forms of social relations and community (13). Like Binx, Will intuits that groups expect conformity to a preestablished role that discounts him as a unique person. Therefore he must either "disappear" into the group or abandon it. As a child he was a loner at camp, and though in college he tried to become a regular Princeton man—joining a good club, making the boxing team, even imitating "a certain Princeton way of talking"—he funks the attempt and quits school. Later, he works briefly as a law clerk, wanders across Civil War battle sites in an amnesiac stupor, and finally lands a job working underground as a "maintenance engineer" at Macy's, living alone at the YMCA.

Significantly, his one brief relationship comes from his extra job "as compan-ion to lonely and unhappy adolescents, precocious Jewish lads who played band instruments and lived in the towers along Central Park West" (19).

Will's longing for relation leads him to psychoanalysis in the hope of devel-oping "group skills." Yet he becomes so successful at role playing and adapt-ing that he all but "disappeared" into the group and "became someone else" (20). For a while "he became an Ohioan," sitting around a cozy lodge in ski pants with "people-likers," until his spirit revolted and drove him back into isolation. Percy's depiction of Will's plight is comic, to be sure, but also a dev-astating critique of modern American culture as the "logical" outcome of the Cartesian spirit Tocqueville so astutely recognized more than a hundred years earlier. Tocqueville saw the American passion for groups as the necessary reac-tion to the loneliness and terror masked beneath the cultic worship of individ-ualism (*Democracy in America*, 114–18). Following Tocqueville, Percy's ironic narrator asks the probing question, "Is it not true that the American Revolu-tion has succeeded beyond the wildest dreams of (Anthony) Wayne and his friends, so that practically everyone in the United States is free to sit around a cozy fire in ski-pants? What is wrong with that?" (22).

Will's alienation from those who "go about satisfying their needs and achieving goals" becomes so intense that he constantly feels bad in this "good environment."[8] But given his "objective" habit of mind, he sees his depres-sion as a symptom of personal derangement, not as a sign of general cultural malaise. Yet when his analyst suggests that his mood is a sign of his sensitivity to living in perilous times, Will rejects such easy apocalypticism. Threats of annihilation are not the problem; lack of ontological coherence is. His dread comes from "the prospect of living through an ordinary Wednesday morning" (23). Will longs for someone of authority to tell him how to live, but lengthy psychoanalysis under Dr. Gamow is of no avail. All the therapist can offer is another version of role playing—the fake "community" of group therapy—hardly adequate to Will's predicament. After five years of psychoanalysis he concludes that Dr. Gamow can tell him nothing about himself that he doesn't already know. After he rejects Dr. Gamow, "a father of sorts," and "his sweet alma mater, sweet mother psychoanalysis," Will tries to manage his life by using an even more reductive formula, that of scientism: "I am indeed an en-gineer, he thought, if only a humidification engineer, which is no great shakes of a profession. But I am also an engineer in a deeper sense: I shall engineer the future of my life according to scientific principles and the self-knowledge I have so arduously gained from five years of analysis" (41).

Will's plan to "engineer" his life scientifically is quickly subverted by desire, when he "falls in love" with Kitty via the telescope. Will spies on Kitty and the "Handsome Woman," Sutter's ex-wife, Rita, when they meet or exchange hidden notes in Central Park. Percy triangulates this action to reveal its deeper significance by juxtaposing Will's other telescopic object of interest—a peregrine hawk preying on pigeons—with his spying on the women, creating "two bearings." As Rita and Kitty prey on each other, so also will they both prey on Will, for different reasons. Once he meets the Vaught family and begins to visit the sick Jamie in the hospital, Will becomes enmeshed in his own and the culture's general sexual malaise. When he meets Kitty he believes that being "in love" and marrying her will solve his problem of desire, his alienation, and the paralyzing sense of "pure possibility" by giving him both someone to cherish and a concrete way to live. Will's plan is to act according to an ideal of "honor" in his relationship with Kitty by following the code inherited from his forefathers. But such a code is an abstract fabrication; it leaves out "flesh" and the ambiguous mystery of sexual desire. Nevertheless, Will believes in it as the solution to his life: "What he wanted to tell her but could not think quite how was that he did not propose country matters. He did not propose to press against her in an elevator. What he wanted was both more and less. He loved her. His heart melted. She was his sweetheart, his certain someone. He wanted to hold her charms in his arms. He wanted to go into a proper house and shower her with kisses in the old style" (71). Though Will does declare his love for Kitty, Percy makes clear that the romantic dream of marrying her and living in the "old style" of southern gentility and honor is a delusion in the post-Christian culture of the 1960s. For one, the anomalous and manipulative sexuality of Kitty and Rita Vaught is enough to defeat Will's plan, as we shall see.

Will's hope to "engineer" his life and live happily with Kitty is undermined also by his own disordered consciousness. When another fugue episode strikes and he wanders aimlessly through Central Park, Percy skillfully reveals his disorientation by semiotically linking inner and outer "confusion," past and present, in Will's mind. The signs he receives are important clues to Will's life, clues that he must eventually understand. In the park, sounds of gunfire from a Harlem riot trigger Will's first extended recollection of his father on the night of his suicide years earlier. When he finds a note containing a Montaigne quotation hidden in the bench where Kitty and Rita exchange messages, Will recalls how his father would quote the French skeptic philosopher on such a summer night. Then he "sees" his father in his "mind's eye": "The man walked up and down in the darkness under the water oaks. The boy sat on the porch steps and minded the Philco, which clanked and whirred and plopped down the old 78's and set the needle hissing and voyaging. Old Brahms went abroad in the summer night. The Great Horn Theme went abroad, the very sound of the ruined gorgeousness of the nineteenth century, the worst of times" (99–100).

On that night, Will's father had reached the point of final despair, just before killing himself. Will's "repetition" here in his memory of that night reveals that what drove lawyer Barrett to suicide was his dismay over the collapse of the stoic code of honor held by the aristocratic southern community, the code young Will now plans to follow in his relationship with Kitty. Percy reveals that at the heart of this collapse is his father's confusion over sexual behavior and ethical values, and a sense of the bankruptcy of religion. Noting the lovers' cars parked on the levee, Mr. Barrett remarked, "They fornicate and the one who fornicates best is the preacher." To him, moral hypocrisy and sexual malaise afflict everyone, white gentry and Negroes alike. "One will pick the worst of the other and lose the best of himself. Watch. One will learn to fornicate in public and the other will end by pissing in the street. Watch," he says (100). But sensing this moral collapse, all lawyer Barrett can offer his son as solution to the problem of desire is his own dualistic ethic:

> "Go to whores if you have to, but always remember the difference. Don't treat a lady like a whore or a whore like a lady."
> "No sir, I won't."
>
> "If you do one, then you're going to be like them, a fornicator and not caring. If you do the other, you'll be like them, fornicator and hypocrite." (101)

Although Will tries to follow his father's advice by treating Kitty like "a lady" and proposing marriage in "the old way," the total failure of such an ethic is exposed comically when he takes Kitty to Central Park on this very night. Their humorous sexual failure, like that of Binx and Kate on the train, reveals that the dualistic code of sexual behavior authorized by his father is no match for the mystery and terror of real sexual experience.

In Central Park, with Harlem burning in the background, Will and Kitty retreat to a "cave," where their mutual sexual confusion confounds the secret tryst. Kitty tenderly agrees to marry him and begins to mouth clichés about love, "being cherished" and protected, but the true motive behind her sexual aggressiveness becomes clear.

"Besides, I want to prove something to myself," [Kitty] said.

"Prove what?"

"A little experiment by Kitty for the benefit of Kitty."

"What experiment is that?"

"Let me tell you, there is nothing wrong with Kitty," she said. (109)

Kitty's "experiment" (the term is aptly scientific) with Will, of course, is to prove to herself that she has "normal" heterosexual feelings, despite her attraction to Rita. For his part, Will is confused by her sexual advances, so discordant with his own desire and his father's advice about how to conduct sexual relations in an "honorable" way: "The puzzle is: where does love pitch its tent? In the fine fervor of a summer night, in a jolly dark wood wherein one has a bit o' fun as the English say? or in this dread tenderness of hers?" (107–8). When Kitty undresses before him, he wonders if love is "a sweetness or a wantonnesse" (110). The tryst fails when Will's sinuses become blocked and Kitty suddenly turns sick and vomits. As with Binx and Kate on the train, "flesh poor flesh," neither enjoyed like pagans nor sanctified by sacrament, comically subverts Will's romantic dream of "being in heaven."

Faced with their sexual failure, Will thinks nostalgically about his Richmond kinsman who, during the Civil War, attended balls and cotillions, danced with southern belles, and "did not feel himself under the necessity, almost the moral, of making love—." Will tries to evoke what he imagines was a "simpler" time when an ideal sexual code of honor seemed to obtain, "[when] even under the conditions of siege he did not feel himself under the necessity, or was it because it was under the conditions of siege that—" (112). Will hopes to be as "honorable" now as he imagines his kinsman to have been. But here the siege is the riot in Harlem, the modern legacy of racial conflict unresolved by the Civil War. Will and Kitty are a hundred years removed from the antebellum South. The code of honor is no more viable for Will in the confusing 1960s than it was for his kinsman or his father. But still the romantic idealist, Will persists, telling Kitty, "I must speak to your father" about his marriage proposal, like any honorable gentleman.

The sexual malaise dramatized in Will and Kitty's encounter in the park is, as I have argued, Percy's sign for what happens when the sacramental mystery of spirit-in-flesh is abandoned, and real (i.e., semiotic) relations are reduced to the merely functional. Sutter's understanding of the displacement of the Real (pace Whitehead) points to this.[9] The dualistic code of honor Will's father proclaimed in his advice to Will about sex is an attempt to hold out against the truth of this collapse, but it fails. Yet given the abandonment of sacramental

mystery and the collapse of the stoic code, Percy sees the "humanism" of Sutter's ex-wife, Rita, as a more destructive threat to real community. Again, Percy
links this threat to its most blatant symptom in the culture, perverse sexual relations. When Will asks Kitty about her relationship to Rita, she says, ambigu-
ously, "It is not quite what you think" (113). She denies any sexual attraction to
Rita, claiming that she is only attracted by Rita's "selfless" devotion to the Indians and their native culture, and by her love of beauty and art. But Kitty also
admits that she cultivated Rita's friendship during the crisis in Rita's marriage
to Sutter, though "she knew exactly what effect [hers and Rita's] friendship was
having." She also admits that she "knew how to make Rita like me and I did
it" (118). Behind her mask of innocent youthfulness, Kitty is a calculating but
confused sexual manipulator in her relations with both Will and Rita, and not
Will's dreamed-of ideal little housewife-to-be. After the Central Park episode
and the failure of her little sexual "experiment," Kitty coyly puts off his direct
questions about their marriage.

Rita's role is ominously symptomatic of the culture's malaise. When Christ
as the center of community is abandoned, Percy suggests, one type of "displacement" of values that occurs is Rita's form of humanism. As one who either rejects the real Christ of history or reduces the Good News to "myth,"
Rita would herself replace Christ as a "savior" of the world. In this sense, she
anticipates the Fedville scientists of *Love in the Ruins* and *The Thanatos Syndrome*, as well as the demonic would-be "savior" Lance Lamar. Rita's so-called
"selfless" devotion to the Indians and their native culture is, as Val recognizes,
a form of idolatry, an attempt to corrupt the spiritual integrity of the native
Indian culture by abstracting its mysterious historical reality and appropriating it as "myth." Her New York apartment is decked with Navajo trappings as
she explains the "holida" rite of the Huichal Indians in her "mythic voice." In
her marriage to Sutter she was a practitioner of what he calls the "sacrament
of the dispossessed"—lewdness—until Sutter began to practice it flagrantly
with other women. Rita deviously manipulates Will to keep him from Kitty
and tries to maneuver Jamie to keep him from Sutter, all the while masking
her deceit with heartfelt "concern" for others. Because of her lies, Will is left
stranded in New York when the Vaughts leave for the South.

Will's return to the "New South" in search of the Vaughts—the
happy, prosperous, hypocritically "Christian" South—enables Percy to map
with deadly satire the broader landscape of fractured community in America
and its metaphysical incoherence. Hitchhiking, Will is picked up by Forney

Aiken, a famous white photographer who has tinted his skin dark in order to "pass" as a Negro and examine black communities in the South from within. He plans to call his account of this experience "No Man Is An Island." A romantic who believes in the primordial myth of a "return to nature," Aiken sees modern society as having disturbed the balance in nature and uprooted man from the earth (126). A "return" is needed, he argues. Disagreeing, Will affirms a postlapsarian view: "Except I would suspect that even if one picked out the most natural surroundings he might carry his own deprivation with him" (127). His "deprivation" or fall, as Percy argued in *Lost in the Cosmos*, is ontological, not social or environmental (LC, 106–9). When they arrive at Aiken's Bucks County home, the prototypical American exurbia, Will finds himself in the midst of a poolside party with role-playing show-biz types who speak in confusing, elliptical half-sentences. When he swims with Aiken's daughter Muzh, just returned from a college year abroad, she talks of "having transcended Western values" and asks him about the transvaluation of values. Disoriented and weak from hunger, Will nearly succumbs to sexual desire for her but saves himself by leaping from the pool, throwing combinations of punches, and taking a cold shower. The general sexual malaise is underscored when Will learns that one of the guests has just finished a six-month jail term for sodomy, and when Aiken praises his friend Mort Prince's novel *Love* as about "———ing . . . a beautiful piece of work . . . a religious book" based on "one simple credo: saying Yes to Life wherever it is found" (137). When Will later reads the novel, he discovers that it is "about orgasms, good and bad, some forty-six," ending with the cliché affirmation: "And so I humbly ask of life . . . that it grant us the only salvation, that of one human being discovering himself through another and through the miracle of love" (138). The dead language of cliché combines with a parody *solitude à deux* in this ludicrous exaltation of the "sacrament of the dispossessed."

The next day Aiken and Will journey to Levittown to pick up Mort Prince, who is to accompany Aiken on his foray into the South. Levittown, the post–World War II middle-class enclave constructed as a model American community, stands as another sign of the failed ideal of community, what Tocqueville predicted as the outcome of the gospel of American individualism. Here in Levittown, a "most commonplace environment," Mort Prince elects to live "like Descartes among the Burghers of Amsterdam," getting along with his neighbors, yet "descend[ed] within himself" to exercise "that last and inalienable possession of the individual in a sick society, freedom" (140). But Levittown turns out to be a bastion of white racism, not a harmonious community.

When they arrive, Aiken and Will are mistaken for a block-busting realtor and his Negro client, and Will is hit in the nose during a skirmish with a mob of angry residents before the confusion is cleared up. Behind their pleasant facades, American communities, as typified by Levittown and Bucks County, are a shambles of hypocrisy, rage, sexual self-indulgence, and violence.

Will escapes Levittown and the clutches of Forney Aiken and Mort Prince with his dream of "engineering" his life and finding happiness in marriage to Kitty still intact. Approaching Richmond, where his kinsman fought a century earlier, Will fantasizes romantically about a "return" to antebellum community or its modern equivalent: "I am returning to the South to seek my fortune and restore the good name of my family, perhaps even recover Hampton plantation from the canebrakes and live out my days as a just man and little father to the faithful Negroes working in the field. Moreover, I am in love with a certain someone. Or I shall marry me a wife and live me a life in the lovely green environs of Atlanta or Memphis or even Birmingham, which, despite its bad name, is known to have lovely people" (151). But the "home" he journeys toward after being reunited with the Vaughts is not the *locus ameonous* Will longs for. In a déjà vu he sees that it is "not quite like home . . . with this spooky stage-set moss and Glynn marshes," but more like "an old house revisited" (161). The "old house" to be found and confronted, of course, is the house where his father committed suicide. As yet unaware of this, Will nevertheless feels spiritually dislocated in the New South, especially when his dream of love with Kitty again dissolves into sexual confusion. His attempts to "engineer" his riven self again collapse under the pressure of conflicted desire.

For one, Will discovers that he does not "love" Kitty much, sensing that she is under the spell of Rita. Nevertheless, he proclaims his love to her on Folly Beach, even though it does not "sound right." When Will still determines to "court her in the old style" as an honorable gentleman, he discovers Kitty's own sexual confusion over whether to act as charming sweetheart to an honorable suitor or as alluring sexual temptress. Will intuits her predicament; moreover, their self-consciousness in their muddled "roles" further separates them, as "he saw that she was out to be a proper girl and taking every care to do the right wrong thing" (167). He can even sense the invisible presence of Rita in their tryst: "What, you worry about the boys as good a figure as you have, etc. So he was the boy and she was doing her best to do what a girl does" (167). No *solitude à deux* is possible. Yet Will tries to overcome his disillusionment and "be both for you [Kitty], boyfriend and girlfriend, lover and father. If it is possible" (167). Will, the man of "pure possibility," thinks "it might be possible for them *to enter here and now into a new life*" (175) (italics mine). Percy's language of religious conversion here is ironic, of course, since Will would not become his true self in this "new life." Rather, he would act out a pastiche of roles adopted to suit Kitty's whims. For her part, Kitty has been so indoctrinated into Rita's sentimental humanism that she now argues that sex is "beautiful" and "anything two people do together is beautiful if the people themselves are beautiful and reverent and unselfconscious in what they do. Like the ancient Greeks who lived in the childhood of the race" (179). To further befuddle Will, Kitty proclaims that she will be either his "whore" or his "lady," whichever suits him. But most of all, she wants to become a "Tri-Delt." Like Binx Bolling on the train (and later, Lance Lamar), Will is totally perplexed by her anomalous sexual morality and his own inner division: "But what am I, he wondered: neither Christian nor pagan nor proper lusty gentleman, for I've never really got the straight of this lady-and-whore business. And that is all I want and it does not seem too much to ask: for once and all to get the straight of it" (180).

Beyond exploring Will's personal dislocation when he returns to his homeland, Percy shows that the "New South" is as fractured and strife torn a community as those in New York, Ohio, Bucks County, and Levittown. Ostensibly "happy, victorious, Christian, rich, patriotic and Republican," its citizens are equally victims of Descartes, "solitary and shut-off to themselves." Their "cities, rich and busy as they were, looked bombed out" (185). Though Will is determined to be happy, the "happiness" of the South drives him "wild with despair." His psychological and physical symptoms of dislocation become exacerbated; his memory lapses increase as he is assaulted by déjà vu, and his knee jerks uncontrollably. The Vaught mansion, a garish "castle" adjacent to a golf course, is a haven of despair peopled by "solitary and shut-off" beings. Here, the role Will is expected to fill is to fit in as Jamie's companion, attend school and marry Kitty, then take a job at Poppy Vaught's Rebel Chevrolet agency and work with Lamar Thigpen and his son Junior, a fraternity boy and "glum fornicator." Disgusted by the failures of his elder children—Sutter's disgrace as physician turned seducer, and Val's conversion to Catholicism— Poppy Vaught sees Will as the "ideal" son (in-law) he cherishes in order to fulfill his own paternal self-image. Yet Will is unable to fit in and feels more "at home" among the Negro servants in the kitchen than with any of the Vaughts.

And what of the Negroes in this "happy" South of fractured community? Long victims of racism, discrimination, and disenfranchisement, the
blacks' condition is another symptom of failed community in America, as
Percy would explore more fully in *Love in the Ruins*. Here, in his dealings
with the Vaughts' Negro servants, Will perceives in them a "vulnerability"
resulting from decades of oppression. In the black youth David Ross, full of
naive schemes to make money selling ice-cube dispensers, Will sees an "innocence" that leaves him prey to the whites who are quite willing to "violate"
Negroes. Listening to Ross, Will thinks: "But Oh Christ, David, this goddamn
innocence, it's going to ruin us all. You think they're going to treat you well,
you act like you're baby brother at home. Christ, they're not going to treat you
well. They're going to violate you and it's going to ruin us all, you, them, us . . .
you're going to ruin us all with your vulnerability" (198). David Ross's schemes
for success echo the dream of finding happiness through material prosperity,
the "American Dream" pursued by the whites, and will have similar disastrous
results: a deep spiritual dislocation. In contrast to Will, Jamie's sister Val sees
racism in America and the mystery of black-white relations in the biblical
terms of a vision of history, sin, and God's divine plan. Val, who teaches black
Tyree children in her community in North Carolina, has a vision that extends
from the South to all America: "It's God's terrible vengeance upon us . . . not
to loose the seven plagues upon us or the Assyrian or even the Yankee, but just
to leave you here among us with this fearful vulnerability to invite violation
and to be violated twenty times a day, day in and day out, our lives long,
like a young girl" (198). The image of the "rape" of the Negroes—a telling
sign given the novel's concern with sexual malaise as the sign of disordered
community—is a moral challenge to America to create a community of *caritas* and care for the vulnerable. Val responds to this call when she builds her
community among the Tyree children, as we shall see.

As I stated earlier, Percy triangulates Will's search for himself and a place
in the world primarily through his relations to Val and Sutter Vaught. Their
antithetical diagnoses and responses to the state of the community are incorporated as "possibilities" within Will's consciousness, helping to shape his
development. Will's first meetings with Val, and then Sutter, occur near the
center of the novel, a "ground zero" for determining the direction of his future. Confused by Kitty's behavior and Rita's promptings to him to take Jamie
out West, and caught in the dialectic of animosity between Rita and Sutter,
Will meets Val, who enjoins his help in a special mission. Knowing that Will
may be with Jamie when he dies, she commands him to tell Jamie about the

"economy of salvation" and see that he is baptized. Val's authoritative command, rooted in the sacramental vision and belief in the mystical community,
contrasts starkly with Sutter's impotent skepticism and Rita's "humanism." After announcing the "good news" to Will, Val remarks on Jamie's attraction to
science and its misguided hope of discovering a community of extraterrestrial
beings as a "clue" to earthly existence, a theme Percy would develop later in
Lost in the Cosmos. Jamie has been reading books about "radio noises from the
galaxies," regarding which Val comments, "I've noticed . . . that it is usually a
bad sign when dying people become interested in communication with other
worlds, and especially when they become spiritual in a certain sense" (211). Val,
the voice of real community in the here-and-now, distrusts "so-called spiritual people," preferring instead ordinary sinners and their mysterious ways.
After telling Will of the local Klan leader who donated a Seven-Up machine to
her community, she wonders, "Do you think it is possible to come to Christ
through ordinary dislike before discovering the love of Christ? Can dislike be a
sign?" (211). Val knows that in the topsy-turvy, malaise-ridden world of devalued signs, it may just be possible that hatred of the tawdry could be an avenue
to Christ. But Will is only confused by her mysterious words and alarmed by
her charge that "Jamie's salvation may be up to you." Consequently, he refuses
to take responsibility for his friend's baptism (a decision he later reverses). He
protests against being involved in any "Catholic monkey business." He cannot
fathom whether "her request [was] true Catholic gall, the real article, or was
it something she had hit upon through a complicated Vaught dialectic? Or
did she love her brother?" (212). To Will her words are a mystery. Angry at her
presumptuousness, Will asks how she can make such a request. Val's enigmatic
response pinpoints the "economy" of salvation, the way of repentance, conversion, and the sacraments: "It's like the story about the boy who got slapped
by quite a few girls but who—well. But it's extraordinary how you can ask
the most unlikely people—you can ask them straight out: say, look, I can see
you're unhappy; why don't you stop stealing or abusing Negroes, go confess
your sins and receive the body and blood of Our Lord Jesus Christ—and how
often they will just look startled and go ahead and do it. One reason is that
people seldom ask other people to do anything" (213). Val's message calls for
a community based on charity, and thus subverts the pride of individualism
so engrained in American culture. Moreover, her prophetic message invokes
the authority of the bringer of "good news" who bears witness to the truth.
Percy complicates Val's sign by linking talk of confession, communion, and a
life of charity to sexual overture—boy asking girl—perhaps as Percy's sly way

of suggesting the real relation between sexual desire and the search for God, as in the case of St. Augustine. But the befuddled Will cannot grasp the meaning of her signs.

After Val leaves, Will has his first encounter with Sutter, a paternal figure of authority to whom he is attracted as one who might provide him with answers to his predicament. He believes Sutter "knows something he doesn't know," and wants Sutter to tell him how to live his life. Hearing a gunshot, a sound that in his mind echoes the shot he heard when his father committed suicide, Will enters Sutter's room to find that he has not shot himself but instead a portrait of the Old Arab Physician, Abou Ben Adhim, affixed to a poem by Leigh Hunt. Sutter despises Hunt as an "anti-Christ," an exponent of the Godless sentimental humanism he holds responsible for "all the meretricious bullshit of the Western world" (217). Like Val, the astute Sutter sees the hypocrisy and bankruptcy of modern Christendom and secular humanism. Unlike Val, his response is flagrant satyrism, which leads him inevitably to the brink of suicide. Sutter asks Will about his own sexual behavior and interests, his belief in God, and his father, but he adamantly refuses to tell Will "how to live his life." To Will, Sutter is a mysterious man who seems to be "onto" something about modern life. Perhaps he can provide clues to Will's condition. But the doctor refuses to be Will's guru. Trapped in his own dualism, Sutter's only "advice" is a dead-end echo of the advice Will's father gave him years earlier: "Fornicate if you want to and enjoy yourself but don't come looking to me for a merit badge certifying you as a Christian or a gentleman or whatever it is you cleave by" (225). Sutter sees the sexual malaise at the heart of debased modern relations, but he has no answer when Will tries to ask him what he "cleaves by." His satyrism exhausted, and walking a tightrope above the abyss of suicide, Sutter truly does not know.

As we see, Will's hopeful return to the New South to "engineer" his life, find happiness in marriage, and discover who he is and what he is supposed to do with his life dissolves in chaos and confusion. The South he discovers is rife with racism, soon to explode into violence over integration at the local college. His fiancée Kitty has become a "changling . . . not absolutely certain of her own sex," transformed from shy girl–sexual adventurer into bubbly sorority girl and cheerleader. Equally confusing is Will's own ambivalent sexual attraction to her—whether to treat her as southern lady or as whore. His increasing sense of dislocation intensifies his déjà vu, memory "gaps," and fugues. Focusing on the fragmented state of Will's consciousness, Percy creates a series of triadically interacting episodes to reveal Will's condition and its broader cultural significance as a sign of American spiritual malaise.

For example, Will becomes increasingly absorbed in reading about the Civil War and the southern "foul-ups" that brought defeat (225–26). Enfolded semiotically within this "return" to the past are Will's present dilemmas: Kitty's attempts to lure him into the racist world of college Greek life; the increasing social turmoil over rumors of a black student coming to enroll; Jamie's restlessness in the face of his impending death; and Sutter and Rita's deadly struggle over the destinies of Jamie and Kitty. In the midst of these conflicts, Will experiences a crucial "return" to the night of his father's suicide. He again recalls his father walking up and down (like Binx's father) at night in front of the house, listening to Brahms, grieving over the moral collapse of the South, particularly over the Snopes-like racists he so nobly fought against. On that night the boy Will tried to convince his father to come inside, fearing his assassination by enemies. But his father remained defiant and exposed. He proclaimed, "I'm going to run them out of town, son, every last miserable son of a bitch" (238). We see now that in Will's day the racists of his father's time have become respectable racists like Junior Thigpen, as lawyer Barrett had predicted. But Will's recollection of this night with his father fades; it remains a "clue" only half-discovered. Sleepwalking in the Vaught house, he climbs to the attic, a palimpsest of the attic where his father committed suicide. He thinks he has heard a shot, leading him there, but discovers nothing in the Vaught attic. The full meaning of this clue in the memory of his father will come to him later.

Percy shows that the immediate clue to Will's present life is embedded in his relationship with his dying friend, Jamie Vaught. Three options, or ways to be, are presented to him as he faces Jamie's impending death. Each option represents a "possibility" for Will; together they expand the semiotic meaning of the developing action.

While Val seeks baptism for Jamie, Rita wants him to return to Teseque, a locus of myth and humanism, where he can "achieve as much self-fulfillment as he can in the little time he has left. I [Rita] desire for him beauty and joy, not death" (244). Rita the manipulative "do-gooder" humanist discounts God and serious religious questions, which both Val and Sutter recognize. Sutter warns that a return to the "beauty and joy" of Teseque would be "death." Sutter himself wants to take Jamie to the desert, where once before he and Jamie almost perished. Sutter sees such a trip as a "religious experience" to the eremetical place where the ultimate questions of death, God, and suicide can be faced directly. Such a quest, he believes, is infinitely preferable to the vapid humanism of "self-fulfillment . . . beauty and joy" that Rita offers. Sutter once lived this life and came to see its emptiness. As he recalls, while married to Rita they

became "self-actualizing people and altogether successful . . . in our cultiva-
tion of joy, zest, awe, freshness, and the right balance of adult autonomous
control and childlike playfulness" (246). For them "self-actualization" meant
absolutizing sex, aiming for the perfect physical union through a mastery of
technique. But as with Binx and Kate on the train, "flesh poor flesh" eventually
failed them. As Sutter sardonically observes, "Being geniuses of the orgasm is
the hardest of tasks, far more demanding than Calvinism" (246). Rita and Sutter's maneuverings over Jamie's last days only further confuse Will. He "could
not quite make this pair out and wished to get another fix on them. Val was
his triangulation point" (243). In contrast to Rita and Sutter's plans, Val's call
to baptize Jamie signifies the sacramental life and entry into the mystical community of redeemed souls. Caught amidst these conflicting pulls, Will must
find his own path. At this decisive moment, he chooses to follow Jamie. In this
commitment to his dying friend, he turns away from Kitty to become a "one
for others" (as Binx finally did). The friendship between Will and Jamie now
becomes the key relation that propels Will forward and out of the traps that
had awaited him in his return to the South. Now his will is directed toward
helping Jamie and away from the deadly life offered under the Vaught roof.

Will's commitment to Jamie also reveals Will's own need. In one sense,
Jamie is Will's double, an alter ego and sign of his own predicament. Both
are "sick" with scientism, victims of Cartesianism. Jamie's fascination with
math theory and extraterrestrial voices mirrors Will's attempts to "engineer"
his own life. But unlike his young friend, Will comes to see the futility of such
abstract posturing in the face of death, and the profound questions of meaning
that facing death raises:

> If Jamie could live, it was easy to imagine him for the next forty years engrossed
> and therefore dispensed and so at the end of the forty years still quick and pud-
> dingish and child-like. They were the lucky ones. Yet in one sense it didn't make
> much difference, even to Jamie, whether he lived or died—if one left out of
> it what he might "do" in forty years, that is "add to science." The difference
> between me and him, he reflected, is that I could not permit myself to be so
> diverted (but diverted from what?). How can one take seriously the Theory of
> Large Numbers, living in this queer not-new not-old place haunted by the god-
> dess Juno and the spirit of the great Bobby Jones? (240–41)

Will's insight is reminiscent of Binx's refusal to be diverted by abstract science
from the "wonder" and mystery of being in the world. But Will is too confused to be able to name the "what" he won't be diverted from. Still, in this

important insight, he anchors himself in the concrete present and rejects the "objective" escape.

Having found the New South to be another "good environment" where he feels terrible, Will decides to head West in search of Jamie and Sutter. He leaves Kitty behind, though he is still enough of a romantic to plan his return to the idyllic Gold Medallion home in the "ferny Episcopal woods" she has chosen for them, complete with a cavelike "foc'sle" where he can retreat. But Will already senses that this might be a haven of despair, seeing himself "as a crusty but lovable eccentric who spied through his telescope at the buzzards and crows" and spending his time "feeding the chickadees for the next forty years" (285). Will intuits the same fate he imagined for Jamie if his friend lived another forty years. Neither way of life is an answer to their deepest longings.

Percy develops Will's journey westward by employing a complicated set of semiotic triangulations that link his personal quest to the spiritual malaise of the nation at large. In the South, the social fabric begins to tear under the pressure of two hundred years of racial injustice. During the riot that ensues at the college, Will is knocked unconscious at the foot of the Confederate monument. Before he fades, he recalls his earlier failed attempt to blow up a Union monument at Princeton, a quixotic southern gesture. But now the civil rights movement and racist reactions are threatening to "blow up" both North and South, exposing the nation's illusory unity and harmony. Using Sutter's notebooks as his lens, Percy again points to sexual malaise as sign of the deeper spiritual disorder. In an entry that echoes Binx Bolling's dismay over the modern devaluation of sexuality, Sutter argues: "Where I disagree with you, Val, is in you people's emphasis on sin. I do not deny, as do many of my colleagues, that sin exists. But what I see is not sin but paltriness. Paltriness is the disease. . . . Lewdness is sinful but it derives in this case not from rebellion against God (Can you imagine such a thing nowadays—I mean, who cares?)—but from paltriness" (292). Like Binx, Sutter emphasizes the collapse of the meaning of sin as a metaphysical reality; sex is now regarded as just a fulfillment of physical "needs." "Paltriness" is all that remains when the sacramental reality of virtue and the notion of sin are "emptied" of substance, now that "flesh" is separated from real being and reduced to mechanics and manipulation. Given this situation, Sutter chose flagrant lewdness over the hypocritical "Americans who practice it with their Christianity and are paltry with both" (292). He describes the hypocrisy as "Main Street, USA = a million-dollar segregated church on one corner, a drugstore with dirty magazines on the other, a lewd movie on the third, and on the fourth a B-girl bar with condom dispensers in

the gents' room. Delay-your-climax-cream. Even our official decency is a lewd
sort of decency" (292). Percy's counterperspective to Sutter's pessimistic analysis of America's moral collapse is the reality of a genuine community based
on charity: Val's mission among the Tyree children, teaching them language
to open them to the "good news" of salvation. Will encounters this alternative
as he heads westward.

Percy underscores the importance of Will's visit to Val's mission through
a pattern of signs that links him to the site. As well, these signs suggest a
historical-evolutionary process at work in the culture. As he approaches the
mission, Will recalls that it was once the site of the old Phillips Academy, a
venerable southern school that once taught the pagan classics and military
science. Will senses that he or his father or perhaps his grandfather once attended the academy. It is strangely familiar to him as an ancestral "home,"
though now it looks like a "lunar landscape" and has been converted into a
Catholic mission school. Will's meeting with Val becomes an encounter with
Christian mystery itself, a sign of the living reality of the Incarnation in the
here-and-now, though he is unable to fathom it. When he arrives Val is feeding a chicken hawk, a countersign to the preying peregrine hawk Will observed
in the novel's opening scenes in Central Park. The nun is completely absorbed
in feeding the hawk, which "scandalized him slightly, like the Pope making a
fuss over a canary" (297). As a detached objectivist, Will cannot understand
her humble attention to a lowly, ordinary, and mean bird. Her action indicates
her total attentiveness to the living mystery of being, as well as her posture
of care and feeding of the "least." When he learns from Val that Sutter and
Jamie have come and departed, Will is anxious to leave but remains transfixed
by her small actions. Held by her attention to the chicken hawk, Will suddenly becomes conscious of time itself and gains a clue to his own temporal
dislocation—his amnesia, déjà vu, and fugues: "The task, he mused, was to
give shape and substance to time itself. Time was turned on and running between them like the spools of a tape recorder. Was that not the nature of his
amnesia: that all at once the little ongoing fillers of time, the throat-clearings
and chair-scrapings and word-mumblings, stopped and the tape ran silent?"
(297). Will feels that his amnesia signifies a mysterious relation to the present,
to presentness. His amnesia is powerfully strange because on the one hand
it "erases" the past, heightens the present, and allows for the possibility of a
new beginning, but on the other hand it leaves one disoriented and without a
context of meaning derived from the past. By intersecting Will's thought about
time with Val's humble action, Percy suggests that Will, like the culture at large

under scientism, has suffered a loss of a sense of Christ's real presence in the ordinary realities of the everyday world. Lacking that sense, Will is separated from the definitive historical event, the Incarnation.

Seizing the moment, Val enjoins Will to give Jamie a "good shaking" when he finds him, since she knows he is "feeling sorry for himself and has taken to reading Kahlil Gibran, a bad sign even in healthy people," the book undoubtedly a gift from Rita. Against this romantic, sentimental "prophet" Percy sets Val's Christian faith and her prophetic mission to teach the language of truth to the Tyree children. Whereas Will notices the physical poverty of her shabby mission school, Val emphasizes the deeper spiritual poverty of the children: their lack of language. "I mean they're dumb, mute," she says. "Children eleven and twelve can't speak. It took me six months to find out why. They're brought up in silence. Nobody at home speaks. They don't know thirty words. They don't know words like pencil or hawk or wallet" (299). As Percy argued in many essays, language is the defining human characteristic—the gateway to consciousness and being, to naming the world and placing oneself in relation to it, and thus to community with others.[10] Through Val's faith and her vocation Percy links the power of words to the Incarnation of the Word, to the sacraments, and thus to mystical community. Though Will does not understand her, Val links the acquisition of language to its ultimate value for her—to give the children the power to hear the "good news" of the meaning of their existence, and especially to hear about the gift of the Eucharist. When Will asks why she remains there, Val replies:

> "I think I stayed not so much out of charity as from fascination with a linguistic phenomenon—that was my field, you know. It has to do with the children's dumbness. When they do suddenly break into the world of language, it is something to see. They are like Adam on the First Day. What's that? they ask me. That's a hawk, I tell them, and they believe me. I think I recognized myself in them. They were not alive and then they are and so they'll believe you. Their eyes fairly pop out at the Baltimore catechism (imagine). I tell them that God made them to be happy and that if they love one another and keep the commandments and receive the Sacrament, they'll be happy now and forever. They believe me. I'm not sure anybody else does now." (302)

Here, Percy indicates the radical triad—God, incarnate Word, and mankind—at the center of his vision of community: the gift of language linked to the gift of Logos and to the sacramental gift of life, the Eucharist. Yet Will, who prides himself that he "knew how to listen and he knew how to get at that most secret and aggrieved enterprise upon which almost everyone is embarked," cannot grasp the mystery behind Val's words. He fails to understand her story of her own conversion, how she was "half dead" until a nun asked her to join the convent and devote her life to God. Nor can he grasp the mystery that her conversion did not automatically change her nature; she is still "mean as hell." Confused, Will only wants to escape her hard scrutiny and the obligation to see to Jamie's baptism she has charged to him. Nevertheless, he does donate money to her mission before leaving.

Set against Val's sacramental vision in Will's mind is Sutter's agnostic critique, spelled out in the notebook entries Will reads after leaving the mission. Sutter accepts his sister's conversion but believes that she has "sold out" by her commitment to a hypocritical society:

> It is you [Val] who concerns me. You are wrong and you deceive yourself in a more serious way. You have cancelled yourself. I can understand what you did in the beginning. You opted for the Scandalous Thing, the Wrinkle in Time, the Jews-Christ-Church business, God's alleged intervention in history. I can understand this even though I could not accept the propositions (1) that my salvation depends upon the Jews, (2) that my salvation comes from hearing news rather than figuring it out, (3) that I must spend eternity with Southern Baptists. But I understand what you did and even rejoiced in the scandal of it, for I do not in the least mind scandalizing the transcending scientific assholes of Berkeley and Cambridge and the artistic assholes of Taos and La Jolla. (307–8)

But Sutter cannot accept the scandal of the Incarnation and the life of charity in the broken, deranged world that it commands: "You reversed your dialectic and cancelled yourself. Instead of having the courage of your scandal-giving, you began to speak of the glories of science, the beauty of art, and the dear lovely world around us! Worst of all, you embraced, Jesus this is what tore it, the Southern businessman!" (308). Sutter argues that even if Val's Christianity were to reconcile all the warring elements in the culture, even if all accepted Christianity, it would not matter because they "are going to remake the world and go into space and they couldn't care less whether you and God approve and sprinkle holy water on them . . . because they'll know it makes no difference any more. All you will succeed in doing is canceling yourself. At least have the courage of your revolt" (308–9).

Though Sutter's critique of modern American culture is partly accurate, he cannot understand how Val's life as "the one for others" in a community of charity does not mean that she has "cancelled" herself. On the contrary, her self-emptying in order to follow the will of the Father and Christ is, for Percy, the path to true self-discovery. In addition, her actions are not "cancelled out," because they are invested with sacramental meaning and power that in the mystical-semiotic community extends from the concrete to the transcendent, from the here-and-now to the eternal. Sprinkling holy water, or feeding a chicken hawk, resonates with the mystery of grace that Sutter the rationalist-dualist cannot see. Lacking this vision, he tries to create his own profane "sacrament" of sex, which fails him. Nevertheless, Sutter's critique does express Percy's sense of the dilemma of the modern searcher-unbeliever who cannot abide living in the hypocritical culture. Paradoxically, there is a dimension of the religious in Sutter's questionings. But his response to the broken world is to remain alienated and withdrawn, except for occasional trysts. He protests to Val: "The reason I am more religious than you and in fact the most religious person I know: because, like you, I turned my back on the bastards and went into the desert, but unlike you I didn't come sucking around them later" (308). Val's *acsesis* engages the human community; it is the paradox of transcendence *through* time and history, the true way of the cross. Sutter's claimed *acsesis* rejects community; it is a mock transcendence that only leads to suicidal despair. As Will peruses the notebooks, he senses that Sutter will not be an adequate guide for his life. The physician's "wisdom" is flawed, like that of his own father, as he will soon discover.

Before journeying west, Will returns to his ancestral home in the Delta, a move that brings him closer to discovering the roots of his riven personality, and a clue to the mystery of how to live in the world. Percy carefully triangulates episodes of past and present in a complex semiosis that leads Will to his crucial discoveries. As he approaches home, he recalls evenings spent walking with his father, talking of the "expanding universe" and taking "pleasure in the insignificance of man in the great lonely universe" (309). His father recited "Dover Beach," Matthew Arnold's sentimental tone poem of nineteenth-century loss of faith, and spoke of his grandfather the high sheriff and "the days of great deeds." Percy interweaves these memories with Will's immediate problems. Pseudo-"Negro" Forney Aiken now appears in Ithica with actors and a Negro playwright to stage a "morality play" at a local festival. Will recalls having seen one of the Negro's plays, about a homosexual couple living on the Left Bank in view of the "gleaming towers of Sacre Coeur." The play's characters, two young men concerned about "the loss of the holy in the world," decide to "have [their] own Mass," that is, homosexual intercourse. Percy's satire here, the homosexuals' travesty of the eucharistic sacrament of community, again underscores the spiritual desecrations of the times. But when the group of show people is harassed by local police, Will acts to help them escape, punching Deputy Beans Ross, as "for once things became as clear as they used to be in the old honorable days" (325). But the scene is farcical, and Will's "heroism" is hardly the grand and dangerous deed of his forefathers.

Will's return home leads him to confront the devastating memory of his father's suicide. Only now will he fully comprehend its meaning for him. Percy triangulates this double return, in fact and in memory, with the immediate scene of Will's aunts watching Bill Cullen's show *Strike It Rich,* a sign of the enduring popular American Dream of success. Will indeed does "strike it rich," but in a more profound sense. Seeing the house, he recalls the night of his father's suicide, with lawyer Barrett pacing and listening to Brahms while Will sat watching with "dread in his heart" (329). That night, the boy naively thought they had achieved "victory" because his father's enemies had left town. But his father, in despair at the general collapse of honor, is inconsolable. "We haven't won, son. We've lost . . . we've lost it all, son" (330). Then he proclaims: "I don't have to choose that" and turns away for the last time, ignoring his son's plea to "wait." When Will asks him, "Why do you like to be alone?" the good stoic father answers, "In the last analysis, you are alone" (331). Trapped in the dualism of an abstract, romantic "honor" that cannot tolerate "paltriness," lawyer Barrett has reached the solipsistic dead end of the Cartesian vision. He rejects a *solitude à deux* bond of love with Will and refuses his son's need. "Don't leave," Will cries, but his father ascends to the attic to take his life with the double-barreled shotgun.

Yet as he recalls this fateful night now, Will discovers the central clue to his life, and the "answer" to his father's despair. Likewise, it is Percy's "answer" to the dualism afflicting the entire culture, a clue to how to live in the world. Will touches the hitching post and in so doing touches the heart of the incarnational mystery of spirit-in-matter, the semiotic real. With his hand touching "the tiny iron horsehead of the hitching post," down to the "warm finny *whispering* bark" where the oak twined around it, he thinks:

> *Wait.* While his fingers explored the juncture of iron and bark, his eyes narrowed as if he caught a glimmer of light on the cold iron skull. *Wait.* I think he was wrong and that he was looking in the wrong place. No, not he but the times. The times were wrong and one looked in the wrong place. It wasn't even his fault because that was the way he was and the way the times were, and there was no other place a man could look. It was the worst of times, a time of fake beauty

and fake victory. *Wait.* He had missed it! It was not in the Brahms that one looked and not in solitariness and not in the old sad poetry but—*he wrung out his ear*—but here, under your nose, here in the very curiousness and drollness and *extraness* of the iron and the bark that—he shook his head—that—. (332) (Italics mine)

Percy's careful conjunction of signs here—light, whispering, hearing, touch—point to the incarnational revelation. Will "wrung out his ear" so as to hear the "whispered" message of real meaning, the truth of real being conveyed, as it were, straight from the horse's mouth. The "extraness" in the iron horsehead is a sign of the spirit indwelling in matter, the irreducible "inscape" and mystery of its unique being, yet a mystery whose meaning can be signified, known and named (even if only as "extraness"), as in fact Will does here. Such signs, for Percy, have their full valuation from the living divine Word who entered history and is present. Although Will is not able here to perceive this ultimate theological sign relation, he does grasp the truth of incarnational vision. The revelation comes as a grace of insight he receives as a gift, an intuition of spiritual presence opposite to the abstract "vision" provided by the telescope. As such, the revelation in the iron horsehead anticipates Will's direct involvement in the mystery of Jamie's baptism later. Here at home, what he does grasp of the mystery before him is enough to enable him to see the flaw in his father's stoic dualism, as he will soon recognize the same flaw in Sutter. Knowing their flaw, he will reject the suicidal "logic" of both men, which led them to abandon community with "paltry" fellow humans and choose death instead.

Having gained these insights into his father, the times, and implicitly his own problem, Will heads to New Mexico. In setting the ending of the novel in the American West, Percy situates the meaning of Will's journey within a landscape whose signs are on the one hand, profane, and on the other, deeply religious. The West, one of the most important tropes in Percy's novels and essays, is on one level a symbol of the great secular American Dream of freedom and self-realization, the locus of the romantic myth of Edenic community so powerful in the culture. But negatively, it signifies the end-all locus of the abstracted solitary spirit that Tocqueville saw in the Cartesian heart of the American experiment. At the same time, it is the "ground zero"—the intersection of place and time, from the Incarnation of Christ to the "end of the modern world"—that focuses the central metaphysical problem of the novel. When he arrives in Sante Fe, Will thinks of it as "the locus of pure possibility . . . [where] what a man can be the next minute *bears no relation* to what he is or what he was the minute before" (356) (italics mine). As a young man still prone to abstraction and often paralyzed by "possibility," Will sees it illusorily as the place of pure potentiality. But the real question is, What concrete actions will derive from this potentiality? This place offers both the worst and the best possibilities for America and humankind. Against the played-out historical background of Revolutionary and Civil War heroes Will left behind in the East, Percy sets the new American "frontier heroes" for the 1960s: the atomic scientists at Los Alamos, such as Robert Oppenheimer's community of nuclear physicists and engineers. Significantly, Sutter connects Oppenheimer with the legendary western hero Doc Holliday, both loners who came west to invent destructive weapons. As Will reads in the notebook now, Sutter came to see this significance of the desert through his earlier failure there: "*Genius loci* of Western desert did not materialize. Had hoped for free-floating sense of geographical transcendence, that special dislocatedness and purity of the Southwest which attracted Doc Holliday and Robert Oppenheimer, one a concrete Valdosta man who had had a bellyful of the concrete, the other the luckiest of all abstract men: who achieved the high watermark of the 20th century, which is to say: the device conceived in a locus of pure transcendence, which in turn worked the maximum effect upon the sphere of immanence: the world" (349–50). The purely possible "maximum effect" achievable by the transcender-scientists, of course, is the destruction of the human community. Transcenders worship power over the world, the antithesis of the incarnational vision, wherein real transcendence occurs only through humble service to another, and "power" is perfected in weakness. Through Sutter's notebook, Percy signifies the novel's final setting of New Mexico as the possible terminal point of a culture driven by scientism and the destructive use of technology. The dream of a great secular American society can be instantly reduced to a wasteland. The Los Alamos scientists stand as the ultimate transcendent, solitary "engineers" whose lives in their abstraction "bears no relation" to the real human community.

But there is another "possibility" of meaning signified in Percy's western landscape, one also open to Will Barrett (and, by extension, America). Sante Fe, with the surrounding Sangre de Cristo Mountains, is also a locus of hope. It is Christ's desert, the place of spiritual challenge where, in the eremetical tradition, men and women came to "empty" the striving, egoistic self into an open relation to God and to live in love and charity among fellow believers. This "remnant" community of faith in solitude, a *solitude à trois* with God and mankind, is the alternate "possibility" to the destructive individualism and power over nature personified by the Los Alamos scientists. And this community of faith lives here-and-now, in Val's work among the Tyrees and in the sacramental community represented by the priest who administers to the dying Jamie.

Will has come to Sante Fe from "the bloody immanence of the South" hoping to find Sutter and Jamie. He remains convinced that Sutter has "something to tell him" about how to live his life. For his part, Sutter has returned with his brother to the site of their earlier "religious experience," which failed. Sutter admits cynically that, unlike St. Anthony, he found his "true vocation" at the Sangre de Cristo guest ranch—seducing lonely women. The earlier trip to the desert "didn't work." Depressed and beset by sexual demons, he collapsed in despair until "saved" by Rita. Now he has come to the desert again to face the demon of suicide, and also, he claims, to help Jamie face the stark reality of his own death, which for Sutter is an option preferable to dying at home or with Rita in Teseque.

Sutter understands that Will is afflicted with "transcendence," but he knows also that Will has made an important breakthrough: recognizing his own abstractedness. "Yes, Barrett has caught a whiff of the transcendent trap and has got the wind up," Sutter says. "But what can one tell him? What can you tell him, Val?" (353). Sutter rightly refuses to "explain" Will's problem to the engineer, believing that he would probably take it as a "solution" to the question of how to live. Sutter knows Will's tendency to objectify and that such "a posture is self-defeating," but he does not know of Will's crucial revelation at the iron horsehead. In fact, Will still wavers between the incarnational insight he gleaned from the horsehead and his "transcending" tendencies. In another of the notebook entries he finds Sutter's description of the dilemma (in which Percy's voice describing the dilemma of post-Cartesian searchers can be heard clearly):

> Even if you were right. Let us say you were right: that man is a wayfarer (i.e., not transcending being nor immanent being but wayfarer) who therefore stands in the way of hearing a piece of news which is of utmost importance to him (i.e., his salvation) and which he had better attend to. So you say to him: Look, Barrett, your trouble is due not to a disorder of your organism but to the human condition, that you do well to be afraid and you do well to forget everything which does not pertain to your salvation. That is to say, your amnesia is not a symptom. So you say: Here is the piece of news you have been waiting for, and you tell him. What does Barrett do? He attends in that eager flattering way of

his and at the end of it he might even say *yes*! But he will receive the news from his high seat of transcendence as one more item of psychology, throw it into his immanent meat-grinder, and wait to see if he feels better. He told me he's in favor of the World's Great Religions. What are you going to do about that? (353–54)

As a typical modern victim of Descartes, Will is inclined to reduce the "good news" given to him—the sign in the iron horsehead—to an item of knowledge *sub species aeternitatis,* applicable to anyone anywhere, as Percy indicated in "The Message in the Bottle." Given that this is a problem in the age's devaluation of signs, Sutter's pessimistic response is that we are "doomed to the transcendence of abstraction." But reading this entry now, Will sees the flaw in Sutter's dualism (hence, something of his own abstracted self): "Where he probably goes wrong . . . is in the extremity of his alternatives. God and not-God, getting under women's dresses and blowing your brains out. Whereas and in fact my problem is how to live from one ordinary minute to the next on a Wednesday afternoon. Has this not been the case with all religious people?" (354–55). Gifted with the iron horsehead insight, Will is now "onto" a new way to be, to stick himself into the world. Most important, Will criticizes Sutter's dualism as he did his father's precisely from an incarnational perspective. The real challenge, he sees, is to live in the here-and-now, in flesh and spirit.

In the final scenes of the novel, Percy focuses Will's new development through his triadic relations with Sutter, Val, and Jamie Vaught. Though the signs are subtle, Will has changed in important ways. For one, he is now "the one for others" in regard to Jamie; Will engages himself directly in the youth's dying. Moreover, as this bond with another becomes stronger, his self-absorption and his psychic afflictions diminish. He abandons interest in the telescope, the instrument of his "objective" self. His amnesia disappears and he can now "remember everything," giving him a firmer hold in the here-and-now; his déjà vu and fugues dissolve; and he begins to make specific decisions about his future. Yet Percy's depiction of these important changes in Will is always tinged with mystery. True to the semiotic reality of the situation, Percy incorporates "possibility" and an open-ended dimension into the signs and actions that structure the ending of the novel. Semiotically, the "ending" is just a new beginning.

Percy's concern with the community at large is revealed again through the debate between Sutter and Val. Echoing the epigraph from Guardini, both Sutter and his sister perceive, and welcome, the demise of hypocritical Christendom. Earlier, Sutter said, "Christ should leave us. . . . We have no hope of recovering Christ until Christ leaves us" (372). Though he agrees with Val that "Christianity should be done for, stove in, kaput, screwed up once and for all" so that "the air would be cleared and even that God might give us a sign," Sutter refuses to believe that God's word and call to service is alive *now* within the flawed American community. He and Val agree that they must "watch and wait" for some sign of spiritual renewal. But in the meantime—the present— Val does not hesitate to act in the light of faith, but works with both a Klan leader and the Tyree children. In her faith commitment Percy suggests the need to see the present devalued state of community for what it really is, and yet to work to transform it. As Sutter says of Val, "But she changed, you see. *She became hopeful*" (378). But for himself, Sutter sees only three options: to live as a genuine Christian, to live what he sees as the bankrupt life of a "good citizen" in modern secular society, or to "die like an honest man" (379). See- ing the alternatives, his own inclination, of course, is toward the third option, which would repeat the desperate choice Will's father made.

As for Will, though he has rejected Sutter's despair, he still believes that the physician is "onto something" because he sees "the prime importance of the religious dimension in life," something Will never learned from his father. Although he still hopes that Sutter can tell him "how to live," Will comes to his own tentative conclusions on the matter. He determines to marry Kitty, live in Captain Andy Mickle's home, and try to become "a fair member of the com- munity. God knows the place could use even a small contribution of good will and understanding" (384). Will's statement, voiced in the clichés of democratic humanism, might seem to suggest that he has chosen the "death" of social conformity Percy criticized in the Lovells in *The Moviegoer*. In fact, Will even echoes one of Nell Lovell's clichés: "To make a contribution, however small" (385). But this is to ignore Percy's realism and open-ended semiotic. Will's plan to marry Kitty reflects vestiges of the southern "gentleman of honor" still em- bedded in his character. This code conflicts with his earlier recognition that he does not love Kitty. His inner struggle over that conflict is yet to come. (We learn later, of course, in *The Second Coming*, that Will escaped the clutches of Kitty.) Here, the key point is Will's interior disposition to make even a small contribution "of *good will and understanding*" (384) (italics mine). His inner desire is like Binx's vocation of "listening to people and helping them along and being helped along" in their common journey. In short, Will concludes that marriage, monogamy, and a life within community and helping others is preferable to the alienated detachment of his father (a "proud and solitary man") and of Sutter. Sutter's abrupt announcement that he plans to kill himself after Jamie dies shocks Will into confronting the essential question of life, and as the narrator reports, that moment of recognition marks for him "the beginning for the engineer of what is called a normal life." Will believes that his own nervous afflictions have been caused by a "lack of relationship—"; he concludes hopefully that for "the first time I think I might really live like other men—rejoin the human race" (385–86). The option of suicide he sees in Sutter galvanizes Will to choose life—and life with others—as preferable, however it might develop.

Will's becoming a "one for others" in community is solidified in the penultimate scene in the novel, the baptism and death of Jamie Vaught. Percy develops an intricately complex semiosis in this action, as we shall see, to suggest the full range of the meaning of community. It is the quintessentially Peircean triadic relation, here extended into religious mystery, because the central sign is the sacrament of baptism, the sign of mystical community. This sign-action opens for the dying Jamie the real possibility of eternal life in the communion of saints. Yet Percy avoids the stereotypical deathbed conversion scene, not simply because it would be bad writing, but because in a real sense, the mystery of the action is "unsayable," except insofar as its possibilities of meaning can be inferred from the signs. As Binx Bolling remarked when he saw the Negro businessman leaving church on Ash Wednesday, it is impossible "to say" how God's presence and grace may be entwined in the black man's progress in the world. Thus Jamie is not shown as explicitly—verbally—accepting Father Boomer's words about the promise of salvation. But the dying boy's small physical gestures—his signs—do suggest his receptivity to the priest's words and to the sacrament. And he *does* receive the sacrament, with help from Will.

As Peirce and Percy hold, every triadic sign relation or act of communication presupposes a prior triadic relation and creates a new one, with the components—sign-giver, receiver, signified, and coupler—interacting dynamically in an open-ended continuum of meaning. Thus the organic "web" of sign relations is always expanding in meaning. Percy's dramatization of Jamie's final hours is set within such a semiotic web, with the principal characters and events interacting in this dynamic way. By using this strategy, Percy is able to "relate" (in a double sense) the immediate, visible human community—the here-and-now of a hospital room—to the mystical community that extends from the present into the eternal. And although he is not a believer, Will is intimately involved as both witness to and participant in this event. Through this involvement Percy plants the "seed" of a clue to the meaning of his heretofore erratic and confused life. As always in Percy, the hint of meaning comes first through recognition of one's bond with another.

At Jamie's request, Will telephones Val, who again charges him with the responsibility of seeing to her brother's baptism, at least until she arrives. Reluctant to accept her charge, and angered at the imposition, Will nevertheless explains the commission to the priest in the hospital hallway. Significantly, Sutter does not intervene and try to stop the priest. When Father Boomer asks Sutter directly whether he concurs with Val's wish to have Jamie baptized, Will says "Yes," and Sutter replies, "By all means stay, Father" (401). When the priest tries to tell Jamie the "good news" of salvation, Jamie turns to Will for validation—"Is that true?" Will becomes the coupler in their exchange. When Will tells the priest that Jamie wants to know why he should believe the good news, Father Boomer simply says, "If it were not true . . . then I would not be here. That is why I am here, to tell you" (404). The priest himself is a living sign of the reality of divine presence, arriving at the moment of Jamie's most dire predicament, a voice of authority to be accepted or rejected. To further signify the meaning of this moment, Percy creates a wry eucharistic sign—a "Holsum bread truck"—that passes outside just as the priest asks, "Do you accept these truths?" After a silence, he explains the meaning of baptism of desire. "If you do not now believe these truths, it is for me to ask you whether you wish to believe them and whether you now ask for the faith to believe them" (404). Jamie looks to Will before fading into delirium, and *"He nodded to the engineer"* (404) (italics mine). When Jamie mutters unintelligible responses to the baptismal questions, Will brings water, and the priest baptizes Jamie, promising him that "you will be with our Blessed Lord and Savior and that you will see him face to face and see his mother, Our Lady, see them as you are seeing me" (406). Like Binx's promise to Lonnie Smith's siblings, the priest affirms Jamie's resurrection and eternal life.

Jamie's finger "stirred" against the priest's thumb and "stirred again" when Father Boomer asks Jamie to pray for him and for Will. When the priest asks Will what Jamie said, Will answers, "He said 'Don't let me go.' . . . He means his hand, the hand there." The priest responds, "I won't let you go" and continues to hold Jamie's hand as he dies (406).

The touch of the hand here is an incarnate sign of grace, echoing Will's touching the iron horsehead at his incarnational moment on the night he relived his father's death. And unlike Will's father, who would not "wait" with his son, Father Boomer holds Jamie's hand to the end and will not let go. (Later, when the priest is leaving, Will wrings his hand "warmly" and thanks him.)

These final brief moments of *solitude à trois* between Jamie, Father Boomer, and Will also recall Kate's holding the flower in her hand on the streetcar as a sign of Binx's loving presence. In this brilliant scene, Percy infuses the grim fact of death—the stench-filled body of Jamie—with the signs of hope for his final resurrection in the community of saints. Using Will's perspective as mediator-coupler, Percy unflinchingly reveals the poverty of our human condition yet also opens this ordinary scene to the possibility of a deeper reality transfigured by grace.

In the final scene in the novel Percy returns, appropriately, to Will's immediate problems. Unlike in the ending of *The Moviegoer,* there is no confirmed *solitude à deux* for Will and Kitty as there was for Binx and Kate. Although Will, the once disoriented engineer stuck in "pure possibility," has now determined to live a "normal" life by marrying Kitty and working in Pappy Vaught's car agency, the prospect cannot be encouraging, given what we know of Kitty and the New South. Yet most striking about Will after Jamie's death is his new power to act and his commitment to others, especially to Sutter. Although Will seems unclear about what "happened back there" in the hospital room, his witness to and role in the baptism-death is, Percy suggests, a decisive experience for Will, coupled with his discoveries about his father and Sutter. Gifted with new signs, his consciousness and *will* are changed. When he stops Sutter and the physician refuses to tell him what to think about "what happened" in the hospital room, Will says, "you're right. I don't need to know what you think" (407). Will takes charge of informing the Vaught family of Jamie's death, plans to meet them at the airport, and agrees to handle final arrangements for Jamie's body. When he learns that Sutter plans to return to the ranch, presumably to make good on his suicide threat, Will commands him to "wait" and says, "Dr. Vaught, I want you to come back with me." The scene, of course, is a reprise—and a reversal—of the night of his father's suicide, when lawyer Barrett rejected his son's plea to wait, rejected the boy's need and love in favor of suicide. Here, Will's open admission of need—"I need you. I, Will Barrett . . . need you and want you to come back. I need you more than Jamie needed you. Jamie had Val too"—is enough to make Sutter wait (409).

Will's admission of "need" and Sutter's response in waiting for him suggests the mysterious relation between them. Will knows that, though a depraved and riven creature, Sutter is nonetheless onto "the prime importance of the religious dimension in life" and the spiritual ills of the times. Will and Sutter thus share a common spiritual need. Will has already seen the "trap of abstraction" personified in Sutter (and in himself) and has been able to confront it in order to live and act in the here-and-now of a "Wednesday afternoon." Will's presence here deters Sutter from suicide. Will *interests* Sutter, and in him he may see a younger, more hopeful version of himself. As Sutter slows the Edsel to wait, Will's strength "flowed like oil into his muscles and he ran with great joyous ten-foot antelope bounds" toward the car (409). The future is open. The connection holds.

Percy once described young Will Barrett as much "worse off" than Binx Bolling, no doubt because of his troubled family past, his confusions over his psychic disturbances, and his isolation and lack of relation to any centering religious or philosophical perspective (Con., 13). Certainly this is true. Yet Will has undoubtedly come to some sense of greater inner coherence by the end of the novel, as Percy leaves him literally on the road in Sante Fe, ready to act and start a new life. Will's resilient spirit and determination to search for true meaning in the world are a sign of hope. But as for the American community depicted in *The Last Gentleman*, it seems "worse off" than in *The Moviegoer*. In his second novel, Percy expanded his viewpoint from the relatively narrow worlds of New Orleans and, briefly, Chicago in *The Moviegoer* to the broader landscape of North, South, and West, sharpening his critical analysis of the deep spiritual disorder in the country at large. The hope for community signified by Val Vaught's mission school is a marginal force overall, though a true incarnation of the real mystical-semiotic community. It stands as an important "remnant" (Percy would become increasingly interested in remnant communities) in the culture represented in the novel, a sign of divine presence. The many social fissures evident in *The Last Gentleman*—endemic racism and violence, destructive individualism, materialism, conformity, sexual license, idolatry of one sort or another, all offspring of the Cartesian spirit—are the major fault lines that undermine the romantic illusion of "one nation under God," thus foreshadowing the catastrophic breakup of society depicted in Percy's third novel, *Love in the Ruins*. But signs of the divine presence remain, in the abiding word and promise of salvation, in the sacraments, in the "inscape" spirit of iron horseheads and sprinkled water, and in the real possibility of love between humans who are ready—as Guardini suggested—to reach out to each other amidst the rubble.

CHAPTER THREE

The Thread in the Labyrinth

Love in the Ruins

As if in fulfillment of Romano Guardini's prophesy about "the end of the modern world" that Percy used as epigraph to *The Last Gentleman,* his third novel, *Love in the Ruins,* depicts a society that seems on the verge of un-raveling into complete anarchy and barbarism. Published in 1971, this futuris-tic satire set at a time "near the end of the world" reflects the social upheaval in American communities in the late 1960s, especially the widespread racial strife. But as in *The Last Gentleman,* the social ills in the nation are symp-toms of a deeper metaphysical disorder. Percy's protagonist, Dr. Tom More, is a "bad Catholic," a man who has abandoned his religious faith for dreams of scientific fame and personal happiness through "love" with women—that is, through the gratification of physical desire and romantic longing. Dr. More, a myopic "seer," serves as the complex narrative lens through which Percy ex-amines the conflicts between religious belief and secular power in a culture now dominated by the ideology of scientism. More's vision is both prophetic and myopic. He is "onto" the ills of the time and his own flaws, but he is also an even more flawed victim of Descartes than is Binx Bolling or the young Will Barrett. As a lapsed Catholic, and unlike his predecessor Will, More *knows* the true alternative of sacramental life, but his disordered will and romantic desire for love and fame leave him nearly helpless before the world's temptations. But a series of trials, a purgatorial rite of passage, eventually sets him on the road to recovery.

As Percy's subtitle—"The Adventures of a Bad Catholic at a Time Near the End of the World"—suggests, the novel's action takes place at a time *near* the collapse of the social order. The scope of Percy's vision in *Love in the Ruins* is much broader and more satiric than in his first two novels, and much more explicitly philosophical. The "world" about to end is not simply the strife-torn American community, which in fact does not collapse. The "world" ending is Western Christian society as Percy now understood it to be dominated by scientific humanism. In this collapsing society, the quest for autonomous power in all forms has separated Christianity from the divine Word and its command for truth, love, and charity, and from the sacramental heart of real community.

The "disaster" has already occurred, and Percy set out to map its causes and aftershocks through a broad, deeply religious, comic vision. Thus he described his third novel as an attempted comic synthesis of modern thought, like Dante's in his time, an attempt to "account for the monstrousness which the 20th century has unleashed upon the world, not the bomb but the beastliness." He wished to answer the question: "why does humanism lead to beastliness?"[1] The "modern world" Percy saw collapsing was based on what he called a "consensus anthropology," defined as the Western democratic-technological humanist view of man as a higher organism invested in certain traditional trappings of a more or less nominal Judeo-Christianity.[2] The inherent contradictions in this anthropology (man as higher organism versus child of God) cause it to explode, unleashing human beastliness. Percy's intent in *Love in the Ruins* was to expose those contradictions through satire. Percy explained in a *Publishers Weekly* article, "I wanted to explore how the boat could go under while we are still using terms like 'the dignity of the individual' and 'the quality of life.' The meaning of such terms have slipped their moorings. It is the job of the satirist to detect these slips and to exaggerate them so that they become known to everybody."[3]

Percy's focus here on the devaluation of language points to the relation between a corrupted semiosis and the general collapse of the social community. As Percy argued, scientism and its stepchild behaviorism are based on strictly causal-dyadic principles of understanding the world and human relations. Using the diagnostic weapons of the satirist, Percy the Peircean triadist ridicules the absurd but nonetheless dangerous contradictions of the scientistic "humanists." At the same time, he fashions signs and actions that open Tom More's world, and the readers, to the possibility of renewed links to the true semiotic-mystical community.

For Percy and his protagonist Tom More, a primary sign of the unleashed beastliness in modern civilization is the epic slaughter of World War I, especially the Battle of Verdun, a slaughter carried out by "humane gentlemen" on both sides. Thus in one sense the word "near" in the subtitle looks backward to the Great War as the coup de grâce of Western Christendom. As well, it also looks forward to the "end time" of history and the human social order, the triumphant return of Christ's second coming, and the fulfillment of mystical community under God. Percy's increasing concern with the larger historical movement and its deeper theological meaning is evident here. But in the novel's present time, Percy focuses on a Tom More living through the "in-between" time of personal predicament and of "waiting," the typical situation of the Percy hero searching for community in a world fraught with potential disaster, but also with possibilities of love, joy, and hope.

On first reading *Love in the Ruins* appears to be a more diffuse, sprawling, and disjointedly episodic novel than either *The Moviegoer* or *The Last Gentleman*. In one sense this is true. The "fractured" form of the novel mirrors the disordered times. But on a deeper semiotic level, form and idea are integrated. Percy created an intrinsic relationship between Tom More's fallible point of view (his disordered consciousness), the disrupted chronology of the narrative line, and the spiritual malaise in the culture he wished to analyze. For Percy, as I have noted, the contradictions in the "consensus anthropology" and the rampant beastliness of the twentieth century signify a deeper metaphysical disorder, as in both earlier novels. He stated the matter precisely in his companion essay to the novel, "Notes for a Novel about the End of the World":

> The wrong questions are being asked. The proper question is not whether God has died or been superceded by the urban-political complex. The question is not whether the Good News is no longer relevant, but rather whether it is possible that man is presently undergoing a tempestuous restructuring of his consciousness which does not presently allow him to take account of the Good News. For what has happened is not merely the technological transformation of the world but something psychologically even more portentous. It is the absorption by the layman not of the scientific method but rather of the magical aura of science, whose credentials he accepts for all sectors of reality. Thus in the lay culture of a scientific society nothing is easier than to fall prey to the kind of seduction which sunders one's very self from itself into an all-transcending "objective" consciousness and a consumer-self with a list of "needs" to be satisfied. It is this monstrous bifurcation of man into angelic and bestial components against which old theologies must be weighed before new theologies are erected. Such a man could not take account of God, the devil, and the angels if they were

standing before him, because he has already peopled the universe with his own hierarchies. When the novelist writes of a man "coming to himself" through some such catalyst as catastrophe or ordeal, he may be offering obscure testimony to a gross disorder of consciousness and to the need of recovering oneself as neither angel nor organism but as a wayfaring creature somewhere between. (MB, 113)

Percy's statement aptly describes the disordered state of narrator Tom More's consciousness.[4] Unlike in *The Last Gentleman,* in which Percy presented Will Barrett's often disordered consciousness from the perspective of a bemused third-person narrator, here he situates the point of view completely within the muddled mind of protagonist More as he makes his "confession." This shift to an interior, sometimes delusional, point of view coincides with the achronological, fragmented structure. More's inner confusions—his free-floating fantasies, reveries, memories, delusions, whims, and prophetic insights—are mirrored externally in the episodic structure of the novel. Just as More observes that the "center" of the social community "did not hold," so also the center of More's consciousness does not seem to hold. Percy's form and narrative voice make transparent the danger of a loss of coherence in the culture itself. So also, the semiotic community is in danger of being reduced to a babble of warring, meaningless voices. The Christic center of culture did not hold. Percy's remark cited earlier, that Will Barrett's muddled consciousness suggested Eric Voegelin's notion of historical (i.e., Jewish-Christian) versus cyclical (pagan classical) time, now comes to be writ large in the very form of *Love in the Ruins* (Con. 13). In the novel's voice and form, Percy points to the general aftereffects of the culture's separation from the decisive event that gives meaning and structure to history—the Christian Incarnation.

Percy traces the roots of the "gross disorder in consciousness" manifested in Tom More and his fellow citizens beyond Descartes to its origins in early modern history. To use Steiner's phrase, this was the time of the beginning of the separation of "the Word from the world," and the rise of the "objective" spirit (*Real Presences,* 93–94). In philosophy and linguistics, the realist ontology that had "centered" thought by affirming the ultimate authority of the Logos and the power to name truth began to give way to the erosions of nominalism.[5] In *Love in the Ruins,* Tom More must face the dire consequences of nominalism in his struggle with Dr. Buddy Brown in The Pit, where the debate centers on language. Nominalism, as Peirce and Percy both saw, finally precludes any notion of *real* (i.e., nonmaterial) semiotic relations and

thereby undermines community. Language, man's unique power to symbolize, to name the truth of reality and thereby form relations of meaning with
God and with other humans, threatens to devolve into a functional tool for
manipulation and power.

For Percy, as we have seen, philosophical realism was inextricably linked
to the sacramental view of reality and the truth of mystery, the interpenetra-
tion of spirit and matter. But under the nominalist-scientistic dispensation, as
the novel particularly shows, the real becomes reduced to solely quantifiable
and manipulable natural "laws." A deformed anthropology governs, one that
sees human beings not as sacred and inviolable creatures made in the image
and likeness of God but as "organisms in an environment," defined strictly by
behavioral criteria. The overt acts of violence Percy points to in the novel—
wars, social revolutions, riots, assassinations—are signs of the deeper spiritual
violence done to humans under scientism in its attack on the mystery and
absolute value of the person, and on mystery itself. Later, in *The Thanatos
Syndrome*, Percy would link one of the century's most horrific examples of
systematic violence, Nazism and the Holocaust, to an attack on the Word itself
through its most visible sign, the Jews. Here he concentrates on the demonic
"powers and principalities" that Father Rinaldo Smith identifies as the source
of chaos in *Love in the Ruins*. Satan's emissary, the consummate nominalist
Art Immelmann, threatens to destroy Tom More and implode the world. But
in spite of this threat, the center and real possibility of community nonetheless holds.

Tom More is an heir to both traditional Catholic belief and to the
new spirit of scientism. His link to the traditional Jewish-Christian ontology
is signified by his collateral relation to Sir Thomas More, the great sixteenth-
century saint, scholar, dutiful child of God, and citizen of the community.
The saint's philosophical romance, *Utopia* (i.e., "nowhere"), imagines an ideal
community without private property ownership. Against this fictional ideal
More measured the many defects of his own society. However, in the minds
of later secular humanists, what for More was an imagined ideal became the
secular dream of an actual utopian social order to be created by reason and
science. The disastrous consequences of this vision, which is based on a gnostic
attempt to transcend history and human imperfection, are now manifested in
the rampant chaos of Dr. Tom More's world. Nevertheless, both More and his
community still possess a "remnant" link to the God-centered, sacramental
vision professed by his saintly ancestor, as we shall see.

Yet for all his prestigious and important connection to St. Thomas More, Percy's failed physician is as much a "son" of Sir Francis Bacon as of the saint and martyr. Prior to Descartes, Bacon's *Novum Organum* (1620) defined the new epistemology, metaphysics, and linguistics that became the guiding philosophy of secular humanism. Bacon's work had as its aim the "reform" of mind itself, toward making it an instrument for observing, mastering, and manipulating nature. His dictum that "knowledge is power" signaled the rejection of speculative learning and the realist philosophical tradition of the Scholastics in favor of *techne*, the power to govern and shape nature toward strictly pragmatic ends.[6] Any notion of metaphysical forms as being the true reality, or of semiotic community as the impenetrable mystery at the center of existence, is routinely excluded from consideration. Most important, Bacon's organon called for a revolution in language equal to the new orthodoxy of scientism. Language was to be purged of the metaphysical generalizations and distinctions about being that had been developed over centuries of learning and that were the centerpiece of Scholastic epistemology. Instead, language was to be stripped down for utilitarian, empirical purposes. Reductive language matched reductive vision. Yet this separation of words from divine revelation and the incarnate Word, this splitting off of concrete experience from prophetic truth, opened the door to the relativism that, in Percy's view, led to the incoherence and dehumanization that is Tom More's other legacy as twentieth-century man. More's desire to cure mankind of its imperfections with his ontological lapsometer, a neurobiological diagnostic tool, is the delusory child of Bacon's perverse utopian dream.

In *Love in the Ruins* Percy houses this perverse utopian dream of community in Fedville, the government-supported center that promotes scientism in all its forms. Fedville is one of the "powers and principalities" threatening to destroy Percy's romantic dreamer-physician. The spirit of scientism that was an important leitmotiv in *The Moviegoer* and *The Last Gentleman*— seen in Percy's satire of Dr. and Mrs. Bob Dean's sexual mechanics and in Sutter Vaught's brooding over the alienated scientist—now is fully exposed as the destructive agent undermining any real human community. Ostensibly offering the promises of individual freedom, respect, and self-fulfillment, Fedville's *Zeitgeist* is in fact fundamentally totalitarian. At this so-called center of humanism, doctors and technicians subject persons to "therapeutic" manipulations based on strictly behavioral principles, applied through the Skinner Box and at Love Clinic. These devices are supposed to condition subjects to fulfill their "needs" and "adapt" to the environment as organisms. Such

practices ignore the central truth of the mystery of semiotic relations by reducing language, the unique human power, to dyadic codes and commands
for manipulating humans. Failing adaptation, the "non-functional" elderly
face extermination at the "Happy Isles." Although Percy presents these efforts
with much satiric humor—such as Ted and Tanya Tennis's vigorous attempts
to make "flesh, poor flesh" into a well-oiled sexual machine—his concern for
the "emptying out" of the self in modern scientistic culture takes a more ominous turn in this novel. The diminishments of being under scientism noted by
Binx Bolling and Sutter Vaught are now expanded into a large-scale, authorized program of managing behavior, run by secular visionaries using technological power in the service of their gnostic dream of social order. Percy's
depiction of Fedville here foreshadows his last novel, *The Thanatos Syndrome*,
in which the experiments of Fedville scientists are linked to the deadly practices of German physicians during the 1930s, and ultimately to the Nazi regime
as archenemy of the divine Word in modern history. Implicitly and explicitly,
Percy exposes the true relation between the secular dream of a "perfect" society
and the totalitarian nightmare of racial purification and genocide.

As the novel's central action reveals, Fedville's perverted vision of the self
and society is manifested in what for Percy is the major sign of a deranged
social order: the corruption of language. As Percy once remarked, language
is the pathology of the twentieth century. Fedville's jargon is the offspring of
linguistic nominalism, a fact seen clearly in Tom More's debates with Drs. Max
Gottlieb and Buddy Brown over the meaning of terms such as "the dignity of
the individual," "guilt," "freedom," and "the quality of life" (LR, 110–11, 186–
87). Such expressions have become separated from real meaning; now they
are simply "markers" in a verbal "exchange" in which meaning is assigned
subjectively by the speakers. Hence, no common basis for understanding or
community of knowledge is possible, as More quickly realizes when he presses
his colleagues to define what they mean by such buzz phrases. For Percy the
realist, Fedville's babble is the logical outcome after centuries of nominalistic
declension from the divine Logos at the center of truth. Thus Fedville's activities, and its claimed justifications, are truly demonic, as the novel makes
clear. If as Percy and Peirce believed, mankind is truly made human through
language, through the power to name and symbolize the real, then the devaluation of that power at Fedville signifies a radical diminishment of humanity
itself. Thus it is no accident that the central "debate" over the fate of Mr. Ives
pivots on the issue of language and meaning.

Tom More's anomalous relation to Fedville and what it represents is a sign of his own fractured being. A more self-aware victim of Descartes than Will Barrett was, More suffers from the very dualism he diagnoses, here called "angelism/bestialism." As is clear, his dream of saving mankind with his lapsometer and achieving universal fame links him to the gnostic scientists at Fedville and their dream of "transcending" the human condition through *techne* and power. Were he to become such a "savior," More would replace Christ and the hard wisdom that salvation comes through the cross of suffering, grace, and repentance, for Percy the only genuine path to transcendence. But like his predecessors Binx Bolling and Will Barrett, More also has a good nose for "merde"; that is, for seeing all of the derangements in his society and in himself. This intuitive sense signifies his inextinguishable desire for truth, his most redeeming quality, even though he often fails to follow his insights. Paradoxically, what will save More from the destructive alienation of "angelism" is the flesh—human desire—even though he often cannot bring his will into line with what he knows in his heart to be the true source and goal of his longing, which is ultimate union with God. Instead, he prefers the physical satisfactions of desire—sex and alcohol. But More also knows that desire and the flesh link him to a world that has been transformed by Christ, a sacramental world in which grace is available. He recognizes that the Eucharist, the sacrament of community, is "the thread in the labyrinth." He admits that attending mass and receiving communion with his daughter, Samantha, a practice he abandoned after she died, were "the best of times . . . we having received communion and I rejoicing afterwards, caring nought for my fellow Catholics but only myself and Samantha and Christ swallowed, remembering what he promises me for swallowing him, that I would have life in me, and I did, feeling so good that I'd sing and cut the fool all the way home like King David before the Ark" (212, 241). But in the time present of the novel More has abandoned the sacramental life out of despair at his daughter's death. Nevertheless, the "voice" of truth within him helps him resist a complete slide into bestialism. He believes the wisdom of St. Thomas Aquinas, that "knowing is man's happiness." This spirit of truth—his commitment to words that mean and name the real—enables him to recognize and finally expose the contradictions in the Fedville ideology, as well as name the very temptations that entrap him, and confess his faults. More's narrative journey, then, like that of St. Augustine in *The Confessions*, is two stranded. His tale is both a dramatic rendering of his experiences and a retrospective account of his spiritual progress from beyond the "end" time, one that records his ongoing trials as a wayfarer whose true end is union with God.

Percy's novel opens amidst the ruins of an America once imagined mythically as a paradise community that would reverse history and tradition. In the myth, America would be a new society in which individual human freedom could be fully realized. This gnostic dream, clothed in nominal Christian beliefs, was to be achieved by reason, work, and scientific progress. As Tocqueville recognized, that dream was philosophically rooted in Cartesian dualism, a vision that held out the promise of transcending the harsh realities of history. Tocqueville understood how in America the ideals of freedom, individualism, and self-fulfillment were liable to degenerate into self-interest, solipsism, and a moral autonomy that would undermine any hope of communal harmony. "Not only does democracy make every man forget his ancestors, but it hides his descendents and separates his contemporaries from him; *it throws him back forever upon himself alone and threatens in the end to confine him entirely within the solitude of his own heart*," he wrote in *Democracy in America* (2.99) (italics mine). Tocqueville also noted how in this solitary condition Americans would easily fall prey to forces of conformity, manipulation, and group think. Tocqueville's Americans are paradoxically both loners and joiners. Thus the problems of the self and its relations to "groups" Percy depicted in Binx Bolling and Will Barrett are here generalized into the warring ideological factions that erupt in *Love in the Ruins*. When Tom More first comes to himself in a grove of pines on July Fourth, in the "dread last days of the old violent USA and of the Christ-forgetting Christ-haunted death-dealing Western world," he ponders its meaning in relation to some providential design of history: "Is it that God has at last removed his blessing from the USA and what we feel now is just the clank of the old historical machinery, the sudden jerking ahead of the roller coaster cars as the chain catches hold and carries us back into history with its ordinary catastrophes, carries us up and out toward the brink from that felicitous and privileged siding where even unbelievers admitted that if it was not God who blessed the USA, then at least some great good luck had befallen us, and that now the blessing or the luck is over, the machinery clanks, the chain catches hold, and the car jerks forward" (3–4). In *The Moviegoer*, Binx spoke while riding to Chicago of the "peculiar gnosis of trains." Here, Percy's railroad metaphor suggests that the gnostic dream of America was an aberration from real history and that the collapsing country has now rejoined the roller coaster train of history. In truth, of course, America never transcended history. From the beginning, the colonists' brutal treatment of indigenous peoples and of dissenters testified to the harsh truth that the evils of the past had not been overcome. Added to this has been the history of racial injustice, greed, and exploitation of natural resources. That

More sees the current collapse in Edenic terms suggests both the power of the myth and his own partly skewed vision, since he too is one of the scientific "pioneers," even though his ostensible goal may be nobler. Whether God has withdrawn his blessing or whether America's luck simply ran out, the dream has collapsed. Instead of a cohesive society, America is a balkanized world of reactionary enclaves—the conservative town, the Edenic exurbia of Paradise Estates where More lives, the prelapsarian Honey Island retreat, the Negroes' Happy Hollow, and Fedville. In all, "principalities and powers are everywhere victorious," as More explains; demonic forces reign throughout the culture.

More wonders if the cause of the collapse of America was racism, the evil that brought disaster to the garden. Echoing Faulkner's "The Bear," he offers a mytho-theological interpretation of American history as paradigm of the Fall:

The poor U.S.A.!

Even now, late as it is, nobody can really believe that it didn't work after all.

The USA didn't work! Is it even possible that from the beginning it never did work? That the thing always had a flaw in it, a place where it would shear, and that all this time we were not really different from Ecuador or Bosnia-Herznagovina, just richer. Moon Mullins blames it on the niggers. Hm. Was it the nigger business from the beginning?

What a bad joke: God saying, here it is, the new Eden, and it is yours because you're the apple of my eye; because you the lordly Westerner, the fierce Caucasian-Gentile-Visigoths, believed in me and in the outlandish Jewish Event even though you were nowhere near it and had to hear the news of it from strangers. But you believed and so I gave it all to you, gave you Israel and Greece and science and art and the lordship of the earth, and finally even gave you the new world that I blessed for you. And all you had to do was pass one little test, which was surely child's play for you since you had already passed the big one. One little test: here's a helpless man in Africa, all you have to do is not violate him. That's all.

One little test: you flunk! (54)

Percy suggests through More that the racism splintering America (the novel was written during the racial turmoil of the late 1960s) is a manifestation of deeper spiritual ills. Pride and greed, already engrained in many of the first settlers, found especially fertile ground in the land of opportunity, watered by secular notions of self-affirmation. John Winthrop's ideal of a national community based on Christian charity finally proved impossible to sustain in such a bountiful setting. But More protests: "No! No fair! Foul! The test was too much! What do you expect of a man?" Driven by his own messianic pride,

More arrogantly proposes to revive and fulfill the dream through his own scientific prowess: "But wait. It is still not too late. I can save you, America! I
know something! I know what is wrong! I hit on something, made a breakthrough, came on a discovery! I can save the terrible God-blessed Americans
from themselves! With my invention! Listen to me. Don't give up. It is not too
late. You are still the last hope. There is no one else. Bad as we are, there is no
one else" (54–55).

More's hope of saving America from its spiritual sins through science is
obviously a delusion. He is unwittingly possessed here by the "powers and
principalities" that reign across the land. (He will only gradually come to recognize this personal demon later when his alter ego, the satanic Art Immelmann, appears.) Moreover, More's belief that Americans are "the last hope"
and that there is "no one else" to save the world is filled with the myopic pride
of election, the claim that Americans are the "chosen race." Having abandoned
"the thread in the labyrinth," More no longer believes that Christ is the true
"last hope" or that divine grace and the sacraments are the means of salvation,
not secular science. Neither does he admit that the cost of recovery is humble repentance and acceptance of the cross. Having lost "the thread," his link
to the sacraments, More has sunk into extremes of angelism-bestialism. The
love he once possessed degenerates into a lust for sexual gratification, alcohol,
and fame. He "left off eating Christ in communion, and took to sipping Early
Times instead and seeking the company of the fair sex, as they used to say"
(23). Though he freely confesses this failure, More nevertheless claims to know
"how to be happy and make others happy" by his invention, the "ontological
lapsometer." Using it, he hopes to diagnose and eventually cure mankind of its
dualism. His dream is to overcome the Cartesian dilemma and solve the riddle
of the mystery of being. But in fact, even were such a "cure" possible, it would
only condition humans to adapt to the mundane world, eliminating any spiritual longings or need for God. In the most radical sense, it would dehumanize
its subjects. More's intended role as self-appointed "world-savior" thus becomes the role of Antichrist, one who would displace the genuine Christ of
real presence and deny the action of grace.

Percy reveals the myopia of More's vision of a new world community in
several ways. One is through the significance of the lapsometer itself, a symbol
of the ambiguous power of science as well as its limitations. As an instrument,
it is based on a perverse adaptation of behaviorist and semiotic principles. It
uses encephalographic techniques to measure the electrical activity of separate centers of the brain. At the same time, it uses the principle of "location

by triangulation" to try to correlate the electrical activity in the brain with psychological states of "terrors and rages and murderous impulses" (27). As an advanced instrument of neurobiology, it tries to "read" the spirit and then quantify it objectively. Any such simple correlation of physical responses to psycho-spiritual states is reductive of real human mystery. It does not account for the "third," human language (and implicitly, divine presence). Thus More's own inclination to reductive behaviorism is embedded in the instrument. Yet at the same time, the lapsometer is moderately and temporarily useful for diagnosing and alleviating some symptoms, if not the radical condition of humans as fallen, alienated creatures. It does help More save Mr. Ives by getting him to speak. But as a device geared to manipulate human beings as organisms, it is at odds with the mystery, sovereignty, and free will of the person. It cannot identify the true locus and goal of desire. More's link to Fedville, and his hope for federal funding to perfect his invention, exposes the larger dangers in such manipulation. That danger becomes clear later when, in a wildly comic scene in The Pit, the satanic Art Immelmann triggers a riot by misuse of the lapsometer, unleasing chaos through violent "behavior modification."

More's vision is also skewed by his bestial appetites. In despair over the loss of his family, he now searches for "love" with three women—Lola Rhoades, Moira Schaffner, and Ellen Oglethorpe. Percy counterpoints these relationships to the life More had with his wife, Doris, and Samantha as three possible options to replace the community of love and faith, the *solitude à deux* bonds, he has lost. As the novel unfolds, More's experiences with these women are interspersed with irrepressible and recurrent memories of Samantha, a vital link in his consciousness to the "thread in the labyrinth." Lola Rhoades, the lusty Texas cellist, enters his life at a time of triumph and despair. On Christmas Eve, More celebrates the initial success of his lapsometer by a night of drinking at the country club. Despite his success, he is filled with loneliness and unappeased longing. Drinking gin fizzes causes his eyes to swell shut during a sexual tryst with Lola in a sand bunker, nestled against her like a "blind babe." Saved by Lola Rhoades, Willard Amadie, and Dr. Dusty Rhoades, More returns home and attempts suicide after watching an aged Perry Como's Christmas show. More is again saved by his friend Dr. Max Gottlieb, but his new relationship with Lola portends a future disaster. Marriage to Lola—her wish as well as that of her father and of More's mother—would be a deathly escape into a false pastoral nostalgic dream. As a retreat from the ruins of the present world, Lola offers a life of sensuality and song at "Tara," a fake movie-set southern mansion, coupled with the romantic illusion of salvation from the social collapse by living "close to the land." To his great credit, More eventually rejects this sham Eden in favor of work within the present community. The truth of his broken human condition will finally dispel the romantic mists of Tara and the dream of a return to nature and innocence. The return to a simple and purer world remains a staple in the romantic myth of America, but Percy's satire reveals that no such pastoral paradise ever existed or ever will. As he makes clear, what really saves More after his tryst with Lola and his suicide attempt is his honest confession of his own sinfulness: "Later, lust gave way to sorrow and I prayed, arms stretched out like a Mexican, tears streaming down my face. Dear God, I can see it now, why can't I see it other times, that it is you I love in the beauty of the world and in all the lovely girls and dear good friends, and it is pilgrims we are, wayfarers on a journey, and not pigs, nor angels. Why can I not be merry and loving like my ancestor, a gentle pure-hearted knight of our Lady and our blessed Lord and Savior? Pray for me, Sir Thomas More" (104). Clarity of vision, repentance, and hopeful prayer momentarily replace lust and despair. More's link to the mystical community remains alive in memory and still faintly holds.

More's relationship with Moira Schaffner threatens him with spiritual disaster in a more subtly perverse way than his relationship with Lola Rhoades, though both represent escape from the real. A "popsy" from Love Clinic, a practitioner of *techne* in sex, Moira is a vapid, amoral romantic who longs to escape to the decadent "ruins" of old western ghost towns and small hotels with wishing wells. Constantly mouthing clichés, she would trade her sexual favors indiscriminately to fulfill her childish, self-indulgent fantasies. Yet what is more threatening to More than just her shallow romanticism is his perverse attraction to her, which he does not recognize. Percy creates in Moira a corrupt "double" of More's daughter, Samantha, to emphasize that his lust for Moira represents a corruption of religious love. In truth, Moira and More's relationship is a form of pedophilia, a theme Percy would explore more fully and seriously in *The Thanatos Syndrome*. Percy makes clear the perversity of their relationship through a pattern of debased sacramental imagery. More's love for Samantha is linked semiotically to faith and their receiving of the sacraments, especially the Eucharist, what he calls their "eating Christ" together at mass. In contrast now, as Moira sits childlike in his lap in the motel room, she tells More that he smells like her "Uncle Bud."

> "You're a lovely girl," I say, holding and patting her just as I used to pat Samantha
> when she had growing pains.

"Do you love me?"
"Oh yes."
"How much?"
"Enough to eat you," I say and begin to eat her kneecap.

"Could we live in Paradise?"
"Certainly."
Eating her, I have visions of golden cockerels glittering like topazes in the morning sun of my "enclosed patio." (242–43) (Italics mine)

More says he is especially fond of "eating" her "biscuit" knees. The image is unmistakable. He has left off eating the body of Christ, the life-giving sacrament, in favor of "eating" Moira's body, as Lance Lamar will do later with his wife, Margot. In *The Last Gentleman* Sutter Vaught called lewdness the "sacrament of the dispossessed." Here, dispossessed of the Eucharist, More enacts a lewd "sacrament" of sexual fulfillment. Sexual gratification becomes for him the profane goal of human desire and longing. In addition, Percy emphasizes Moira's significance as a sign of the idolatrous sexual desire that pervades American culture, which "feasts" on such pedophilic icons by objectifying women and debasing sexual relations into "need" fulfillment: "She's the girl of our dreams, Americans," More thinks, "the very one we held in our hearts as we toiled in the jungles of Ecuador. . . . My throat is engorged with tenderness. Planning a house she is, marking the margins of *House Beautiful*. She's beautiful too. . . . Her golden deltoid curves in a single strong arc, a whorl of down marking its insertion. Now she turns a page and supines her forearm to hold the spine of the magazine: down plunges the tendon into the fossa at her elbow. Sweet fossa. I kiss it" (329).[7] More's own inclination to objectify is revealed in his medical description of Moira's body. Significantly, desire has "blown his speech center," reducing him to an abstract "dissector" of her charms on the one hand and a lewd sexual predator on the other. But fortunately, grace comes in the memory of Samantha, recalling him to his human self and leaving him in tears, asking, "Why does desire turn to grief and memory strike at the heart?" (129–30).

More's third relationship, with his Presbyterian nurse Ellen Oglethorpe, eventually enables him to find a new home, a new family, and a revived career—in short, a place within the ordinary community. As many commentators have noted, Ellen is the voice of ethical conscience, one who believes in "doing right" more than believing in God. Although her role in More's interior religious journey is limited, she does provide a center of love and commitment in marriage that helps save him from despair and the extremes of angelism-bestialism. As in the case of Binx and Kate, marriage to Ellen situates More within a world where he can fulfill his vocation as husband, father, citizen, worker, and fellow wayfarer "helping others along in their journey and being helped along." Moreover, his newfound stability in marriage, family, and work helps him to reconnect with "the thread in the labyrinth," the sacramental life. As we shall see, this sacramental life, a truer vision of America within the context of redemption history, dominates Percy's final vision of More in the epilogue of the novel. But this last state of qualified hope comes only after More's trial by combat with the "powers and principalities" within himself and in the culture, in the life-or-death struggle over Mr. Ives.

Percy focuses the life-death struggle and the theme of malaise or death-in-life on the central issue of the corruption of language. His spokesman is the prophetic Father Rinaldo Smith, the somewhat batty but faithful priest of a remnant community. Through him Percy links the modern corruption of language to an abandonment of belief in the incarnated Logos, and the "emptying out" of meaning that ensues. Standing in the pulpit at mass, before the schism in society has occurred, Father Smith falls silent, then proclaims that "the channels are jammed and the word is not getting through" (175). Echoing Percy's argument about the "restructured" modern consciousness in "Note for a Novel about the End of the World," the priest claims that demonic powers—Satan—have "jammed" the lines of communication so that the "good news" cannot be heard. After committing himself to the hospital, Father Smith tries to explain the matter to More and Dr. Max Gottlieb:

> "They've won and we've lost," says Father Smith.
>   "Who are they, Father?"
>   "The principalities and powers."
>   "You are speaking of devils now, Father?" asks Max.
>   "That is correct."
>   "Now what tactic, as you call it, has prevailed?"
>   "Death."
>   "Death?"
>   "Yes. Death is winning. Life is losing."
>   "Ah, you mean the wars and crimes and violence and so on?"
>   "Not only that. I mean the living too."
>   "The living? You mean the living are dead?"

"Yes."

"How can that be, Father? How can the living be dead?"

"I mean their souls, of course."

"You mean their souls are dead," says Max with the liveliest sympathy.

"Yes," says Father Smith tonelessly. "I am surrounded by the corpses of souls. We live in a city of the dead." (176–77)

The priest links spiritual death to the "jamming" of the divine Word, God's "good news" to mankind, by the reigning demonic powers. The image of "jamming" is appropriately both technological and semiotic. With the possibility of divine revelation "evacuated" by scientism, words are reduced to mechanical "exchanges." The authority of the divine Word has been replaced by a nominalism under which words have only relative meaning, seen in the "doublespeak" of the Fedvillians. But Father Smith is a true namer, and he points to the source of this spiritual death, the "father of lies" who is bent on confusion and destruction. More must contend with this adversary in the person of Art Immelmann, the demon he must see and name clearly if he is to recover his life.

Percy's emphasis on the threatening ascendancy of satanic power in the culture, and his clear intention to name it here, represents a significant development from his first two novels. Binx Bolling and Sutter Vaught both mention the problem of the dissolution of the meaning of "sin," how the very word and concept seem to have lost their force in modern society. But in *Love in the Ruins,* Percy chose to dramatize and personify that threat explicitly in the satanic Art Immelmann. St. Thomas Aquinas claimed that Satan has no being; the devil is the negation of being. Yet as Rene Girard points out in *I See Satan Fall Like Lightning,* Satan operates in the world as a parasite on true being, working by disguise, deceit, and often by a mock imitation of the good (182–93). Such is the "character" of Art Immelmann in the novel, tempting More as a "double" figure bent on helping More "fulfill" his dreams of scientific and sexual conquest.

More's initial failure to recognize Immelmann as Satan mirrors the debilitated spiritual condition of the culture. If, as Father Smith argues, the transmission of the "good news" is jammed, then so also is the ability to recognize the Adversary. He seems to "disappear" from the modern secular consciousness (his most artful trick), and Percy suggests that this "disappearance," like the concept of "sin," is directly linked to the devolution of language from realism into nominalism. Satan cannot be named *as* Satan under such a relative perspective. Percy shows the demonic consequences of this devaluation in the calculated deceit of the elusive Immelmann and in the activities at Fedville, where human life itself is at stake. Percy focuses this theme specifically in More's defense of Mr. Ives, a linguist whose life More saves by getting him to talk and thus "prove" his humanity.

As one of the reigning powers and principalities, Immelmann is a master of the corrupted word and a "facilitator" of egoistic human desires. Parodying Satan's temptation of Jesus, he offers More worldly power and fame in the form of funding to perfect and manufacture his lapsometer. The temptation More faces to become a scientific "savior" of mankind is irresistible to his vanity. Percy underscores this by depicting More as a flawed redeemer, trapped in bestialism and despair. Drinking with Leroy Ledbetter, More sees his own reflection in the mirror:

> In the dark mirror there is a dim hollow-eyed Spanish Christ. The pox is spreading on his face. Vacuoles are opening in his chest. It is the new Christ, the spotted Christ, the maculate Christ, the sinful Christ. The old Christ died for our sins and it didn't work, we were not reconciled. The new Christ shall reconcile man with his sins. The new Christ lies drunk in a ditch. Victor Charles and Leroy Ledbetter pass by and see him.
>
> "Victor, do you love me?"
>
> "'sho, Doc."
>
> "Leroy, do you love me?"
>
> "Cut it out, Tom. You know better than to ask that."
>
> "Then y'all help me."
>
> "O.K., Doc." They laugh and pick up the new Christ, making a fireman's carry, joining four hands. They love the new Christ and so they love each other.
> (145)

As the "new Christ" More would presume to reconcile mankind to its fallen state, using the lapsometer. No more longing for God or eternal life. No need for grace or repentance. Science replaces Christ and the cross as the way of redemption. As Girard notes, one of Satan's cleverest guises is to pose as a world savior, offering an illusion of salvation based on deception and violence (*I See Satan*, 180–81). Yet More cannot resist this Faustian temptation.

Neither can he resist Immelmann's offer to facilitate his lustful appetites. The devil, who personifies More's own messianic desires, buzzes the shaky physician with the lapsometer to "stimulate the scientist-lover" and induce him to "love faithlessly but truly" and win fame. Immelmann says: "so that in the same moment one becomes victorious in science one also becomes victorious in love. And all for the good of mankind! Science to help all men and a happy joyous love to help women. We are speaking here of happiness, joy, music, spontaneity, you understand. Fortunately we have put behind us such unhappy things as pure versus impure love, sin versus virtue, and so forth. This love has its counter-point in scientific knowledge: it is neutral morally, abstractive and godlike" (202). Massaged by the lapsometer, and confused by Immelmann's alluring gospel, More signs the contract just before entering The Pit for his duel with Dr. Buddy Brown over Mr. Ives.

In the debate between More and Dr. Brown over whether Mr. Ives is to be euthanized, Percy focused the central question raised by the dominant scientistic ideology: is a human being a sovereign child of God with the power of human language, or merely an adaptable organism? Percy's answer to this question will not come from Fedville's behavioral theories but from a semiotic demonstration of man's power to know truth and symbolize it triadically through language. Mr. Ives, we learn, rebelled against the benign conformity of the senior citizens' ersatz community, the Golden Years Center in Tampa, by refusing to participate in organized group activities and by defecating on "Flirtation Walk." He now sits in a mute, catatonic state, leading behaviorist Dr. Brown to assume that he is senile and therefore a candidate for extermination at Happy Isle Separation Center. But More is able to reduce Mr. Ives's anger, the cause of his silence, and get him to speak. His rage, he explains, was directed against the distracting programmed activities of the seniors' center that prevented him from pursuing his solitary avocation—that of being a linguist and a writer. Mr. Ives protests: "Doctor . . . how would you like it if during the most critical time of your experiments with the Skinner box that won you the Nobel Prize, you had been pestered without letup by a bunch of chickenshit Ohioans? Let's play shuffleboard, let's play granddaddy golf, Guys and Gals a go-go. I mean is there any reason why a retired person should not go on his own way and refuse to be importuned by a bunch of chickenshit Ohioans?" (219).

Mr. Ives, it turns out, is a Peircean semiotician, which is Percy's "answer" to the reductive ontology of scientism. Mr. Ives had been searching for the "fountain of youth" in Florida, but not the mythical source of "eternal life" of the legendary Ponce de Leon. Rather, he was searching for language clues to decipher the signs on the Ocala frieze, a medal struck by the Spaniards to commemorate the parley between Narvaez and the Indian leader Osceonanta. Percy thus suggests that the "eternal" youth of vital life comes through the human power of language and "parleying," not through some magical waters. As More says, echoing St. Thomas Aquinas, man's greatest joy is knowing. Mr. Ives now explains how he planned to make "direct pairings of glyphs and Spanish words" in order to decipher the frieze. In short, his search is governed by triadic principles, connecting signs in order to uncover meaning. Searching at a "big spring" near Tampa, he found the gold coin and then related the signs to help decipher the frieze: "What they did was take one of their old medals showing a salamander on one side and scratch a proto-Creek glyph on the reverse. My hypothesis was that the glyph meant fish. It worked" (218). As triadic signifying helps decipher the coin, Mr. Ives's explanation demonstrates his humanity. Moreover, the coin symbolizes a real historical event, a "parley" in fact, as opposed to the airy hypothesizing of the Fedville ideologues.

By getting Mr. Ives to talk, More is able to save him from euthanasia so that he can return home to Lost Cove, Tennessee, and pursue his studies until he dies. In More's success with Mr. Ives, Percy offers hope for the recovery of the human through language, the true "fountain of youth." Mr. Ives's discovery of meaning through a triadic relating of signs echoes Helen Keller's discovery of the meaning of "water" at the well-house, Percy's central example of triadic behavior in his seminal essay "The Delta Factor" (MB, 3–45). Life comes in the human power to know, name, and celebrate the real through shared signs, the bedrock of genuine community. But More's triumph with Mr. Ives is short lived. Chaos breaks out in The Pit when Immelmann distributes lapsometers to the staff and students and they zap each other. Loosed from self-control, they collapse into violent, bestial behavior. The powers and principalities again reign.

The scene of chaos that erupts in The Pit is a microcosm *in extremis* of the disorder beyond Fedville, the general confusion in More's society that raises Percy's central question: "How does humanism lead to bestialism?" The "humanism" espoused at Fedville is shown to be radically antihuman and based on a false ontology. Trapped amidst these ruins, More now is faced with several dangerous options. Life with either Moira Schaffner or Lola Rhoades offers escape from the difficulties of the here-and-now, an abandonment of responsibility to the community, in favor of sensual delight. A similar option is presented by Hester, the social dropout who renounced Judaism for the mock prelapsarian world of a Honey Island commune. Alternatively, Art

Immelmann tempts him to flee the broken world of America for a life of wine, women, song, and fame in Copenhagen. Standing as a force against these temptations is Ellen Oglethorpe, the Presbyterian nurse who frequently "clears" More's blurred vision and recalls him to his responsibilities as a man and a physician—"Chief . . . You're not living up to the best that's in you" (237). But most important to More's future is the memory and the living presence of Samantha, an insistent "voice" of grace in his head. She is More's link to the sacramental life, to Christ and the invisible community of saints.

After the debacle in The Pit, More's memories of Samantha recur with increasing frequency to disrupt his planned assignations with Moira and Lola. As he did with young Will Barrett's memories of his home and past, Percy places these recollections strategically throughout the novel to reveal More's true spiritual condition. Memories of his daughter and the life she represents become the semiotic links in More's consciousness to the larger mystical community that is the "home" of true being. These are not merely memories of a "paradise lost," of the happiness of marriage and family before the death of Samantha and the defection of his wife, Doris. Rather, they are signs of his growing awareness of his failure of faith when faced with Samantha's death. For example, while waiting to begin a tryst with Moira, More again recalls hearing mass and receiving communion during the early days of his marriage to Doris:

> Sunday morning I'd leave her and go to mass. Now here was the strangest exercise of all! Leaving the coordinate of the motel at the intersection of the interstates . . . descending through a moonscape countryside to a—town! . . . to some forlorn little Catholic church up a side street just in time for the ten-thirty mass . . . for here off I-51 I touched the thread in the labyrinth, and the priest announced the turkey raffle and Wednesday bingo and preached the Gospel and fed me Christ—
>
> —Back to the motel then, exhilarated by—what? by eating Christ or by the secret discovery of the singular thread in this the unlikeliest of places, this geometry of Holiday Inns and interstates? back to lie with Doris all rosy-fleshed and creased of cheek and slack and heavy-limbed with sleep, cracking one eye and opening her arms and smiling.
>
> "My God, what is it you do in church?"
>
> What she didn't understand, she being spiritual and seeing religion as spirit, was that it took religion to save me from the spirit world, from orbiting the earth

like Lucifer and the angels, that it took nothing less than touching the thread off
the misty interstates and eating Christ himself to make me mortal man again
and let me inhabit my own flesh and love her in the morning. (241–42)

Like Mr. Ives's triadic discovery, More's recovered memory is historical and
concrete, anchored in time and space. But in addition to being historical, the
"thread in the labyrinth" is the mystery of the Incarnation and redemption
signified in the mass and Eucharist, his link to the possibility of full humanity—"to make me mortal man again and let me inhabit my own flesh and
love her in the morning." The communion is both sign and means of grace to
overcome the dualism of angelism/bestialism that threatens to destroy him.
But More's discovery here is incomplete. Only later will he discover the secret
link between Samantha's death, his despair, and his leaving off eating Christ
in favor of "feasting" on Moira.

Still trapped in his involvement with Moira, Lola, and Immelmann, More
does nonetheless summon the strength of will to pray, calling on his saintly
ancestor for help. When captured by the revolutionaries, he escapes from
"prison," the old St. Mary's rectory, by unscrewing the air-conditioner vent
with the sword from the statue of St. Michael and then sliding like a newborn
child into "the hot bright perilous world" (295). Prayer brings renewed power.
More important than his escape from the "Bantus," however, is his eventual
overcoming of the satanic Immelmann by again calling on his namesake in
prayer. Whereas earlier in the novel More could only recall the saint wistfully
and lament that he did not live like him, More will soon invoke his ancestor's
aid against the Adversary. But the power to renounce Immelmann comes to
More only *after* a frank admission of his perverse "use" of Samantha's death,
and his confession of the sin of malice. Just before Immelmann's offer to take
him to Denmark, More recalls how, before her death, Samantha challenged
him about his failure to attend mass and warned him about "the sin against
grace," the refusal to believe in and love God. Recalling this challenge, More
admits that he abandoned faith in the face of her death. Percy casts this insight in terms of the mysterious relationship between More's consciousness,
his foreknowledge, and actual events:

> I wonder: did it break my heart when Samantha died? Yes. There was even the
> knowledge and foreknowledge of it while she still lived, knowledge that while
> she lived, life still had its same peculiar tentativeness, people living as usual by
> fits and starts, aiming and missing, while present time went humming, and fore-
> knowledge that the second she died, remorse would come and give past time its

bitter specious wholeness. If only—If only we hadn't been defeated by hum-
drum humming present time and missed it, missed ourselves, missed everything. I had the foreknowledge while she lived. Still, present time went humming. Then she died and here came the sweet remorse like a blade between the
ribs. (353)

More's insight here is a crucial epiphany in the novel, and another of Percy's
meditations on the modern problem of time. It recalls Will Barrett's anxious
thoughts about the fleeting present as being like a running spool of tape and
foreshadows Lance Lamar's somber view of present time as a "tapehead" between past and future. Here, More admits that his foreknowledge of Samantha's death incapacitated him to live in and accept the "present" of their time
together. His foreknowledge signifies his gnostic impulse, the pull of his abstractive consciousness or "angelism" to transcend time.[8] More's angelic foreknowledge of Samantha's impending death fixates him on her physical demise.
Lacking sufficient faith, he cannot see her death in the sacramental context of
faith and hope in the final resurrection of the body. Moreover, foreknowledge tells him that remorse will come and give time a "bitter *specious* wholeness" (italics mine). More's life since Samantha's death, as he intuits, has been
a gnostic attempt to separate past from presentness, producing an illusory
"wholeness." Even his remorse is "sweet" because it served as an excuse for
self-pity. The "blade between the ribs" is suffering unredeemed. More has de-
spaired of the present, the incarnate here-and-now, as he will soon admit. In
short, his riven state of angelism-bestialism undermined his weakened religious faith in Christ's Incarnation and his commitment to the sacramental life.
    Percy makes the semiotic connection between More's recognition of the
"problem" of modern time and the sacramental theology of the Incarnation
clear. When Samantha was alive, she and More shared a time of joy in their
mutual faith and in eating the body of Christ together. When she died, More
turned away from the Eucharist. Instead, he has "fed" on her death as an excuse for despair. "But is there not a compensation, a secret satisfaction to be
taken in her death, a delectation of tragedy, a license for drink, a taste of both
for taste's sake?" he asks (353). The "secret satisfaction" points to More's continuing spiritual *acedia*. For all her gnostic flights, Doris saw her husband's
refusal of faith and his use of Samantha's death to justify despair: "Doris was
a dumbbell but she could read my faults! She said that when I refused to take
Samantha to Lourdes . . . The truth was that Samantha didn't want to go to
Lourdes and I didn't want to take her. Why not? I don't know Samantha's

reasons, but I was afraid she might be cured. What then? Suppose you ask God for a miracle and God says yes, very well. How do you live the rest of your life?" (353–54). More is able now to admit his failure *and* the need for forgiveness, what he and Doris refused each other when their daughter died: "Samantha, forgive me. I am sorry you suffered and died, my heart broke, but there have been times when I was not above enjoying it. . . . Is it possible to live without feasting on death?" (354). Acknowledging that he has "feasted" on death rather than on Christ, More receives the grace to call on his namesake and renounce Immelmann once and for all: "*Sir Thomas More, kinsman, saint, best dearest merriest of Englishmen, pray for us and drive this son of a bitch hence*" (355). Momentarily, the father of lies disappears in a puff of smoke.

As More's partial recovery is a sign of hope for him, so also does Percy create cautionary signs of hope for the larger community, the possibility of a recovery of its ordinary humanity. Five years after the disaster of July Fourth, the black revolutionaries' utopian dreams of a "new society" have failed, though the Bantus have now taken control of Paradise Estates by asserting their property rights. The blacks now hold the upper hand economically. Still, Percy suggests that a deeper spiritual transformation must occur before a genuine community of the races will emerge. Speaking to the revolutionary Uru, More says: "Well, you're right about one thing. I couldn't help you now even if you'd let me. We're not talking about the same thing. We're talking about different kinds of trouble. First you got to get where you're going or where you think you're going—although I hope you do better than that, because after all nothing comes easier than that, being against one thing and tearing down another thing and talking about peace and brotherhood—I never saw peace and brotherhood from such talk and I hope you do better than that because there are better things and harder things to do" (352). Through More, Percy suggests that the dream of the black revolutionaries may turn out to be another version of the secular dream of personal "freedom" and material success so embedded as myth in the American psyche. Economic justice is imperative, but if it fails to touch the core of charity on which genuine community must be founded, it will be little better than the secular consumerism of white society. This is the *spiritual* challenge facing the blacks. Fortunately, there are signs that the thread of common charity still holds, as we shall see. More important, there are clear signs of the presence of God and his word in the here-and-now ordinary world. That Percy wishes to affirm this deeper hope is clear from the setting and final action of the novel.

Just as the chaotic events of most of the novel are set within the context of

America's secular history, signified by Independence Day, July Fourth, Percy sets the epilogue within the Christian liturgical scheme of salvation history—Christmas Eve and the celebration of mass on the feast of the Nativity. While *The Moviegoer* ended with a similar liturgical focus (Ash Wednesday), *Love in the Ruins* echoes St. John's Revelation by introducing the theme of a "remnant" community, a small group of believers faithful to the divine word. However, echoes of the *Book of the Revelation* do not portend an impending apocalypse in a literal sense, though More mistakenly thought so at the beginning of the novel. As Gary Ciuba has argued, the "apocalypse" has already occurred in human consciousness (*Walker Percy,* 163–64). What exists now is the "in-between" time—the present—when believers must "watch and wait," live with hope in the ordinary world, and attend to the signs of Christ's presence in the here-and-now. The Epiphany season celebrates that pivotal event in Christianity, the coming of the savior who offers not political freedom but freedom from sin and death, the "principalities and powers" governing humanity. For the "good news" preached by Jesus in the Sermon on the Mount offers a concrete yet transforming vision of human community based on charity. More explicitly than in *The Moviegoer* and *The Last Gentleman,* Percy emphasizes this spiritual ideal as a present and real possibility in the remnant community shown in the epilogue.

In the end, having set the overall action of the novel within the larger liturgical context, Percy links that context to More's journey in the ordinary world of human aspiration, failure, and hopeful endurance. Along with his wife, Ellen, and two children, More lives among a remnant community of believers and nonbelievers in the old Quarters, once slave dwellings. He is a changed man, a "poor but kingly man," no longer detached from present time, not casting ahead with bestial longings and desire for success and power. Instead, he lives and works modestly. Like Eliot's Fisher King, he fishes in the bayou, "the mystical element," and when he lands "a great unclassified beast of a fish," he thinks of Christ's second coming: "I thought of Christ coming again at the end of the world and how it is that in every age there is the temptation to see signs of the end and that, even knowing this, there is nevertheless some reason, what with the spirit of the new age being the spirit of watching and waiting, to believe that—" (365). More rejects the temptation to apocalypse and its attempted transcendence of time and history; indeed, he affirms the mystery of Christ's possible presence, the "mystical element" where fish can signify the true fisher of men. While he has not abandoned his desire to perfect the lapsometer, his dream is now refocused. Fame and power are no longer his goals; instead, he desires to discover truth for its own sake and to benefit mankind. Thus Percy suggests the proper goal and limits of science, contrary to the destructive ideology of scientism. Apropos this focus, Percy reminds us that More once wrote a paper on the compatibility of science and religion that included discussion of the transubstantiation, a central argument in the debate over language and the meaning of the Christ's Incarnation. As More now proclaims: "What I want is no longer the Nobel, screw prizes, but just to figure out what I've hit on. Some day a man will walk into my office as ghost or beast and walk out as a man, which is to say sovereign wanderers, lordly exile, worker and waiter and watcher. Knowing, not women, said Sir Thomas, is man's happiness" (361).

More now lives a new "ordinary" life as working physician, husband, father, and committed citizen of the community, having like Binx Bolling found a way to "stick himself" into the world. That world is one in which people "still stop and help strangers lying in ditches having been set upon by thieves or just plain drunk" (363). More himself has organized "SOUP," a group of southerners and others dedicated to preserving America from the ruinations of northern secularists and consumers. Moreover, he agrees to serve as his black friend Victor Charles's campaign manager in his bid for Congress. But his most important commitment and sign of his new life is his reestablished link to "the thread in the labyrinth," the sacramental life and the community of saints.

Earlier, alone and in despair, More attempted suicide at Christmastime. Now he goes to confession to Father Smith in preparation for midnight mass. More proclaims that he has not lost his faith, although he admits he does not feel sorry for his sins. Still, he is ashamed of them, and since this is sufficient, he receives absolution and penance from the priest. At mass, he receives the Eucharist—"I eat Christ, drink his blood"—and prays with the congregation, "confessing the sins of the Church and asking *for the reunion of Christians and of the United States*" (377) (italics mine). Again Percy emphasizes the link between the eucharistic center that holds, the incarnate Word, and the hope for the coming of genuine community among men. More's vision has cleared, and although he is not entirely free of angelistic and bestial impulses, he is free to live again as a human being, still struggling with desire but full of hope for final salvation.

Percy's open-ended "ending" of *Love in the Ruins* suggests an enfolding of his bracing satirical criticism within a larger religious comic vision in the manner of Dante. Tom More's partial recovery and his new direction affirm the possibility of reconciliation—always a comic movement—of man being reconciled to his humanity and thus overcoming the "tempestuous restructuring of consciousness" through grace and humility. More is open once again to hearing the "good news," harbinger of reconciliation with God. But Fedville, a factitious community dedicated to manipulation and killing, remains powerful, and though the satanic Immelmann has been dispatched, his numbers are still legion. In *Love in the Ruins* Percy took dead aim at the machinations of the "principalities and powers" of scientism and its threat to humanity. He exposed its reductive "anthropology" and the historical roots of its errant philosophical assumptions. And this achievement itself was a triumph made possible by the power of the word to name truth—the enduring "thread" in the labyrinth of delusion and self-deception—which is the most hopeful sign in the beleaguered American community Percy imagined.

CHAPTER FOUR

The Worm of Interest

Lancelot

Speaking of his fourth novel with interviewer Zoltan Abadi-Nagy, Percy said: "*Lancelot* might have come from an upside-down theological notion, not about God but about sin, more specifically the falling into disrepute of the word 'sin'. Lancelot wouldn't be caught dead looking for God, but he is endlessly intrigued by the search for evil. Is there such a thing—malevolence over and beyond psychological and sociological categories?"[1] Percy's statement reveals the central theme in *Lancelot:* the question of the meaning of evil in an age dominated by the ideology of Cartesian scientism and by relativism in language. The word "sin," as intuited by Hawthorne's Young Goodman Brown and by Faulkner's Addie Bundren, has now become a "name." How the question of the meaning of sin and evil is understood and evaluated will determine the meaning of community established in Percy's novel. If the meaning of "sin," what it signifies as a word-sign, has been nullified in Lancelot's modern world, then so have the meanings of repentance, forgiveness, and reconciliation. Without sin, there is no need for repentance or forgiveness, for there is nothing to be forgiven or reconciled. Certainly there is no need to be reconciled to God. Neither is there any need for an incarnate divine redeemer to offer the means for reconciliation. Likewise, without sin the ideas of the sacramental life, of a mystical community that extends through and beyond human time, and of salvation history become meaningless. If, as Percy suggests, the word "sin" has fallen into disrepute, if in fact this emptying out has occurred, then the idea of semiotic community—of *real* relations of meaning—is also nullified.

In *Lancelot,* Percy transforms the religious writer's age-old concern with the mystery of evil into a concern for the mystery of its "disappearance," as befits the age. But in fact the novel reveals that evil's so-called disappearance is an illusion. What has become occluded in the culture is the power to clearly see and name evil as evil. *Lancelot* probes this epistemological crisis in order to overcome it. The disjunction of words from truth is dramatized brilliantly in the person of narrator Lance Lamar himself, so that his "search" for sin ultimately finds its true meaning within his own character. That he cannot fully see it reveals Percy's sense of the direst possible consequences of the Cartesian dilemma—a person so self-absorbed and cut off from real connection to the world that the result is monomania and spiritual obliviousness. Fortunately, Percy also offers a way to move beyond the dilemma—the way of community.

At first glance it may seem that *Lancelot* is a radical departure from Percy's earlier novels, especially the high-spirited humor and broadly farcical satire of *Love in the Ruins.* Yet Percy's attention to the collapse of the meaning of sin in modern Jewish-Christian culture and the implications of that collapse was persistent. Both Binx Bolling in *The Moviegoer* and Sutter Vaught in *The Last Gentleman* brooded over the meaning of sexual "sin" in a world that denies its moral and theological significance, as indeed Lance will. In *Love in the Ruins* Tom More implicitly defended the meaning of sin and guilt in his arguments with the Fedville qualitarians, and his own actions dramatize the need for repentance, the sacraments, and grace. At the same time, Percy presented in More the figure of a "maculate" Christ, a mock savior who would try to reconcile mankind to sinfulness, and this image of the half-blind, would-be redeemer foreshadowed Lance Lamar's plan for a secular, purified community.

In *Lancelot* Percy inverted the motif of the search that was central to *The Moviegoer,* here making Lance's search for sin the main action in the novel. Moreover, he concentrated the search within the mind and voice of a single narrator, narrowing and intensifying the focus to a character who is—in great part—possessed by the demonic "powers and principalities" that threatened the world of *Love in the Ruins.* Lance, as we shall see, is a more savage and desperate "victim" of Descartes than any of his fictional predecessors. As readers we are situated within the cell of Lance's mind as he recalls and relives the catastrophic events of his life for his listener, Percival/Father John. His recollections are subject to all the rationalizations, delusions, contradictions, and half-truths of any monologist, intensified here by his disturbed mind. Percy's narrative strategy forces the reader's engagement in a much more immediate and challenging way than in his earlier novels. As readers we become trapped in the tangled action and web of implication that the novel creates, ourselves searching for meaning. We are both engaged by and resistant to the spell of Lance's monologue as we search for the truth through and beyond Lance's own search for the meaning of his experiences.

The narrative of *Lancelot* is complicated further by the character and silence of the listener, Father John. The priest's name points to his hieratic identity. Lance calls it "a good name" and asks, "is it John the Evangelist who loved so much or John the Baptist, a loner out in the wilderness? You were a loner" (8). Both namesakes are apt. The priest's identification with the precursor of Christ suggests his own wandering in a desert of doubt after the collapse of his missionary work in Africa. It also points to his "coming" forth to speak at the end of the novel, to bring the prophetic Word and a new vision to Lance. By casting him as a prophetic witness, of course, Percy also aligned him with the author of the fourth gospel, John the Evangelist, who most explicitly related the coming of Christ to the origin of the Logos in the divine Godhead: "In the beginning was the Word, and the Word was with God; and the Word was God. He was in the beginning with God" (John 1:1–2). The divine Logos is the source and guarantor of all signs, the fountain of the Word enfleshed in Christ and his gospel of love, expressed in the ultimate triad: God the Father, Son, and Holy Spirit.

Significantly, Peirce regarded the gospel of John as the most profound expression of the purpose and goal of the human semiotic community. Reacting against mechanistic theories of evolution, he affirmed a cosmic divine love, called *agapism*, as the force driving the evolutionary process. John, the "ontological gospeller . . . made the One Supreme Being, by whom all things have been made out of nothing, to be cherishing-love" (CP, 6.287). As Raposa concludes, Peirce saw John's insight as "the essence of a theosemiotic" (144). Evolution is a psychical and spiritual process whose ultimate goal is community with God, the source of love. Percy's Father John stands as a silent witness against the mechanistic vision of history and human destiny proffered by Lance in his misreading of signs. The renewed priest embodies the patient love and fidelity to truth that may in the end help Lance evolve beyond his own self-centered, destructive vision.

Although the occasional critical suggestions that Father John is only a figment of Lance's imagination are too extreme, as a character he is in a profound sense a "double" of the narrator. He is a "voice" of conscience within Lance; as well, he is the sign of the Holy Spirit that contravenes the demonic power at work in Lance. In *Love in the Ruins* anger drove Mr. Ives to silence, and Tom More dreams of "bridging the dread chasm" between body and soul caused by Cartesian dualism (181). In *Lancelot* Percy creates a "dread chasm" between Lance's anger and Percival's silence, which will finally be bridged only by the words of healing grace. Lance's anger is abstractive, a move toward the transcendent role of the righteous one. Percival must "watch and wait" for the inevitable collapse of Lance's pose, and then offer help. Thus together narrator and listener embody the full scope of Percy's moral and theological vision. Father John is silent, but not absent; he is a real presence in the semiosis of the novel. His silence compels our involvement as participants in the triadic progression of meaning between narrator (Lance), listener (Percival), and reader. We are intimately engaged as witnesses, interpreters, and judges of the evolving relationship between priest and narrator, especially as we see Father John resist Lance's attempts to persuade him to his viewpoint. Thus the priest's silence throughout most of the novel is a brilliant technical strategy that is perfectly coincident with Percy's vision. Why? Because his "silent" witness is the real, invisible core of spiritual meaning at the heart of triadic communication. Moreover, his faithful presence is a hopeful sign of a real *solitude à deux* between Lance and his friend—an open-ended, mysterious relation that may eventually transform Lance.

Any attempt to understand *Lancelot*, then, must first come to terms with Percy's complex narrative strategy, as well as with Lance's vision. For all its distortion, Lance's monologue has its measure of truth, which must be recognized. It is a mistake to label Lance *simply* as a madman, demagogue, murderer, or fascist. Such categorizing is precisely one of the reductive thought patterns of the scientistic age as well as of Lance's thinking, a fact that Percy both exposes and resists by narrative strategies that affirm the reality of mystery. Lance may well commit violent and perverted deeds, but for all that, he is, like Conrad's Mr. Kurtz, a representative figure of the age, the "age of interest." Lance is "us," *in extremis*. As we shall see, he is a Cartesian dualist blinded by his own "objectivity" and reductive mode of thought. Such a mode of thought, as I have argued, undermines the truth of real semiotic community, a fact that is especially important for understanding Lance's failure to see his own responsibility for his failed marriage to Margot. Yet on a deeper level, Lance comes to embody the spirit of the Antichrist, the demonic accuser-"savior" who offers mock salvation from sin.

Finally, another complication is the fact that throughout *Lancelot* Percy inverts or parodies many familiar themes and motifs developed in his earlier novels. For example, the theme of awakening to a new life through ordeal, of

being "on to" something and searching for meaning (Binx Bolling, Will Barrett, Tom More) is inverted here. Lance awakens to a "new life" of deceit and
plotted revenge; he searches unsuccessfully for the meaning of "sin." The *solitude à deux* community discovered by Binx and Kate, Tom More and Ellen
is parodied here in the sexual relationship Lance describes between him and
Margot, and in his proposed relationship with Anna the rape victim. The epistemological quest for knowledge and self-knowledge seen in Binx, Will Barrett, and Tom More is frustrated greatly here by Lance's egotism and reductive mode of thought. In addition, the theme of conversion through hearing
a voice of authority, as seen in the case of Val Vaught, is suborned here into
Father John's silence on the one hand, and Lance's fascist demagoguery, the
"authoritative" fascist anti-Word, on the other. Many other inversions of familiar themes and motifs could be cited from *Lancelot*. Uniting all of these in
the novel is a seeming "emptying out" of triadicity itself. For beyond the central vital relation between Lance, Father John, and the reader, Percy creates a
dizzying array of parody triangular relations between the characters that constantly seems to mock the possibility of the real thing—genuine community.
    These complex strategies, I believe, should not be seen as Percy's effort
to complicate the narrative so as to stay one step ahead of the adroit reader.
More probably they suggest a crisis in Percy's own life and thought, a darkening mood in the dark age of corruption, the post–Nixon administration era.
Lancelot, it seems to me, is Percy's most dangerous novel. By inverting these
themes and motifs from earlier works, Percy emphasized the dire condition of
the culture—the *near* collapse of meaning, of the power of truth, and of language itself as a force to create genuine community. In this sense, Father John's
silence implies a threatened drowning out of the divine Logos, the ground
for truth and community. Yet against this somber reading of the times Percy
does affirm, in hope, the possibility of "new life" in the relation between Lance
and his "recovered" priest friend, and perhaps with the survivor–rape victim,
Anna. In spite of Lance's circuitousness and distortions, the relationship between Lance and Father John is one in which two people strive to uncover
and name truth. Affirming that possibility, and language's power to uncover
meaning, is the ground for measuring, naming, and partially overcoming the
metaphysical and linguistic crisis of the age. The central fact to be held in mind
is that, notwithstanding his claims to the contrary, Lance's narrative is a "confession." More accurately, it can be called a preconfession or self-examination
(again echoing St. Augustine), and that movement at least *provisionally* opens
the door to the power of sacramental grace.

Lance Lamar's tale is focused on two interwoven searches, one past and one present. The first, undertaken roughly a year before the novel opens, was to prove objectively his wife Margot's adultery. This search evolves in Lance's mind into a quest to prove the reality of sin, which if proven, would presumably give some meaning, and in his eyes moral justification, to the pain of jealousy he feels. The second search, unfolding in the "present" of the novel, is a quest undertaken with Father John to discover why Lance's search for the meaning of sin failed. The two searches interact dynamically in the shifting chronology as the narrative unfolds. Meaning develops through this interaction in an evolving semiosis. Lance's role as lone narrator creates lacunae or gaps in his perspective, so the reader, aided by Father John's implied reactions, comes to see the meaning of Lance's searches in ways that he cannot see.[2] Since Lance alone narrates, all of his comments are potentially distorted, consciously or unconsciously. In this respect *Lancelot* is *about* the problem of interpretation in a culture in which semiotic community—the world of shared signs—is threatened with collapse. Still, the principal clues to the meaning of Lance's searches, and his failure, are embedded in his perspective as narrator.

Percy intimates how Lance's narrative perspective is restricted and skewed in the opening set piece of the novel. From his narrow cell window Lance can see "nothing more than a patch of sky, a corner of Lafayette Cemetery, a slice of levee, and a short stretch of Annunciation Street." By leaning into the embrasure, he can also see part of a sign with the letters:

Free &
Ma
B.

Lance speculates on what the sign might read—"Free and Easy Mac's Bowling? Free and Accepted Mason's Bar?"—but he cannot find an answer (2). Both the setting and the sign are triads that, from his angle of disadvantage, Lance is unable to interpret. His vision is too narrow. In the setting, Percy triangulates cell, cemetery, and Annunciation Street. The cell suggests Lance's closed mind and heart, while the cemetery suggests the death and resurrection of the body signified in the feast of All Souls Day, celebrated the following day. The third in the triad, Annunciation Street, denotes the coming of the redeemer Christ announced in the message delivered to Mary, the Blessed Mother. But locked in his spiritual cell, Lance cannot see this possible sign relation. To him it is only physical landscape. Percy suggests that the signs that point to a reality beyond the physical world are enigmatic and "unstable" in the current atmosphere of disbelief and literalistic vision.

As he cannot read the depths of possible meaning in the landscape, neither can Lance interpret the triad encoded in the phrases on the sign. Lance wants to "be" ("B"). He wants to claim a true identity and justify his life. He wants to understand himself and his actions through a colloquy with others, Father John and Anna. In addition, he wants to be "free." He hears the song about freedom sung by the lovely girl on the levee, and freedom is a central principle of his proposed New Order in Virginia. But genuine freedom will only come about when he understands his relation to his mother, Lily—"Ma"— and to women and human sexuality as well. Although the coupling of signs is suggested by the "&," Lance cannot unite the three elements to interpret their meaning for him. Their possible semiotic relation eludes him. The triad is literally "broken," with each element listed successively, rather than in triangular relation. Lance's inability to fathom both landscape and sign in this opening scene underscores the reductive nature of his vision. Nevertheless, as Percy presents them, the signs remain open ended for Lance to eventually plumb their triadic relation, with help from others.

Another way that Percy emphasizes Lance's distorted perspective is through his reaction to his first major discovery, that he is not the father of his daughter Siobhan. Lance describes his reaction as being like "that of a scientist, an astronomer say, who routinely examines photographic plates of sectors of the heavens and sees the usual random scattering of dots of light" (9). He then explains how one day the astronomer discovers a dot "out of place" in the heavens, tracks its course, and discovers that it will strike the earth catastrophically in two months. So also Lance discovered a sign "out of place," Siobhan's blood type, revealing the "catastrophe" that he cannot possibly be her father. His reported response is that "the worm of interest turned somewhere near the base of my spine" (29). Although the fact of Siobhan's blood type is scientific proof of paternity, Lance still proceeds, like the astronomer, to try to verify the circumstances surrounding her illegitimacy.

Lance's self-comparison to the astronomer is a clue both to his personal vision and to the Cartesian spirit of the age. As in his earlier novels, Percy uses the images of astronomy, star-gazing, and telescoping as signs of the objectivist approach to reality that dominates the culture of scientism.[3] Binx Bolling's father was a stargazer, as was Lance's father; Will Barrett has his telescope; Tom More's lapsometer is a would-be telescope of the human psyche.

Lance's self-image as astronomer-scientist aligns him with the Baconian tradition as one given over to a detached, "objective" view of human realities. But his deep emotional response to the discovery of Margot's infidelity, hidden in the early part of the novel—his visceral anger and jealousy—reveals a dualism that makes him another "victim of Descartes." Despite his detached and seemingly unemotional "interest," Lance feels pain in the flesh, the body. The duality of his reaction is, as I have suggested, itself a symptom of both his and the age's malaise—the "angelism-bestialism" Percy treated satirically in *Love in the Ruins.*

The significance of Lance's initial response to the discovery cannot be overemphasized. As Percy argued in many essays and interviews, the detached posture of the scientist exempts him from recognizing his real semiotic relation as an incarnate creature to the world he observes (LC, 160–67). Lance is so inclined, and much of Father John's task is to recall him to his true relation to the community. Moreover, Lance's objective-observer stance is antithetical to mystery, to the "extraness" of spirit in things that Will Barrett discovered in the iron horsehead as a clue to meaning and living in the present. The reductive viewpoint Lance assumes precludes any vision of the incarnate world as truly sacramental, although later he offers his own debased notion of sexual "feasting" as sacramental, as Tom More did. As an erstwhile believer, More understood that he needed "flesh" to keep him human. Lance's dualism dooms him to desacralize flesh into an object of false worship and manipulation.

Such is the perspective of a culture dominated by scientism and technology, Percy suggests, an "age of interest." As Jacques Barzun argued years ago, an age dominated by the cult of "the interesting" implies a separation of self from moral value and a sense of personal involvement in society (*Uses and Abuses of Art,* 106–9). Genuine forms of communal understanding and value are replaced by spheres of "interest" and voyeuristic observation as the primary modes of interaction with reality. Furthermore, in an age dominated by scientism such a perspective finds its inevitable expression in pornography (LC, 175–94). Pornography employs technology in an attempt to "see" human sexual behavior but in the process reduces and desecrates the mystery of human sexuality. It literalizes the body by separating it from the unique person; flesh becomes manipulable matter. Using his objective viewpoint, Lance becomes precisely such a voyeur-pornographer in his search to "see" Margot's adultery. Lance thinks this is the way to "know" her and to know "sin," but his deeper purpose is to humiliate her, humiliate Woman, who in his heart is his real betrayer. He would capture or possess Margot's spirit, and in this Lance is satanic. Yet this does *not* resolve the deeper mystery that at some hidden level he may also love her, or at least long to love her.

Lance's pornographic voyeurism suggests the broader cultural implications of the marriage of scientism and technology, as Percy developed them later in *Lost in the Cosmos*. Lance prates of "freedom" throughout his narrative, but Percy shows implicitly the link between Lance's pornography (the perspective of "interest") and a totalitarian mentality. The reductive "emptying out" of the mystery of the person that occurs in pornography also signifies the denial of individual freedom. Percy explores this more fully in *The Thanatos Syndrome,* in which pornography and pedophilia are linked explicitly to the Blue Boy project of behavior control, to the experiments of German physicians in the 1930s, and to the Nazi regime. But the seeds of Percy's concern are well sown in *Lancelot*. Lance's evolution from pornographer to murderer to would-be despotic ruler of a fascist "New Order" reveals the potentially fateful conse-quences of scientism. Totalitarian social order, abetted by technology, stands as the inhuman antitype of genuine community and the invisible mystical com-munity.

Lance's claim of detached "interest" in the discovery of Siobhan's illegit-imacy masks the deeper mystery of his felt response and his personal stake in the discovery. When Father John prods him to examine his relationship to Margot by asking him repeatedly how he felt, Lance claims that "the usual emotions" do not apply, except for a "kind of dread at the discovery" and "a curious sense of expectancy, a secret sweetness at the core of dread" (41). We recall the "sweetness" Tom More felt at the death of his daughter, Samantha, which he later realized was an excuse for his despair. Lance does not recognize a similar malice in himself. Instead, he compares his feelings to the time he dis-covered his father was a thief, when as a child he found ten thousand dollars in kickback money in his father's sock drawer: "What I can still remember is the sight of the money and the fact that *my eye could not get enough of it.* There was a secret savoring of it *as if the eye were exploring it with its tongue.* When there is something to see, some thing, a new thing, there is *no end to the seeing.* Have you ever watched onlookers at the scene of violence, an accident, a killing, a dead or dying body in the streets? Their eyes shift to and fro ever so slightly, scanning, trying to take it all in. There is no end *to the feast*" (42) (italics mine). The conjunction of images—seeing, tasting, feasting—like More's "feasting" on his daughter's death, reveals the perverse desire behind Lance's search to "see" Margot's adultery. As in *Love in the Ruins,* feasting on sexuality here is a deathly counterimage to the Eucharist, the sacrament of community. In *The Last Gentleman,* Sutter Vaught recognized the implications of this when he noted that in the absence of belief in the Christian sacraments, the exaltation of the body and physical sex would take their place in a dualistic culture. Physical sex, as Percy argued later, becomes in the culture of scientism a desperate means by which the self tries to affirm its "reality." But such "reality" is a reductive parody of the semiotic real.

Initially, Lance wants to see the two events—the discovery of his father's thievery and of Margot's adultery—as comparable. But then he quickly distinguishes the two events and his relation to them. When he discovered his father's dishonor, although "the world fell to pieces," the revelation gratified because it undermined the exalted standard of honor he was expected to fulfill as a southern gentleman. "For if there is one thing harder to bear than dishonor, it is honor, being brought up in a family where everything is so nice, perfect in fact, except of course oneself" (42). Lance saw a reflection of his own fallen self—*his* act of stealing from his father's drawer—in his father's dishonor, so the discovery is paradoxically liberating. Father and son are bound together as fallible creatures, as they are united later as cuckolds and sexual impotents. But recalling the episode now, Lance's doesn't question his mother's "honor," though it was she who told him to take the money from his father's drawer. Lance fails to mention Lily's duplicity here, a clue to his blindness to her effect on his character and actions. As a child, he could not see her role as a revered but tainted idol in the impossible code of honor that still imprisons him. Later, when Lance's suspicion of his mother's affair with Uncle Harry develops, it combines with his knowledge of Margot's infidelity to produce a profound sense of anguish and anger at the dual "failure" of woman.

Regarding his present feelings, Lance insists to Father John that the discovery of Margot's adultery "involved something quite different" from when he discovered his father's thievery. Instead of relating Margot's act to his own sense of dishonor, as he did with his father, Lance separates himself from it as an objective observer. The "worm of interest" takes over:

There was a sense of astonishment, of discovery, of a new world opening up, but the new world was totally unknown. Where does one go from here? I felt like those two scientists—what were their names?—who did the experiment on the speed of light and kept getting the *wrong* result. It would just not come out right.

The *wrong* result was unthinkable. Because if it were true, all physics went out the window and one had to start from scratch. It took Einstein to comprehend that the *wrong* answer might be right.

One has first to accept and believe what one knows theoretically. One must see for oneself. One has to know for sure before doing anything. I had to be sure about Margot, about what she had done and was doing now. I had to be absolutely certain. (42–43)

Lance's reaction—his posturing as scientist-observer—deflects Father John's question about how he felt. Instead, like engineer Will Barrett he wants to hold the world at an objective distance—"One has to know for sure before doing anything"—a stance that precludes genuine self-scrutiny and a sense of personal involvement. So Lance avoids the obvious questions: Why is the blood type evidence not sufficient? More important, why doesn't he ask Margot directly about her actions and talk to her about their marriage? The "chasm" between word and world that Tom More bridged through language in Mr. Ives's case is here maintained by Lance. Rather than choosing the personal approach—talk with Margot—Lance prefers the more "objective" approach of stealthy observation.

Viewed from a psychological angle, the answers to the question raised by Lance's adopted strategy are extraordinarily complex. They are bound up with the mystery of Lance's character, partly obscured in the dark recesses of his soul. However, one clue can be found in Lance's dualism; specifically, in the relationship between his "scientist's" perspective and the incarnate world of flesh against which he stands. As a victim of Descartes, Lance's character strongly mirrors aspects of the philosopher's own personality, particularly his intellectual detachment from human community. In *The Flight from Woman*, Karl Stern traced the connection between Descartes's dualism and certain decisive events in the philosopher's life (75–107). Descartes's described method of arriving at basic certitudes through doubt exalted scientific knowledge as the single criterion for truth and thereby devalued "poetic knowledge, i.e. knowledge by interiorization" (77). (Descartes's epistemology is opposite that of Peirce's way of knowing by abduction, "guessing," and musement. Percy implicitly applied Peirce's method to fiction writing in his essay "The Novel: Dying Art or New Science.")[4] Poetic knowledge, Stern argues, is "acquired by union *with* and attachment *to* the object; scientific knowledge is acquired by distance and detachment *from* the object. The poetic relation to nature is one of imbeddedness; the scientific is one of confrontation" (86). The relation to nature through poetic knowledge implies an acceptance of materiality, of mystery, and of one's irreducible connection to the world. As Stern demonstrates, Descartes's dualism and his objective stance of dubiety toward the world were deeply rooted in the traumas of his personal life. Descartes's mother died when he was a year old. The effect on Descartes was a "total cleavage between the carnal and the spiritual in the image of woman." In such cases the image of woman is dichotomized into "prostitute-madonna." The victim of the trauma suffers from "an inability to combine sexual relations and 'higher friendship' in the same person (woman)" (92). Stern suggests that Descartes's disastrous adult intellectual attachment to "lofty, non-carnal women" may well represent his attempts to recover "the remote mother, the one who left him in the cold" (96).

Stern's argument seems especially pertinent to understanding the psychological dynamics of Lance's behavior. What I wish to emphasize here, however, is Stern's insight into the relationship between the man's character and the intellectual stance or method he adopts. For Descartes the early loss of the mother, who provided "the certainty of carnal presence," shattered his sense of himself as an incarnate being. As an adult philosopher he argued the need to "doubt sensible things because they have deceived us" (100). Stern then points to the inextricable connection between the two:

> The certainty of the flesh which is the foundation of all certainty *had* to be conjured away—because it was here where the terror and pain of abandonment lurked. To the man who was to make *the act of doubt* the basis of all inquiry, doubt had supplanted trust a long time before conceptual thinking. . . . Reality, perceived primarily through the flesh, meant dread, and therefore ratiocination, the pure *cogito*, became an impenetrable armor.
>
> [T]he ideal of the *cogito*, of *mathesis universalis*, means *denial*, a defense against the flesh because the flesh is synonymous with anguish, and the clear fission between mind and body is an *isolation*, a setting apart and rendering innocuous of all that which spells dread. (100–101)[5]

There are obvious similarities between the origins of Descartes's method as described by Stern and Lance's method of inquiry into Margot's infidelity. Lance begins by asserting an *a priori*, though factitious, "doubt." From his observer's stance, Lance uses the technology of "seeing"—videotapes—to witness her adultery and satisfy "the worm of interest." Using this strategy he tries to distance himself from the felt anguish of his carnal relationship to Margot, his involvement in the world and the flesh. Like Descartes, Lance's method serves as both a defense against the pain of the flesh and a way to try to dominate the world through a "scientific" demonstration. He attempts to gain power over nature, reducing her as a woman to an object in an experiment. His mistrust of the carnal world reveals his hatred of its dubiety and mystery. Eventually, as we see, the core of his mistrust and hatred will be directed against his own flesh, against sexuality itself. But here, the so-called "dishonor" of woman, the failure of the maternal, is too painful for him to confront by talking directly to his wife. Lance does not seek truth, which would demand self-scrutiny of his own mysterious relation to Margot, so much as he seeks *evidence* by which to judge and condemn her perfidy.

Lance's response to his felt loss is similar to but more perverse than that of Descartes. Hidden deep in Lance's soul is his sense of grievance over the loss of and manipulation by his mother, Lily. Initially, Lance has less to say about his mother than about his father, but what he does recall is most revealing. His memories of Lily are not fond. He recalls her as not beautiful but pale, a secret alcoholic in later years (like him). She liked to jab him in the ribs, saying "I'm going to get you," an action that recalls Emily Cutrer's jabbing at Binx to "get" him, and the "knife in the ribs" of sweet dread Tom More felt at Samantha's death. Lily's aggression suggests that she resents her maternal tie to her son and perhaps resents motherhood itself. When her spirit appears to him on the night of the murder, she again "gets him" by handing him the Bowie knife, "point first in the same insistent joking way my mother bore her fists into my ribs." Her aggression reveals the wish to destroy, perhaps out of hatred of her own failed marriage and her sexual betrayal. Her wish to destroy her son is the visible sign of her perfidy. Yet Lance is convinced that with the gift of the Bowie knife he can exact revenge on Jacoby by "doing what she wanted me to do" (243). What he does, of course, is savagely cut Jacoby's throat.

Lance's profoundly alienated yet submissive relation to his mother undermines his own sense of identity, and this cleavage resembles Descartes's life as Stern describes it. One sign of this cleavage is the detective role Lance assumes toward Margot. In *Lost in the Cosmos* Percy correlated the self's desire for hiddenness, disguises, and erasure to the role of detective in mystery novels. (Lance is an avid reader of Raymond Chandler novels.) As Percy implies, the "anonymous" role of the detective is akin to the observer stance of the scientist (155). Appositely, Karl Jaspers's insight into Descartes, who called himself "the philosopher with the mask," seems a fitting description of Lance's detective posture: "Descartes seems rather like hiddenness itself. It is not only because of his cautiousness that he remains opaque. There is something weird about his hiddenness because it does not hide anything that one might reveal by interpretation. The very fact that Descartes' personality is not open to our eyes tempts us to seek the secret of his soul. But instead of finding it one feels compelled to look for hidden meanings in what he says, *only to find an ambiguity which does not hide anything but seems to be part of his own character*" (quoted in Stern, *Flight from Woman*, 91).

The fundamental mystery of Lance's character and his Cartesian "separation" from the world shapes every aspect of his thought and action. For example, like Descartes, Lance splits the image of woman into "madonna-prostitute." Unwilling to accept the reality of actual woman as mysterious being, Lance in resentment schemes to "see" Margot's adultery. Given Lance's original deprivation, we are led to question whether Lance is capable of love at all. Father John probes the hidden wound of Lance's loss by asking repeatedly, Did you love her? in hopes of leading his friend to healing recognitions. But Lance is more interested in exercising power over the world and over woman. Shaped by what Stern calls a "neurosis of destiny," he plans eventually to create a New Order of society in Virginia, with Anna as the "New Woman."

Lance's dualism likewise governs his general views of human sexuality and evil. Self-contradiction combines with evasiveness and rationalization throughout his narrative. He equates the astronomer's discovery of the out-of-place star with Margot's infidelity. Both, he claims, are "incommensurate" catastrophic events: "the end of the world following upon the out-of-place dot is her ecstasy inferred from the O" (21). From this he infers a larger metaphysical correlation: "Beyond any doubt she was both beside herself and possessed by something, someone? else. Such considerations have led me to the conclusion that, contrary to the usual opinion, sex is not a category at all. It is not merely an item on a list of human needs like food, shelter, air, but is rather a unique ecstasy, ek-stasis, which is a kind of possession. Just as possession by Satan is not a category. You smile. You disagree? Are you then one of the new breed who believe that Satan is only a category, the category of evil?" (21). Here Lance argues that the sex act is unique and therefore irreducible to a category of behavioral needs. From a metaphysical viewpoint, Lance is correct. Since it involves human subjectivity, the sexual union is a unique mystery. But Lance's comparison of it to possession by Satan is revealing. He chooses to equate the sexual with the demonic rather than signify its unique ecstasy by analogy to "possession" by the divine.[6] Hidden from his eyes is his deeply rooted instinct that sex—the flesh—is evil and unredeemable. As a true Cartesian, Lance is anti-incarnational, anti–enfleshed Word, as we see later. But given Lance's view that the sexual is not a category, it follows that any attempt to "see" it (comprehend it objectively) is a perversion of that mystery. Yet that is exactly the perverse goal of his search. Lance's "flight" is not only from woman. His flight is from the world and the Incarnation—Christ's divine being enfleshed in the body of the world and signified in the Eucharist. In short, he is a soured romantic like Sutter Vaught.

Yet despite his metaphysical accuracy, Lance's claim for the uniqueness of the sex act and demonic possession is only half true from a semiotic viewpoint. In refusing to categorize the sex act as merely a human need like food or sleep, Lance rightly rejects, at least in theory, the behaviorist view in favor of unique mystery. However, the sex act and demonic possession can both be *named* for what they are and so are not "unspeakable" as Lance claims. Mystery can be named as "mystery," and the mystery of evil is precisely Percy's subject in the novel. Margot's act can be named "adultery," just as Lance's action later can be named "murder." As a realist, Percy believed that "generals" (categorical statements) name real categories of being. Without generals, meaning and shared communication are impossible, and shared meaning is the heart of community. In terms of his own actions, then, Lance's claim for the unique mystery of the sex act is contradictory, since he is clearly determined to "see" its meaning objectively. But this quest is also undercut fortuitously by his *present* bond with Father John as Lance searches for the meaning of his failure. Moreover, Percy suggests that the contradictions in Lance's positions are a quality of the age, like the contradictions in the claimed "value of life" arguments by the Fedville qualitarians. Lance's monologue thus embodies the very "slippage" of meaning in a culture caught in an epistemological crisis, a culture, for example, in which murder and mutilation can be labeled abstractly as "aberrant behavior." The age of interest is also the age of euphemism.

While the searching relationship between Lance and Father John creates the possibility of a real triadic bond based on truth telling, Lance's first search to uncover sin through Margot's adultery parodies the genuine quest in both aim and method. Lance assumes the roles of detective and actor, playing the part of gracious southern host to the movie company while secretly plotting how to uncover Margot's adultery. At one point, Lance even adopts a Peircean strategy of triangulation to pursue his goal. For example, Lance spies on the group by standing in the dark parlor next to the dining room and using a pier mirror as a triangulating "lens" through which to observe them unseen while searching for clues to their relationship. But since he stands "outside" the hidden relationship between Margot-Merlin-Jacoby, he cannot as yet fathom it. Lance's quest is further complicated and confounded by Percy's clever use of several triangular relations that are based on power and manipulation rather than genuine triadic, intersubjective relations. Among these are Lance-Mother-Father; Father-Mother-Uncle Harry; Lance-Margot-Merlin; Lance-Margot-Jacoby; Merlin-Margot-Jacoby; Lucy-Raine-Troy Dana; Lance-Raine-Margot. To these one can add Percy-Lance-Reader; Percy-Text-Reader, and so on. The effect of this complex strategy is to deepen the mystery and frustrate the objective quest Lance has undertaken, as well as any simple reading of the novel's meaning.

In a similar way Percy inverts the self-discovery-through-ordeal theme familiar in his other novels. Lance claims to be "reborn" to a new life with the discovery of Margot's adultery; he even cleanses himself thoroughly. But this is a parody of genuine purgation, conversion, and "resurrection"; at the end of the novel he still needs a true awakening to "news" of his predicament. Claiming a "new vision," he converts Margot's act into a search for sin, calling it a search for the "Unholy Grail." Lance's analogy to the grail quest is especially revealing, given his perverse goal. In appropriating and inverting the legend, Lance focuses on the object/deed itself (the cup equals "sin") rather than on the way of life—love, forgiveness, charity—necessary to achieve the cup of salvation. Always a romantic at heart, he envisions himself as a heroic knight questing for meaning in an age of unbelief, but his skewed vision is focused on accidentals rather than substance. What Lance doesn't see is that the inner meaning of the grail quest derives from the eucharistic presence signified by the cup, not from the object itself. Similarly, the substance of "sin," being spiritual, is not to be seen by discovering Margot and Jacoby in the act of adultery. However, we must acknowledge that Lance's quest does have its measure of value, as Percy suggested. In an age dismissive of the reality of sin, that Lance tries to take evil seriously is important. His anger and anguish over the devaluation of moral behavior in the culture may in some mysterious way eventually lead him, like Val Vaught, to a sense of his own true place in that fallen community, and the need for healing grace.[7]

Lance's perversion of the grail quest legend also reveals his rejection of the Word made flesh and the sacramental view of reality. He cancels out Jesus' message of love of the Father and of fellow humans, of salvation through repentance. He admits that he doesn't love his children; he declares so-called "family love" to be an anachronism. He calls his love of his first wife, Lucy, "a dream," part of the defunct "romantic age" (i.e., a false ideal). While he talks of creating a new life with Anna, he doesn't speak of loving her. As for loving Margot, Lance says that "the best thing we'd always had between us was a joyous and instant sex" (71). As other critics have noted, Lance tries like Sutter to elevate human sexual relations to an absolute, saying, "Margot's love was enough for me" (see Ciuba, *Walker Percy,* 185–91). He rejects the view of those saints who claim that "the love of God is even better" (129). In a revealing speech, he rhapsodizes over the joys of sexual union, attempting to sacralize woman in one of his typical half-truthful proclamations. Speaking of the lover, he says:

> then one fine day [he] discovers that the great starry heavens have opened to him and that his heart is bursting with it. It? She. Her. Woman. Not a category, not a sex, not one of two sexes, a human female creature, but an infinity. o = inf. What else is infinity but a woman become meat and drink to you, life and your heart's own music, the air you breathe? Just to be near her is to live and have your soul's own self. Just to open your mouth on the skin of her back.
>
> What else is man made for but this? I can see you agree about love but you look somewhat ironic. Are we talking about two different things? In any case, there's a catch. Love is infinite happiness. Losing it is infinite unhappiness. (137)

Lance's apotheosizing of woman as like a gift from the "starry heavens" who becomes his "meat and drink" suggests his paradoxical mental habit of degrading true realities, rendering them as absolutes. In this, he enacts what Alfred North Whitehead called the "displacement of the Real." Later, in describing a sexual tryst with Margot in the tourist cabin Asphodel, the elevation-degradation of the flesh becomes explicit: "She stood naked before the mirror, hands at her hair, one knee bent, pelvis aslant. She turned to me and put her hands under my coat and in her funny way took hold of a big pinch of my flank on each side. Gollee. Could any woman have been as lovely? *She was like a feast. She was a feast. I wanted to eat her. I ate her.* That was my communion, Father—no offense intended, that sweet dark sanctuary guarded by the heavy gold columns of her thighs, the ark of her covenant" (182) (italics mine). Like Tom More's eating of Moira Schaffner's "biscuitlike" knees, Lance's equation of sexual fulfillment with the sacrament of Eucharist reveals his profane displacement of spiritual communion to physical gratification. Such is the inevitable result of a dualism that separates or excludes spirit from the act of sexual union.

And what if Lance's "love" as sexual sacrament fails, as it failed Binx and Kate on the train? Lance admits under Father John's questioning that after a time he became impotent with Margot, that he has not "felt pain" for a long time, and that "for years [I] had not allowed myself to feel anything" (69–70). When passion faded and Margot turned to other interests, Lance anesthetized himself from the pain of loss and from the world itself. His physical impotence signifies a general *acedia* that has overtaken his life. But beneath this torpor lies a deep resentment of Margot, who as a woman has tried like his mother to make him into her image of what she wants him to be—a southern "gentleman." Lance resents this manipulation yet also regards Margot as his possession. (Hence his anguish over another man "possessing" her.) His resentment soon erupts into jealousy and a desire for revenge, the dark energy behind his search. But as we come to see, Margot's sexual betrayal is for Lance the betrayal of the flesh itself, *his own* as well as hers and all humanity's.

Lance's first attempt to "see" Margot's infidelity fails. Using Elgin to spy on the movie group at the Holiday Inn, he discovers their shuttling between rooms throughout the night. But Margot's claim that she fell ill after midnight raises doubts in Lance's mind. Doubt or mystery cannot be countenanced by Lance. "Can one ever be sure of anything?" he asks, and then more pointedly, "Are people as nice as they make out and in fact appear to be, or is it all buggery once the door is closed?" (139). In typical dualist fashion he wishes to reduce mystery to an either-or dichotomy, rejecting the ambiguous reality of "niceness" *and* "buggery." Thus he rails against Catholicism for what he claims is its "dissolving" of moral clarity into a "sorrowful solution" wherein "all distinctions" are subsumed under an ethic of mercy and forgiveness. Yet although Father John resists this oversimplification, Lance remains bent on "knowing-by-viewing" Margot's betrayal and punishing it (139).

Lance also justifies his plot to catch Margot in adultery by assuming the role of religious quester. He claims to be serving "God's cause" by undertaking "the only quest appropriate to the age," the search for evil. Echoing Binx Bolling, Lance claims to be "onto something": "I was like Robinson Crusoe seeing a footprint on his island after twenty years: not a footprint but my daughter's blood type." "Sin", replaces the mythical grail as the object of his quest, and Lance quickly reduces it to sexual sin: "Could it be possible that since the greatest good is to be found in love, so is the greatest evil? Evil, sin, if it exists, must be incommensurate with anything else. . . . There is only one kind of behavior which is incommensurate with anything whatever, in both its infinite good and its infinite evil. That is sexual behavior. The orgasm is the only earthly infinity. Therefore it is either an infinite good or an infinite evil" (146–47). Yet in calling human love the "greatest good," Lance excludes the love of God. The sexual orgasm is not, as Lance claims, an "infinite." Neither is sexual sin an "infinite" evil. Just as he has eliminated the mystery of divine love, Lance reduces the mystery of human love to physical and emotional gratification. In so doing, he misses the spiritual reality of human love, just as he will miss discovering the meaning of sin later. His assumed role as quester who is serving "God's cause" is another mask for his deep, half-conscious desire for vengeance against those he feels have impugned his honor and robbed him of his manhood.

Once his plot to discover Margot's infidelity through Elgin's spying fails, Lance sets in motion his scheme to videotape activities in the bedrooms at Belle Isle. Percy interweaves Lance's description of this scheme to Father John with telling revelations of his true design. Lance the putative quester becomes a demonic prophet and pseudo-redeemer, unleashing his most vicious attack on Christianity and the moral rot of the age. Through Lance's diatribes, Percy again contrasts two visions of human community—Christian and pagan stoic, as in *The Moviegoer*. Yet despite the contradictions and personal vitriol in Lance's diatribes, they do set forth the moral dilemmas of the age as Percy saw them. Lance announces emphatically to Father John, "I cannot tolerate this age. What is more, I won't. That was my discovery: that I didn't have to" (163). To him, systems of religious and ethical belief that once gave order and meaning to the community are now bankrupt. Christianity destroyed itself, he argues, by its wishy-washy acquiescence in modern corruptions. Likewise, the stern, unambiguous (he thinks) abstract "code of honor" his ancestors lived by has also collapsed. Lance says he could live by his ancestors' code, "crude as it was, though I do not think men should butcher each other like animals" (164). Nevertheless, his murder of Jacoby repeats such acts of butchery.

In the face of what Lance sees as the present collapse of values, he proposes a "new order of things" based on "a conviction and a freedom," a "stern code" under which "gentlemen," upholders of the code, would practice "a gentleness toward women and an intolerance of swinishness . . . and above all a readiness to act" in defense of the new order. For this, he argues, "you don't need a society" (166–67); each knight of the New Order will recognize and accord with each other instinctively. Lance claims that his proposed New Order is founded on individual freedom. But in fact, as Cleanth Brooks noted, it is a fascist order, based on racism and intolerance, repression (especially of women), and violence.[8] Its claimed "virtue"—a stern and moral code—is a radical, inhuman oversimplification of mystery and real personal freedom. What is missing from his code, of course, is any notion of genuine love, compassion, or forgiveness, any ethic of charity as the basis of community. Although he disdains the Nazis for their political ineptitude in dealing with the Jews (but not for their persecution of the Jews per se), Lance bases his New Order on the same dehumanization, will to power, and brutality as the Third Reich, and he masks it in a similarly gnostic rhetoric of "purification" of society, of "salvation" by force. Lance's attempt to subvert real community and freedom is revealed further in his warped depiction of Christianity. He condemns the Catholic Church for not remaining "true" to itself, yet the church he regards as once true is a romanticized image of "Mont-Saint-Michel . . . the Archangel with the flaming sword," and "Richard Coeur de Lion at Acre" (167). His heroic militaristic vision serves as trappings for his stoic code, completely dismissing the Christian ideal of the suffering servant, the sacramental life, and the hard demands of charity in the ordinary community of sinners. So he tells Father John: "Don't speak to me of Christian love. Whatever came of it? I'll tell you what came of it. It got mouthed off on the radio and TV from the pulpit and that was the end of it. The Jews knew better. Billy Graham lay down with Nixon and got up with a different set of fleas, but the Jewish prophets lived in the deserts and wildernesses and had no part with corrupt kings" (168). In this typical distortion of the truth, Lance ignores the fact that Jesus mingled with sinners, preached the gospel of redemption to them, and called for faith, repentance, and inner conversion, not the law of a stern code of stoic morality. Likewise, he ignores the fact that the Hebrew prophets witnessed and spoke against "corrupt kings" and kingdoms, and thus were deeply involved—through the word—with the community. Dismissing Christ, Lance claims himself to be a righteous prophet, calling for a return to the "desert" or wilderness from which to start the New Order. He imputes to himself the power to preach the "good news" of the New Order because he can "speak with authority. Was that not the new trait that people noticed about your Lord, that he spoke with authority," he asks (170). But Lance's claim of "authority" corrupts the word as enfleshed divine authority into the anti-Word of self-righteous demagoguery.

While it is easy to see the fascism in Lance's vision of a New Order and the demonic violence that fuels it, we cannot simply dismiss his ravings as being those of a demented fanatic. Lance's attack on the contemporary culture of Christianity (as distinct from its sacramental essence) echoes in kind if not degree similar criticisms made by Percy in his other novels and essays. At issue here is Percy's concern over the devaluation of the Christian *kerygma* within modern consumerist-technological society, whereby it becomes just another item for consumption. As Percy argued, the radical nature of the "good news" is unheard or almost inaudible in this culture, or else pandered as vapid benevolence (MB, 142–49). His concern with the collapse of *that* true community and meaning is registered accurately, if vehemently, in Lance's diatribe. So also, Percy's concern with the genuine religious search (if even for "sin") and the need for a "return to the desert," which echoes the desert motif in *The Moviegoer* and *The Last Gentleman*, must be taken seriously as a call for renewal. It echoes Romano Guardini's prophesy about the impending collapse of cultural Christendom in *The End of the Modern World*. But the key difference is that Lance's apocalypticism rejects the hope for love and redemption in the present ordinary world, in favor of a future totalitarian "utopia." The force of Lance's angry voice surely reflects Percy's ambivalence over the dissolute state of American society, as well as a yearning for radical renewal. As well, Lance's fury may reflect Percy's pessimism over the unlikelihood of such renewal. Lance's insane "final solution" is, of course, not the answer. But to complicate matters further, Percy does suggest that Lance's angry condemnation *does* in some mysterious way help to revitalize the faith of his friend, Percival/Father John. Listening to Lance, he turns "pale as a ghost," and the next time he visits, he is reinvested in clerical garb. Might this not suggest the mystery of good emerging paradoxically from evil, as the "first fruits" of Lance's search for sin?

As Lance pursues his quest to uncover Margot's adultery and "see" sin and to fathom why he had to see it and why this search ultimately failed, Percy deepens the mystery of Lance's character. Although Lance's objective stance precludes self-knowledge, his inner being becomes more transparent. Increasingly his monologue dissolves into a tangled web of half-truths, rationalizations, and contradictions. For example, Lance claims that he "lived for love" with Margot, but he equates this with "possessing" her as if she were a bawd. Sex with Margot is "a homecoming" for him, her body "a habitation." But secretly he resents her defrauding of his identity by casting him first as a "big raunchy Sterling Hayden" and then as a stereotypical southern gentleman, scion of a plantation and memoirist (179). He does ask her to leave Belle Isle with him when the hurricane approaches, but this seems an attempt to recover a lost "treasure," a possession of which he has been robbed. Lance comes closer to the truth about himself when he asks the question, "If I loved her," why did the discovery of her infidelity cause a pang of pleasure within me?" (178) Lance's perverse pleasure at loss recalls Tom More's similar feeling at the death of his daughter, Samantha. Like More, Lance is "feasting" on Margot's adultery as a way to justify his despair. So also does Lance feast on sin and death—his perverse "sacraments"—as the envious man or malicious man feasts on the failure of others to blindly exalt himself.[9] Yet he cannot bring himself to ask Margot directly. When he hints at his suspicion and she lies, telling him she doesn't "mess with anybody," he muses: "But here's the real question: Did I want her guilty or innocent? And if she were guilty and I knew it—and I knew it as surely as I know that my blood type A plus B does not equal Siobhan's O—why did I want to hear her say it? Why did I believe her denial? Which is better, to have a pain and find no cause or to locate the abscess, loose the pus?" (186).

Behind Lance's question lies Percy's deeper probing of the mystery of human desire, the body, and "the world" that resonates throughout all his novels. Binx Bolling, Will Barrett, and Tom More all suffer the pangs of longing and of desire for physical union. At the end of *The Moviegoer* Binx almost "falls prey to desire" and to despair, until union with Kate gives him a bond in marriage. Tom More recognizes that the true goal of human desire is union with God, though he has difficulty matching insight to willed action. Lance's case is far more complicated than that of his predecessors. He is the most wounded "victim of Descartes," the most extreme dualist. Hidden deep inside Lance is the truth that he resents Margot *as woman* because she lured him into the feast of sex. She became the object of his incommensurate desire. This "entrapment" brought home the inescapable knowledge of his own bodily desire, his physical humanity, which he both resents and has tried to transcend, as Descartes tried, by "objectifying." The real cause of Lance's anguish is the mystery of his own sexual nature, which he holds "beneath" his detached intellectual self. Thus his anguish over Margot's "sin" is a mask for his contempt and rage at his own incarnate human nature.

Lance's predicament regarding human desire and longing is the focal point of Percy's views of the semiotic self and of the meaning of the sacramental in *Lancelot*. In explaining the "demoniac self" in *Lost in the Cosmos*, Percy followed Kierkegaard in affirming that Christianity "first brought the erotic spirit into the world" (175). To be more precise, Christianity spiritualized flesh and human desire, specifically through Christ's Incarnation, his establishing of the Eucharist, and his bodily resurrection. It identified the sensuous-erotic as a spiritual force, a "qualified spirituality" and not just a biological drive. Human desire, the sensuous-erotic as a spiritual force, is rebellious and needs to be ordered and directed toward its proper end. It is important to see that Lance's desire for Margot is not simply driven by a need for physical gratification. Rather, his sexual desire signifies a deeper spiritual longing, but one that is misdirected by his egoistic need to "possess" her. Rejection of the incarnate body is, by extension, a rejection of the Body of Christ signified by the Eucharist. Lance's resentment of his own physicality is of a piece with his resentment of Christianity, that most "fleshly" belief. So also, Lance's willed "emptying" of himself into the gnosis of stoicism parodies the *kenosis* of Christ. Lance would now be the "world savior," setting out to redeem mankind in his proposed New Order.

Christianity's positing of the sensuous-erotic as a spiritual force recognizes the struggle between the "flesh" as spiritualized and the proper goal of human longing—union with God. To this view Percy added his own semiotic perspective, which sheds additional light on Lance's predicament. In his "Semiotic Primer of the Self" Percy argued that the self as sign-user can name and identify anything in the cosmos—except itself (102–9). The self is a mystery to itself, but it can know something of itself through its relation to the world, and only *with* another. In this way the self can be "informed" of who and what it is as a creature. Christianity identified the unique predicament of the semiotic creature. Man is a unique person, a unity of flesh and spirit, a "wayfarer" in the world who can yet know his predicament and the true end of human desire. But as Percy argues, the traditional ways for the self to identify or be informed about itself—through myth and religion, or through Jewish-Christianity in particular—have been discredited or radically devalued in the age of scientism. Humans are now seen as "autonomous," free to choose any "self" or mode of being. But because of its fundamental nature as a semiotic spirit, the self cannot escape being "informed" in some way. Percy goes on to say that the "autonomous" self, lacking any real governing principle for the sensuous-erotic spirit, becomes "possessed" by its power in such a way that inevitably leads to violence. Desire, driven by the spirit of the sensuous-erotic *in* the flesh, is perverted toward destructive ends (175–98).

Lance Lamar is such an "autonomous" and possessed self. Having either wittingly or unwittingly rejected the real substance of sacrament (the Eucharist as semiotic event in which the physical is mysteriously spiritualized), Lance feeds perversely on the "language" of sacrament by misappropriating it to describe his own ends, his physical "possession" of Margot. Cunnilingus becomes his eucharistic sacrament. He thus becomes the "demoniac," possessed by the desacralized erotic spirit, unable to see what informs his thought and actions. Lance hates the very predicament of his life in the flesh, feels betrayed by his own desire, and this hatred inevitably turns to violence against the world.

Lance's predicament, of course, exemplifies in full force the meaning of the Cartesian defection from the Christian Incarnation, the sacramental life, and the real mystery of human nature. Ultimately for Percy, unless Christ sanctified flesh in the Eucharist, unless desire is sacralized and directed toward its true end of union with God, unless consciousness is grounded in an awareness of corporate, communal identity with others, then there is no avoiding the "derangement" (a favorite Percy word) of dualism. Having rejected this vision, and hating his own sexual being as much as anything, Lance in the end projects that hatred onto God as the author of his predicament, the creator of life itself:

> Didn't your God say that unless you become as innocent as one of those [children], you shall not enter the kingdom of heaven? Yes, but what does that mean? It is obvious he made a mistake or else played a very bad trick on us. Yes, I remember the innocence of childhood. Very good! But then after awhile one makes a discovery. One discovers there is a little secret that God didn't let us in on. One discovers your Christ never did tell us about it. Yet God himself so arranged it that you wake up one fine morning with a great thundering hard-on and wanting nothing more in life than a sweet hot cunt to put it in, drive some girl, any girl, into the ground, and where is the innocence of that? Is that part of the innocence? If so, he should have said so. From child to assailant through no doing of one's own—is that God's plan for us? Damn you and your God. Between the two of you, you should have got it straight and had it one way or the other. Either it's good or it's bad, but whichever it is, goddamn say so. Only you don't. You fuck off somewhere in between. You want to have it both ways: good, but—bad only if—and so forth. Well, you fucked up good and proper, fucked us all up, for sure fucked me up. (188)

Lancelot's dualism becomes explicit here. For him, human sexuality is a trap invented or permitted by God, who could have arranged creation otherwise. In effect, Lance wants to strip human existence of spiritual content—of choice and responsibility, of possible redemption, and of any idea of love that doesn't reduce to physical desire. By the same logic, human relations, for Lance, are grounded finally in power manipulation. Ethical nuances are flattened in favor of "rational" either/or, clear-cut meanings. Christianity is denounced for its affirmation of personal freedom and responsibility, its notion of the ambiguity of sin and ethical judgment. Lance mocks this reality: "I won't have it your way with your God-bless-everything-because-it's-good-only-don't-but-if-you-do-it's-not so bad" (189). Instead, he pledges allegiance to a simple pagan stoic code of stern righteousness and "honor" among men, enforced by the power of the sword. Leaders will enforce this ethic "not for Christ's sake but for their own sake" (191). As for women, Lance claims that the New Woman "will have perfect freedom" to live as lady or whore. But when Father John protests such a simplification, Lance replies, "The hell with them. They won't have anything to say about it" (191). When the priest again raises the question of love, Lance answers, "Don't talk to me of love until we shovel out the shit" (192). Finally, Lance's contempt for the present world and of a God whose Son entered it to redeem it leads him to challenge Father John in terms of their opposing visions: "[It will be] your way or my way." In his view, given the present state of American society, there is no other alternative.

For Percy, as we have seen, triadic sign relations are always the foundation of real human communication and community. They are the means for an intersubjective union between persons. Percy emphasizes Lance's defection from this truth through the detached technological method—the secret videotaping—he employs to uncover Margot's sin. In making the video-tapes Lance becomes at once pornographer, voyeur, "objective" scientist, and film producer, though he claims to despise Hollywood and its denizens. Both videos show the perversion of triadic relations—here, intimate sexual rela-tions—in a double sense: between the subjects filmed, and between Lance as observer and those subjects. Percy's inverted use of double triads, including graphic linear triangles that reduce the "actors" to stick figures, emphasizes this perversion. Furthermore, the technical failure in the video-taping process, which causes the images to appear as distorted negatives, bodies emptied out and "blown apart" by magnetic force, underscores the dehumanization in the scenes. In a fitting kind of antirepresentation, all the subjects are reduced to wavering protoplasmic images, nonselves moving through a surreal dark-as-light netherworld.

In the first "feature," Lance discovers the sexual triangle involving Merlin, Margot, and Jacoby. But in this parody of communion, the conversation is distorted or fragmented, so that Lance has to guess at the meaning of half-sentences and broken phrases. He observes what appears to be an affair-ending scene between Margot and Merlin, partly due to Merlin's sexual impotence. At least this is how Lance interprets the garbled conversation, though he may also be injecting his own fears of impotence. What is clear is that Margot is pursuing an affair with Jacoby, in spite of Merlin's warning that she is being manipulated for her money. Thus, to his added humiliation, Lance discovers that Margot's adultery is indeed a triangle, but one that now excludes him entirely. When Merlin leaves, Jacoby enters and Lance watches as he and Margot make love, their negative body images and voices fusing in the video like fluid electrons. By seeing Margot's adultery, Lance presumably has the "proof" of sin that he desired.

In the second "feature," Lance watches a ménage à trois encounter between the actors Troy Dana and Raine, and his daughter Lucy. It is a "rough swastika-ed triangle" in which Lucy is being acted upon "like a patient." Percy's signs here grimly suggest an analogy to the Nazi physicians who experimented, sexually and otherwise, on helpless "patients" in another perversion of technology. As in the scene with Margot and Jacoby, male and female voices merge confusedly; likewise, the male-female sexual roles in the ménage become blurred as the actors "feed" on each other. Yet watching both videos with "interest," Lance reveals no personal feelings of rage or disgust at the devastating betrayals he has witnessed. Instead, he tells Father John, perhaps disingenuously, that "what I mainly remember of the tapes is not the tapes themselves but the day outside" (197). Nevertheless, the tapes confirm Lance in his plan for revenge, to move from passive observer to righteous avenger in the name of "honor."

Having decided to destroy Belle Isle, Lance dispatches Elgin and his family, Tex, Siobhan, and Lucy, and then sets his plan of revenge in motion, piping methane gas into the mansion as the hurricane approaches. The recent videotape revelations confirm him in despair. Against Father John's silent appeal, Lance argues that "the truth is, nobody understands anyone else, and nobody is reconciled because nobody knows what there is to be reconciled. Or if there is something to be reconciled, the way it is done in the movies, by handshakes, level-eyed looks, expressions of mute understanding, doesn't work" (214). Lance rejects the hope for genuine communication or any healing of broken trusts through forgiveness. His argument is illogical, of course, since he now presumes to understand Margot's actions completely without having talked to her. But what the search has truly revealed is Lance himself. His self-appointed role as "objective" sleuth and voyeur discloses his own blindness. The denial of his own humanity in order to follow "the worm of interest" issues in a demonic self that Percy signified by Lance's increasing "coldness" as he approaches his revenge. Drugs help to anesthetize him from personal suffering as well as from human compassion. The amphetamines provided by Raine help create "a little space between me and the pain," but only marginally: "How do you get comfortable with a sword through your guts? I didn't expect a solution or even relief. I only wanted a little distance: how does one live with it . . . being stuck onto pain like a cockroach impaled on a pin? . . . It became a *problem to be solved* (223–24)" (italics mine). Drugs also create the illusion of freedom and self-discovery. Raine stupidly tells him, "You feel absolutely free to choose, to plan and act. You become your true self" (221). But in fact at this point Lance is furthest from his true self, far from freedom, since his planned vengeance is determined rigidly by the past that has shaped him, unwittingly, toward the role he is about to fulfill, that of a slave to the code of "honor."

Percy reveals Lance's blind servitude to the past through a series of disjointed recollections and fantasies. The first is the apparition of "Our Lady of Camillias," a madonna-whore figure who embodies Lance's dualism toward woman. She is a corrupt version of the knight's lady of the quest. She brings him the dark truth of his mother's adultery with Uncle Harry, and his father's cowardly acceptance of it: "She lived for love. Literally. Unless she was loved, she withered and died. Maury understood that. God, what understanding he had! And he also understood his own limitations and accepted them. He understood her relationship with Harry and accepted that. That man was a saint" (227). Her revelation reminds Lance of his father's theft and, implicitly, their mutual loss of "honor," a wound Percy links semiotically to Lance's locker room initiation as a "young Comus knight" into the krewe headed by his Uncle Harry, a once potent "knight" now become an old, fat salesman. In his deranged state of mind Lance even wonders if perhaps Uncle Harry is his real father. Whatever the truth, these memories underscore the degeneration of the ideal of the grail quest in Lance's mind. Both father and uncle have failed as models of the honorable knight-hero, so Lance feels compelled to avenge the many betrayals of the code and try to succeed where they failed. Therefore he quickly displaces them in mind with more heroic images from the past, that of his great-great-grandfather who fought at Lee's side in the Civil War, and of his uncle who fought in the Argonne. Thinking of his own son's refusal to serve in Vietnam, Lance laments to Father John how the days of great battles and heroic deeds have collapsed into the moral quagmire and irresolution of the present.

In the face of this decline Lance now proposes to resurrect the heroic ideal with his Third Revolution and the establishment of the New Order community in Virginia. In *Love in the Ruins* Tom More saw how the gnostic dream of America as utopian paradise exploded in the face of history's tough realities and human frailty. But now Lance proposes to revive this dream-vision, signified by a purified hero, a youth with a rifle "standing in a mountain pass above the Shenandoah Valley" (237). He is the quintessential "innocent" male American archetype—stoic frontiersman, hunter, warrior, conqueror—turning his back on the corruptions of history, on community with woman, setting off alone in search of an Edenic wilderness in which to exercise freedom and power. In Lance, the romanticized myth of the past has become a gnostic vision of the future. All of his romantic longings are distilled in the song he imagines hearing young men singing:

> Oh Shenandoah, we long to see you
> How we love your sparkling waters
> And we love your lovely daughters
> From these green hills to far away
> Across the wide Missouri. (238)

Ironically, Lance believes he is reacting against "every abstract *disincarnate* idea ever hit upon by man roaming the wilderness in search of habitation" (236) (italics mine). Yet he is blind to his own absorption in the disincarnated ideal. But when Father John interrupts his reverie by abruptly asking the serious question about women's place in the New Order, Lance expounds a second version of his theory of history. This version, we see, is a viciously misogynistic and deterministic countervision to the Christian incarnational vision of history and community. God Himself, Lance argues, is the creator of Original Sin, and the "sin" is the human condition itself, specified by human sexuality. Thus his pseudo-scientific sexual theory of history concludes with the belief that the "great secret of the age is that man has evolved, is born, lives, and dies for one end and one end only: to commit a sexual assault on another human being or to submit to such an assault" (239). Woman is the "omega point" in Lance's evolutionary scheme, determined by nature to "find happiness and the meaning of life itself" in being assaulted by a man. God is to blame for this condition, from which no redemption is possible. In Lance's reductive vision, the insoluble conflict between abstract "ideal" and human desire leads inevitably to violence, as Percy described later in *Lost in the Cosmos*. Lance's demonic vision of history denies all human and religious values. Unable to accept the mystery of being-in-the-flesh, of existence in time, he reduces all distinctions of meaning to the common denominator of biological drives. But in his typically contradictory fashion, Lance's subsequent actions repeat the adulterous and violent acts that he both condemns as judge-prosecutor, on the one hand, and implicitly rationalizes as biologically determined on the other.

Percy makes clear that Lance's revenge scheme is fueled by forces he does not recognize when the image of the Lady of the Camillias melds into an image of his mother and she hands him the Bowie knife. Now armed with this "sword," he prepares to assume the role of avenging knight against all the forces of evil around him. Although his mother was guilty of the original abandonment of Lance that helped shape his ambivalence toward women and the world of flesh, he is now willingly "doing what she asked me to do" (243). The corrupted ideal figure of woman he might logically be expected to hate now becomes the femme fatale of his life. Since Lance is blind to his own ambivalence toward women, seen in his obsession with the lady-whore duality, he dooms himself to act out the dualism by taking revenge against the flesh in the name of the ideal of honor. In his delusion, Lance thinks he will recover his own power by punishing the betrayers who stole his "possessions"—Margot and his daughter Lucy. Likewise, he hopes to reinvest the concepts of "sin," "honor," and "freedom" with meaning in a world that has become a moral and linguistic wasteland. But Lance's detachment and his failure to see his own real complicity in this sullied world preclude such recovery. Even now, as he recalls the murderous events at Belle Isle, he tells Father John that "the most unpleasant experience of that night" was the "damn fiberglass" (247).

As other critics have noted, Lance's regression to the role of dutiful southern son to the "lady" mother figure becomes clear in his sexual assault on the actress Raine. When she calls him a "big mother," Lance gazes at her childlike form, his "thumbnail against tooth." He remains aloof and watchful, "thinking of the queerness of the present-here-and-now moment." He continues: "Other times belong to someone or something or oneself and smell of someone or something or oneself. The present is something else. To live in the past and future is easy. To live in the present is like threading a needle. It came to me: our great locker-room lust had no relation to the present. Lust is a function of the future" (253). Lance's observation echoes in part Will Barrett's discovery of the mystery of presentness when he stood outside his family home, touching the iron horsehead. Will discovered that his dualist father had missed the "extraness" (spirit in sign) in the present that was incarnated in the solid iron of the horsehead, a clue to "how to live" without despair. But here, Lance's partial insight into the mystery of living in the present is quickly dismissed when he sees the sign of his daughter Lucy's sexual fall, her sorority ring, on Raine's finger. Then, as in his first discovery of Margot's infidelity, the "little worm of interest" stirs in him. As he guides Raine's hand to fondle him, Lance smiles because "I discovered the secret of love. It is hate. Or rather the possibility of hate. The possibility of hate rescued lust from the locker-room future and restored it to the present" (254). Almost at once "interest" coalesces with sexual desire and the wish to "know" Raine, but not as the intimate communion of knowers united in love. This is "knowledge" as power exercised against woman, a vengeful sexual assault. Now the claimed defender of honor and scourge against adultery becomes himself an adulterer, a participant in the perverted triangular relation. He who tried to sacralize sex as an absolute now uses it as an instrument of hate.

After his sexual assault on Raine, and still blind to his true motives, Lance pursues his desire to "see" sin. But as he recalls this now for Father John, he admits, "I didn't see what I wanted to see after all," though he cannot fathom why. "Why was it so important for me to see them, Margot and Jacoby?" he wonders. "What new sweet-horrid revelation did I expect to gain from witnessing what I already knew? Was it a kind of voyeurism? Or was it a desire to feel the lance strike home to the heart of the abscess and let the pus out? I still don't know. I only know that it was necessary to know, to know only as the eyes know. The eyes have to know" (255). Since sin is spiritual, and since the very concept presupposes a real relation of meaning to God, "seeing" sin as Lance wishes to do is not equal to "knowing" sin. Lance's detachment and blindness make such knowledge impossible for him to attain, since in his contradictory way he has already "emptied" the act of meaning. Consequently the end of his quest for the Unholy Grail becomes a brutal parody of the genuine religious search.

In the murder scene Percy emphasizes Lance's perversion of the triad of word, flesh, and spirit signified by Christ's Incarnation and the sacraments. The bed the lovers lie in is "like a cathedral, a Gothic bed," and poised beside it, Lance listens like "an unconsecrated priest hearing an impenitent confession" from a voice that "rose and fell in a prayer-like intonation." What he hears is the repeated phrase: "God. Sh—God. Sh—." For Lance, the reductive dualist who cannot countenance mystery, "love [must] require the absolute polarities of divinity-obscenity."[10] Human love is "an absolute and therefore beyond all categories," so Lance concludes, "Why not then curse and call on God in an act of love?" (256–57).

Since he now has discovered the lovers in bed, Lance would seem to have fulfilled his announced purpose to "see" Margot's sin. But his real purpose is revenge against the whole enfleshed world. Percy emphasizes this truth and the demonic root of his quest when Lance joins the adulterous triangle by mounting the "two-backed" beast to attack Jacoby. In his delusion, Lance relishes the fight as though he were reviving the "code of honor" he imputed to his ancestor's alleged knife fight and dismemberment of an enemy. But the fantasy of "honor" is destroyed by Lance's gratuitous mutilation of Jacoby. Paradoxically, the act of revenge turns out to be self-inflicted. The man who presumed to unravel the mystery of sin with cold, detached objectivity, like Ethan Brand, now discovers his own death of feeling: "What I remember better than the cutting was the sense I had of casting about for an appropriate feeling to match the deed. Weren't we raised to believe that 'great deeds' were performed with great feelings—anger, joy, revenge, and so on? I remember casting about for the feeling and not finding one. Yet I am sure the deed was committed, because his voice changed. His voice dropped a foot from his mouth to his windpipe and came out in a rush, not a word, against my hand holding the knife" (262). The cold banality of Lance's description reveals his inability to see or feel any dimensions of reality beyond the literal. His sense of reality seems almost entirely gone. With Jacoby dead, Lance tells Margot that he loves her and that together they can start "a new life." But he fails to see either the source of his aggrieved being—carnal woman as sign of the flesh—or his own sexual malaise. Margot points to this truth when, just before the mansion explodes, she tells him, "With you I had to be either—or—but never a—uh—woman" (265). But Lance does not understand her point, and when Belle Isle explodes, he proclaims, "for the first time in thirty years I was moved off the dead center of my life. Ah then, I was thinking as I moved, there are still great moments. I was wheeling slowly up into the night like Lucifer blown out of hell, great wings spreading against the starlight" (266).

Lance construes the analogy between himself and Lucifer as a heroic one, but in misappropriating George Meredith's poetic image he misses the deeper truth of Satan's confinement within his own egotism, his self-chosen hell of isolation from God.[11]

The last chapter of *Lancelot* presents two opposing visions of history and community—Lance's fascist New Order on the one hand, and Father John's planned return to the ordinary life of a parish priest in Alabama. When released from the Center for Aberrant Behavior, Lance intends to move to Virginia (taking the Bowie knife) and begin a new life with Anna and Siobhan away from the morally bankrupt world he sees around him. His proposed community à trois, a kind of ironic remnant community, is to be based on the rigid code of honor he enunciated earlier to Father John. Lance's planned new community is of course gnostic, ahistorical, and anti-incarnational, a place "stripped of the past" where he and Anna can be "the new Adam and Eve of the new world," which Lance identified with a romantic vision of the American frontier. In his warped view the "old life" of history was based on the "great secret" of the "ignominious joy of rape and being raped." Lance proposes to transcend that historical circumstance and create a "new dignity between man and woman" (272). Redemption from history will be achieved by the fascist leader-savior. But the so-called "dignity" Lance claims he can create in man-woman relations recapitulates the false, idealized model of woman Lance the dualist holds. She is not to be a real, free person. Lance's disincarnate view of woman undermines any chance for genuine community with another. By association, Percy links the prospect of dehumanization that Lance's scheme implies to the Nazi vision of a desacralized "purified" order, another program of "purification" that ended by murdering millions in an assault on the incarnate Word.

But Anna, the rape victim Lance has opened communication with, refuses to join him in Virginia on his terms. She knows his plan would deny her full humanity as woman (as he denied Margot's). Enraged, Anna denounces Lance's plan as an insult to her integrity: "Are you suggesting . . . that I, myself, me, my person, can be violated by a *man*? You goddamn men. Don't you know that there are more important things in this world? Next you'll be telling me that despite myself I liked it" (272). Yet despite Anna's vehement rejection, Percy suggests some hope for future change in Lance. Anna (grace) will allow him to live in her Virginia barn, and Father John believes that she will join Lance and Siobhan at some time to "begin a new life." But she will not go on his terms. Percy also suggests this hope in the fact that Lance did indeed help Anna overcome the solipsism/silence of her own posttrauma despair. With his help Anna has begun to speak and to affirm herself as a woman on her own terms. An incipient *solitude à deux* is nonetheless possible. Words as signs may yet bridge the "abyss" in Lance.

Earlier in his conversation with Father John, when Lance raged against the present moral pollution he sees in America and how to confront it, he said, "it will be your way or my way." Both agree that a moral revolution is needed. But the priest affirms the need for an inner revolution of the heart, to be effected not by the will to power of a secular code of honor but by humble submission to the divine will and acceptance of sacramental grace. Thus Father John's plan, which Lance speaks of almost contemptuously, is to "take a little church in Alabama . . . preach the gospel, turn bread into flesh, forgive the sins of Buick dealers, administer communion to suburban housewives"

(277). The priest's commitment is to sullied history and the real present, yet a present whose reality incorporates the mystical-eternal in the ordinary, temporal world. The "tapehead" of present time running is the elusive mystery of divine presence here and now. At the center of Father John's vision of community is the scandal of the word made flesh in the Eucharist, the communion he will dispense to Buick dealers and suburban housewives. This community is based on charity and forgiveness, the command to serve God and fellow humans, and the hope of final resurrection in the community of saints. At the end of the novel Percy leaves open the two contending visions of Lance and Father John for the reader to consider. What is clearly suggested, Percy again echoing Guardini, is that the hypocritical "modern age" must soon come to an end, and that the community must "start over" to begin to rediscover its true humanity.

Starting over, and the mystery of Lance's future, is the keynote in Percy's final view of his protagonist in the novel. Lance's pretentious plan to begin "a new life" in Virginia is undercut by the fact that he has not undergone that radical personal change—conversion—to even make a "new man" possible. He is still very much the old Lance, trapped in egotism, isolation, and self-righteousness, as yet unaware of his crippling dependence on the past. Still isolated from humanity and spiritually frozen, he now feels only "numbness and coldness . . . a lack of feeling . . . except a slight curiosity about walking down that street out there . . . I feel nothing now except a certain coldness" (274). Lance admits that he found "nothing at the heart of evil," that his search ended in failure. Deeper self-scrutiny would have provided the answer. Instead, he concludes that there "is no unholy grail just as there was no Holy Grail" and that everything resolves to an "interaction of molecules" (275). But Lance cannot finally accept this reductive vision. His own moral sensibility revolts against it, since such a view destroys his own meaning. Thus his search for meaning, to "see" and unravel the mystery of evil, circles back to the mystery of his own being, which he has yet to explore.

Father John, by contrast, has changed in the course of their "silent" colloquy through the mystery of his encounter with the demonic forces in Lance. Having failed as a missionary, the priest will now start his life over again in a God-centered life of service, in community with other sinners. Lance has yet to change and may never change. Still, Percy offers the real possibility for Lance for a different "starting over" than the one he imagines in Virginia. For the first time in the novel, the priest's words become explicit in the text. Listening, Lance has come to realize that Father John knows something about him that he does not know. The relationship is the classic triadic semiosis, of knowing oneself *with* another, through language. Lance feels a *need* for his companion if he is ever to understand himself. The priest's final "Yes" indicates that he is now ready to help Lance discover what he needs to see about himself. Throughout the novel Father John listened with quiet patience to the horrors of Lance's monologue. He listened in love and compassion; that is, he sustained the *solitude à deux* relationship between them, which is the heart of all human community. He has withstood the defilement of words—and of the Word—by Lance's vitriol, half-truths, evasions, rationalizations, and monomaniac delusions. Now, perhaps, he is ready to deliver the "good news" that, unlike the Bowie knife, both lacerates *and* heals. Perhaps Lance is ready to listen.

Early in this chapter I said that *Lancelot* was Percy's most dangerous novel. From what we know of his personal life, it seems clear that he was undergoing a profound spiritual crisis during its writing.[12] *Lancelot* reflects this in incalculable ways, hinted at in Percy's wry description of it as a "post-menopausal novel" and his admitted "closeness" to Lance Lamar as a character.[13] But beyond the personal, the novel depicts Percy's dark sense of the deeper crisis of the times, and not just the political, social, and religious hypocrisy and corruption he witnessed. Rather, he felt the threatening dissolution of the epistemological foundations of community itself—how we know and share experience through language—especially the "emptying out" of spiritual and moral categories of meaning and value. Such a situation threatened to make a mockery of the basic premises of Percy's theosemiotic vision: belief that human beings *are* human by triadic exchanges of meaning; that together they can name truth; that "love," "hate," "virtue," and "evil" are meaningful concepts that derive their truth and value from a God whose word is guarantor of an ultimate triad of Father (Author-ity), Son (Incarnate Word), and Holy Spirit (Divine "copula")—a community of the Real in which we humans participate mysteriously. In *Lancelot* Percy imagined and dramatized that threatened collapse.

Percy's decision to narrate the novel entirely through Lance's monologue was a daring gamble. Lance's distorted, reductive monologue, coupled with Father John's silence, undermined the *spoken* triadic relation between speaker and listener, the *solitude à deux* bond in word. Father John, the listener, is virtually erased from the narrative as a voice. But as I have argued, he is a strong presence in the novel. This narrative situation in part dramatizes the "disappearance" of the Word as a force in the culture. This threat is reflected, as I have argued, in the parody inversion of key Percyean themes in the novel— themes of the search, communion in love, conversion and awakening to "a new life," revelations through signs, and so on. At the same time, Percy gives full voice to the distortions, rationalizations, and reductions we see in the speeches and actions of Lance and the other characters.

But viewed semiotically, Father John as silent witness *becomes* the mysterious copula in the triad of meaning the novel creates between text and reader. He is the "spark" through which Lance's warped monologue reaches that larger, invisible but real community of meaning, wherein Lance's words may be judged ultimately as true or false. Percy gambled that the reality of that community would, in however muted a fashion, shine through in the novel. That affirmation was Percy's sign of enduring hope, for Lance Lamar, for the readers, and for the culture at large.

CHAPTER FIVE

The Gift of the Word

The Second Coming

Speaking with obvious pride of his fifth novel, *The Second Coming,* Percy said: "I like to think, half-seriously, that this may be the first unalienated novel written since Tolstoy" (Con., 190). In a later interview, Percy was more explicit about his sense of the novel's achievement in overcoming alienation. Concerning the love that Will Barrett and Allison Huger find, he said: "One lonely person finds another lonely person. From this very loneliness, this existential alienation, there is possible a true communion, which in a way is even better than it used to be. What do the French call it? *Solitude à deux?* And between the two they create a new world. At the end of *The Second Coming* it takes place *through the recovery of Christianity*" (More Con., 74) (italics mine). Percy's claims for the novel are far reaching. In addition to Will and Allie's overcoming of alienation by their *solitude à deux* love, he claims that their union occurs *through* a recovery of authentic Christianity. If true, this recovery would represent an important breakthrough in his fiction. Percy often insisted, echoing the Psalmist, that the novelist must "sing a new song" and "make it new"; that is, he must find a new language with which to express the truth of twentieth-century humankind's spiritual predicament, *and* the possibilities of "recovery" or redemption from that predicament.

In this respect, *The Second Coming* is Percy's most ambitious novel. In it he attempted to synthesize Christian incarnational theology with his version of Peircean triadicity to create a theosemiotic vision that would express his belief in the divine presence in the ordinary world. "Theosemiotic," as I have noted, is a term used by Raposa to describe the self's movement toward God by becoming attuned to the presence of the divine maker in the world. According to Raposa, for Peirce "the universe is God's great poem. . . . Fragments of its meaning are accessible to the human intellect, most especially to a genuine community of inquirers devoted to discovering that meaning" (*Peirce's Philosophy of Religion*, 144). Robert S. Corrington explains the concept more fully: "God is fully semiotic and the signs of the divine are to be found throughout the innumerable orders of nature. . . . Theosemiotic lies at the heart of all forms of semiosis. . . . Signs thus become open at both ends. In addition to their correlation with objects and interpretants, signs represent the body of God in nature. The universe of signs is also the universe of divine action and growth. . . . Theosemiotic is the culmination of semiotics precisely because of the spiritual core at the heart of each sign" (*Introduction to C. S. Peirce*, 207). Moreover, to understand Percy's theosemiotic method and his vision of community in *The Second Coming*, we can recall that as a realist like Peirce, he affirmed the idea of "possibility" as an integral dimension of the real and therefore of the notion of community. As Joel Weinsheimer noted in the passage I cited earlier, for Peirce "the real consists in the habits, the beliefs, the possible acts of mind and body it produces. It is the idea of possibility that must be emphasized. The real consists not in what you or I or anyone else thinks it is. . . . Rather, the real is what all who inquire *would* think and *would* continue to think, if inquiry *were* carried far enough."[1]

Percy set out in the novel to dramatize the real possibilities of new community: on the semiotic level, by creating an intricate web of potentially theophanic signs; on the personal level, through the love of Will and Allie; and on the social level, through the founding of a community based on charity. This was a breakthrough novel for Percy, a way to move beyond the dark enclosure of *Lancelot* and offer a clearer way to resolve the predicament of alienation that haunts each of his earlier novels. Moreover, *The Second Coming* also would be a breakthrough for novel writing itself, as Percy's "half-serious" remark suggested, a way to expand the novel beyond mere diagnosis of the modern malaise and suggest ways of therapeutic recovery from personal and social derangements in the community at large. The affirmation and hope implicit in these breakthroughs is grounded in Percy's belief in the human power to symbolize, to know and name our predicament, and with the aid of divine grace, to combat the death of spirit. Yet for Will Barrett and Allison Huger, many obstacles stand in the way of their recovery, as we shall see. But their modest triumph together fully justifies the hope that Percy encoded in the novel.

The Second Coming also presented Percy with perhaps his most difficult technical challenge as a novelist: incarnating his theosemiotic vision in an aesthetically convincing way. One can illustrate this challenge by a brief comparison. In each of his previous novels the Christian sacraments, the traditional signs of divine presence in the human community, are represented explicitly. Lonnie and Binx discuss penance and the Eucharist, attend mass and receive communion; Jamie Vaught is baptized on his deathbed; Tom More goes to confession and receives communion with his daughter Samantha; Father John plans to minister communion to suburban housewives and Buick salesmen. These traditional Catholic signs are part of the vital semiosis of each novel, pointing to each novel's possible extensions of meaning and evoking the mystical community. But in *The Second Coming* there is only one brief reference to the traditional sacraments, an oblique allusion to the Eucharist that comes during a crucial scene in the novel. The "world" Percy depicts in the novel is largely a decadent "Christian" community in which the traditional signs and language of belief and religious commitment have been, at best, emptied of meaning, and at worst, appropriated and manipulated by the purveyors of a bland, desacralized simulacrum of genuine faith. In this world, the "good news" has either become old news or slogan. Almost everything we see in this representative fictive world—its hypocrisy, its vapid pietistic language, its conformity and devaluation of the inner quest for faith—seems to justify Lance Lamar's angry attacks on society in *Lancelot*. In short, *The Second Coming* seems to record the emptying out of traditional sacramental meaning that existed, however marginally, as a real spiritual dimension in Percy's earlier novels. How write a novel of spiritual recovery, and what Percy specifically called "a recovery of Christianity," in the face of that collapse?

The Second Coming is Percy's most thoroughly Piercean novel. If in the end Will and Allie create a new world "*through* the recovery of Christianity," as Percy maintained, then writing the novel constituted something of a "recovery" in both religious and artistic terms. Lance Lamar and Sutter Vaught both argued that the traditional sacraments were "emptied out" of meaning. Their arguments clearly reflect Percy's own concern with the status of the sacraments in a scientistic-dominated culture. Percy answered that challenge in *The Second Coming* by employing Peircean triadicity to invest the signs of the novel with sacramentality in a more thoroughgoing way than in any of his previous novels. The novel's signs are profoundly mysterious, and their mystery and open-endedness is itself a way out of the trap of scientistic consciousness Percy named as a dominant characteristic of the age (MB, 113). Stated differently, triadic sign making to create mystery is the manner in which the novel—and protagonist Will Barrett—uncovers God's being in the world. That being is "present" in sign and action; theosemiotic is embedded in the language. The dramatizing of this incarnational action fully justifies Percy's claim of a new world *through* the recovery of Christianity. The overcoming of alienation in *The Second Coming* is not just Will and Allie's triumph. It is a triumph for the novel itself in overcoming alienation, and it looks forward to the "new world" in which science and faith could be reconciled through Peircean semiotics, which Percy hypothesized in his Jefferson Lecture.

Percy's plan, then, was to create a complex web of signs that shapes the action and inner movement of the novel and incarnates his theosemiotic vision. Form and vision were to be coextensive. The heart of this "new song" or semiosis is mystery, the mystery of the nonmaterial coupler or "jumper" that Percy first discovered in Helen Keller's breakthrough into languaged consciousness, the paradigmatic experience of triadic relations and naming (MB, 33–39). At the center of this seminal event is the mystery of divine love, the gift of the word communicated to humankind in divine revelation and then in the coming of the Word into history and the human community.[2] Percy's "new" novel, in effect, would instantiate in fiction the mystery of the coming of that Word into the world, manifested in the relationship of Will and Allie.

My use of the term "mystery" is not meant to suggest some obscurantism in Percy's novels. Viewed from the standpoint of a realistic semiotic, mystery refers to the truth that, as Peirce argued, every triadic sign is open ended. As we have seen, every triad of sign meaning both presupposes another triad and anticipates or "opens" the sign to further developing triads of meaning. Triadic signs exist in a continuum or web of meaning, constantly evolving toward higher or more expansive revelations of the truth of being. Thus, in the concrete situation of the interpreter/sign user, as in Will Barrett's case, the experience of interpreting signs is itself one of mystery, of searching out clues, a search that propels the interpreter toward deeper insights into his or her "situation" in the world.

Semiotically, Will's recovery occurs when he becomes a true namer of being, in the manner of Percyean triadicity. In this recovery Will's words and his naming become linked to the coming of the divine Word. Throughout the novel his consciousness and the voice of the narrator evolve in a process of triadic interaction to chart Will's progress toward self-discovery and movement toward God. Aided by the grace of Allie's loving presence and her "new language," Will breaks through the mold of decadent talk and the deadening influence of his father's rhetoric. Thus in this novel Percy chose to bypass the traditional Catholic sacramental signs, largely devalued in the culture, and instead create an intricate web of fresh and open-ended signs to suggest the real possibility of divine presence and agency within the natural, human world. In this way, as I have suggested, the patterns of triadic semioses would serve to literally incorporate in the text a vision of possible spiritual renewal, without slighting either the possibility for failure or the cost of such recovery. Will and Allie are still damaged creatures at the end of the novel. But their loving relation helps them to begin to overcome the fracturing effects of alienation (i.e., the Cartesian predicament)—spirit separated from matter, consciousness from will, word from being, desire and longing from redeeming love—that have beset them and almost all of Percy's characters. In *The Second Coming* Percy's triadic sign relations and their widest spiritual implications receive their most achieved expression in fictional form.

Percy's strategy of recovery in the novel, then, entailed creating a triadic relationship between Will and Allie "coupled" with signs of the divine presence. To help achieve this technically, Percy also developed a triadic pattern of narrative perspectives that evolve as Will and Allie develop throughout the novel. For example, Will's troubled and somewhat deranged inner consciousness is counterbalanced by the voice of a more "rational" and bemused, but not omniscient, narrator. And within Will's mind, the doom-ridden presence and voice of his father contends with the questioning intuitive consciousness of Will's searching self. As the novel unfolds, Will's intuitive mind begins to grasp intimations of a divine presence, a God-father whose spirit mysteriously infuses the ordinary world.

Percy also structured the novel in such a way as to inform the underlying triadic movement toward recovery and reconciliation. Initially, he alternates separate chapters on Will and Allie before bringing them together and interweaving their lives. More significantly, Will's interior development proceeds triadically. His consciousness evolves through a dynamic interaction between crucial memories and his present life, leading him to new self-knowledge. Events from the past (e.g., hunting with his father) triangulate with present events (e.g., golfing with friends) in his mind, forcing him to interpret clues from both experiences as signs of his immediate predicament. Will must first come to understand what his life has been before he can name what it presently is, a process complicated by the insistent inner voice of his father, who offers him deadly advice. Later, Will turns to challenge another father—God—in search of answers to his life, and the two fathers—one vociferous, and one silently present in signs—become contending forces that shape Will's fate. Allie becomes the incarnate "link" between the divine Father and Will; Allie is the benevolent "mother" and lover who is the matrix of loving communion in their *solitude à deux.* With Allie, Percy found a way to express the ultimate communal relation between humans and God through the word, the sign of love made flesh in the love of his two protagonists. Such love creates charity, which, for Will and Allie, extends to the community at large at the end of the novel. The idealism of such a movement is reminiscent of *The Tempest,* wherein self-discovery and reconciliation also keynote the possibility of a "new world." But as in Shakespeare's play, Percy's ideal is tempered by an understanding of the hard truths of human fallibility—the capacity for regression, self-delusion, and evil. Still, *The Second Coming* offers a real glimpse of what "might be," a vision of community such as Peirce envisioned as eventually "possible," like the ideal community St. Paul imagined in his first epistle to the Corinthians.

Will Barrett's search to recover a genuine self, and Percy's search to create a new semiosis, to "sing a new song" and express the inner spirit of Christianity, are coextensive throughout *The Second Coming.* But Will is a lost self as the novel opens, even more subtly a victim of Descartes than Percy's earlier protagonists. Initially it appears that his life has been a resounding triumph. A successful lawyer who married well, he now lives comfortably as a retired widower in North Carolina, the "most Christian state" in the "most Christian country" in the world. Surrounded by friends who esteem his character and good citizenship, Will has been awarded the local "Rotary's man-of-the-year award for service to the community" (5). His time is spent playing golf, socializing with friends, overseeing St. Mark's Convalescent Home (founded and financed by his late wife, Marion), and managing his car dealership. Yet something is deeply amiss in Will's life, and signs of that disorder erupt in the opening scenes. As always in Percy's fiction, ordeal triggers a spiritual crisis and intensifies self-awareness. While golfing, Will falls down in a bunker, the first of many falls. This initial sign is mysterious and paradoxical. While Will may be suffering from some neurological disorder, Percy also suggests that his fall is symptomatic of a sudden wrenching of the inner spiritual equilibrium of his seemingly well-balanced life. The mystery deepens later when it is discovered that medication to balance his pH factor and make him "normal" also diminishes his inexplicable desire and "longing." As with Binx and Lance Lamar, desire is the key to his spiritual search. Here too Percy anticipates what would become a major theme of his final novel, *The Thanatos Syndrome*—the pharmacological pacification of subjects and the elimination of "longing" at the expense of full humanity.

In the new awareness triggered by his fall, Will finds that his life and the lives of those around him are "farcical," and his reaction is to contemplate suicide. Percy's choice of the word "farcical" is exactly revealing. Etymologically it means "to stuff," and indeed, Will and Marion stuffed their lives with good works as much as she stuffed herself with food. Percy here suggests St. Paul's argument that good works alone are not sufficient for salvation (Romans 3–4). In this suggestion he introduces the complex theological and ethical issue of the meaning of "good" actions in relation to the social/mystical community. A lifetime of good deeds has not brought Will a genuine sense of *felt* belief; later, he comes to see that his own pro forma "religious" commitment to help society was merely a reaction against his father's despair. Neither has his life of good deeds brought him any close communion of love with fellow humans or with God. Throughout his "successful" life he has remained alienated, aloof, and "cold." His acts of goodwill, dissociated from his deepest personal desires and a true self, seem fraudulent to him. Now Will feels a sense of personal hollowness at the core of his benevolence. His "remoteness" from his charitable deeds reveals an insidious Cartesian split in his being. The discovery is devastating, and escape by suicide seems an honorable option to a "farcical" life.

Will's fall causes dislocations of memory, a state "opposite of amnesia," in which "he remembered everything." Will's anamnestic condition is paradoxical. On the one hand, it denotes a recovery of signs by which he will uncover the past in order to overcome it. On the other hand, it threatens to trap him in a solipsistic self-consciousness that paralyzes him when he needs to act in the world. Percy's exploration of this mystery—of the relation between self-consciousness, memory, and action—is of course a major theme throughout his fiction. As he remembers "everything," his world suddenly becomes charged with signs, and "everything reminded him of something else" (9). Climbing through a fence to retrieve a golf ball sliced out of bounds, Will hears a sound that "reminded him of an event that happened a long time ago. It was the most important event in his life, yet he had managed until that moment to forget it" (3). Presumably this "most important" event in Will's life is the childhood hunting trip he took with his father, but Percy clothes Will's anamnesis in mystery. Could it be a hallucination, as one doctor suggests? Could it be a neurological disorder, a lesion in the frontal lobe of the brain, "the seat of memory," one that triggers "association response"? Or could the source be metaphysical and hieratical, a transcendent sign offered to Will in the face of his "farcical" predicament? In the semiosis of the text all three possibilities— psychological, neurological, and metaphysical—exist within the mystery of Will's self-consciousness.

The possibility of the hieratical dimension of these signs that begin to flood Will's mind is reinforced by his memory of another "most important" event in his youth, a countersign to the hunting trip memory. Will recalls how as a youth he fell down in a "wedge-shaped salient of weeds," overcome with longing for Ethel Rosenblum, a smart Jewish classmate who rivals him for academic honors. The patch of weeds, "shaped like a bent triangle," suggests a triadic relation of possible love and/or sex between them. In addition, her Jew-ishness further links her to Will's obsession with the meaning and importance of "the Jews" in history. He marvels at how rapidly Ethel can solve math equa-tions, factoring them down to the ideal triad of "unity, symmetry, beauty." But life for Will is not so symmetrical. The patch of weeds is a "bent" triangle, and his collapse there only reveals his insatiable longing for sex, love, and commu-nity. Still, the memory of the Jewish girl is a brief intuition of an ideal *solitude à deux,* a triadic *locus amor* such as that imagined by St Paul. Will thinks: "Ethel, let's me and you homestead this leftover land here and now, this non-place, this surveyor's interstice. Here's the only place for us, the only place *not Jew or Gentile, not black or white, not public or private"* (8) (italics mine). Will's intuition of the ideal here anticipates his later discovery of the "good" place and the woman to love in Allison Huger, a place from which to try to rebuild community.

Percy's evocation of the "Jewish" link through Ethel Rosenblum early in the novel is also a central sign of the link between Will's personal memory, history, and the final goal of the journey. The Jews are history's memory, as Owen Barfield said, and through the Jewish people the divine Word entered the world and is present in the here-and-now. Will will journey through per-sonal memory to discover the divine gift in the here-and-now with Allie, so that by the end of the novel he will point himself "toward Jerusalem." But at the outset of his trials, in his addled mental state, he can only lament the lost chance with Ethel and imagine apocalyptically that the "Jews" are fleeing North Carolina as a "sign of God's plan working out."

In his focus on Will's longing for Ethel Rosenblum, or what his doctor calls the "sexual component" in his disorder, Percy again returned to the problem of human desire that so confounded Binx, the young Will Barrett, Tom More, and Lance Lamar. Here, eros is linked to "Jewishness" and to woman in order to suggest that Will's path to recovery from his Cartesian self will be tied to his discovery of the living word and to love—the coupling of the "it" and the "doing," flesh and spirit—in his relationship with Allie. But initially, his anamnesis only reawakens his unappeased longing and an awareness that he has lived a life defrauded of genuine selfhood. As he later sees, only "one event had ever happened to him in his life. Everything else that happened afterwards was a non-event" (52). That "one event" was his father's attempt to kill him, and Will's first "fall" in body and mind on the golf course stirs him to examine the lifelong effects of that event.

Will learns that he has spent his life trying to avoid the event's meaning—refusing to *name* it—in various ways. He has refused to live in the present, instead either casting ahead into the future (e.g., making plans) or backward into the past, unconsciously trying to escape his paternal legacy. Thus he "misses his life" and thinks now that his own and the lives of those around him have been only "farcical" diversions. Of course, this is not entirely true; Will has done good work. Rather, it reflects Will's distorted mental state and his tilt toward suicidal pessimism. But he does acknowledge truthfully that much of his life has been a role constructed as a reaction against his past. He left the South and became a successful Wall Street lawyer to escape that past and the memory of his destructive father. He married Marion Peabody because he enjoyed pleasing her, not out of deep love. His life as husband and father has been, to a great degree, a mask of self-deception that insulated him from the painful truth. He confesses that he loved neither his wife nor his daughter, Leslie. He has carried out the external motions of life smoothly and successfully while living in an isolated "cave" of the self. This truth is brought home to Will by his enemies—the ghostly voice of his father trying to persuade him that all life is finally senseless, and his cantankerous neighbor Ewell McBee, an alter ego who sees through Will's benign, gentlemanly mask to his selfish core. Ewell's accidental near-miss rifle shot, which echoes the hunting episode with overtones of an assassination attempt, shocks Will into recognizing his defrauded life (17).

Percy suggests that Will's predicament is that of the age as well, or indeed any age. He is, he discovers, like others, "never a hundred percent themselves." Unlike the cat in his garage, fully at one with its being, humans are "too often these days . . . two percent themselves, specters who hardly occupied a place at all. How can the great suck of self ever hope to be a fat cat dozing in the sun?" (16). The simple answer, of course, is "Never," given human self-consciousness. Yet Will's naming of the problem is at least a first step toward self-knowledge. "There was his diagnosis, then. A person nowadays is two percent himself. And to arrive at a diagnosis is already to have anticipated the cure: how to restore the ninety-eight percent?" (16).

Will's sense of diminishment has also been hidden from him by his absorption in "planning" the future. Marion's charitable projects, while commendable, are one example. Will's life as husband was reduced to the role of legal adviser and helper, adjunct to her many plans. After Marion dies, Will is threatened by others' constant efforts to manage his future. Here Percy again satirically attacks the many contrived forms of community in America, which become diversions from the "great suck of self" and the question of life's meaning. Will must contend with his daughter Leslie's and the modish priest Jack Curl's plan for a "love and faith" community, as well as Leslie's later plot to keep him in the convalescent home. Will's neighbor Ewell McBee wants to involve Will in a sex and video scheme, while his golfing friend Jimmy Rogers wants to recruit him for the seniors golf tour. Moreover, his ex-girlfriend Kitty Vaught Huger schemes to seduce Will, literally and professionally, to help her plan Allie's future as a psychiatric patient and gain control of Allie's inheritance. As Will becomes aware of these threats and of the defrauded life he has led, he sees, as Lance Lamar did, that the challenge to becoming a free being lies not in the past or in planning a future but in the here-and-now present. And for Will that challenge is focused on trying to understand his relationship to God. "Perhaps, he thought, even God will manifest himself when you are bent far enough out of your everyday lifeline" (67). Will's everyday lifeline had included playing the role of a Christian as part of his "successful" life. In a colloquy with his father's ghost, he admits: "I even tried to believe in the Christian God because you didn't. . . . I did all that and succeeded in everything except believing in the Christian God" (73). Now Will must seek a new approach and a new language by which to explore a possible relation to God. Rejecting his father's despair and the secular humanism of his friend Lewis Peckham, Will begins to search for his own meaning and for an encounter, however strange, with God the father. But such a search demands a return to the deadly scene where his life was initially defined—the hunting trip with his actual father when he was twelve.

Once his ordinary lifeline is bent when he slices "out of bounds," Will begins to recover the event he has suppressed for forty years. Signs again create echolalia—stepping through the barbed wire fence, seeing a hawk overhead, holding his golf club like a shotgun. When his father rebuked him for mishan-

of his predicament through the multiple possible meanings encoded in key
signs. For example, Will thinks he has found the "buried treasure," the fatal
"truth" about life his father wished to convey—that he too would eventually
come to despair. Like all of the important signs in the semiosis of the novel, the
"buried treasure" is multivalent. Later, the "buried treasure" is the iron stove
that Allie uncovers, as well as her inherited fortune and her "treasure island."
Will finds a treasure of knowledge buried in the Lost Cove cave that he enters
in search of ultimate knowledge of God, and then receives the treasure of the
gift of Allie and her love. The sign also suggests the buried treasure of salvation
in Christ's parable (Matt. 13:44), as well as the treasure of the word and the
power of naming by which Will finally comes to claim a true self in the world.
But at first Will believes that his father's treasure of spoken "truth" is offered in
order to save him. "Was he trying to tell me because he thought that if I knew
exactly what happened to him and what was going to happen to me, that by
the mere telling it would not then have to happen to me? Knowing about what
is going to happen is having a chance to escape it" (62). But of course Will is
mistaken, since he has not yet discovered that his father planned to kill him.

During his second golf outing, Will clings to the belief that his father only
meant to warn him of his future struggle by telling him of his difference from
others and of the struggle with despair he would face, so Will concludes, "it's
not your [his father's] fault" (73). He sees his father, as Binx saw his father, as a
victim of the times, an age when "men held allegiances unto death and love of
war and rumors of war and under it all death and your secret love of death, yes
that was your secret" (72). Will's predicament is symptomatic of the century's
obsession with death that Tom More saw signified in the Battle of Verdun.
Yet here Will seems resigned to his father's fatalism. He decides, "I don't hate
you. We're together after all" (74). But at the same time Percy superimposes
this memory of his father's talk with the appearance of "a figure" standing
behind a poplar, or what may be "a trick of light, a pattern in the dappled
leaves" (71). As Allen Pridgen and other critics have shown, throughout the
novel Allie is associated with sacramental signs—light, water, air—and eventually with God incarnate.[3] To cite one example: sunlight reflects from her
"house of glass," the greenhouse, which is "big as an ark," with a copper hood
shading the front door like "a cathedral porch." Will's initial response to this
apparition-like "figure" is confusion and anger. He is angry at having been
observed unnoticed by the "odd" girl and confused by her strange language.
"Are you climbing on your anger?" she asks. The question appears literally
nonsensical, but it points to how Will's anger, like that of his father and of

Lance Lamar, serves as a mode of detachment and transcendence for Will, his "standing above" the world in cold contempt. Sensing his resentment at exposure, Allie adds, "I wasn't spying or denying. I was afraid" (77). Allie responds to his anger by showing her own vulnerability; when his golf ball breaks her greenhouse window, she feels "concealed and revealed" (76). Percy designs their first meeting as one of mystery, strange response, and Allie's quiet affirmation. Will is attracted by the odd girl who seems to read his inner self and whose words are a fresh "new song" in his head that begins to counterbalance the deathly rhetoric of his father.

As I have noted, Percy's structural technique links Will and Allie within their alternating narratives in the opening section. At first glance, Allie's situation seems opposite that of Will. Whereas he suffers anamnesis, Allie's memory has been erased temporarily by electroshock treatments. "She remembered nothing." Yet they are alike in that both have lived a lifetime of alienation. Like Will, Allie accepted a role defined by others: her mother, Kitty, who obsessively planned her daughter's life; her school mentors, who prescribed good grades as the key to success; and her lover Sarge, for whom "love" meant sexual gratification. Allie worked to please each of these mentors, only to lose her free self in the performances. Others controlled her past life, just as Kitty and Dr. Duk now wish to control her future. Like Will, Allie "flunked" ordinary living (i.e., living in the ordinary present). Both are alienated from existing communities and their manipulative power; both are keenly aware of the dead language such groups use to control and manipulate. Both long for a genuine, affirming love that unites erotic desire with the deepest human need for spiritual communion, a *solitude à deux*.

Yet unlike Will, Allie's "fall" is in the past, and she has already begun to recover her free self. She descended into the cave of herself, withdrew from the manipulative world by hiding in her closet at home, sat alone and refused to participate in "group therapy" sessions, suffered through shock treatments, and finally escaped from the hospital in a bread truck (a eucharistic echo of the Holsum bread truck in *The Last Gentleman*). As the novel opens, she is ready for a "new start," having made the startling discovery that she is "*free* to act for herself" (40). Central to her new start is the creation of a new language, one that empowers her uniquely as a namer. Percy was rightly pleased with his achievement in creating Allie's strange speech, noting its similarities to certain aspects of schizophrenic talk—nonsensical puns and rhymes, illogical tropes and syntax, and so forth (Con., 188, 191, 307–8). Yet her speech also suggests

Percy's notions about truth by metaphor developed in his essay "Metaphor as Mistake," the way in which "illogical" analogies can be an avenue to the inscape of being (MB, 64–83). Despite her strange speech, Allie is a linguistic realist. "She took words seriously to mean more or less what they said, but other people seemed to use words as signals in another code they had agreed upon" (34). Her speech is rooted in the belief that, however strangely ordered, words can name truth and be the real foundation of a relation to the world and other beings. She has been driven to her mysterious locution by the slippery nominalism of the age, which regards words as mere tokens in a manipulative exchange, not signs that reveal being.

Allie's linguistic realism is central to Percy's attempt to "sing a new song" that expresses the possible "new life" and the truth of divine Word made flesh in the human community. Like Will, Allie is a serious searcher of language, of the meaning of signs. Inheritor of an island that supposedly contains Captain Kidd's buried treasure, she is not interested in the treasure as money but as a sign-clue in a search. She "thought of it often, not so much to get the treasure as to find it, to *find a sign or a gold bug or a map*" (39) (italics mine). After finding a "treasure" of books in the cellar of the ruined house and reading a passage from *Captain Blood*, Allie thinks: "The words were still clear on the thick yellow pages but the paper crumbled *like bread and a bakery smell rose in her nostrils.* Words surely have meanings, she thought, and there is my trouble. Something happens to words coming to me from other people. Something happens to my words. They do not seem worth uttering.

"People don't mean what they say. Words often mean their opposite. If a person says to you: *I hate to tell you this, but*—she doesn't hate to tell you. She likes to tell you. *This is a good place to make a new start with words*" (82) (italics mine). The triadic interaction of signs here, Percy's linking of Allie's discovery of the "treasure" and the chance of a "new start" to eucharistic images—bread, bakery, even the suggestion of Christ as the true "captain blood"—reinforces her role as a bearer of meaning and grace in the novel. One of her first acts is to give Will a gift—a drink of water—Peirce's prime symbol of the essential triadic exchange. But her greatest initial gift to Will is the "new" words that disarm his anger. In turn, once Allie has found the treasure of a possible "new start" with words, she receives another gift when a stray dog appears, his head "as wide and flat as an anvil" (82). The anvil image echoes the iron horsehead in *The Last Gentleman*, which young Will recognized as a sign of the indwelling spirit, "extraness," in ordinary things that was a clue to understanding and rejecting his father's despair.

Allie's escape and new beginning came after she recognized the destructive power Dr. Duk and her parents exercised over her. Like the young Will in *The Last Gentleman,* her "trouble" was with people. When she refused to participate in "group," Dr. Duk ordered shock treatments. Her parents plan to make her a permanent psychiatric patient. Allie recognizes the manipulative intentions behind their platitudes of care and concern. Dr. Duk's words, a pastiche of clichés, and his attempts to give Allie a "language structure" are as phony as his role playing as an "English" gardener and bird-watcher. When he proposes electroshock, Allie says, "*No buzzin cousin. . . . Fried is crucified*" (103). She calls a visit by her parents "a bang by the gang," a "rape" of her sovereign being. To resist, she withdraws deeply into herself to a center of warmth and light, in contrast to the core of "coldness" Will retreated to on the day of the hunting accident. Allie's center is symbolically identified with a search for God, the source of warmth and light. In her "center" she discovers the freedom of personal sovereignty. Unlike Will's inner move to detachment and mock transcendence, Allie's move is incarnational, a coming into being and action in the here-and-now material world. As she says, "I have to go down down down before I go up. Down down in me to it" (90). The "it" she descends to, as she metaphorically conceives of herself, is the "white dwarf" star Sirius, the hottest star. "One good sign," she says. "I can already feel myself coming down to myself. From giant red star Betelgeuse, Dr. Duk's favorite, trying to expand and fan out and take in and please the whole universe (that was me!), a great gaseous fake of a star, collapsing down to white dwarf Sirius, my favorite, diamond bright and diamond hard, indestructible by comets, meteors, people. Sirius is more serious than beetle gauze" (93). As Gary Ciuba has pointed out, through Allie's wordplay Percy breaks through the false clarity of discursive language and logic to suggest the mystery of her analogical movement toward a divine center of being (*Walker Percy,* 218–29). "*Go-ing. Go-on. Gawain. go-way, gong, God, dog,* I said, not knowing what I meant—do I have to mean something?—maybe just go way, maybe dog—star=Sirius=serious=God—but [Kitty] as usual insisting on making her own strong sense of everything even my nonsense" (94). Though apparently gibberish, Allie's ramblings follow a semiotic track of associations by which she gropes to discover the relation between herself, the cosmos, and God, the first and ultimate sign giver. The triad-shaped diamond, created by intense heat and brilliantly reflective of light, will reappear later as a theophany during Will's discovery of his life.

Although her escape from the sanitarium and move to the greenhouse is the beginning of her freedom, Allie approaches her new life cautiously, still afraid of the manipulative world. When Will returns with a gift offering—avocados and Plagnol oil—she is wary, afraid he might be a part of "the plan" of others to arrange her life. Mistrust is overcome by sharing and a growing bond of mutual respect. Their gifts are sacramentally significant. Allie offers him a drink of water; he in turn gives her food (108–9). Equally important, each feels free to talk or remain silent, reveal or conceal inner mystery. Allie is able to "read" Will's predicament: "You seem somewhat pale and in travail. Is the abomination at home or in the hemispheres?" (110). For his part, Will is able to interpret Allie's strange speech. Allie's suspicions that Will's gifts entail an obligation are allayed by his awareness of her fear and by his circumspection. When Allie reveals her plan to move the iron stove into the greenhouse, Will explains how it can be used to heat water. Later, Allie will use the warmed water to bathe Will after his fall from the cave, the beginning of his new life with her. But naming and sharing the word is the most important sign of their incipient *solitude à deux*. When Will tells her she needs a "creeper" to move the stove, Allie says, "Thanks for the word," and he notes "that she treated the gift of the word exactly like the avocados" (115).

With his partial recovery of the memory of the hunting episode, a way opens for Will to begin to understand his life. His inner search begins, but the way to self-knowledge is also shrouded in opaque and disconnected signs. Touring the nursing home with Jack Curl, Will feels "that now for the first time in his life he could see everything clearly. . . . Something had given him leave to live in the present" (123). Believing that he missed his life by trying to escape his father's despair, Will now determines to face both the fact of mortality and the questions it raises about the ultimate meaning of his life. He believes his father "knew the secret" of life and tried to offer the "gift" of his somber wisdom: "For that was your secret, wasn't it? That it was death you loved most of all and so surely that you wanted to share the secret with me because you loved me too" (126). Will recalls his father's attempt to name the source of his despair:

"The trouble is," the man said, "there is no word for this."
    "For what?"
    "This. . . . It's not war and it's not peace. It's not death and it's not life."
    "What is it? What do you call it?"
    "I don't know."

"There is life and there is death. Life is better than death but there are worse things than death."

"What?"

"*There is no word for it*. . . . What is the word for a state which is not life and not death, a death in life?"

"I don't know." *Where* is the word, the girl in the greenhouse would say, and look around. (126) (Italics mine)

Where is the word, Allie would say. With her incarnational sense, she seeks to locate the word in the world. And as Will thinks of her here in relation to his father's question, sunlight streams through the convalescent home window. But he misses the revealing conjunction of signs here. He remains stuck with his father's despair and Jack Curl's prattled clichés about a "love and faith" community.

"There is no name for this" death-in-life existence, Will's father argued. To him, such quotidian existence is literally unspeakable and unformulable by signs; hence it is meaningless and answerable only by the ultimate silence of suicide. Will is strongly attracted to this fatalism, as he fondles the German Luger and the Greener shotgun inherited from his father. Yet he also struggles against this fatal legacy, hoping to *name* the source of the death in life truthfully and thus render it meaningful. He has an intuitive faith in the salvific power of language to discover meaning. As Tom More said, following Aquinas, the end of man is to know. For all his father's influence, Will resists his fatalism by naming his father's romantic fascination with Nazism, stoicism, and heroic death in a loveless world. His father admired the German colonel from whom he took the Luger, admired Marcus Flavinius and the whole cult of war and conquest, yet never mentioned Buchenwald or the Holocaust, the truly unspeakable events. But Will now asks: "what if there is another way? Maybe that was your mistake, that you didn't even look. . . . You loved only death because for you what passed for life was really a death-in-life, which has no name and so is worse than death" (132–33). Unlike his father, Will chooses instead to become a searcher for meaning, a Peircean open-minded reader of signs that may lead to some hierophany or gift of the word: "I shall put the question—as a matter of form—and I shall require an answer . . . the question can be put in such a way that an answer is required. It will be stipulated, moreover, that a non-answer, silence, shall be construed to mean no" (138).

Believing that he has found the secret of his father's fatalism and found a way to overcome it by questioning God directly, Will is nonetheless still perplexed by the hunting episode. Only while examining the Greener shotgun does he discover the truth that his father intended to murder him and then commit suicide. But still he wonders whether his father pulled up at the last second out of love or failure of love. The answer seems to lie in Will's cold recognition that his father's love of death—the Freudian equation of erotic desire and death—was the only answer he found to despair. Will analyzes the near murder:

> Both barrels. Wouldn't one have been enough? Yes, given an ordinary need for death. But not if it's a love of death. In the case of love, more is better than less, two twice as good as one, and most is best of all. And if the aim is the ecstasy of love, two is closer to infinity than one, especially when the two are twelve-gauge Super-X number-eight shot. And what samurai self-love of death, let alone the little death of everyday fuck-you love, can match the double Winchester come of taking oneself into oneself, the cold-steel extension of oneself into mouth, yes, for you, for me, for us, the logical and ultimate act of fuck-you love fuck-off world, the penetration and union of perfect cold gunmetal into warm quailing mortal flesh, the coming to end all coming, brain cells which together faltered and fell short, now flowered and flew apart, flung like stars around the whole dark world. (148–49)

Sex, death, hate, anger, and destruction conjoin in the language and vitriolic tone of Will's thought, revealing a despair and rage equal to his father's. His "naming" is ferocious, analytical, and apocalyptic, reminiscent of Lance Lamar. As in Lance's case, the tone reveals in Will an unrecognized split between the detached, abstractive man who will mount an intellectual challenge to God, and the enfleshed man who equates sexual desire with death. Will's denunciatory litany here stands in stark opposition to the melding, conciliatory words Allie uses later, when erotic desire is transmuted into love. So after condemning the various forms of "belief" and unbelief he sees around him, Will concludes that his father's suicide may well have been justified. But Will's thought of release through death evokes a new triad of signs in his consciousness. Recalling the "triangular patch" where once he wished to make love to Ethel Rosenblum, and which Percy associated with the Pauline ideal of community, he thinks, "It was the very sort of place, a non-descript weedy triangular public pubic sort of place, to make a sort of love or to die a sort of death" (162). Thus he surmises that his father was right when he questioned: "that these two things alone are real, loving and dying, and since one is so much like the other and there is so little of the one, in the end there remained only the other?" Faced with silence, Will concludes, "Very well, old mole, you win" (162).

Will's deep anger, first revealed by Allie's question "Are you still climbing on your anger?" and here disclosed in his diatribe on his father's suicide, is double edged. On the one hand, it shows Will that he is indeed his father's son. Furious at his insolent servant Yamaichi, he thinks: "I could have killed him. . . . My father could have too: he could have as easily have shot the guide as he shot the dog" (171). But Will also questions the source of such anger. When his father's voice insists "*You're one of us,*" Will agrees, but asks: "Where does such rage come from? from the discovery that in the end the world yields only to violence, that only the violent bear it away, that short of violence all is in the end impotence?" (171). Will's anger leads him to direct the question to the divine father, God, and to challenge Him to respond. Consequently, like Lance Lamar in his attack on God as the creator of human sexuality, Will's real target is a God who lives in impenetrable mystery. Will is tormented by the incomprehensibility of life, the inability to extract clear meaning from a hidden God whose signs are indirect and mysterious. Through Will, Percy here measures the "gap" or semiotic breakdown between the modern searcher and some verifiable signs of God's presence in a culture where sacred signs and sacraments have been largely devalued.

Behind Will's challenge to make God reveal Himself, as we see, is his belief that his father's suicide was meaningless. His death, the narrator explains, "availed nothing, proved nothing, solved nothing, posed no questions let alone answered questions, did nobody good." Will vows not to waste his own death but rather convert "a necessary evil into an ingenious good" (182–83). His plan is a product of his "coldness" and abstraction, an attempt to know the meaning of life without suffering it. His descent into Lost Cove cave will, he believes, resolve the question of God in a way superior to Pascal's famous wager by providing incontrovertible proof, either by forcing God to reveal Himself or by death.

Will explains his plan in a long letter to Dr. Sutter Vaught, enlisting his help to verify his scheme in the event of his death. While the narrator condemns Will's plan as "Madness! Madness! Madness!" the truth is more complex. On one level Percy offers Will's plan as a challenge to the spiritual fecklessness of the times. Like all of Percy's serious searchers, Will acts to find a personal answer to his spiritual dilemmas, to break his "lifelong dependence on this or that person, like my father or yourself" (187). He wishes to act freely in

light of "a growing disgust with two classes of people," hypocritical Christians
and fatuous unbelievers. He classes both groups as "maniacs"—the Christians
because they live contrary to the good news they proclaim, the unbelievers because they refuse to confront basic questions about existence. Against both of
these groups Will poses a third way: to become a searcher for meaning, like
Binx Bolling. As for Pascal's way of fideistic acceptance of God's hiddenness,
Will finds it "frivolous." Instead of blind faith, Will plans to perform a "scientific experiment" with his life to solve the mystery of God once and for all: "My
experiment is simply this: I shall go to a desert place and wait for God to give
a sign. If no sign is forthcoming I shall die. But people will know why I died:
because there is no sign. The cause of my death will be either his nonexistence
or his refusal to manifest himself, which comes to the same thing as far as we
are concerned" (193). Determined to coerce a sign from God, Will mistakenly
compares himself to Jacob (who did not receive a *direct* sign from God). Will's
plan would reduce divine mystery to objective, empirical proof, a "method"
that owes more to Descartes than to Pascal. Abstract and "logical," it leaves
out the historical fact of the Incarnation and the sacraments, since for Will
the signs of Christ in his culture have been co-opted or emptied of meaning.
Yet granted the legitimacy of his search for meaning, in his plan to solve the
question of God "for all mankind" Will imputes to himself a power of knowledge and action that rivals God. His hubris is like Tom More's grandiose plan
to heal mankind with his lapsometer. Nevertheless, his willingness to ask the
essential question, demand a response, and stake his life on the answer denote
a "sanity" and seriousness that commend Will's desire for truth.

Will's descent into Lost Cove cave becomes a strange semiotic journey,
rendered brilliantly by Percy through an elaborate web of interrelated signs
that reveal the mystery of his predicament. Drugged by Placidyl, Will searches
through a mindscape of personal memories, delusions, imaginary scenes, and
imagined colloquies. Though Will's journey is interior, Peirce's full, *real* world
of sign relations shape and inform his progress. Presented in the narrative as
discreet and disconnected fragments, these signs interact triadically to reveal
the inner core of Will's life. He recalls key scenes with his father: the hunting
episode, a fateful trip to Hollywood, his father's odd happiness during World
War I. Scenes of his life with Marion are intertwined: their marriage, returning
from her funeral with his daughter, Leslie; imaginary scenes such as a meeting
with John Ehrlichman and with Confederate soldiers hiding in the cave during
the war. Recurrent signs abound as leitmotiv: war, suicide, failed love, death,

lack of place, and the defrauded, role-playing self. But no direct signs of God appear. Instead, Percy focuses the mystery of Will's search on the multivalent sign of a tiger. On one level, the tiger is nature's primordial beast, which retreated to the cave thirty-two thousand years ago to die. To Will the tiger also portends the great beast of the Apocalypse, unleashed as God's wrath on the Last Day. But the tiger also suggests divine power incarnate in the mystery of Christ the redeemer, like the tigers in Blake's "Songs of Innocence" and T. S. Eliot's "Gerontion."

Will encounters this beast at the nadir of his journey when the sign of the tiger is enfolded within the mystery of his attempt to interpret signs that *may* be hierophanies within the ordinary. At first, the tiger that Will "sees" is ordinary and mortal, with "nothing bright or fearful or symmetrical about him. His eyes were lackluster and did not burn" (221). A "commonplace" animal, he has come to the cave to die, nature's end. Yet in Will's delusion the tiger becomes an ironic double of himself. He imputes self-awareness to the tiger; his eyes are "careworn and self-conscious." He questions the animal: "Haven't you troubled yourself and fretted needlessly over the years? Did you ever really know your times and seasons? What a mystery that you should have come here without knowing! Were you ever really a splendid tiger burning in the forests of the night?" (222). Will's questions, really self-questions, emphasize the decay and death of natural man/beast, death without a final "knowing." But as he explores the beast's hide, signs of a mysterious transformation emerge in his mind. Will feels that "the skin has loosened in preparation for the molt." Strict logic foils him, but like his earlier apprehension of the "extraness" in the iron horsehead in *The Last Gentleman,* he senses that something *more* than natural decay is present: "Molt? Tigers don't molt. Be logical. It can be figured out. Very well. *Whatever is alive here is more than a dying tiger.* Yet it is not a tiger giving birth or a tiger molting and being transformed like a cicada. *It is the same tiger but different*" (222) (italics mine). Is Will's sense of what may be happening simply a delusion, a result of his drugged state? Or is it a sign of the "something more" in reality, the inscape or "extraness" of spirit incarnate in matter, like the iron horsehead? The sign is unclear, and Will does not pursue his intimations of the "something alive here" in the mysterious tiger. Instead, he dismisses it as a "joke," projects his own anxieties onto the tiger double, and smugly forfends mystery: "The joke was that for the first time in the history of the universe it was the man who knew who he was, who was as snug as a bug in his rock cocoon, and the beast who did not, who was fretful, unsure of himself and the future, unsure what he was doing here. The tiger asked: Is this the place for me? Will I be happy here? Will the others like me? Will my death be a growth experience?

"But how can you be dead and grow? Dead is dead" (222). Like his father, Will dismisses the possibility of mystery in the sign of the tiger, though the question "how can you be dead and grow?" suggests the possibility of the transfiguration of the body. Bent on coercing some stupendous, unequivocal revelation, he misses the inscape of the ordinary. "Tiger or no tiger, he thought, it's all the same. The experiment continues. That was no sign" (222).

But the experiment is disrupted by an ordinary toothache that causes a "lightning" flash of pain in his body. The "lightning" foreshadows the lightning flash later during a key epiphany with Allie in the greenhouse. Here, the pain is a direct, visceral sign that returns Will to his senses in the present, leading him to choose life. Percy's subtle narrative deliberately occludes the meaning of the sign in mystery. The narrator simply says: "A clear yes or no answer may not be forthcoming, after all. The answer may be a muddy maybe. . . . Whether it was God's doing or ordinary mortal frailty, one cannot be sure" √ (213). Yet the toothache destroys Will's presumptuous challenge to God. Deep in the cave and wracked with pain, he becomes "sober" and "disinterested," makes the choice to live, and begins his ascent back to the world of sunlight. After falling into the greenhouse, and now being nursed by Allie with water and oatmeal, Will warms himself by the iron stove, where a "fire burned behind amber mica bright as tigers' eyes" (228).

Before Will comes crashing into the greenhouse, Allie "had begun to slip a little" (236). Having demonstrated her own self-sufficiency—moving the stove and making the greenhouse into a home—Allie still suffers loneliness, especially in the late afternoons, a "longens" time that "ensues in a longing if not an unbelonging" (238). Like other Percy characters, Allie's burden is the consciousness of time itself, as when Lance Lamar experienced the present as a "tapehead" between past and future. The word "longing" itself denotes unfulfilled time and inchoate desire. One way Allie deals with the "longens of clock time" is to withdraw into "her dog star Sirius serious self," into solitary subjectivity. But such retreat is destructively solipsistic. Her anvil-headed stray dog, a gifted presence, "does not like her there." He whines until she gets up and begins her nightly ritual, lights a candle, and starts to read. Reading itself, contact with the word, brings her into community (as Percy argued in "The Man on the Train"), and in The Trail of the Lonesome Pine she finds a clue to the path she must follow. In that story, she reads, Hale and June meet at the schoolhouse gate for their first walk in the woods together, hand in hand. Hale points to some boys playing marbles. " 'That's the first sign,' he said, and with quick understanding June smiled" (238). For Allie, the sign in the story is of serendipitous relation, of the need for shared love and understanding with another, a *solitude à deux*. Making a home and life alone for herself will not satisfy Allie's human longings; she discovers that "late afternoon needs another person" (239).

Allie's loneliness leads her to consider the meaning of sexuality and love. Sexually experienced from her life with ex-lover Sarge, she knows when she was "doing it" with him "it did not seem to be the secret of life" (239). Allie wishes to inhabit the mystery of love in sexual union, the mystery of word in deed. In Allie's physical/spiritual longing Percy again echoes the theme of the incommensurability of spirit in matter that so baffled and enraged Lance Lamar. Allie has already learned that mechanical sexual intercourse is no answer to the self's longing for communion. Thus she is puzzled by various definitions of love offered by "great writers," wondering, "What does all that *mean?* These people are crazier than I am!" (241). None can explain the connection between "being in love" and "doing it," the mysterious copula linking the physical and metaphysical dimensions of sexual union. Allie realizes that a home or true "place" means communion with another, but her experience with Sarge and her family has been a loveless denigration of self. Allie must find another person in the world who is compatible with her serious/Sirius self. Through his carefully woven web of signs—God=Sirius/serious, the "extraness" of the tiger, the "secret of life"—Percy suggests that a triadic relation with another, with the divine spirit as source, will initiate a second coming for Will and Allie to recover their lives together.

Such a second coming for both also entails grounding their lives in the human community in love and charity, the incarnational move into a wider range of relations beyond a *solitude à deux*. Will's descent into the underworld cave brought him enough self-knowledge to choose life over death. His challenge to God produced ambiguous signs, not clear answers. While being nursed back to health, he tells Allie he descended into the cave to "get out of himself," that he did not find the tiger ("the tiger wasn't there"), but that "there was more than the tiger." When she asks if he found an answer to his yes-or-no question to God, Will says "yes," but when asked what it was, he replies, "I don't know" (246). Still, he does know what he must do, and he is prepared to act. Percy suggests that part of the revelation he received in the cave was a discovery of his own "cold" detachment from life, dating from the hunting episode. Will now believes he must love and care for others and act on their behalf (262). He begins to move toward living and acting in the ordinary world, rejecting both isolation and the "heroic" catastrophic death his father chose. Likewise, Allie comes to see that she need not "do something extraordinary, be somebody extraordinary," but that "the trick lay in leading the most ordinary life imaginable . . . in itself a joy in its very ordinariness" (247).

As she helps Will recover, Allie slowly begins to realize her love and need for him, finding a happiness that appeases her immediate "longens." Percy conveys this through a tightly woven web of signs in an extraordinary love scene. When Will disappears and she finds him fallen on the path, Allie hoists him back to the greenhouse and warms him with her own body "as if he were her cold dead planet and she his sun's warmth" (256). Nestling with Will, she wonders if this is "it" and whether she will "for the first time in my life get away from my everlasting self sick of itself to be with another self and is that what *it* is and if not then what?" (257). The "it," of course, is the love Allie is discovering, but Percy makes clear that it is human love transfigured by divine grace. Their love becomes a mysterious union of word and deed, one that heals the Cartesian split that has afflicted Percy's characters throughout his novels. Allie imagines the self-discovery as analogous to approaching the ocean. Percy's oceanic image, here a positive sign that is antithetical to the closed inwardness of closet and cave, suggests freedom, power, and openness. When Will says there is "something you need to know," Allie thinks:

> What I need to know and think I know is, is loving you the secret, the be-all not end-all but starting point of my very life, or is it just one of the things creatures do like eating and drinking and therefore nothing to dream about? Is love a filling of the four o'clock gap or is it more? Either way would be okay but I need to know and think I know. It might be the secret because a minute ago when you held me and I came against you, there were signs of coming close, to *it,* for the first time, like the signs you recognize when you are getting near the ocean for the first time. Even though you've never seen the ocean before, you recognize it, the sense of an opening out ahead . . . a quality of sound, a penultimate hush marking the beginning of the end of land and the beginning of the old uproar and the going away of the endless sea. (258–59)

Words are at the center of their loving relation, a coming together in which the word *is* act, the incarnate mystery at the heart of their *solitude à deux.* Lying together, their bodies make a "diamond," a triadic analogue to Allie's earlier diamond-hard-dog-star=God, a sign repeated in Will's subsequent epiphany. He tries to explain to her what he learned in the cave and what he plans to do: "When he began to talk she found that she could not hear his words for listening to the way he said them. She cast about for his drift. Was he saying the words for the words themselves, for what they meant, or for what they could do to her? There was something about the way he talked that reminded her of her own rehearsed sentences. Was she a jury he was addressing? *Though he hardly touched her, his words seemed to flow across all parts of her body.* Were they meant to? A pleasure she had never known before bloomed deep in her body. Was this a way of making love?" (262) (italics mine). Will tries to explain to her what he "learned in the cave," how his life had been "phony" and that now he sees "this gift of yours and mine . . . by God? by her? (!!!!!)," while Allie is attuned to the message of his love being communicated through and beyond his spoken words, harmonizing their being like Allie's music, the Schubert Trout Quintet.

That their *solitude à deux* is infused with divine presence is underscored by Percy's hierophanic signs. When Will asks what happened to her "sister Val," Allie says that Val now teaches in a school in *Pass Christian* run by "*Little Eucharistic Sisters of St. Dominic*" (262) (italics mine). Lightning flashes overhead. Suddenly, as they exult over the name of the religious order, and Allie recalls Val's healing visit to her in the sanitarium, she has a stunning revelation:

> "The good is all over me, starting with my back. Now I understand how the two work together."
> "What two?"
> "*The it and the doing, the noun and the verb, sweet sweet love and a putting it to you, loving and hating, you and I.*" (263) (Italics mine)

In the signified eucharistic context Allie intuits the union of word and act at the core of love as the "secret" of human fulfillment of the self, an analogue of incarnated divine love.

Lightning crackles around the greenhouse, so that it "was like living inside a diamond. . . . A ball of light rolled toward them down the center aisle of the greenhouse as lazily as a ball of yarn . . . '*Jesus Christ*,' she said." As Will holds her close, Allie feels the true center of her life: "Ha, she said to herself, maybe he didn't find what he was looking for but I did. Ha. Maybe I'm nuts and he's not but I know now what I want. . . . I am in love. Ah ha, so this is what it is, this 'being in love.' This is what I want. This him. Him. . . .

"Lightning struck again. The glass house glittered like a diamond trapping light. *Jesus, she thought,* doesn't he know we could get killed? But he was humming a tune—the Trout?—and keeping time with his fingers on her shoulder" (264–65) (italics mine).

Allie's discovery of the mysterious coupling of the "it" and the "doing" in her love with Will echoes Helen Keller's discovery of triadic meaning in her well-house experience. Allie discovers the *relation* between being and doing, matter and spirit. In effect, she discovers the mystery of love that is the heart of the Incarnation, the triad of being-doing-saying made flesh through the mysterious action of the "coupler," the Holy Spirit. Will and Allie's human love is a sign of enfleshed divine love. Hence Percy could legitimately claim that the novel overcame alienation *through* a recovery of Christianity, through the sign. For his part, Will confirms the new direction of his life—he will "do what is expected of me. Take care of people who need taking care of," a commitment to community like Binx's dedication to helping others along in their journey at the end of *The Moviegoer.*

But Will's discovery of his new life and his resolve to act is threatened unless he confronts and *names* the force of death that has ruled his life since the fateful hunting trip. On a subsequent trip West with his father, Will realized that "they couldn't be pals" (270). But his reaction then was to distance himself coldly from the world. Only through the crisis in the cave and his new relation to Allie is he able to realize fully his deathly condition. His father felt the death in life of the age but was reduced to silence, impotence, and despair, declaring, "there is no name for this." But Will becomes a true namer who affirms the human power to *know* and define being. His stunning epiphany comes in the parking lot of the country club immediately following his interlude with Allie in the "diamond" greenhouse where they were surrounded by crackling lightning: "Ha, there is a secret after all, he said. But to know the secret answer, you must first know the secret question. The question is, who is the enemy? Not to know the name of the enemy is already to have been killed by him. *Ha,* he said, dancing, snapping his fingers and laughing and hooting, *ha hoo he,* jumping up and down and socking himself, *but I do know. I know. I know the name of the enemy.* The name of the enemy is death, he said, grinning and shoving his hands in his pockets. Not the death of dying but the living death" (271). Will then identifies the enemy as the "father of lies . . . the devil himself," over whom he now triumphs because "I know all your names" (272). Percy's echoing of signs here looks backward to Father Rinaldo Smith's naming the "principalities and powers" as the enemy of the "good news" in *Love in the Ruins,* and forward to the priest's (and Percy's) naming of Satan as the demonic archenemy of Christianity in history in *The Thanatos Syndrome*. Will names the "devil himself" as the source of the devaluation of the sign; that is, the undermining of the ultimate triad of meaning between God's word and man that is concretized in the "coupler" of the Incarnation. And against the "powers and principalities" of deceit stands the human power to know and to name truly. In an action analogous to that of Christ when he named Satan, Will exercises the power of the word to name truth. Against the two alternatives of life in death (war) and death in life (peace), he poses "a third thing—love," a delta of being here identified with "love of truth" (272). Intoning a long litany of the various forms of death in this century, Will declares, "it will not prevail over me because I know the names of death. . . . It is a matter of knowing and choosing. To know the many names of death is also to know there is life. I choose life. . . . Death in the form of death genes shall not prevail over me, for death genes are one thing but it is something else to name the death genes and know them and stand over against them and dare them" (274). Affirming himself as a "truth seeker," Will categorically rejects his father and the culture of death.

Percy underscores the theosemiotic significance of Will's breakthrough in consciousness by the mysterious revelation he receives as he rests in the backseat of his Mercedes. In this epiphany, signs that encapsulate his past and point the direction of his future interact triadically within his mind as *present* realities—"All at once he knew what had happened and was going to happen" (275). First of all, Will finds himself in a "desert place," echoing the triangular patch of weeds where he longed for Ellen Rosenblum, as well as the desert of the West he crossed, full of teenage longing, with his father. Then the desert becomes a "real place," the springhouse where he retreated after his father's suicide. The springhouse, of course, suggests the well-house where Helen Keller discovered the mysterious "delta factor"—the triad of naming, knowing, and "saying" truth that signified her breakthrough into language and human identity. But in Will's case, at age twelve, no breakthrough occurred. Instead, he "coldly" and cunningly retreated into silence before the world, acting only to please others.

Will was discovered in the springhouse by D'lo, the Negro cook, who grieved over him but was also angry at his withdrawal from her. "You poor little old boy, you all alone in the world. Your mama dead, your daddy dead, and ain't nobody left in the house but you and me" (275). Will rejected her attempts to console him, already withdrawn into the "cold" center from which he will act for forty years. "He knew how to please people, even black people.

He was everybody's nigger. He was even the niggers' nigger" (276). D'lo intuited both the boy's need and his refusal: "You poor little old boy, you don't
know nothing. You don't even know what you need to know. You don't even
know enough to know what you ain't got" (276). But Will has already elected
to become the abstracted Cartesian and stoic son of his father. It takes nearly a
lifetime of fraudulent "pleasing others" before he can recognize and name it.

The "spot" or place Will sees in his mind next becomes a "patch of grass" in
a bunker at the country club, which then evolves into a subdivision, a "spot"
that now is the weedy corner of a lot where a house was built for Sam Gold,
a Jew. The place or spot, of course, again recalls the weedy triangle of Will's
passion for the Jewess Ethel Rosenblum, a sign of his "missed" life. Now he
wonders: "Though Sam Gold was a Jew, places meant nothing to him. One
place, even Jerusalem, was like any other place. Why did he, Will Barrett, who
was not a Jew, miss the Jerusalem he had never had and which meant nothing
to Sam Gold, who was a Jew?" (276). Percy's intricate web of signs—Jewishness
(Ethel/Sam), place (Jerusalem), Will's longing (now for the definitive place
of Jewish-Christianity)—suggests that these links in consciousness reveal his
deepest need for connection to the ultimate source of naming and knowing, the God of Israel and the incarnate Word. All "places"—weedy triangle,
bunker, subdivision lot, Jerusalem—become one under the sign of the God
who entered time and place to transfigure the ordinary world with signs that
point to the mystical. Thus the "spot" is transformed again into an anticipa-
tory sign of Will's longing for God, for some revelation of the ultimate loving
father and source of being. The subdivision becomes a shopping center for
twenty years, but now "it was deserted." Projecting ahead to a time and place
where he "came to," Will finds himself "lying on the spot amidst the ruins of
civilization," but with signs of renewal—grass sprouts and water runs. He is
not alone: "something moved and someone spoke. Maybe it was D'lo. No.

"Was it Allie? No, nobody. *No, somebody was there all right.* Someone spoke:
Very well, since you've insisted on it, here it is, the green-stick Rosebud gold-
bug matador, the great distinguished thing.

"The ocean was not far away.

"As he turned to see who said it and who it was, *there was a flash of light
then darkness then light again*" (277) (italics mine). The confluence of these
portentous signs is the only answer Will receives from his challenge to God
to reveal Himself. In the allusions to *Citizen Kane*, Poe, Hemingway, James,
and Tolstoy, Percy suggests the longing of the searcher for the treasured life, as
well as the path to death that Will finally rejects.[4] This inner semiotic journey

ends with allusions to the ocean and flashes of light/lightning, recalling Allie's discovery of her "very life" and her intuition of coming close to "it" (love) as being like "getting near the ocean." As well, the flash of light echoes the play of hierophanic lightning (and Allie's cry, "Jesus Christ") in the diamond-like glass greenhouse when Will and Allie confirm their love.

Even though Will and Allie find the true center of themselves and a *solitude à deux* in the greenhouse, under signs of the ultimate gift giver, the formidable challenge remains for them to find a life together *in the world*, not in isolation. How can they preserve their sense of recovered identity through being in love in the face of the numbing, manipulative society around them? How can they exercise their new power of freedom for the good of others? How can the *solitude à deux* expand outward into meaningful action in the larger community? What threatens is the fact that, as maimed creatures, they are both susceptible to relapse when not with each other, Will because of his neurological disorder, and Allie because of her pull toward inwardness and isolation.

The challenge is posed immediately by those "closest" to Will and Allie, those who would manipulate them for their own ends. Having jettisoned her dentist husband, Kitty Huger attempts to rekindle the flame of lust with Will and insinuate herself into his vast fortune. She continues to scheme to commit Allie permanently to the sanitarium and gain legal control of her inheritance. A fatuous believer in popular notions of reincarnation, Kitty argues that Allie is "not of this world," is "disembodied" from the present because she was a courtesan in a previous life, a Union spy during the war. (Percy's spoof of reincarnation here has serious implications. Kitty's belief in the myth of "the Return" signifies that gnostic, mythic view of reality promoted by Joseph Campbell and others, a view that tries to categorize all behavior and cultural signs and implicitly denies the historical uniqueness of Christ's Incarnation. As we see later, Percy critiques this vision more fully in *The Thanatos Syndrome* in his analysis of Nazism as a myth.) At the same time, Will's daughter, Leslie; her husband, Jason; and Father Jack Curl plot to gain control of his inheritance, the Peabody fortune, in order to build "love and faith" communities worldwide. Leslie also contrives to shuffle off Will permanently to St. Mark's home, while his golf friend Bertie plans his future on the senior circuit golf tour.

To compound his difficulties, Will has begun to "slip," both literally and figuratively. When he returns home to find it stripped of his personal belongings, he falls down in the bedroom, weak and disoriented. The room holds an ominous emptiness, a sense of "someone present or someone absent" (288).

The light that earlier signified Allie and hierophany now seems to have emptied of significance: "Above him the bar of sunlight stretched out straight as a plank. Motes drifted aimlessly in and out of the light. The bar of sunlight seemed significant. He sat up and shook his head. No, things do not have significances. The lazer beam was nothing more than light reflected from motes he had stirred up. It was not 'stark.' One place is like any other place" (288). Will's lapse here is one of vision; he views the light as an objectivist would, not as a triadic sign of spiritual reality. So also, *this* place—the axis point of potential revelation—is categorized in his mind as without uniqueness, just like "any other place." In the closet, an echo of Allie's closet retreat, Will finds the new trappings of identity—cardigan sweater and loafers, pipe and Bible— Leslie has prepared for his future role as "an agreeable youngish old man, like young Dr. Marcus Welby" (289). Recognizing the death in life signified by these trappings, Will rebels from such a role, but initially in favor of the death option proffered by his father. Boarding a bus for Georgia, he plans to return to the definitive place of his youth and confront his life once and for all. The "third way" of love with Allie he discovered earlier seems forgotten, as Will becomes an "other" dissociated from his true self:

> The other was going back to Georgia to find something he had left there, to find a place where something had happened to him. Or rather hadn't happened to him. All these years he had thought he was in luck that it didn't happen and that he had escaped with his life and a triumphant life at that. But it was something else he had escaped with, not his life.
>
> His life—or was it his death?—he had left behind in the Thomasville swamps, where it still waited for him. With a kind of sweet certainty he knew now that it was there that he would find it. Finding the post oak—he knew he could walk straight to it—*and not coming out of the swamp at all* was better than thrashing around these pretty mountains, playing in Scotch foursomes, crawling into caves, calling on God, Jews, and tigers. No, it was in Georgia that he would find it. And it was in Georgia that he would do it. (296–97) (Italics mine)

Bent on committing suicide, Will is saved by a gift—an evocative sign of Allie—when he sees "a single gold poplar which caught the sun like a yellow-haired girl coming out of a dark forest," the same triad of sunlight, girl, and tree that caught his eye when he first met her near the golf course. "Once again his heart was flooded with sweetness but a sweetness of a different sort, a sharp sweet urgency, a need to act, to run and catch. He was losing something. Something of his as solid and heavy and sweet as a pot of honey in his lap was being taken away" (297). Gifted with this sign, Will reverses himself, choosing life over death and future over past, now determined that "it's not going to end like this or in a Georgia swamp either because I won't stand for it and don't have to" (298). But when he is found wandering, and then hospitalized with what is diagnosed as a form of temporal lobe epilepsy, others take control of his life again so that he feels his "life was out of his hands," and he is returned to St. Mark's home.

The ending of *The Second Coming* has sparked considerable critical reaction, especially regarding Percy's literary intentions and execution. John Edward Hardy has raised questions about Will Barrett's relation to the Episcopalian Father Weatherbee as the priestly authority in his new life (220–24). Other critics have expressed uneasiness about the serendipitous ending, particularly the romance of Will and Allie and what is seen as Will's (and Percy's) manipulation of Allie to serve the ends of solving his alienation.[5] More broadly, dissatisfaction has been expressed over Percy's neat "tying up" of the complex thematic strands of the novel.

Although Percy's resolution of the theme of alienation is seemingly serendipitous, the ending of the novel is realistic in the deepest sense of the term. That is, what characterizes the language and action is several elements: a semiotic realism that opens the concrete signs to the *possibility* of divine presence and action in the immediate world (i.e., a theosemiotic perspective); the truth of mystery encoded in those signs; and the heightening of Will's consciousness of his existence within that real world of mysterious signs and his new will to act in it with freedom and hope. As I shall argue, Percy's unending "ending" is a powerful affirmation of the theosemiotic vision. This theosemiotic vision is the real ground for the community of charity that Will and Allie propose at the end of the novel. The evolution of this vision is meticulously developed by Percy in the denouement of the two wayfarers' journey.

Initially, Percy frames the final union of Will and Allie and their commitment to a new community within a context that shows alternative plans or ways "to live." These plans are manipulated by others; consequently, they are a threat to their freedom. Maneuvered into the convalescent home by Leslie, Will faces a death-in-life existence of passive care, conversation with other patients, and TV watching. Moreover, his medical condition and its symptom—"inappropriate longing"—make him begin to second-guess his desire for Allie. His longing is hardly "inappropriate," but Will does not yet recognize its true goal, union with another in love and with God. Instead, he reluctantly

considers the possible truth of the empirical, "scientific" diagnosis. "Did it all
come down to chemistry after all? Had he fallen down in a bunker, pounded
the sand with his fist in a rage of longing for Ethel Rosenblum because his pH
was 7.6?" (307). His life could now become a tranquil idyll of relaxation, for
if his unappeased desire is only a matter of chemical imbalance, then he can
be managed back to "normalcy" with drugs. As for his undertaking any larger
social role, Leslie and Jack Curl have already planned to use Will's inheritance
to underwrite ecumenical meetings to "reunite Christianity" and build "love
and faith communities" across the world. Such gestures are fruitless without
individual conversion, and Percy's satire seems directed at the American al-
liance of money, proselytizing, and vapid religious clichés (to judge by Jack
Curl) forged to "market" brotherhood and reconciliation. If so, they seem
yet another version of what Tocqueville saw as American boosterism and religious conformity, a target of Percy's satire since *The Moviegoer*. Such schemes
threaten personal freedom, as well as the solitary dimension of the individual's
search for God.

Although seemingly trapped in the convalescent home, Will moves toward
understanding the meaning of his situation by rejecting any simplistic interpretation of his condition and by following the mysterious signs given to him.
When he meets Father Weatherbee, the retired Episcopalian priest whose pas-
sions include toy trains and Apostolic Succession ("it happened"), Will sees
"something in his eyes," perhaps a clue that he "knows" something Will needs
to hear. For John Edward Hardy the issue of Father Weatherbee and apostolic
succession is a contentious one because it makes the validity of the priest's
powers questionable, at least for Percy as a Catholic (22–24). Allen Pridgen,
by contrast, sees the priest as an addled-brained romantic who has retired to
the play world of toy trains and naive myths about the "simple" Mindanoan
natives he once ministered to. Therefore, for Pridgen, he has no good news for
Will to hear (*Walker Percy's Sacramental Landscapes*, 136–38). What does Percy
want us to make of Will's relation to the priest, since it is so crucial to the end
of the novel?

Percy's handling of this relationship is, I believe, consummately realistic
within the semiosis of the novel. In their final meeting, as Father Weatherbee gazes at him with his "bad eye" and his "good eye," Will asks himself:
"Could it be that the Lord is here, masquerading behind this simple silly holy
face?" (360). Will's question points directly to the mystery of Father Weatherbee's presence in Will's life at this time. What characterizes the question as
stated—and left unanswered, so that Will has to interpret and act on it—is the

openness and possibility encoded in the sign. The priest *is* silly and romantic, but he may *also* be the bearer of a sign of divine presence. The mystery of the priest's significance is precisely Percy's point; it is the real sign as clue, and as such it contains both fact and possibility. That is the real condition Will must apprehend and journey through, toward meaning. Percy makes this point again in Will's question when he sees two attendants nonchalantly helping a patient: "Does goodness come tricked out so as fakery and fondness and carrying on and is God himself as sly?" (349). The question is a version of Binx Bolling's musing about being "onto" God. In short, Father Weatherbee is another mysterious sign, like the Negro businessman leaving church on Ash Wednesday, who is there as a possible clue to lead Will along in his search for a new life. Percy uses the "silly" priest to underscore God's mysterious action in the world, without explicitly linking that action to Catholicism or to the formal sacraments as he had done in earlier novels. In this way, he was able to, semiotically, "make it new" in *The Second Coming*. Thus Percy leaves unresolved whether Will and Allie do marry, whether the priest will perform the ceremony, whether the couple will become members of the church, or whether Father Weatherbee does possess valid priestly powers under apostolic succession. What is crucial for Will is that, for him, the priest is a believable sign pointing him toward what he needs to know, what he deeply wants (Allie and God), and what he needs to do.

Once he understands how he has been manipulated by others into the cozy world of St. Mark's, Will rebels against such deathly accommodation. His decisive recognition of this new predicament occurs while he is watching *King Solomon's Mines*, a movie about a search for treasure in a "remote unexplored country." Will recalls how he believed he had escaped his father's despair by accommodating his life to others. Now he sees his mistake:

> I thought he missed me and he did, almost, and I thought I survived and I did, almost. But now I have learned something and been surprised by it after all. Learned what? That he didn't miss me after all, that I thought I survived and I did but I've been dead of something ever since and didn't know it until now. What a surprise. . . .
>
> He killed me then and I did not know it. I even thought he had missed me. I have been living, yes, but it is a living death because I knew he wanted me dead. Am I entitled to live? Ah, but there is a difference between feeling dead and *not knowing it*, and feeling dead and *knowing it*. *Knowing it* means there is a *possibility* of feeling alive though dead. (324) (Italics mine)

Knowing the full truth of the past, Will now turns to his future. Rejecting suicide, he thinks, "I can shuffle off among friends and in comfort and Episcopal decorum and with good Christian folk to look after every need" (325). But abruptly, after what is a clear recognition of the truth of his situation, Will decides to leave the convalescent home and to plan his own life freely. Watching the search-for-treasure movie, he "stood for a moment gazing at a tarantula in Deborah Kerr's tent. Was there a whole world of meaning, of talking and listening, which took place everywhere and all the time and which no one paid attention to, at least not he?" (325). Will becomes Peirce's triadic reader of signs. Crossing the golf course, he kicks down the rotted fence-post boundary, sign of his past, and returns to Allie and the greenhouse. Declaring their mutual love *and* need, a need entirely "apart from the needs of society and the family as a unit, or the group," Will and Allie enter "a new and happy land" (327–28).

In the idyllic union of Will and Allie, Percy stresses their sexual, semiotic, and spiritual harmony. Each attends lovingly to the other's body, having discovered the "it" (spirit) that unites the "doing" and the "being." This incarnated triadic harmony of word, flesh, and spirit overcomes Lance Lamar's Cartesian view of flesh and desire as God's perverse "trick" on humanity. Human love, here apotheosized in their union of flesh, becomes the earthly sign of the divine love that is the ultimate goal of the heart's desire for community. Moreover, their needs are complementarily joined. As Will says, "I need you for hoisting and you need me for interpretation" (329). Allie's strange words that "mean more than other people's" resonate in Will's deepest self, since they are purified of the "dead" language he has listened to most of his life. United with Allie in love and word, he is finally able to silence the determining voice of his father when he again beckons him to suicide: "Come, what else is there?

"Go like a man, for Christ's sake, a Roman, here's your sword . . . get up and go out to the car and get it and go to the empty corner of grass and fence where nobody's been. We like desert places" (337). But Will resists his father's satanic temptation to the desert of suicide. Strengthened by his love for Allie, he throws the Greener shotgun and the Luger into the gorge. His focus now is on the future, on a new life with Allie, and on acting constructively in the community.

Percy's resolution of the alienation that beset Will and Allie is thus realistic and open ended. Both are wounded creatures, but both know their "fall" has not been irretrievably determined by biology or history, as Will's father tried to convince him. Allie says, "Our lapses are not due to synapses" (329). Percy emphasizes their new freedom to act in hope, in unison, and in the concrete world at hand to shape a better future. Percy's corporate sign at the end of the novel is the community of charity, based on its citizens' personal talents, needs, failings, and capacities for renewal. Will plans to resume a career in law as a clerk and to use the talents of retirees Arnold, Ryan, and Eberhart to build a new retirement community; Allie will develop a greenhouse business.

Will's developing religious consciousness at the end of the novel is also set clearly within the context of semiotic realism. Though he claims he is not a "believer"—how could he be, given the "Christian" and agnostic alternatives he sees around him?—he does believe he is "on the track of something" (358). The "something" is his intuition of a divine being who has come into history and transfigured the meaning of all signs. Will's "hunch" is of the real presence of Christ. As he says to Father Weatherbee, "In any event, the historical phenomenon of the Jews cannot be accounted for by historical or sociological theory. Accordingly, they may be said to be in some fashion or other a sign. . . . This goes back to Christ himself, a Jew, a unique historical phenomenon, as unique as the Jews" (357). Although Father Weatherbee may be a "silly holy" man, Will's choice of him, given his present understanding, is carefully discriminated. After acknowledging his unbelief, Will says, "it does not follow that your belief, the belief of the church, is untrue, that in fact it may be true, and if it is, the Jews may be a clue. Doesn't Scripture tell us that salvation comes from the Jews? *At any rate, the Jews are the common denominator between us*" (358) (italics mine). In choosing this priest, Will acts on the faith that the sign of the Jews, and Christ, may *possibly* be the axis of meaning for his life. In this, he explicitly commits himself to the search for the larger mystical community signified in history by Jewish-Christianity and the Incarnation. Having been the recipient of gift-given signs in Allie's love and the diamond-bright sunlight in the greenhouse, he overcomes despair with hope for the new life to come. Will describes himself as a "penitent" to the priest, suggesting that he has come to recognize his cold selfishness to others, and how like Tom More he "feasted" on the despair inherited from his father. Will's penitential attitude is reminiscent of Helen Keller's experience. After her crucial triadic discovery of truth in word at the well-house, Helen Keller returned to the house to find a doll she had broken in pieces. Stricken with sorrow, she repented her willful, destructive earlier life and felt a deep loving relation with the world. Will's new life is one that looks forward in hope as he wonders about the final second coming: "Tell me something, Father. Do you believe that Christ will come again and that in fact there are certain unmistakable signs of his coming in these very times?" (360). Father Weatherbee does not answer directly, but Will intuits a mysterious relation between the old priest, the girl in the greenhouse, and the divine giver of signs who is both here-and-now in the ordinary world and who promised to reveal Himself fully in the second coming: "His heart leapt with a secret joy. What is it I want from her and him, he wondered, not only want but must have? Is she a gift and therefore a sign of a giver? Could it be that the Lord is here, masquerading behind this simple silly holy face? Am I crazy to want both, her and Him? No, not want, must have. And will have" (360).

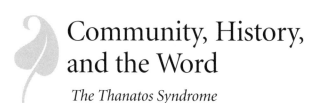

Community, History, and the Word

The Thanatos Syndrome

Near the beginning of chapter 2 of Percy's last novel, *The Thanatos Syndrome*, protagonist Dr. Tom More says: "Small disconnected facts, if you take note of them, have a way of becoming connected. The great American philosopher, Charles Sanders Peirce, said that the most amazing thing about the universe is that apparently disconnected events are in fact not, that one can connect them. Amazing!" (67–68). Later, during his first conversation with More, Father Rinaldo Smith says that words have been deprived of meaning and no longer signify, and that even if matters like the existence of God, heaven, hell, and sin were irrefutably proven, it would "make no difference" because "the words no longer signify" (117–18). These two apparently antithetical statements—one affirming a meaningful relation between events, the second undermining it—are clues to both the central themes and the form of Percy's last novel. In *The Thanatos Syndrome*, Percy examined the triadic relation between community, history, and the Christian Incarnation; that is, the radical connection between present events, their etiology, and history's definitive event: the Incarnation of the divine Logos.

More's first statement affirms Peirce's notion of an invisible web of intelligible sign relations extending throughout history, which for Peirce includes all that *could* possibly be as well as what is or what has actually occurred. In short, the statement points to the community of *real* relations. In the novel, this semiotic web covers a broad expanse of relations that extend from the ancient Hebrews, to Christianity, to the activities of a group of German physicians during the Weimar regime, to Nazism and the Holocaust, and to current events in the Feliciana Parish of the novel. For Percy, these events form an intelligible pattern or continuity of meaning that can be discerned, interpreted, and acted on. At the same time, the second statement by Father Smith points to the condition of semiotic breakdown, a radical disjunction between words and what they are intended to signify. Words have been deprived of meaning, according to the priest, especially their power to relate current and historical events to any meaningful theological, metaphysical, or ethical order. Percy's central character, Tom More, embodies both of these problematic possibilities. He is a representative character of the present age, a victim like most citizens of the culture fractured by the devaluation of language. Yet he is also capable, at least potentially, of interpreting the signs of the times and responding to events as a free and sovereign moral agent. More acts as a Peircean searcher throughout the novel, reading and connecting the disjointed signs in his society in order to fathom the malaise that afflicts it. Through his protagonists More and Father Smith, Percy issues his most bracing and blunt challenge to his readers and to the age. *The Thanatos Syndrome* is his most explicitly prophetic novel.

The devaluation of language and consequent loss of meaning, and the displacement of the self from true being implicit in Father Smith's remark, serve to focus Percy's principal concern: the threat of the spiritual destruction of the individual. For Percy, the power of language and the power of free choice are of the essence of human sovereignty. Both powers are threatened with extermination in Percy's prophetic vision of modern culture in the novel. When asked by Zoltan Abadi-Nagy to name the target of his anger in *The Thanatos Syndrome,* Percy answered: "It is the widespread and ongoing devaluation of human life in the Western world—under various sentimental disguises: 'quality of life,' 'pointless suffering,' 'termination of life without meaning,' etc. I trace it to a certain mind-set in the biological and social sciences which is extraordinarily influential among educated folk—so much so that it has almost achieved the status of a quasi-religious orthodoxy."[1] Masked as free scientific inquiry, this orthodoxy is driven by two hidden dogmas, according to Percy. The first is the denial that humans are absolutely unique because of the capacity for language; that is, the human power to symbolize. The second is the denial that a unique and fatal flaw occurred in human beings as a species, an ontological flaw or "fall" that is distinct from the shaping influences of history and human culture. Percy was careful to distinguish this orthodoxy from what is generally understood as secular humanism. Rather, in its devaluation of life he finds this orthodoxy to be both "anti-human" and nonscientific. It is, in fact, a myth, the myth of scientism that in Percy's view dominates modern Western culture. Under the auspices of this orthodoxy, the individual human self as a sacred, inviolable creature made in the image and likeness of God is threatened with spiritual and actual annihilation.

Centered on the new trials of Dr. Tom More, *The Thanatos Syndrome* is structured to reveal the dialectical struggle between the devaluation of self and word on the one hand, and on the other hand, the hopeful possibilities for discerning events' meanings, for self-knowledge, and for human freedom. Percy appropriated elements of the mystery novel—the search for clues to aberrant or inexplicable behavior and actions—to probe the deeper mystery of the individual's "place" in relation to the weave of history's progressions and regressions. Behind this drama lies the unfathomable mystery of God's agency in human events. Tom More and Father Smith are the focal points of Percy's exploration of these broad concerns, but More's personal difficulties and vulnerabilities threaten to cripple his own power to "connect" the signs and fully relate current events to the theosemiotic center of Percy's parable of history. One way that Percy reveals More's predicament as representative modern man is through the form of the novel itself, structured with many disjointed gaps and fissures, time shifts, and dissociations of mind and memory. Along with Dr. More, the reader must connect the narrative strands and their many signs in Peircean fashion in order to grasp the novel's far-reaching implications, even though More himself may not always comprehend them. Percy's faith in the reader's capacity to interpret the signs, of course, runs counter to Father Smith's claim that words no longer signify. Nonetheless, by focusing the dialectical struggle over meaning through More, Percy was able to dramatize several crucial questions: What constitutes a human being? What is the nature and *telos* of human community? What ethic governs the uses of power, especially political and medical power, to achieve social ends? What relation *now* exists between the direction of human history, divine providence, and the incarnate Logos, particularly if, as Father Smith argues, words and the Word of revelation have been deprived of meaning by a "depriver"? And what hope exists for the "recovery" of the signifying power of language, and thus a recovery of meaning and the possibility of a coherent culture?

Percy's concern with these profound questions reveals a broadening, intensifying, and darkening of vision from his earlier novels. Despite elements of fine comedy (More's servant Hudeen and her daughter Chandra; the regressing of the Belle Ame pedophiles) and beautifully evocative passages (such as More's journey on the river with Vergil Bon and Uncle Hugh Bob), Percy's attention remains riveted on the dire threats to the individual he perceives in modern American society. The social malaise observed earlier by Binx Bolling and Will Barrett has evolved into a general ethos of dehumanization that Percy represents as spread across the century. Although the Blue Boy project turns out to be a quasi-fugitive operation, Fedville's activities are now part of the cultural mainstream, since pedeuthanasia and gereuthanasia have been legally sanctioned by the Supreme Court. The Mr. Ives that Tom More saved in *Love in the Ruins,* and presumably thousands like him, would be helpless against such legal and social forces. Palliative drugs have replaced the crude electroshock that Allison Huger underwent in *The Second Coming,* but the effect is similar (i.e., deprivation of the fully human self). Pharmacopoeia as a way of "engineering" the social order has become the modus vivendi for dealing with "aberrant" behavior or for enhancing human "performance" in idiot-savant fashion. In addition, Percy's earlier sly and suggestive handling of Binx Bolling's and Will Barrett's connection to "the Jews" here becomes an explicit discussion of the meaning of the Jews in history and of the far-reaching theosemiotic significance of the Holocaust as a historical event. What Percy depicted with exuberant comedy in *Love in the Ruins*—a zany, misguided but resilient society—now becomes a community of "zonked out" citizens whose lives are but a "dream" of true being, whether or not they are drugged. The fractured Western technological society that Percy criticized through futuristic satire and science fiction in *Love in the Ruins* has now become the menacing present in *The Thanatos Syndrome.* Given this somber perspective, Percy's "cautionary" tale takes on the urgent tone of a latter-day prophesy.

At times Percy's attempt to synthesize all these weighty matters of vision threatens to sink *The Thanatos Syndrome* as a novel. For all its imaginative inventiveness, in places it shows signs of being too ingeniously plotted and over-manipulated in order to drive home Percy's serious message.[2] Fissures threaten to open up between the complex pattern of interrelated ideas Percy wishes to explore and the dramatic exigencies of specific scenes and actions. Thematic purpose sometimes seems to override fictional plausibility or to be rendered too explicitly, as for example in the characterization of Lucy Lipscomb, or in the convenient "tying up" of subplots and ancillary themes. Transparency of intention sometimes shows through in the pivotal scenes between More and Father Smith. Percy's more pointed strategy was no doubt informed by the depth of his concern and perhaps a growing sense of the need for directness and shock in order to convey his prophetic message about the times to a largely indifferent audience. In this respect his strategy resembles that of Flannery

O'Connor, a writer whose presence looms large throughout *The Thanatos Syndrome*. Yet such weaknesses in the novel are offset by Percy's powerful analysis of the death-wish pathology of the twentieth century, of the spiritual roots of the disorder, and its manifestations in the corruption of language. Moreover, the novel's vigorous defense of the individual's sacred, inviolable uniqueness, of free choice, and its affirmation of a community of charity serve as important thematic counterforces to the threat of human deprivation that Percy saw facing the culture.

Unlike his predecessors Binx Bolling, Will Barrett, and Lance Lamar, Tom More is not a searcher of the great questions of life—the existence of God, evil, the soul, and the meaning of history. The absence of such concerns in More is itself one measure of the deprivations of the age. To him large philosophical or theological questions would ring hollow or sound like academic wordplay in the culture of linguistic deprivation. But More is an ethical man, a beleaguered but skilled psychiatrist-diagnostician who must still try to discern the meaning of events. Most important, he must decide on his personal response to the two opposing visions of the human self and of community that confront him. One vision, represented by qualitarians Drs. Bob Comeaux and John Van Dorn, is the ersatz "humanist" vision of a man-made utopia in which evil and human imperfection will be eliminated through the application of reason and technology. In this vision, humans are looked on as higher organisms in the chain of biological species. Against this stands the Jewish-Christian vision of persons as flawed yet sacred children of God, and the all-inclusive community of charity represented by Father Rinaldo Smith and St. Margaret's hospice. In this latter view a human's truest being is rooted in the mystical community that extends through history into the eternal. A lapsed Catholic, More must finally choose which of these antithetical visions he will serve. These alternatives are the main challenge to his humanity and, for Percy, the main challenge to Western culture near the end of the twentieth century.

By profession More is a man who believes in the power of the word as an instrument for understanding, communication, and self-discovery. But from the opening of the novel More sees signs of deprivation in his patients that portend some deep disorder. As a psychiatrist, he is a self-proclaimed "old-style Freudian analyst" who believes in the therapeutic value of talking and listening, contrary to the new-age neurological technicians who treat pathological symptoms with drugs. More counts himself as one of those who "like our mentor Dr. Freud believes there is a psyche, that it is born to trouble as the sparks fly up, that one gets at it, the root of the trouble, the soul's own secret, by venturing into the heart of darkness, which is to say, by talking and listening, mostly listening, to another troubled human being for month, years—. We have been mostly superseded by brain engineers, neuropharmacologists, chemists of the synapses" (13). More's faith in traditional psychotherapy is grounded as well in the teachings of Dr. Harry Stack Sullivan, the eminent psychiatrist who held that "*Each patient this side of psychosis, and even some psychotics, has the means of obtaining what he needs, she needs, with a little help from you*" (16). More's faith combines Peirce's belief in the human community of triadic sign users with Sullivan's affirmation of the healing power of psychoanalysis, by which an individual can begin to recover a true sense of self. To More, Sullivan's principle is "the pearl of great price, the treasure buried in a field, that is to say, the patient's truest unique self which lies within his, the patient's, power to reach and which we, as little as we do, can help him reach" (16–17). As Percy's use of biblical references here suggests, Sullivan and More's principle affirms the possibility of a form of recovery or redemption, or at least its beginnings, through self-examination with the help of another. Again, this principle is the basis of More's belief that "People can get better, can come to themselves, without chemicals and with a little help from you" (17). Stated differently, and in the manner of St. Augustine's *Confessions*, Percy here transforms the idea of the outward "search" in the world shown in Binx, Will, and Lance into the "search within" adopted by psychiatrist More. St. Augustine searched for relation to God through memory and understanding. On a lesser level, More will follow a similar course in helping his patients to find their truer selves. But as the novel opens, More finds his patients and others, including his wife, Ellen, to be deprived of this unique, self-conscious sense of being.

    More first notices the signs of deprivation in three subjects: patient Mickey LaFaye, his former patient Donna S——, and the black custodian Frank Macon. Each exhibits a "mild fond vacancy" without "the old terrors," a loss of self-awareness, the main symptom of which is their simplistic, elliptical manner of speaking. Their once-normal speech has regressed to the level of dyadic exchanges of signals; they seem no longer capable of fully human (i.e., triadic) conversation. Real triadic exchange, as Peirce and Percy argued, requires a rule-governed syntax, but More's patients "speak" in two-word codes.[3] None of them needs a "context"—a place or *umvelt*—within which to talk or answer questions; none seems to relate a question asked to his or her personal self.

Good empirical diagnostician that he is, More suspects a suppression of cortical function in the "major speech center, the locus of self-consciousness, the 'I,' the utterer, the 'self' " (22–23).[4] After several additional case studies, More summarizes their common symptoms: changes in personality; a more open, casual expression of sexual feelings; a simplistic, telepathic speech; a lack of human context; and idiot-savant responses, contrary to the normally fallible workings of human judgment and memory. More's subjects' loss of self is also denoted by their free-floating abstraction from time and place and a loss of any sense of themselves as concrete historical beings. More's initial diagnosis of cortical suppression is medically accurate but only symptomatic, and therefore limited. For Percy, of course, their condition is a sign of the more widespread dehumanization of the person promoted under the abstract theories of self and society preached by the scientistic qualitarians. Apropos of this creed, Dr. Van Dorn's model for the new mode of being in the world is that of "artificial intelligence," humans responding abstractly to external stimuli or signals, like computers. Such a model is the new form of "angelism" made possible by the wedding of technology and pharmacology, seen in the NA-24-12 added to the drinking water to enhance the performance of subjects. The detachment of spirit from body More detected in the "riven selves" of his patients in *Love in the Ruins* has been "upgraded" here into a technocratic instrumental model of man re-created in the image and likeness of a machine. Likewise, the counterpart to angelism in *Love in the Ruins*—bestialism—is revealed here in the "presenting" sexual postures of Mickey, Donna S——, and Ellen when they "come on" to More, and later in the pedophilia at Belle Ame.

Having observed the signs of his patients' and Ellen's dehumanization, More sets out to discover the specific source of their regression to subhuman behavior. Once the source is uncovered with the help of epidemiologist Lucy Lipscomb, More must then decide how to act. But his power to act is compromised by many factors: his own flawed character; his estranged family situation; his seduction by his cousin Lucy Lipscomb; and the job offer he receives to join the qualitarians at Fedville, an offer made under threat of reincarceration in the prison where he has served time for illegal drug dispensing. Yet even though More does eventually discover the source of his patients' regression to be the Blue Boy project of adding heavy sodium to the Feliciana water supply, and even though he halts the project, Percy makes clear that this scheme itself is only symptomatic of a much broader condition. Deprivation of humanity extends well beyond the immediate victims of pharmacological doping. In fact, most of the main characters in the novel, whether doped or not, are either victims or victimizers under the pervasive "thanatos syndrome," the general drift toward death marked in the novel. As I have suggested, Percy developed a broad web of interrelated signs in the novel to connect the immediate events in Feliciana Parish to World War I, the Nazis, the Holocaust, Supreme Court decisions, and the larger utopian dream signified by the Fedville qualitarians.

Specific examples of this thanatopsic condition can be seen in Drs. Comeaux's and Van Dorn's refashioning of their own identities into prefabricated social roles: Comeaux's affected name change from Como, and Van Dorn's reinvention of himself as ersatz "southern gentleman." On a more humorous level, even Chandra, the daughter of More's black cook Hudeen, works to transform herself into a television "anchorperson," a female Dan Rather with a flat, midwestern voice. Near the end of the novel, More notices a similar deprivation of self in the fond vacant gazes of the retirees from Ohio and Canada that he meets at the trailer park in Florida. Seeing them, More wonders if Western civilization didn't really end with World War I. And as we discover, both Father Smith and More have been infected with the thanatos syndrome. As a youth Father Smith became enamored of the death cult of the German Schutzstaffel and secretly wished to join them. More's drift toward the death of self is seen in his seduction by Lucy Lipscomb, the heiress of Pantherburn whom Percy links symbolically to the deadly romantic stoicism of the old South.[5] Lucy also tempts More to compromise his own freedom and integrity and join the Fedville team. As astute as they are, Father Smith and More must come to recognize their own infection with thanatos and struggle to overcome it.

Seeing the deprivation of the human as a general condition, Percy argues through Father Smith that the real source of this deprivation is Satan the depriver. As Rene Girard has pointed out, one of Satan's cleverest ploys is to mask himself as one concerned for the welfare of humanity; that is, as a "savior" of the world or promoter of a more "perfect" and "humane" community (*I See Satan*, 178–81). Satan's real interest is in power and the destruction of the individual human soul. He is the "father of lies" who promotes the ethos of false "tenderness" and "concern" that infects the many personal, cultural, and historical relations Percy develops in the novel. This ethos was clearly identified by Percy's fellow writer Flannery O'Connor in a statement that Father Smith echoes later in the novel. In her introduction to *A Memoir of Mary Ann* O'Connor stated:

discussion of transsignification in the introduction. It is the root of the novel's theosemiotic vision. Since the risen Christ is the one who acts in the eucharistic sacrifice, through the signs of bread and wine, the mass cannot be "evacuated" of meaning (Powers, *Eucharistic Theology*, 171–72). Christ is the living word who is act, and the Eucharist is the sign of this active presence in the world. Thus through Father Smith's argument that words have been deprived of meaning, Percy subtly suggests the direct relation between the rejection of the incarnate Word, Christ, and the general malaise of the deprivation of meaning in language and signs. But Christ as eucharistic Word cannot be deprived of meaning, though satanic forces like the Nazis have tried throughout history. Moreover, the real presence of the divine Logos in the world verifies the human person as a unique being. Therefore, Percy suggests through the priest that the attempted denial of Christ's real presence is both ontologically and linguistically at the root of the human deprivation More witnesses in his patients and other citizens of Feliciana Parish. In this deprived community, the Word made flesh, the source of the individual person's spiritual integrity, has been displaced by various secular "theories" of humankind.

Father Smith's point about the devaluation or deprivation of language and what it infers about the modern predicament cannot be overemphasized. As George Steiner has pointed out, "It is this break from the covenant between word and world which constitutes one of the very few genuine revolutions of spirit in Western history and which defines modernity itself" (*Real Presences*, 94). Steiner's argument presupposes the covenant between the divine Logos and humankind. This logocentric tradition denoted an order, coherence, relationality, and intelligibility to experience rooted in a belief in an ultimate source or Authority for the covenant of language. As Steiner says, the "archetypal paradigm of all affirmations of sense and significant plentitude—the fullness of the meaning of the word—is a *Logos*-model" (119). The *Logos*-model entails "the central supposition of 'real presence'" (96). The logocentric tradition at the heart of the covenant between word and world constitutes "the Hebraic-Hellenic copula on which our *Logos*-history and practice have been founded. 'The age of the sign,' says Derrida, 'is essentially theological'" (119–20). For Percy, the *Logos*-based covenant between word and world is specified historically in God's covenant community with the Jews and their election as the chosen people. It is further specified, as I have argued, in the Christian doctrines of the Incarnation of the divine Word, the resurrection of Christ, and in the mass and sacraments, especially the Eucharist. As Steiner points out, the doctrines of the Incarnation and the Eucharist, alien to Hellenic and Jewish perspectives, totally revolutionize the notion of the meaning of meaning and the truth of signs in Western consciousness. "By virtue of the 'substantiation' of the supreme mystery of divine presence and agency in outward form (that of the eucharist) man can and must 'make sense' of the sensory," Steiner says (*Grammars of Creation*, 76).

Yet as Father Smith well knows, we now live in the time of the "after-Word" and the "eclipse of the messianic," to use Steiner's phrases for modernity. The breaking of the covenant and the "deconstruction" of the word proceed at an exponential pace from the late nineteenth century onward. The attack on the logocentric tradition is, perforce, an attack on God as the source of authority and meaning. Again as Steiner notes, contrary to the incarnational theology and aesthetic of the Eucharist, deconstruction is "theoretical" in its attempt to undermine the epistemological assumptions of real presence in language (*Real Presences*, 116). Thus it is consonant with the other "theorists" who offer abstract models of self and society. The breaking of the covenant of the word will eventually find its most violent expression in the attempt to exterminate the "people of the Book" in the Holocaust. As Father Smith will argue, the Holocaust was the result of "the sign which could not be evacuated" (TS, 126).

Father Smith informs More that the breakdown of coherent meaning is now so advanced in modern Western culture that it "is not a question of belief or unbelief. Even if such things were all proved, if the existence of God, heaven, hell, sin were all proved as certainly as the distance to the sun is proved, it would make no difference" (118). Rational demonstration or "proof" would not avail because the very ground of meaning, of a community of truth discoverable by language, has eroded. The priest attempts to demonstrate the point by giving More two examples of triadic sign relations to enforce his argument. In the first, he shows More how the location of a fire is determined by triangulating coordinates between the smoke sign, his location in the fire tower, and the location of a fire watcher in a second tower. The sign is clear, easily interpreted, and can be acted on accordingly. However, Father Smith notes that it is "unlike word signs" (120).

Father Smith is a semiotic realist, a believer in the existence of true realities and relations in the world that are not dependent on what we think of them. For the priest, under the current deprivation words have lost their power to signify true realities "out there" in the universe. To demonstrate his belief that, with one exception, word signs have been evacuated of meaning, Father Smith gives More a free-association test in which More responds to words like "Irish" and "Black" by making general categorical associations with those words, such as, "Bog, Notre Dame . . . Africa, niggers, minority, civil rights—" (122). However, More responds to the word "Jew" by naming specific relations with Jews he knows or has known, "Real persons." From this Father Smith concludes that the Jews are "the only sign of God which has not been evacuated by an evacuator." The Jews, he argues, cannot be "subsumed" or abstracted into a category. "Since the Jews were the original chosen people of God, a tribe of people who are still here, they are a sign of God's presence which cannot be evacuated. Try to find a hole in that proof!" (123). (The evolution of Percy's protagonists' search for "proof" is significant—from Binx Bolling's search for scientific "proofs" of the universe's meaning to Lance's search to prove the existence of sin, and to Will Barrett's cave-dwelling attempt to prove God's existence or nonexistence. Unlike those searches, Father Smith's "proof" is grounded in faith, historical reality, and semiotics, not in reason alone or egoistic searching for self-confirmation.) The priest affirms a continuity between the Jews as "the original chosen people of God" and Christianity, despite Judaism's rejection of Christ as redeemer. Citing St. Paul, Father Smith proclaims that "salvation comes from the Jews." Consequently, he explicitly links the promise of salvation given to the Jews to the Christian sacrament of the Eucharist as the visible sign of God's enduring presence in the world. The Eucharist is God's spiritual gift to the believer so that the believer may have life, the true antidote to the thanatos syndrome. "Unless you eat my body and drink my blood, you will not have life in you," Father Smith recites (125).

However, More himself is a sign of the broken covenant of words and does not fully grasp the priest's argument. To help his friend understand, Father Smith proceeds to connect or triangulate the meaning of the Jews as an ineradicable divine sign to their tragic fate in history, and then to the present activities of the qualitarian theorists at Fedville. His message is intended specifically to show More the moral choices he faces. The historical uniqueness of the Jews and the Christian Incarnation, the priest explains, is the scandal that is obnoxious to theorists: "This offends people, even the most talented people, people of the loftiest sentiments, the highest scientific achievements, the purest humanitarian ideals" (126). The naming of the Jews as the chosen "people of God" and the instrument of salvation, and the Christian Incarnation, by virtue of their specific historical uniqueness, can neither be explained by rational human categories of meaning nor eradicated from human consciousness. Christ's promise of redemption to humankind from the primordial estrangement from God, proclaimed in the scriptural word, is an offense and an obstacle to the theorists of history and language. To the theoreticians, such an obstacle was dealt with only, finally, by violence. As Steiner points out, the de-valuation of the human is signified in the devaluation of language, a fact seen explicitly in the "monstrous inflation" of propaganda, the "embezzlement of diction," and the wholesale undermining of language's truth function that accompanied Nazism (*Grammars of Creation*, 270).

Consequently, Father Smith concludes that the Holocaust was the result of "the sign which could not be evacuated" (126). Because that unique sign—the Jews and the Christian Logos—was not subsumable under theory (i.e., not reducible to an item in a category), he calls the Holocaust "a myth." In naming it a myth, the priest means, among other things, that the theoretical argument for genocide was based on the myth of Aryan superiority, the perverse millenarian goal of a "purer" race and society purchased at the expense of individual persons. Nazi "theory" of the sovereign state was a demonic extension of the Weimar physicians' theoretical arguments for the destruction of life deemed "without quality." Perverse theory was coextensive with corrupt language, the expression of nationalistic goals as a mask for killing. For Father Smith, such demonic theories, practices, and language now hold sway in American society, as exemplified by the qualitarians and the Blue Boy project. The priest warns More that he is a member of the "first generation of doctors in the history of medicine to turn their backs on the oath of Hippocrates and kill millions of useless old people, unborn children, born malformed children, for the good of mankind." Eventually, he says, "you're going to end up killing Jews" (127–28).

Percy's linking of these signs—the assault on the Jews and on the divine Logos, the assault on individual persons in the name of theory, and the de-valuation of language—reveals his concern with the extent to which secular theory has now become the reigning ideology of Western liberal culture. Father Smith says pessimistically that even if God, heaven, hell, and sin were "proved," it would make no difference. The subsuming mind, as Percy argued in "Notes for a Novel about the End of the World," is virtually incapable of "hearing" the good news. The logical outcome of subsuming humanitarian theory, the priest insists, will be the gas chamber. For Father Smith, a human-itarian lover of mankind, like Walt Whitman, or a theorist of mankind like Rousseau or Skinner, may be harmless. But a combination of the two, with the power to put theory into practice, is another matter: "If you put the two together, a lover of Mankind and a theorist of Mankind, what you've got now is Robespierre or Stalin or Hitler and the Terror, and millions dead for the good of mankind. Right?" (129).

Although Tom More seems not to fully comprehend the significance of Father Smith's argument, being more concerned with the priest's strange behavior, his words nevertheless register in More's consciousness throughout this scene. Through this exchange of signs, Percy establishes a growing bond of communion between the priest and the psychiatrist. A clue to this important connection is given just before More leaves the fire tower, when Father Smith asks him if he has ever told him about the year he spent in Germany before the war, living with "an eminent psychiatrist whose son was a colonel in the Schutzstaffel." When More answers "yes," the priest adds, "Last night I dreamed of lying in bed in Tubingen and listening to church bells. German church bells make a high-pitched silvery sound" (131). More has already heard the story of the priest's German experiences, and as we soon discover, that story, now lodged in More's memory, will influence his thoughts and actions in profound ways. As well, the priest's explicit arguments about the deprivation of language, the Jews, the Holocaust, and the Eucharist become shaping forces in More's mind as he struggles over the Blue Boy project and his other personal difficulties.

More's important first conversation with Father Smith in the fire tower immediately precedes his trip to Pantherburn to visit Lucy Lipscomb, his epidemiologist cousin who plans to help him discover the cause of his patients' regression. The visit marks a critical turning point for More as man and physician. At Pantherburn he discovers his wife's presumed infidelity, drinks heavily, and is seduced by Lucy. Yet together they also discover that the cause of the patients' regression is the Blue Boy project of filtering heavy sodium into the Feliciana water supply. The discovery presents More with a clear moral challenge, since such "zonking" of citizens without their knowledge runs counter to his belief in personal freedom and the therapeutic power of psychoanalysis. But at Pantherburn More is too afflicted by his own pull toward thanatos—despair—to make out clearly what is happening and what he must do.

Percy's development of the Pantherburn episode is complex, yet also a key to his strategy for linking signs and themes across the novel. The episode is focused through More's consciousness, and Percy presents him realistically as a post-Christian man with a free-floating mind often dissociated from time and place. This is not the Tom More of the epilogue of *Love in the Ruins*, wherein he was shown as the shriven sinner receiving the Eucharist at Christmastime and happy in his marriage. Now he is the embattled humanist who dispensed drugs illegally to truck drivers out of "compassion" for their weariness during long hauls. The older More seems *almost* as deaf to the "good news" and to Father Smith's signs as everybody else. To underscore More's disorientation and susceptibility to moral regression, Percy creates an elaborate web of triadic sign relations that reveals the physician's personal predicament as well as that of the times. Key to this strategy is Percy's semiotic melding of More's night at Pantherburn with Father Smith's experiences in Germany.

That More's night at Pantherburn will be a dangerous descent for him is signaled by the small mental "disruptions" he experiences, the déjà vu feelings that reveal his gnostic disjunction from present time. The first déjà vu occurs when he meets Lucy in the parking lot, which triggers a memory of youthful courting in the car and foreshadows More's "return to the past" while at Pantherburn (106). The second occurs when he arrives at Pantherburn, triggered by the smell of Lucy's cotton shirt. The third déjà vu, evoking the "tragic tinkle of bad news, the sweet sorrow to come," occurs just before Lucy reveals that his wife, Ellen, has contracted herpes while he was away in prison (156). More's sad discovery is followed by a strange free-association "dream" of past and present family experiences, of the Civil War, and of Germany. The events are real, part of the web of signs within his consciousness. When he is awakened by Lucy, he says, "I go back to sleep, *as if* I had dreamed the whole thing, panzers, nukes, bad water, Alice Pratt—but not Lucy" (169) (italics mine). Later in the novel, Percy relates More's "dream" to Father Smith by using a parallel phrase, just before the priest's confession: "I was dreaming of Germany. . . . No, not dreaming. It happened. I was wide awake . . . what I had was this peculiar dream which was not a dream" (236–37). In melding the two men's experiences through interrelated signs, Percy underscores the truth that, whether hallucination, déjà vu, fantasy, actual or imagined memory, their "mutual" experiences confirm a real spiritual bond between them. As More cited Peirce earlier, "apparently disconnected events are in fact not, [and] that one can connect them." But whether More will be able to connect the signs and act responsibly is jeopardized by his own weakness during his "dark night" at Pantherburn.

Drinking heavily after he learns of Ellen's perfidy, More remembers visiting Pantherburn twenty years earlier, recalls the "child's silver cup that Uncle Rylan used for a jigger," and how the "silver spoons made a tinkling sound against the crystal" (159). As drinking frees him from "the necessity of time," he remembers visiting at Christmastime as a child and listening to the "doom talk. As a child I associated the pleasure of doom with the tinkle of silver against crystal" (160). The association of "doom talk" with his family past, and the "pleasure" taken in such talk signify the thanatopsic ethos Percy saw at the heart of both the old southern stoic world and that of Weimar and Nazi Germany. Both societies are grounded in romantic myth, in Father Smith's (and Percy's) sense of the term "myth"; both are antihistorical, anti-incarnational. As in *Love in the Ruins*, More's pull toward despair makes him especially vulnerable to the seductions of alcohol and sex. Lucy's "mothering" of him with bourbon and Alanone, like his earlier "mothering" by Moira and Lola in *Love in the Ruins*, leads him passively into adultery with her. His regression is underscored by the fusion of despair-death-war-sex motifs, as More thinks how "the English Lipscombs [Lucy's ancestors], must have spoken exactly the same way, with the same doomed conviviality and the same steady tinkle of silver against crystal, when the Americans came down the river two hundred years ago in 1796 and up the river with Silver Spoons Butler in 1862" (161). (As we see later, Percy closely links More's reveries with Father Smith's memory of Germany by repeating signs in both passages: silver, crystal, church bells, featherbed, and forest.) Uncle Hugh Bob's nostalgic prattle about the "glories" of hunting and war (he especially admires the Roman, Confederate, and German armies) and of casual sex reinforce the patterns of despair, doom worship, killing, and stoic death that are part of More's and the culture's morbid legacy.

More's recollection of a featherbed he once slept in at Pantherburn triggers another "memory" of waking in a featherbed with a bolster in Freiburg "to the sound of church bells . . . a high-pitched crystalline sound, *eine Klingel*, yes, almost a tinkling" (162). As mothering Lucy now covers him in bed and "warms him," he "recalls" another sexual tryst in the Schwarzwald with one Alice Pratt, a lonely southerner from Montgomery, Alabama. In this romanticized encounter, the young More's fear of "touching" the girl is overcome when a column of panzer tanks suddenly appears and they are forced to hide: "We lie on a soft bed of needles and watch an entire panzer division pass. I am Robert Jordan lying on the pine needles. I hold her. She wants me to. When the panzers are gone, we look at each other and laugh. We have been given leave by the German Army and Robert Jordan" (163). War machines, the threat of "doom," and stoic death (Hemingway's Robert Jordan) in this fantasy have "given leave" to their tryst. Now, caught in the aura of doom at Pantherburn and his despair over Ellen, like his earlier despair over his daughter Samantha's death years ago, More passively acquiesces to intercourse with Lucy. "Her mouth is on mine. She, Alabama-German-Lucy-Alice, is under the comforter and I under her, she a sweet heavy incubus but not quite centered. Her hair is still damp. She needs centering" (163). The "doom" of this seduction, for More, is signified by sexual inversion—Lucy as evil spirit "incubus" seducing the "sleeping" More.

More's free-floating consciousness also "recalls" scenes from his ancestral past—Miss Betts reading his grandmother's journal entries from the Civil War; his kinsman Rylan's death in the war at Cross Keys, Virginia; memories of his stay at Fort Pelham prison and of former psychiatric patients. Past and present, actual and imaginary events all become for More a confused jumble of signs that, in his drugged state, he is unable to fully interpret. But the recurrent signs of war, sex, hunting, and death all point to his immersion in the ethos of doom. Percy underscores this when More awakens the next morning and realizes that his "memory" of being in Freiburg and the Schwarzwald with Alice Pratt is false. He declares, "I've never been in Germany" (166). In More's specious "memories" of Germany, Percy conflates some episodes from More's own past with Father Smith's tales of his youth in Germany, which in fact More has already heard. Yet this relation does not account fully for More's imagined tryst with Alice Pratt in the Schwarzwald, nor for the uncanny echoing of images between More's reverie and the priest's later confession. While Percy's deliberate fusing of the two men's "experiences" underscores More's present confusion, it is also intended to show the "presence" of Father Smith as a moral authority and preceptor in More's mind. The priest's role as guide becomes explicit when he later tells More, "You will have to choose." He must choose to be either for or against life.

Despite his personal debilitation on the first night at Pantherburn, More begins to grasp the full implications of his patients' symptoms once he, Lucy, and Vergil Bon Jr. discover the shunt pipeline for diverting the heavy sodium solution into the water supply. By correlating high NA-24 levels with symptoms observed in his test cases, More and Lucy identify the source of his patients' dehumanization. Uniquely human symptoms like "anxiety, depression, stress, insomnia, suicidal tendencies, chemical depression" are abated, causing "a regression from a stressful human existence to a peacable animal existence" (180). But despite the discovery, More's power to act is hampered by his personal struggles over his relation to Ellen and his own adultery with Lucy, as well as by the looming crisis in his professional life. As a parolee, he is at the mercy of his guarantors at Fedville, especially Bob Comeaux, who wants him on the team of qualitarians. More important, as the leading expert on the use of isotopes to affect cortical function, More is already complicit in the project as a pioneer theorist in the whole ethos of pharmacological manipulation of

human behavior, despite his claimed allegiance to traditional psychoanalysis. As in *Love in the Ruins*, More's ambivalent relation to technological scientific "progress" reveals his own separation from "the center"—the Jewish-
Christian Event—that did not hold. Yet More does realize his implication in
the Blue Boy project, however tangential, and this knowledge sharpens his
sense of the moral dilemma he now faces.

Percy focuses More's dilemma during his long conversation with Comeaux
after being released from the Clinton jail, where he was held on a bogus
charge of trespassing. Driving along in his Mercedes Duck with Straus waltzes
playing on the car stereo, Comeaux announces his plan to hire More for the
"team." Comeaux personifies the "theorists of mankind" Father Smith warned
More about. The trappings of his fabricated identity as nouveau "southern
gentry"—his German car and love of romantic German music—are ominous
signs that Comeaux is the intellectual heir of the Weimar physicians whose
theoretical arguments for killing individuals in order to create a "utopian"
community paved the way for Nazism and the Holocaust. In short, Percy affirms that the scientistic consciousness that produced the Holocaust is alive
and present. Comeaux now claims that he and More have the same goals:
"Healing the sick, ministering to the suffering, improving the quality of life
for the individual regardless of race, creed or national origin" (190). He enu-
merates the "benefits" of the Blue Boy project: reduction in street crime, child
abuse, teen pregnancy and suicide, chemical dependency, AIDS, and homo-
sexuality. More broadly, Comeaux suggests the possibility of chemically solving all human pathologies, thus eliminating "wars, insanities, perversions"
through "cortical control" (195).

Through Comeaux Percy expresses the latest model of secular "humanist" ideology. Comeaux's plan is a pharmacological version of the old gnostic
dream of human perfectibility. Like the prototypical scientist and would-be
savior Alymer in Hawthorne's "The Birthmark" whom Flannery O'Connor
named in her introduction to *A Memoir of Mary Ann*, Comeaux would "correct" mankind's fallen state, eliminate imperfection, but at the cost of individual freedom. Such "salvation" needs no God or God-man; history can be overcome by scientific transcendence. For theorists like Comeaux, community is
humanly fashioned and controlled; it is not a covenant with God. But behind
such romantic utopianism lies the perverse vision of a master race and the
terror and annihilation of "aberrant" subjects. For such qualitarians, human
"imperfection" is merely hereditary or cultural, not ontological; for them, being is always manipulable by theory. As for language, man's uniquely human

power, Comeaux would reduce it to "graphic and binary communication—
which after all is a lot more accurate than once upon a time there lived a wicked
queen." Yet More recognizes that such a means of communication reduces
human (i.e., triadic) language, the root of consciousness, to dyadic signal-
ing. He tells Comeaux, "You mean they use two-word sentences" (197). Loss
of human language, the triadic relation between sign givers, undermines the
ground of genuine community, the intersubjective "knowing with" another
human that creates a shared world of meaning. But to eliminate the anxieties
of self-consciousness that being human entails, Comeaux extols "artificial intelligence" and binary exchanges as the language of the future.

Mindful perhaps of Father Smith's earlier warning during his first visit to
the fire tower, More questions the qualitarians' violation of individual civil
rights by doping subjects without their permission. "You're assaulting the cor-
tex of an individual without the knowledge or consent of the assaultee" (193).
This issue cuts to the ethical core of human freedom and dignity, the respect
for the sanctity of the person that is the bulwark against enforced social conformity and, ultimately, terror. But as a scientist once involved in research on
cortical manipulation, More's own position is equivocal. He is "the father of
isotope brain pharmacology," Comeaux insists, and as such More is already
"one of us" (200). Comeaux's subsequent job offer to More comes as both
bribe and threat—join the qualitarian team or risk being returned to prison.
To compound More's problem, his cousin Lucy argues that he has "no choice"
but to accept Comeaux's job offer, and tells him that he should "work from
within" the system. Her encouragement is duplicitous, however, since she also
wants him for herself. With his doped and errant wife gone to another bridge
tournament in Fresno, More now balances vulnerably on the razor's edge of
choice. What helps him find direction after his dark night at Pantherburn is
the discovery of pedophilia at Belle Ame and his second long conversation
with Father Smith.

In their first conversation Father Smith argued that the logical end
of secular theory about mankind and "tenderness" would be terror. Degradation of the sacredness of the person takes many forms in Percy's novels, one of
which is sexual rape. As Percy argued in *Lost in the Cosmos,* pornography and
rape are manifestations of the objectification and theorizing of the self, a form
of violation that has become a conspicuous feature of technological society
(175–98). Pornography and rape are the perverse corollaries to the theorizing
of a "perfect" self, based on principles of power and manipulation. The board-

ing school, Belle Ame, operates on such principles. When More and Lucy come to rescue his children Tommy and Margaret and Claude Bon, he immediately confronts Van Dorn with evidence of the Blue Boy project. Van Dorn's justification for doping with heavy sodium echoes that of Bob Comeaux: to combat the evils of crime, teenage suicide, drug abuse, and AIDS and allow subjects to be "human enough to achieve the ultimate goals of being human" (218–19). His argument is strictly theoretical and instrumentalist. In his view the so-called "humanitarian" end of a utopian community justifies the means to achieve it, regardless of individual choice. When More asks him to define "the ultimate goals" of being human, Van Dorn's answer is "excellence," based on "the tough old European Gymnasium-Hochschule" model of hard work and discipline, *but* enhanced by performance drugs. His private "theory of the nature of man" is a mechanistic, pseudo-Freudian doctrine of sexual energy as the basis of human creativity and excellence, energy that can now be liberated by the "science" of drug enhancement. Recalling the demonic Art Immelmann in *Love in the Ruins,* Van Dorn proposes Don Giovanni as a model of the "sexual genius." But Percy's move here from the gimmicky lapsometer as instrument of manipulation in *Love in the Ruins* to pharmacological "enhancement" indicates his somber sense that the perverse "dream" of social pacification may be an increasingly more widespread and acceptable feature of American life.

The stark truth, as More and Lucy soon discover, is that Belle Ame is a school for sexual perversion and pedophilia. Idealized theory is a mask for sexual violation, "tenderness" turned into horror in the name of human "fulfillment." Van Dorn believes sexual repression is the root cause of failure—a barrier to "excellence." But just as the Blue Boy project signifies in extremis a broader social malaise, so also does Belle Ame. In Van Dorn's theoretical argument for achieving the "ultimate goals" of humanity through "scientific" and sexual liberation, Percy voices a popular secular vision of the goal of personal self-fulfillment and community. Belief in the inviolable sacredness of the individual, and in man's eternal destiny, has been displaced by an ethos that promotes "natural" human fulfillment alone. The popular Enlightenment-romantic notion of human perfectibility is here "scientifically" updated by Van Dorn and his cohorts. But the sexual violence at Belle Ame reveals the ineradicable capacity for evil in human beings. "Natural" man is neither inherently human nor moral. Lucy Lipscomb tries to convince More that their drug-induced sexual liaison was "natural" and should continue. So also, in the footnote to his confession later, Father Smith remarks that he was not by "nature" horrified to discover pedeuthanasia at Eglfing-Harr hospital. He had to *learn* the meaning of horror. Animals are not horrified by brutality; such a reaction can only be human. Percy's dark vision here of the abnegation of human feeling, conscience, and will points to the broader issue of cultural anesthetization—citizens "zonked out," detached, "zapped," and stunned looking—in the face of numbing violence and terror in the twentieth century. No amount of "human engineering" will eliminate such evil. Van Dorn's theoretic attempt to create a higher species instead creates its antitype, bestial man reduced to pongid primate behavior, as More discovers in the pornography and rape at Belle Ame.

More's discovery of pedophilia at Belle Ame immediately precedes his second visit to Father Smith, and the two episodes are decisive in More's ethical development. While his own children are saved from the pedophiles, More now sees the full extent of the Blue Boy project's danger, which is nothing less than the wide-scale drug pacification of citizens, whether at prep school, at Angola prison where the inmates are drugged, or in the parish at large. For More, public and personal crises become intertwined. His strained relationship with his absent wife is already complicated by his own infidelity and by Lucy's pressure to capture him for herself and for a position at Fedville. But even though Comeaux's threat of reincarceration hangs over him, after his visit to Belle Ame More is determined to close down the school and the Blue Boy project. His second visit to Father Smith confirms his resolve. Percy's triangulating of these episodes—More's first visit to the priest, his "German" dream at Pantherburn, and his second visit to Father Smith—reinforces the bond between More and the priest, as well as the real semiotic relation between current events in Feliciana Parish and their historical antecedents.

After telling the priest about the pedophilia and doping at Belle Ame and the Blue Boy project, More says, "I am not sure what I should do" (234). He has, in part, already decided what to do, but he wishes to confirm his own judgment as well as induce the priest to talk. Prodded into speaking, Father Smith begins to talk of a recent recollection that "was not a dream but a complete return of an experience which was real—as if I were experiencing it again"— that is, his experience as a young man in Germany (235). As we saw earlier, Percy links the priest's recollection of his actual experience in Germany to More's imagined reverie of his "experience" in Germany with Alice Pratt in the Schwarzwald forest. Images of dreaming and waking, piney forests, church bells with a silvery sound like struck crystal, goose-down bolsters and featherbeds connect the two episodes. Although one is imaginary and one a memory of an actual experience, in the semiosis of the novel both are real signs of what is and "could be," what is real and possible in a continuity of sign relations. The relation between these episodes now suggests the growing influence of the priest in shaping More's thoughts and actions. (Near the end of the novel, speaking of Father Smith, More asks himself, "Am I beginning to think like him?") Nevertheless, the two "experiences" are different in important ways, beyond the fact that one is an actual memory and the other imagined. More has already absorbed parts of the story of the priest's trip to Germany, to the point that he "remembered" them as part of his own past during the night at Pantherburn. But unlike More's fragmented and confusing "memory" of the Germany he has never visited, here the priest discerns and *interprets* the meaning of his German experience, unlike More's incoherent reverie at Pantherburn. Specifically, he describes how it shaped his character and perhaps his decision to become a priest. A spiteful youth, Father Smith grew up disaffected from his parents and scornful of religious "believers." Alcohol gave him a way to "enjoy" his spite. The experience of seeing the pedeuthanasia room in Germany during the war did not change his fundamental character, but it surely helped lead him to work in the hospice. There, among the dying patients, he can speak and hear truth. Beyond his personal story, Father Smith connects the signs in his experience to show More the historical and theosemiotic links between Weimar and Nazi Germany and their direct relation to current events in Feliciana Parish. His purpose is prophetic, to warn his physician friend of the significance of his choices. Saying he has "never told anyone," the priest tells More, "I'm afraid this concerns you. I didn't want to tell you, but I'm afraid I have to. There is something you need to know" (238). What More "needs to know" is the full historical impact of the crisis he faces.

Father Smith's prophetic role here focuses the central paradox of the novel. On the one hand, the priest has voiced Percy's deep concern for the devaluation of language, that "words no longer signify," that the "covenant between word and world," to use Steiner's phrase, has been ruptured in modernity. The logical conclusion to such an argument would be solipsism and silence. Communication, hence community between humans, would no longer be possible. But on the other hand, Father Smith *does* speak the language of truth, *does* relate and interpret the meaning of his experience, to More, as well as of course to the readers. Thus the priest's telling More "what he needs to know" confirms Harry Stack Sullivan's belief in the therapeutic power of talking and listening. This belief in the real possibility of communication and community is the affirmation of Peirce's, as well as Percy's, hope for the recovery of the human. It is based on the belief that, despite the devaluation, the "covenant between word and world" is not irrevocably broken.

The paradox of language bears particularly on the meaning of the Holocaust as a historical event, as Percy develops it in the novel. The question of the devaluation of language in relation to the Shoah is especially vexing and acute and has been the subject of considerable debate among Holocaust survivors and scholars. The "unspeakable" horror of the Shoah exposed the radical poverty of language. The "emptying out" and deprivation of language, seen for example in theories of racial superiority and in Nazi propaganda, was coextensive with the systematic process of dehumanization, especially for the Jews. After the death camps, language seemed powerless to signify such previously unimaginable events. Silence seemed the only true response. Steiner, for one, sees the Shoah as an inevitable consequence of the progressive attacks on the Western logocentric tradition, the belief in "a theological, canonic world-order" based on "the normative claims of the primacy of language, of its sovereign at-homeness in creation" (*Grammars of Creation*, 282). Steiner conjectures "that the classical and Judaic ideal of man as 'language animal,' as uniquely defined by the dignity of speech—itself a facsimile of the original and begetting mystery of creation—came to an end in the anti-language of the death camps" (283). Steiner terms this the "end of the messianic era." Percy himself was sensitive to this view. Commenting on William Styron's novel *Sophie's Choice*, he expressed admiration for his fellow writer's attempt to convey the horrors of the Shoah, yet also termed it an "incommunicable evil" that is difficult, if not impossible to convey in language.[7]

By contrast, survivor-author Primo Levi flatly rejected the idea of the "incommunicability" of the Shoah. In refuting the notion of the utter devaluation of language, Levi said: "Except for cases of pathological incapacity, one can and must communicate, and thereby contribute in a useful and easy way to the peace of others and oneself. . . . To say that it is impossible to communicate is false; one always can. . . . We are biologically and socially predisposed to communication, and in particular to its highly evolved and noble form, which is language."[8] Levi's affirmation implies that to capitulate to the view of "unspeakability" is to renounce humanity and conspire with the "deprivers of meaning" Father Smith names as Satan. In Levi's view, then, the covenant of word and world is not irretrievably broken. His idea is coincident with Peirce and Percy's anthropological view of man as a unique creature whose essence is to be a sign user. It is the basis for the hope that a community of meaning is an ineradicable and true possibility, despite language's devaluation. For Percy, as indeed for Steiner, the covenant of words is ultimately grounded in the presence of the divine Logos in Judaism and Christianity. Therefore for both authors the attempt to annihilate the Jews is an attempt to erase the Word from human history and consciousness.

To emphasize the prophetic importance of Father Smith's confession and footnote, Percy sets off both formally as "texts" within the narrative. While this creates some awkwardness, this formal "break" does reinforce the interpretive power of language, the power to "read" the meaning of one's personal experience as Father Smith does in the light of history and understand the signs of the times. The priest has come to discern the connection between the Fedville qualitarians and Weimar Germany and the Nazi regime and to instruct More through personal parable. All three events—Weimar, Third Reich, Fedville—are examples of what happens in a culture when the Logos is suborned by secular theory. Whether that theory is "humanitarian" or fascist, the unique individual is subsumed under or sacrificed to an all-consuming ideology. The legitimizing of the "disposal" of the individual on whatever grounds—humanitarian, cultic, nationalistic—reveals its horrible truth in the words of Mother Theresa that Percy quoted in speaking about abortion: "[I]f a mother can kill her unborn child, then I can kill you and you can kill me" (ssl, 311). Yet given a century of deprivation of the individual by "enlightened" secular theory, seduction by such ideologies seems almost irresistible. Father Smith says that it took him years to grasp the lesson of his own blindness and complicity. Yet whether More fully understands the priest's parable is an intriguing mystery in the novel.

As Father Smith informs More, the Germany he and his father visited in the 1930s as guests of a cousin, the eminent psychiatrist Dr. Hans Jager, was a culture already much saturated with "humanitarian" theory. The relatives and friends Smith and his father met were among the cultural elite, intelligent and well educated, decent warm-hearted humanitarians and upright citizens. Their "tenderness" was expressed in their love of romantic music, especially the sentimental songs of Straus and "The Student Prince." The subsuming cult of nationalism and Aryan superiority was summed up in the myth of Das Volk and specified in Helmut Jager's dedication to "the flag and death" as a member of the Schutzstaffel, with its death's-head insignia. In science, Dr. Jager and his colleagues were leading figures in the practical application of "humanist" theory for the "improvement" of society. The young Smith listened to the doctors argue over the study, The Release of the Destruction of Life Devoid of Value, without fully understanding the implications. But he does recall that the debate centered on the *extent* to which euthanasia should be implemented, not on the issue of its fundamental morality. One participant, Dr. Brandt, maintained that "reverence for nation" precedes "reverence for life"; that is, medical killing is justified in the name of the "advancement" of the modern secular state.

The prophetic signs of Nazism were ominously present in Weimar Germany. Yet Percy makes clear that this prevailing ethos was not atypical in enlightened secular Western culture as a whole. As More noted earlier, the thanatos syndrome ruled the battlefields of the Somme and Verdun two decades earlier, when millions of "humane" Europeans and Americans slaughtered each other. Moreover, even as a youth Smith intuited the spiritual kinship between his German relatives and his father, also a lover of music, poetry, the romantic mystique of Heidelburg, drinking songs, and saber scars. The "southern connection" to the morbid culture of post–World War I Europe is grounded in their shared attachment to stoicism, war, and despair, as seen for example in Uncle Hugh Bob's nostalgic obsession with war, hunting, and sex. In his confession to More, Father Smith tells how he later came to see that same love of "heroic" death in himself. He admits that he would have "joined him," his cousin Helmut, if he had been a young German instead of an American.

The young Smith's attraction to the death cult of the Schutzstaffel reveals his own prideful desire for power and domination, as well as his despair. Contemptuous of his father's vapid romanticism and his mother's religious hypocrisy—she has masses said for her enemies—Smith views humanity in general with a mixture of scorn and spite: "Frankly, I found my fellow man, with few exceptions, either victims or assholes. I did not exclude myself. The only people I got along with were bums, outcasts, pariahs, family skeletons, and the dying" (243). His contempt for humanity echoes that of Sutter Vaught and Lance Lamar. Like Lance, Smith turned to alcohol to ease the pain of wounded egotism. As with the younger Tom More, alcohol allowed him to "feast" on despair and enjoy his spite. Yet Smith's misanthropy is fueled in part by his acute recognition of the spiritual bankruptcy and hypocrisy he witnesses around him—the various deprivations of humanity, the role playing and power manipulation, and the wholesale corruption of the language of truth. Consequently, he turns from the living death of modern culture to the "life" and truth telling of the dying. Dying people, he tells More, "were the only people I could stand. They were my kind. . . . Dying people, suffering people, don't lie. They tell the truth. Dying makes honest men of us all. Everyone else lies" (244). In a world where language is devalued, Smith finds the living word among the dying. In the hospice, the *solitude à deux* community that Will Barrett and Allie Huger found in *The Second Coming* becomes a community of the dying, the antithesis of the many pseudo-communities found throughout Percy's fictions. At the hospice, murderous "tenderness" is replaced by genuine compassion, once defined by Flannery O'Connor as being "in travail with and for creation in its subjection to vanity" (*Mystery and Manners*, 165). Smith's knowledge that he is "one of them" (i.e., one of those contaminated with the living death of the spirit and the corruption of language) enables him to see the need for the divine Word and the sacraments. Thus when More asks why he became a priest, he answers, "What else?" (257).

Father Smith makes his confession to More because, he says, "there is something you need to know." Yet how well More "hears" the meaning of the priest's confession remains ambiguous. More claims not to "understand" the connection between Smith's experience in Germany and the "Louisiana Weimar psychiatrists" (252). Signs can connect, as Peirce avowed, but connections can also be missed. In response to the priest's confession, More seems "more interested in his story as a symptom of a possible brain disorder than in the actual events which he related" (252). More's knack for interpreting signs, Percy suggests, is limited by his own tendency to abstraction. The "scientist" in More leads him to extract a medical diagnosis, so he seems to miss the deeper spiritual signs and their historical importance. Sensing More's obtuseness, the priest adds the footnote to reinforce his point. He describes how, while serving with the Seventh Army when it liberated Eglfing-Harr hospital, he discovered Dr. Jager's pedeuthanasia chamber, "a pleasant sunny room" with "a large geranium plant on the window sill" (253). Neither the nurse who shows him the extermination room nor Smith is horrified, merely interested. "Only later was I horrified. We've got it wrong about horror. It doesn't come naturally but takes some effort" (254).

But neither is More horrified now when he hears this tale of the extermination of children at Eglfing-Harr. Rather, he seems unclear about "what you're trying to tell me" and claims that he "couldn't say" whether "we're different from the Germans" (256). Father Smith drives home his point when More asks why he became a priest. "In the end one must choose—given the chance. . . . Life or death" (257). The dire nature of that ultimate choice is precisely what More "needs to know" and face in his own situation. The horrors enacted in the sunny room at Eglfing-Harr, Dachau, Fedville, and Belle Ame, as well as in the Soviet gulags and to the millions of unborn "terminated" under American law, are all one—signs of the reigning thanatos culture in the twentieth century. So also, in Percy's theological perspective, the assault on the individual person is finally an assault on the source and guarantor of the person—the divine Person incarnated in history, as Father Smith's semiotic reading of the meaning of the Jews affirms. For him, as a real sign and sign of the real, the Holocaust *is* still present here and now. But as he leaves the fire tower, More is only thinking of the "smell of geraniums" and how events "in some cases of epilepsy or brain tumor, replay, come back with all the haunting force of memory. And play one false too. I don't recall geraniums having a smell" (257). More seems to reduce the priest's words and behavior to a possible sign of cortical dysfunction and to view his friend as a "case." But although he does not seem to grasp the full significance of Father Smith's words, More does "choose life" and defense of the individual. The priest's confession and footnote do help to reinforce his decision to stand against the qualitarians.

More's immediate plan of action is to expose the sexual perversion at Belle Ame and close down the school. Having connived for a temporary release from the federal holding facility, he returns to Belle Ame with Vergil Bon Jr. and Uncle Hugh Bob to retrieve Claude Bon. There they discover the photographs and videotapes showing Van Dorn, Mr. and Mrs. Brunette, Mrs. Cheney, and the coach engaged in pornographic activities with the children. The horror of these images is intensified by the apparently diffident expressions of the children, as if such violations were just "natural" play. Knowing the evidence may be challenged or disallowed in court, More forces the culprits to drink the molar-strength heavy sodium solution, regressing them to pongid-primate behavior. By the time the sheriff arrives, the pedophiles are "presenting" rearward, *hoo hoo hooing,* and squabbling like apes for dominance, clear evidence of the drug's effects. Percy treats the lengthy episode as ribald comedy, but his underlying point is deadly serious. The dehumanization, drugging, and sexual perversion at Belle Ame "connect" to the larger Blue Boy project of pacification and to the sunny room at Eglfing-Harr, as Father Smith intended.

Pornography and sexual perversion, as both Percy and Flannery O'Connor indicated, are signs of the times in a desacralized culture driven by theory. Long displaced from the Body of Christ and the sacramental meaning of the flesh, the human body and sexuality become the focal points of "abstraction" and manipulation. O'Connor's observation that when tenderness is separated from "the person of Christ," the true source of compassion, it is open to perversion by theorists is especially apposite Belle Ame. Under their reigning theory, "affection" quickly turns to violation, committed by sentimental predators in the name of "natural" fulfillment. O'Connor noted the intrinsic link between sentimentality and pornography, how both posit a mock innocence—denying the fall and need of a divine redeemer—that devolves into terror and violence (*Mystery and Manners*, 227). In a similar vein in *Lost in the Cosmos*, Percy defined the significance of pornography in a post-Christian culture: "Pornography is not an aberration of a few sexually-frustrated middle-aged men in gray raincoats; it is rather a salient and prime property of modern consciousness, of three hundred years of technology and the industrial revolution, and is symptomatic of a radical disorder in the re-lation of the self to other selves which generally manifests itself in the ab-stracted state of one self (male) and the degradation of another self (female) to an abstract object of satisfaction" (10). Percy here points to the relation between the ascendant technological culture and pornography, manifested in the reduction of a genuinely human community to relations of physical exchange. The pornographer operates as an "autonomous" secular being, one "liberated by education from the traditional bonds of religion, by democracy from the strictures of class, by technology from the drudgery of poverty, and by self-knowledge from the tyranny of the unconscious—and therefore free to pursue its own destiny without God" (13). Thus when More confronts Van Dorn with the evidence of pedophilia, Van Dorn speaks as the "autonomous" man in defense of their project: "Once we get past the mental roadblocks of human relationships—namely, two thousand years of repressed sexuality— we see that what counts in the end is affection instead of cruelty, love in-stead of hate . . . we're talking about caring" (302–3). Such "caring" mocks true compassion, and the results of such perverse fulfilling of "natural" man is registered in the abstracted gazes of the child-victims, as it was in the "nat-ural" reaction of soldier Smith and the German nurse at Eglfing-Harr, all anesthetized to the horror. Dehumanization of the person under theoretical "tenderness" signifies the death of the spirit that St. Paul spoke of so eloquently in his letter to the Romans as the real danger to humankind.

More's plan to expose the pedophilia and close Belle Ame succeeds. The pedophiles are arrested, the school is closed, and More escapes being sent back to Fort Pelham prison. Just as important, his threat of prosecution forces Comeaux to close the qualitarian terminal center at Fedville and use the funds to support reopening St. Margaret's hospice, where sick children, the elderly, and the dying will receive palliative care. Yet despite More's real successes, the novel does not end as serendipitously as *The Second Coming*. In keeping with Percy's realistic vision and his cautionary prophetic tone, the ominous threats to human sanctity and freedom persist yet are balanced with the modest possibilities of recovery of the human self. This hope for recovery is instantiated in three ways: through the power of the Holy Spirit in sacrament; through the power of human language to counterbalance devaluations of the word; and through the power of acts of charity as the basis of community life, however "remnant." The center of this hope is thus theosemiotic—words and actions grounded in the eternal Word—and not in secular humanistic theory.

Percy's recovery of some of the pedophiles at the end of the novel—Mr. and Mrs. Brunette, the coach, and Mrs. Cheney all ministering to patients at the hospice—may seem unduly manipulated and comedic. Yet Percy uses it to make his hopeful point about community. For More, it is better to put the culprits to constructive use in the community and help them recover their humanity than to banish them, yet at the same time safeguarding them and others from temptations. The exceptions, of course, are Drs. Comeaux and Van Dorn, whose ironic "recoveries," like Lance Lamar's release from the Center of Aberrant Behavior, serve as an indictment of the broader culture of thanatos. After the qualitarian center is closed, Comeaux escapes prosecution and, according to rumor, now operates a Planned Parenthood clinic in Queens. More ominously, he has been hired as a consultant for "family planning" in China; that is, for "the humane disposal of newborn second children" (345). In his last conversation with More, Comeaux remains the unregenerate theorist. He defends the Blue Boy project and the regressing of black prisoners at Angola to passive "slavery" levels of behavior on the grounds of scientific necessitarianism. Such projects are justifiable, he claims, for the future good of society and of science. Like the German Dr. Brandt, for Comeaux, "reverence for nation," the gnostic utopian ideal, precedes "reverence for life." Dr. Van Dorn eventually recovers his "humanity" by living with the gorilla Eve and relearning signing. But with his power of language restored, Van Dorn becomes a huckster media star, author of the best-seller *My Life and Love with Eve,* and a frequent talk show guest, discussing human sexuality with Dr. Ruth. In contrast to the fresh successes of his adversaries Comeaux and Van Dorn, Tom More barely ekes out a living between private practice and work at the hospice.

As a refuge where the sick and dying are treated as sacred persons, St. Margaret's hospice stands as a counterimage to the theory-based communities of Belle Ame, the qualitarian center, and the general culture of thanatos.

In the broken bodies of the hospice residents Father Smith and his fellow workers find signs of the Body of Christ, the true Word. Just as the persistence of the Jews and the eucharistic mass are the remnant signs of the presence of the living Word in history, so also is the hospice a remnant community of charity amidst history's abattoir. As Girard has pointed out, the etiology of "hospital" associates it with the "house of God," the place where victims are cared for "without distinction of social, political, or even religious identity" (167). Although a small remnant community in a degenerate culture, the hospice is a powerful sign of belief in the absolute sacredness of the person and the true concern for victims that issues only from the reality of the cross and resurrection. Against this genuine community, as Girard reminds us, stand the many neopagan caricatures of a community of concern—the Fedvilles and qualitarian centers—that would usurp the place of Christ by offering "compassion" and self-transcendence through violence and oppression. Such utopian schemes, mock imitations of Christian community, are truly the work of Antichrist, the "great Depriver" that Father Smith names in his final sermon (180–81). Through the stark either/or choice of vision implicit in these opposing images of community, Percy points to the somber reality of present culture. His vision is tough minded and realistic but also limned with small signs of hope.

Typical of Percy's endings, the conclusion to this cautionary tale is open ended, as befits the truth of a Peircean community. Percy's ending is designed to show us where we stand now, historically and culturally, and at the same time suggest the possibilities—hopeful and direful—implicit in our situation. This situation calls his protagonist More (as well as his readers) to an awareness of fateful human choices; indeed, the radical choice for or against humanity. Consequently, the novel's ending is true to the paradoxical reality cited in the two quotations that opened this chapter: that on the one hand, words have suffered deprivation of meaning, and on the other, that signs and events can be connected, and that real meaning can be discovered by humans. Indeed, the possible recovery of humanity that is the novel's hopeful message is grounded in Percy's affirmation of the meaningful "connectedness" of all reality and the human power to discern and name it.

More's affirmation of his own humanity comes in his refusal to join the Fedville team, his undermining of the Blue Boy project and diverting of its resources and subjects to the hospice. In addition, he rejects Lucy's offer to live with her at Pantherburn, recognizing that such a choice would lead him down the suicidal paths of his ancestors. Instead, he returns to his family and is reconciled to Ellen, who, once detoxified, begins to recover herself. But this and other fortuitous events—Lucy's reconciliation with her ex-husband Buddy Dupre, Vergil Bon's financial success with Exxon, and Uncle Hugh Bob's winning the Arkansas National Duck Call for the eleventh time—do not dispel the general spiritual anomie in the culture. Feliciana's citizens have "subsided into a pleasant funk" once the heavy sodium stimulant is removed, but at least they are no longer contentedly regressed subhumans. Hope lies in their return to the realities of anxiety, depression, and failure. The return to their real condition as humans offers the chance, and the choice, to recover their true selves, neither superhuman (angelic) nor pongid-primate (bestial). Yet despite this promise, when More and his family visit Disney World, he finds his retiree neighbors in the trailer park "amiable, gregarious, helpful—but at something of a loss. . . . They stand nodding and smiling, but looking somewhat zapped" (338, 349). In this scene Percy situates More in the deprived present between the coordinates of a gnostic, utopian future—Disney World's "Magic Kingdom" and "Tomorrowland"—and the defining sign of human deprivation and the symbolic "end of the modern world" from the past—the battles of the Somme and Verdun. More's axial point for witnessing this panorama of the modern condition is a "little copse in Fort Wilderness" where he again reads Stedman's *History of World War I,* from a vista that "affords a view of the great sphere of spaceship earth and the top of the minaret-like tower of Cinderella's Castle" (338). Connecting his reading of history to the fond, stunned look of his neighbors, More says: "I experience the sensation that the world really ended in 1916 and that we've been living in a dream ever since. These good fellows have spent their entire lives working, raising families, fighting Nazis, worrying about Communism, yet they've really been zapped by something else. We stand about in the Florida sunshine of Jack Rabbit Run, under the minaret of Cinderella's Castle, they fresh from the wonders of Tomorrowland—Tomorrowland!—We don't even know what Todayland is!—fond, talkative, informative, and stunned, knocked in the head, like dreamwalkers in a moonscape" (339–40).

More's fellow citizens suffer a radical displacement from being, signified by their free-floating displacement from time. Through Father Smith Percy suggested that the cause of this displacement is a "separation" from the axis point of history, the Christian Incarnation. Supplanting this definitive historical sign of the real meaning of human community are the fantastical signs of the gnostic dreamers' impulse to escape history—Cinderella's Castle and Tomorrowland. The "zapped" dream walkers, among whom More counts himself, float through a present deprived of meaning by a destructive spiritual force they neither acknowledge nor understand. But Father Smith knows this force and will come to name it.

One tangible sign of hope, despite the general deprivation, is the living presence of the divine Word and the sacraments. Percy specifies the presence of the unsubsumable Word through More's relationship with his recovering wife, on the one hand, and through Father Smith on the other. When Ellen is detoxified and returns to her "tart, lusty self," she abandons Presbyterianism for Episcopalianism, but then becomes a Pentacostal, speaking in tongues and loving "the Holy Spirit." More recognizes the dualism in her new belief, its implied rejection of real Presence in the fleshly world. He notes: "In her case spirit has nothing to do with body. Each goes its own way. Even when she was a Presbyterian and I was a Catholic, I remember she was horrified by the Eucharist: *Eating* the body of Christ. That's pagan and barbaric, she said. What she meant and what horrified her was the mixing up of body and spirit, Catholic trafficking in bread, wine, oil, salt, water, body, blood, spit—things. What does the Holy Spirit need with things? Body does body things. Spirit does spirit things" (353). When Ellen insists that More and the children will not be saved until they are "born again of the Holy Spirit and into the Lord," More defends the validity of their initial baptism (355). Though no longer a practicing Catholic—he claims he isn't sure now what he believes—More affirms his children to be Catholic and takes them to Christmas mass. The Catholic community in Feliciana has shrunken to a "remnant of a remnant," losing ground to evangelical Christians, who give More "the creeps." Yet the kingdom of God persists here and now in the Word and the sacraments, antitheses to Disney World's fantastical "Magic Kingdom." More still continues to assist Father Smith at mass when needed, which leads Ellen to accuse him of being "still a Roman." But he refuses to serve mass regularly, believing it would be deceitful, given his skepticism.

Percy's open-ended ending enables him to gather all thematic strands and related signs, place them in historical-theological context, and emphasize the elemental choices of life or death that must be made. The focus of his final view of community is Father Smith, the prophetic visionary who interprets the present situation before beginning the mass to celebrate the reopening of St. Margaret's hospice. Speaking on the feast of his patron saint, St. Simon Stylite, Father Smith, like Will Barrett in *The Second Coming,* names the source of human deprivation to be the "great Prince Satan . . . who rules the world" (361). As Christ is present in the Eucharist, so also "the great Prince is here"

(359). Satan, the deceiver, the priest argues, has deprived language of its power to signify truth, the most telling signs of which are the absence of human guilt and the disbelief in Satan. The threatened "evacuation" of these essential human attributes, the recognition of evil and the sense of conscience, is far more portentous than the "zapping" with drugs. What has replaced guilt, the sign of man's capacity for evil and the need of redemption, is "benevolent feeling" and "tenderness." Such tenderness, as Father Smith warns his audience, will lead "to the gas chambers" (361).

Echoing his earlier essay "Notes for a Novel about the End of the World," Percy acknowledges through Father Smith the difficulty of religious belief in a culture governed by secular theory and linguistic relativism. Hence we see the power of Satan, the Great Depriver. The priest tells More: "It is to be expected. It is only necessary to wait and to be of good heart. It is not your fault. You have been deprived of the faith. All of us have. It is part of the times" (363–64). Percy approaches the deeper mystery of God's purpose in permitting such deprivation—prologue to the Holocaust—to occur. But as a novelist, he does not speculate beyond representing the present reality. For Father Smith, despite his pessimistic sense that the capacity for faith has been radically diminished, the other two virtues—charity and hope—are within humans' grasp. If words are devalued, actions nonetheless speak. Charity is the ethic of human community, as shown in the care of the unwanted at the hospice and in the priest's encouragement to "have a loving heart and do not secretly wish for the death of others." In an age that feasts on "the delectation of doom," he enjoins More, "you must not lose hope" (365).

Father Smith's message of hope is linked to a mysterious sign within the present culture, the alleged apparition of the Virgin Mary to six children at Medjugorje. What interests the priest about the apparition and, for him, gives it the stamp of authenticity is the reported appearance of Mary as an ordinary young Jewish girl, not in celestial glory. Her ordinariness, and the message she brings that God has permitted the Great Depriver to "rule" the twentieth century by leaving humankind alone, stand as real clues within the semiosis of the present world, as Percy imagines it. Her ordinary Jewish identity links her to the "unsubsumable" Jews of history, to the divine Word incarnated as a Jew, to the fate of the Jews in the Holocaust, and to the present and future danger of exterminations on "humanitarian" grounds. As a sign, the apparition itself cannot be subsumed or explained under humanist theories of knowledge. The apparition is an encouragement to hope, that Satan will not succeed in destroying the world, and that even if "the world will end in fire . . . the Lord will come" (365). Understandably, More is mystified by the story of the apparition, perhaps even incredulous. But his own actions, as distinct from his mental skepticism, signify that in some mysterious way, the message of hope and charity may well have been received.

As the Jews and the apparition of Mary are unsubsumable real signs, so also are the mass and the sacraments, concrete signs of the Holy Spirit and hope in the present world. Although he is "not sure" what he believes, More responds when Father Smith sends him a coded sign—a "Jewish girl, a visit from royalty. Gifts"—on the feast of the Epiphany, the feast of the "showing forth" of the sign of salvation, the Christ child, and the offering of gifts. In this sign (we recall again that Peirce's central image of triadicity was gift giving) Percy sets the whole question of the deprivation of humanity and the hope of recovery within the context of liturgical time. The feast proclaims the coming of the kingdom of God in the real here-and-now and the promise of final salvation within the community of saints. The historicity of the Jews and of the Christian Incarnation stand as living ordinary signs of humanity's possible redemption and against the secular visions of community that issued in the terror of the twentieth century.

Percy's final scene in the novel expresses this hope of recovery in ordinary human terms, as befits his bemused but resilient protagonist, Tom More. An end becomes a beginning. Now free from heavy sodium, More's first patient Mickey LaFaye has returned to her normal self, anxious and "terrified." But in a colloquy with More, Mickey begins to explore her inner self for the roots of the terror. She begins to search out the possible meaning of the mysterious signs in her dream of a cellar, the smell of winter apples, and "a stranger coming." Mickey thinks the stranger "is part of myself," associated with the terror but "not someone to be terrified of" (371). In the semiosis of the novel, Percy's association of this stranger with the mysterious "stranger" of the Medjugorje apparition, and the "stranger" who arrived in Bethlehem, seems unmistakable. But what is important here is that Mickey, with More's help, is beginning to try to *name* the source of her terror. In their colloquy, More once again affirms Peirce's belief that apparently disconnected events can be connected and understood, as well as Harry Stack Sullivan's belief that every person can discover what he or she needs to know, "with a little help from you." Ordinary human language and a community of relations can, with humility and charity, contend against the deprivations of language and humanity. As Mickey opens her mouth to speak, More's final words are, "Well well well." The Great Depriver does not have the last word.

Epilogue

In the last years of his life Walker Percy intended to write a study of language that would provide the basis for a "new anthropology." The study was to be grounded in Peirce's semiotic, especially the concept of triadicity, and in the fundamental beliefs of Percy's Catholic faith. As he announced in a letter to Kenneth Laine Ketner on February 27, 1989, "I want to use . . . CSP as the foundation for a Catholic apologetic, which I have tentatively entitled (after Aquinas) *Contra Gentiles*" (TP, 130–31). Elaborating on this plan, Percy said: "what I hope to do is use CSP's 'ontology' of Secondness and Thirdness (not Firstness) as the ground for a more or less scientific introduction to a philosophical anthropology. Such an ontology, I think, would debouche directly into the phenomenology of the 'existentialists,' like Marcel, Heidegger, Buber, et al" (131). Percy's bold plan was conceived as no less than an attempt to establish a foundation for the recovery of a coherent intellectual community. The plan would challenge, undermine, and hopefully reverse what Percy and Peirce saw as the more than four-hundred-year domination of Western thought by erroneous scientistic principles. For realists Percy and Peirce, nominalism and its various offshoots and Cartesianism were at the root of those erroneous principles. As I noted in the introduction, Percy went back to the Scholastics, especially John Poinset, to develop realist concepts of language that would challenge these principles. As always for Peirce and Percy, realism in language was the basis for genuine community. Yet for Percy, unlike Peirce, linguistic realism was the intersection where anthropology and "Catholic apologetics" could meet. As we have seen, his belief in humans' uniqueness as creatures

249

who can name and symbolize true realities was, because of his belief in Christ's Incarnation, coincident with his belief in the absolute spiritual integrity of the person.

Percy's plan, as he explained it in his letter to Ketner, held the promise of making possible a new ground of meaning and a new unity in science and the social sciences, one that would be truly anthropocentric and yet situate the person within a community of signs that extended from the immediate to the mystical—in short, an unlimited community. Percy's planned introduction offered hope for the reconciliation of science, the social sciences, and religious faith, a hope he expressed in "The Fateful Rift: The San Andreas Fault in the Modern Mind," the Jefferson Lecture delivered at the National Endowment for the Humanities.

In his plan to develop a new anthropology, and in the hope he expressed for the future of the human community, Percy can be seen as a genuinely evolutionary thinker. The sense of this truth is important to grasp. As a scientist Percy obviously believed in the biological evolution of species. But far more important was his belief in the evolution—and possible devolution—of human consciousness and the human spirit. Percy understood that the evolution of consciousness is intimately linked to the evolution of signs within the living community of meaning where humans are actually and potentially related to each other. For Percy, the truth of realism—the fact that realities exist independently of what we think, and encompass both the actual and the possible—is the ground for the drama of the human journey through history. Viewed from this evolutionary perspective, Percy's various attacks on scientism, behaviorism, and nominalism in language can be seen as his attempt to unmask—or, to use his term, "unhorse,"—aberrant ideologies that are radically anti-evolutionary because they reduce the real context and mystery of existence and diminish the freedom of sovereign persons to respond to that mystery. In contrast, Percy's writings are truly "progressive" in their attempt to expose fallacies of thought and reestablish the communal basis for genuinely *human* evolution.

But if Percy's plan to construct a "new anthropology" in the proposed study called *Contra Gentiles* looked to the future, he was nonetheless clearly attuned to the realities of the present situation as well. What he saw and wrote about was the incoherence and chaos in the modern human community, the many signs of which included the denigration of the spiritual worth of the person, the antinomy of science and religion, the fragmentation of the social sciences, global warfare and mass death, the devaluation of language as an instrument for truth, and the pervasive sense of alienation and despair in the midst of material plenty. As a realist writer Percy was ever faithful to "where we are now"; he was neither utopianist nor apocalypticist. Consequently most of his energies went toward diagnosing the present "incoherence," exposing its contradictory assumptions and dogmas while at the same time suggesting ways to clarify intellectual confusions and point ways to heal the riven self and the community.

Percy died before he was able to write *Contra Gentiles*, and so the great work of intellectual synthesis he had imagined and planned remained unwritten. (That he had earlier considered calling such a work the "New Organon," perhaps as a rebuttal to Bacon's arrogant dismissal of Scholasticism and its metaphysics, reveals his sense of its significance.) Nevertheless, the principal ideas of this synthesis, as I have argued, are evident throughout his writings, implicitly in his fictions and explicitly in his essays and addresses. The idea for such a synthesis is behind his attack on the modern schism between the physical and social sciences in the Jefferson Lecture, delivered nearly a year before his death. In addition, his critique of the schism forms the basis of his vision of the modern self and community in *Lost in the Cosmos*, especially his semiotic primer of the self, which he regarded as one of the most important pieces he had written. Elements of Percy's "new anthropology" surface throughout his essays as well, applied to various social, cultural, linguistic, and anthropological phenomena, as well as to fiction writing itself. Yet his remark to Ketner that he wished to "use CSP" as the basis for a "*Catholic apologetic*" and a "new anthropology" points clearly to the doctrine of the Christian Incarnation as the centerpiece in his proposed theosemiotic synthesis (italics mine). The early draft of the Jefferson Lecture, titled "Science, Religion, and the Tertium Quid," strongly emphasizes the incarnational and sacramental basis of his argument. In the draft version, he compares the scientific and Christian views of reality and explains how the latter affirms a God who, through the Jews, "founded a visible institution, founded upon another man, a member of the same tribe, through whose agency men are provided with a means of worshipping God and receiving certain gifts from him, for example, the Eucharist which, though having the appearance of bread and wine, is believed to be in a real, not symbolic sense, the body and blood of the man-God himself" (TP, 88–89). For Percy, acceptance or rejection of the truth claim of the Christian belief is the fault line for epistemology (hence, for science) and cosmology. Hence the "scandal" of this claim. As he noted, to say that the Christian incarnational view of reality and its insistence on the absolute importance of the particular is only one viewpoint among many is "to use the word *true* analogically and to surrender all truth claims to the scientist" (92). Once this occurs, the particular is deemed relevant only "in order to arrive at generals. No significance can be attached to a particular electron or a particular comet" (94). At the same time, Percy recognized the paradox that the doctrine of Christ's Incarnation conferred an importance on particulars that had propelled scientific discoveries for centuries. But separation from the anthropological root (i.e., from the personal relation between God and creation) had fostered the modern incoherence. Percy hoped to begin to recover "coherence" with his proposed new organon.

For his part, as Michael Raposa has shown, Peirce believed in an ideal of community of truth seekers moving in concert to build the community of signs toward ultimate truth (*Peirce's Philosophy of Religion*, 153–54). Percy accepted such an ideal of community but historicized and Christianized it by looking at the evolution of signs through the lens of Christ's Incarnation to see how *that* fact shaped history and opened a new reality and new possibilities for recovery within the human community. In theological terms, Percy's "new anthropology" was grounded in the possibility of a "new man," aided by grace, a possibility whose true source is the resurrection of Christ from the dead. The discovery of authentic humanity—the person who discovers himself "transparently with another under God"—was thus the real goal of his "new anthropology."

As I noted in the introduction to this study, Percy's acquaintance with Peirce's thought probably began in the late 1940s with the gift of an inscribed copy of *The Unlimited Community: A Study of the Possibility of Social Science*, coauthored by Julius Friend and James K. Fiebleman. This work was a polemical study of, in their view, the disastrous effects of the rejection of a realistic ontology in favor of nominalism in all areas of life in the West— in philosophy, theology, politics, economics, linguistics, and social science. For them, nominalism spawned a turning away from metaphysics and the search for objective truth and replaced them with a "subjectivism of reason" and an individualism that led eventually to an "incoherent" anthropology and social and intellectual fragmentation. Against this ascendant nominalism Friend and Fiebleman offered Charles Sanders Peirce as one of the few modern thinkers who understood the destructive influence of nominalism and who set out in his writings to disprove the prevailing nominalistic doctrines and offer an alternative philosophical viewpoint—realism (43). A central feature of Peirce's realist vision was the ideal of an "unlimited community." It denoted the open-ended community of signs and sign users, that is, the semiotic web that encompassed both actualities and possibilities and propelled the growth of knowledge. Peirce's notion of the unlimited community expressed his evolutionary idealism, his belief in the progressive development of the intellectual community in its pursuit of ultimate truth. For Peirce, as Raposa has shown, the force or energy driving evolutionary progress in the human community was divine love, a force or principle he terms "agapism" (*Peirce's Philosophy of Religion*, 153–54). Peirce's notion of agapism is consonant with the Christian ideal of a community of charity. In attacking the nineteenth-century gospel of greed and individualism, he said: "Jesus, in his Sermon on the Mount, expressed a different opinion. Here, then, is the issue. The gospel of Christ says that progress comes from every individual merging his individuality in sympathy with his neighbors. On the other side, the conviction of the nineteenth century is that progress takes place by virtue of every individual's striving for himself with all his might and trampling his neighbor under foot whenever he gets a chance to do so. This may accurately be called the Gospel of Greed" (CP, 6.293–6.294). Half a century later, Percy would register the disastrous effects of America's having followed the gospel of individualism and greed.

Peirce's semiotic realism, coupled with Percy's Catholic beliefs, gave Percy the basis for his "new anthropology" by providing a way to articulate the traditional notion of the fall and possible redemption of humanity within the purview of a scientific linguistic perspective. This is the vision that informs *Lost in the Cosmos*. Its central semiotic primer expresses Percy's concept of evolution in history viewed in terms of man's unique status as a namer, his loss of that status, and his possible recovery or redemption. Thus in the primer Percy described the human predicament in terms of man's development as a language user. In his semiotic reading of evolution, fairly recently in the history of the cosmos, perhaps 100,000 years ago, humankind achieved a "breakthrough" into triadic behavior with the discovery of the sign and the power of symbolic communication (94–95). No longer was man simply an organism whose behavior was carried out, and could be explained, in terms of material cause and effect (i.e., dyadically). Triadicity brought with it the capacity for *real* meaning and human communication, for knowledge of the world, self-knowledge of one's creatureliness, and the power to name (and thus "create") the world. In short, Thirdness makes genuine human community possible. But as Percy also argued, the breakthrough into triadicity also incurred the inevitable "fall" into self-consciousness, and the inescapable sense of homelessness we experience in the world. The self, gifted with the power to name and to comprehend the world, cannot name itself in any stable way (107). Man the symbolizer suffers an estrangement from the original joyous rapture of being and knows himself to be as a wayfarer or alien adrift in the cosmos. As Percy stated, "The exile from Eden is, semiotically, the banishment of the self-conscious self from its own world of signs" (108).

Much of *Lost in the Cosmos* examines the condition of alienation inherent in the human predicament, and the various guises the self adopts to try to "locate" itself in the world. Most often this involves fraudulent and literally self-defeating attempts to establish or join in community with others through the guises of role playing seen in Binx Bolling, Kitty and Rita Vaught, Mercer, Moira Shaffner, Doctors Van Dorn and Comeaux, and others. To use Percy's language, the self embarks on a continual attempt to hide the "nakedness" it experiences at the core of its being, due to the inability to "formulate" or iden-tify who it really is (109). When the self tries to name itself (define its funda-mental being), all names seem to apply (107). Paradoxically, self-consciousness and the power of language enable human freedom and individuation (I am I and not you) but also incur a sense of separateness, "lostness," and alien-ation from the true source of being. After examining several of the guises the self adopts to cover the "nakedness" of self-conscious alienation, Percy allows one exception. Following Kierkegaard, he affirms the possibility that the self can come to know itself with another "transparently under God." Percy de-fines this as the "theistic-historical" view of the self characteristic of Judaism, Christianity, and Islam: "The self becomes itself by recognizing God as a spirit, creator of the Cosmos and therefore of one's self as a creature, a wounded creature but a creature nonetheless, who shares with a community of like crea-tures the belief that God, who transcends the entire Cosmos and has actually entered human history—or will enter it—in order to redeem man from the catastrophe which has overtaken his self" (112). Unfortunately, as Percy notes, the theistic-historical perspective on the self seems "no longer available" in a "post-religious technological society" (113). Lacking that perspective, the self—and the prospects for human community—seem doomed to failure in Percy's parable. After exhausting various avenues of possible transcendence from its predicament, the self may well become possessed by the demoniac spirit of erotic violence, leading to "War without passion: one billion dead" (191). The "autonomous self" with its human freedom holds within it the ca-pacity for almost unlimited destruction.

After offering this dire possible scenario for the future fate of the human species under scientism, Percy concludes *Lost in the Cosmos,* as he does his novels, by focusing on the present situation and on the ethical choices it presents and demands. In the final section, titled "A Space Odyssey (II)," Percy offers two familiar visions of community for his space travelers to choose between. Although set in an imaginary future, the communities—and the choice—are presented clearly as the moral options Percy sees open to a "post-religious technological society." One is the postapocalypse community proposed by Dr. Aristarchus Jones, who wants to colonize the planet Europa, a satellite of Jupiter, rename it New Ionia, and create a society "based on reason and science." Jones's new community would eliminate "the mistakes of the past," such as "the superstitions and repressions of religion." In this projected utopia, "sexually free and peace-loving" citizens would live in harmony, although children with genetic defects would have to be "excluded" so as not to contaminate the new master race. In short, Jones's plan for community is another version of Lance Lamar's New Order and the gnostic ideal of the qualitarian doctors in *Love in the Ruins* and *The Thanatos Syndrome,* now presented as a remnant vision on which to create a brave new world.

The second option for community is proposed by Abbot Liebowitz, a Jewish-Catholic monk who himself embodies the remnants of the Jewish-Christian tradition. Liebowitz proposes a community of "the people of the Book," to be founded not in distant space but in Lost Cove, Tennessee. It will include all manner of spiritually and physically "defective" believers and non-believers, fallen creatures who nonetheless recognize their wounded condition and live—often fractiously—in the hope of some final redemption from their predicament. Liebowitz offers mass and the sacraments for those who will attend. The covenant between God, the incarnate Christ, and the remnant people still holds. In short, his is the ordinary human community. In his typical "open-ended" fashion, consistent with his view of the present situation, Percy leaves the choice of which model is preferable up to the reader to decide.

While the opposing models of remnant communities Percy offered in *Lost in the Cosmos* are familiar from his other fictions, here he elaborates more fully on the current paradoxical relation between the two viewpoints. His elaboration offers a clue to the hope for community he expressed at the end of the Jefferson Lecture. In a "Thought Experiment" near the end of *Lost in the Cosmos,* Percy offers an exercise in "shifting one's perspective" when thinking about the relationship between Jewish-Christianity and modern scientism. He argues that, on the one hand, the Jewish-Christian view of humanity seems preposterous to the modern scientific consciousness (i.e., scientism) "*precisely to the degree*" that the latter has elevated itself to an "all-construing quasi-religious view of the world" (252) (italics mine). On the other hand, by adopting an "outside" viewpoint by which one observes the modern "scientific" self as it views the world through its perspective, it is possible to see that scientism's perspective is equally preposterous, because the real self is "excluded" when the world is construed entirely by scientism's principles. As Percy states: "The earth-self seeks to understand the Cosmos overtly according to scientific principles while covertly exempting itself from the same understanding. The end of this enterprise is that the self understands the mechanism of the Cosmos but by the same motion places itself outside the Cosmos, an alien, a ghost, outside a vast machinery to which it is denied entry" (254). In the face of the dilemmas inherent in the "preposterousness" of these views, Percy suggests two options, which are not mutually exclusive. One is that, with further advances in science and technology, the Jewish-Christian view of the person will become totally anachronistic and "unbelievable." The second option is that advances in science and technology will only widen the gap between our empirical knowledge of the world, and the unique human alienated self, until "in the end it is this preposterous remedy (the Jewish-Christian view), it and no other, which is specified by the preposterous predicament of the human self as its sole remedy" (254). The second option, of course, expresses Percy's hope for the future: that recognition of the extremity of the modern human predicament may lead to a reversal of perspective and a new beginning. This hope formed the basis of his plan to write a "new anthropology" from a scientific perspective, as a way to begin to bridge the current chasm or "fault" between science and religion.

What is implicit in Percy's hope for a "new anthropology" and a new intellectual community is a rejection of any notion of retrogression from the advances achieved through science and technology. Given the evolution of consciousness, such a "turning back" would obviously be impossible. In his brilliant study of the roots of modernity, *Saving the Appearances: A Study in Idolatry,* Owen Barfield analyzes how the modern idols of scientism and literalism have beguiled us into believing that the material world holds the sum total of truth, including the truth of human existence. This process of idolization was accelerated by the scientific revolution, when the all-construing ideology of scientism began to absorb the modern mind. This absorption was intensified by the *kind* of self-consciousness posited by Descartes when he formulated the mind-body split. But the way to overcome this besetting modern idolatry, Barfield argues, is not by some impossible "return" to a premodern mentality. Rather, Barfield proposes that man the self-conscious creature must come to understand himself as a being not defined and determined by the material world around him but as a free co-creator and namer of the world, a person who is at one with the spirit expressing itself through the "representations," the objects and signs that make up human existence. The way forward, he argued, is *through* and beyond idolatry, by absorbing the best achievements of science and technology and then using them imaginatively to ascend to a higher level in the development of the human spirit. But for Barfield, this will occur *only* through the recognition of our radical relation to God, to the divine Word given to the Jews and enfleshed in history in Christ, his death and resurrection, and in the Eucharist. Speaking of the unity between Word, Christ, and sign in the Eucharist, Barfield says: "In one man the inwardness of the Divine Name had been fully realized; the final participation, whereby man's Creator speaks from within man himself, had been accomplished. The Word had been made flesh. For all who partake of the Eucharist acknowledge that the man who was born in Bethlehem was "of one substance with the Father by whom all things were made; and then they take that substance into themselves, together with its representations named bread and wine. That is after all the heart of the matter" (170).

Walker Percy clearly held to such a view and the perilous hope it expresses. Near the end of the Jefferson Lecture he imagined the possibility of a recovery of men and women as fully human and a reconciliation of our fragmented community. He imagined a future in which: "with this new anthropology in hand, Pierce's triadic creature with its named world, Heidegger's *Dasein* suffering a *Verfallen,* a fall, Gabriel Marcel's Homo Viator, man as pilgrim, one might even explore its openness to such traditional Judeo-Christian notions as man falling prey to the worldliness of the world, and man as pilgrim seeking his salvation" (SSL, 291). Like Barfield's vision of a more spiritualized human being, Percy's "new anthropology" offers the possibility of the "new man" St. Paul speaks of in 15 Corinthians, but only after trial, suffering, and conversion. Paul's model for the new man is, of course, Christ resurrected in glory, in whose image fallen yet redeemed man may rise for all eternity in a spiritualized body. For Percy the sign of the possibility of this transfigured and glorified body is the final answer to Descartes's mind-body split, and he named it explicitly in Binx Bolling's affirmation of a risen Lonnie Smith near the end of *The Moviegoer.* The transfiguration of the body is the ultimate sign of mystical community, enfleshed in the body and blood in the Eucharist, in the broken bodies of the patients in St. Margaret's hospice and in the many signs of the spirit that exist in the mystery of the communal, semiotic world. But as in the ending of *Lost in the Cosmos,* Percy leaves the choice of vision—and the kind of community we wish to create out of the ruins—up to us.

NOTES

INTRODUCTION

1. For example, see Quinlan, *Walker Percy.*

2. Patrick Samway, "Walker Percy the Gift-Giver," *The Delta Factor* 6, no. 1 (1999): 2.

3. Percy extensively analyzed the "fall" in language in his semiotic parable of the self in LC, 85–126.

4. For an excellent analysis of Percy's semiotic perspective, see Weldon Thornton's "Homo Loquens, Homo Symbolificus, Homo Sapiens: Walker Percy on Language," in *Art of Walker Percy,* ed. Broughton, 169–92.

5. O'Connor, "Novelist and Believer," in *Mystery and Manners,* 154–68.

6. Percy, "Decline of the Western," *Commonweal,* May 16, 1958, 181–83.

7. See my essay "Closing the Gap: Walker Percy and the Realism-Nominalism Debate," *Logos* (fall 1998): 11–30.

8. Peirce, "The Fixation of Belief," in *Charles Sanders Peirce,* ed. Wiener, 107–8.

9. Joel Weinsheimer, "The Realism of C. S. Peirce, or How Homer and Nature Can Be the Same," *American Journal of Semiotics* 2 (1983): 225–64.

10. Peirce, "Letters to Lady Welby," quoted in *Charles Sanders Peirce,* ed. Weiner, 383.

11. In contrast to Ketner's view, Raposa argues that it is inaccurate to claim that Peirce denied the existence of individuals. See *Peirce's Philosophy of Religion,* 21–22.

12. Percy, "Interview with Sr. Bernadette Prochaska, F.S.P.A.," in *The Delta Factor* 5, no. 2 (1994): 2.

13. Powers, *Eucharistic Theology,* 172–73. I am deeply indebted to Powers for his superb discussion of transsignification in the Eucharist.

14. In a letter to Ketner, regarding the abortion issue, Percy said: "If one does not grant a religious warrant for the sacredness of human life, one must consider the scientific grounds, i.e., that there is no essential difference between the human organism, genetically or hormonally, before and after birth. Thus, if you allow the destruction of the unborn for however good and private a reason, why not get rid of undesirable 1 year olds, or middle-aged subversive professors for that matter?" (63).

ONE. The Footprint on the Beach: *The Moviegoer*

1. See my essay "Binx Bolling—Walker Percy's Musing Scientist," in *At the Cross-roads,* 13–31.

2. See, for example, Lawson's "Walker Percy's *The Moviegoer:* The Cinema as Cave," in *Following Percy,* 83–108; and "The Dream Screen in *The Moviegoer,*" in *Still Following Percy,* 29–57; and Luschei, *Sovereign Wayfarer,* 64–110.

3. See Luschei, *Sovereign Wayfarer,* 66–67; and Lawson, "Walker Percy's Southern Stoic" and "*The Moviegoer* and the Stoic Heritage," in *Following Percy,* 41–83.

4. See especially Ciuba's discussion of Lonnie Smith in *Walker Percy,* 76–79.

5. See Anne Goodwyn Jones's comments in *Tommorrow Is Another Day,* 1; and Timothy Nixon's "The Exclusionary Nature of *The Moviegoer,*" in *Walker Percy's Feminine Characters,* ed. Lawson and Oleksy, 50–62.

6. Percy's interest in and use of Kierkegaard's concept of repetition is well known. For example, see Luschei, *Sovereign Wayfarer,* 48–52, 93. For an excellent and thorough discussion of repetition in Percy's work, see Dupuy's *Autobiography in Walker Percy.*

7. Luschei defines Kierkegaard's distinction between the three stages—the aesthetic, the ethical, and the religious—in reference to Percy's writings. See Luschei, *Sovereign Wayfarer,* 49–63. Lawson sees Binx as developing from the aesthetic to the ethical stage. See his "Walker Percy's Indirect Communications," in *Following Percy,* 7–23.

8. See Percy's comments on Kierkegaard's essay in "An Interview with Zoltan Abadi-Nagy," in SSL, 376.

9. Allen, *Walker Percy.* Allen sees the father-son relationship as central to Percy's fiction, as do most other critics of his work.

10. See in particular Lawson's two essays on *The Moviegoer,* cited above in note two.

TWO. Ground Zero and the Iron Horsehead: *The Last Gentleman*

1. In several interviews Percy commented extensively on Will Barrett's psychological condition. See his remarks on Barrett's dislocation from time in an interview with Ashley Brown, in *Conversations with Walker Percy,* ed. Lawson and Kramer, 13–14; and his comments to Dewey, 114.

2. I have treated the triangular pattern in greater detail in my essay "The Shot Heard 'Round the Room: JFK and Walker Percy's *The Last Gentleman,*" in *Louisiana Literature* (summer 1999): 89–96.

3. Vautier examines the pattern of triangulation between the narrator, narratee, and the narration that creates the changing dynamics of focus in the novel. See her essay "Narrative Triangulation in *The Last Gentleman,*" in *Art of Walker Percy,* ed. Broughton, 69–95. Vautier's essay does not relate Percy's narrative strategy to a larger theological-semiotic perspective.

4. Allen Pridgen's excellent discussion of the sacramental dimension of the novel parallels my own in several respects. See his *Walker Percy's Sacramental Landscapes*, 49–97.

5. Percy's elaborated argument on the relation between Christianity, science, and pornography was developed later in his discussion of the demoniac self in LC, 175–98.

6. See Lawson's important essay "Will Barrett under the Telescope," in *Still Following Percy*, 112–41.

7. Donne's comment on the effects of the new science:

And freely men confess that this world's spent,
When in the planets and the firmament
They seek so many new; they see that this
Is crumbled out again to atomies.
'Tis all in pieces, all coherence gone;
All just supply, and all relation.
"Anatomy of the World," 199–204

8. In his semiotic primer of the self in LC, Percy distinguished an "environment," the realm of dyadic interacting organisms, from a "world," the realm of triadic sign-users (99–100).

9. Alfred North Whitehead, *Science and the Modern World* (New York: The Macmillan Company, 1926), 64–82.

10. See Percy's "Naming and Being," in SSL, 130–39.

THREE. The Thread in the Labyrinth: *Love in the Ruins*

1. See Percy's review of Richard Hughes's *The Fox in the Attic* in "Hughes's Solipsism Malgre Lui," *Sewanee Review* 72 (1964): 492, 495.

2. Percy, "Walter M. Miller Jr.'s *A Canticle for Liebowitz*," in *Rediscoveries*, ed. Madden, 264.

3. Percy, "The Authors That Bloom in the Spring," *Publishers Weekly*, 199 (1971): 23.

4. Interestingly, Charles Sanders Peirce identified a similar epistemological crisis much earlier in the century when he suggested that in the scientistic atmosphere of modern culture, the human mind's natural affiliation to God, through signs, was being drowned out. See Raposa, *Peirce's Philosophy of Religion*, 139–40.

5. In his 1983 interview with Robin Leary, Percy argued that the philosophical debate between realism and nominalism was more important than the idealist versus materalist debate. See my essay "Closing the Gap: Walker Percy and the Realism-Nominalism Debate," *Logos* (fall 1998): 11–29.

6. Bacon, *New Organon*, 39–53.

7. The link between technology, war, and objectifying women as idealized icons is

particularly significant here. See Percy's later analysis of this relationship in his discussion of pornography, violence, technology, and war in LC, 175–98.

8. See Edward Dupuy's excellent comments on gnosticism and time in Percy's writings, in *Autobiography in Walker Percy*, 93–119.

FOUR. The Worm of Interest: *Lancelot*

1. Percy, "An Interview with Zoltan Abadi-Nagy," quoted in SSL, 383.

2. Obviously, the relationship between Lance and Father John can be seen as a dramatic working out of the Kierkegaardian thesis that the self can come to know itself only with another transparently under God, which Percy cited in LC, 156.

3. Lawson, "Will Barrett under the Telescope," in *Still Following Percy*, 112–41.

4. Percy, "The State of the Novel: Dying Art or New Science," in SSL, 153–68.

5. Speaking as a semiotic realist in LC, Percy insisted on the social, communal origins of the *cogito* and remarked, "What Descartes did not know: no such isolated individual as he described can be conscious" (105).

6. See my essay "Love, Sex, and Knowledge in *Lancelot*," *Mississippi Quarterly* (spring 1986): 103–11.

7. See Percy's comments on Lance's quest in his interview with Zoltan Abadi-Nagy, in SSL, 386.

8. Brooks, "Walker Percy and Modern Gnosticism," in *Art of Walker Percy*, ed. Broughton, 260–73. See also Lawson's "The Gnostic Vision of *Lancelot*" and "Gnosis and Time in *Lancelot*," in *Following Percy*, 196–227.

9. See Percy's discussion of the Envious Self in LC, 57–69.

10. For a more detailed discussion of this theme, see my essay "Love, Sex, and Knowledge in *Lancelot*."

11. George Meredith, "Lucifer in Starlight," quoted in *The Norton Anthology of English Literature*, ed. M. H. Abrams and Stephen Greenblatt, 7th ed., vol. 2 (New York: W.W. Norton and Company, 2000), 1572–73.

12. See Samway, *Walker Percy*, 294–96; and Tolson, *Pilgrim in the Ruins*, 361–94.

13. See Percy's self-interview, "Questions They Never Asked Me," in SSL, 422–23.

FIVE. The Gift of the Word: *The Second Coming*

1. Joel Weinsheimer, "The Realism of C. S. Peirce, or How Homer and Nature Can Be the Same," *American Journal of Semiotics* 2 (1983): 249.

2. As I have already noted, gift giving was Peirce's central example of triadic exchange.

3. Pridgen, *Walker Percy's Sacramental Landscapes,* 121–22, 136–38.

4. I am indebted to Gary Ciuba for his suggestion of Tolstoy as the source for Percy's reference to "the green stick." Tolstoy once imagined a green stick, hidden in a forest, inscribed with words that could destroy all evil in humans.

5. In addition to Hardy's critical view of the ending of the novel, see especially the following: Doreen Fowler's "Answers and Ambiguity in *The Second Coming,*" in *Walker Percy,* ed. Bloom, 115–24; Susan V. Donaldson's "Keeping Quentin Compson Alive: *The Last Gentleman, The Second Coming,* and the Problem of Masculinity," in *Walker Percy's Feminine Characters,* ed. Lawson and Oleksy, 62–77; and Oleksy's "From Silence and Madness to the Exchange That Multiplies: Walker Percy and the Woman Question," in *Walker Percy's Feminine Characters,* ed. Lawson and Oleksy, 122–33.

SIX. Community, History, and the Word: *The Thanatos Syndrome*

1. Percy, "An Interview with Zoltan Abadi-Nagy," in SSL, 394.

2. See, for example, John Edward Hardy's astute analysis of the narrative problems in the novel in *Fiction of Walker Percy,* 225–69. See also Michael Kobre's critique of Percy's use of voice in the novel, in *Walker Percy's Voices,* 194–217.

3. Percy discusses triadic language exchange in several essays in MB. On the matter of syntax, see particularly his essay "Semiotic and a Theory of Knowledge," 243–64. See also LC, 92–94.

4. For a more extensive discussion of the semiotic self, see LC, 94–112.

5. See my discussion of Pantherburn and its connection to southern stoicism in "Disjunctions of Time: Myth and History in *The Thanatos Syndrome,*" in *At the Crossroads,* 102–18.

6. O'Connor, introduction to *A Memoir of Mary Ann,* in *Mystery and Manners,* 226–27.

7. See Percy's comments on Styron's novel in *Correspondence of Shelby Foote and Walker Percy,* ed. Jay Tolson, 257–58.

8. Levi, *Drowned and the Saved,* 89.

WORKS CONSULTED

WORKS BY WALKER PERCY

Lancelot. New York: Farrar, Straus, and Giroux, 1977.
The Last Gentleman. New York: Farrar, Straux, and Giroux, 1966.
Lost in the Cosmos. New York: Farrar, Straus, and Giroux, 1983.
Love in the Ruins. New York: Farrar, Straus, and Giroux, 1971.
The Message in the Bottle. New York: Farrar, Straus, and Giroux, 1975.
The Moviegoer. New York: Alfred A. Knopf, 1961.
The Second Coming. New York: Farrar, Straus, and Giroux, 1980.
Signposts in a Strange Land. Edited with an introduction by Patrick Samway. New York: Farrar, Straus, and Giroux, 1991.
The Thanatos Syndrome. New York: Farrar, Straus, and Giroux, 1987.

SECONDARY SOURCES

Allen, William Rodney. *Walker Percy: A Southern Wayfarer.* Jackson: University Press of Mississippi, 1986.
Almeder, Robert. *The Philosophy of Charles S. Peirce: An Introduction.* Totowa, N.J.: Rowman and Littlefield, Publishers, 1980.
Bacon, Francis. *The New Organon and Related Writings.* Edited by Fulton H. Anderson. Indianapolis: Bobbs-Merrill, 1960.
Barfield, Owen. *Saving the Appearances: A Study in Idolatry.* New York: Harcourt Brace Jovanovich, 1965.
Barzun, Jacques. *The Uses and Abuses of Art.* Princeton: Princeton University Press, 1974.
Bloom, Harold, ed. *Walker Percy.* New York: Chelsea House Publications, 1986.
Brent, Joseph. *Charles Sanders Peirce: A Life.* Bloomington and Indianapolis: Indiana University Press, 1993.
Brinkmeyer, Robert H., Jr. *Three Catholic Writers of the Modern South.* Jackson: University Press of Mississippi, 1985.

Broughton, Panthea Reid. *The Art of Walker Percy: Strategems for Being.* Baton Rouge: Louisiana State University Press, 1979.

Buchler, Justus, ed. *Philosophical Writings of Peirce.* New York: Dover Publishing, 1955.

Ciuba, Gary. *Walker Percy: Books of Revelation.* Athens: University of Georgia Press, 1991.

Colapietro, Vincent M. *Peirce's Approach to the Self.* Albany: State University of New York Press, 1989.

Coles, Robert. *Walker Percy: An American Search.* Boston: Little, Brown, and Company, 1978.

Corrington, Robert S. *An Introduction to C. S. Peirce.* Lanham, Md.: Rowman and Littlefield Publishers, 1993.

Deely, John. *Introducing Semiotic: Its History and Doctrine.* Bloomington: Indiana University Press, 1982.

Delbanco, Andrew. *The Death of Satan: How Americans Have Lost the Sense of Evil.* New York: Farrar, Straus, and Giroux, 1995.

Desmond, John F. *At the Crossroads: Ethical and Religious Themes in the Writings of Walker Percy.* Troy, N.Y.: Whitston Publishing Company, 1997.

Dupuy, Edward. *Autobiography in Walker Percy: Repetition, Recovery, and Redemption.* Baton Rouge: Louisiana State University Press, 1996.

Elliott, Carl, and John Lastos, eds. *The Last Physician: Walker Percy and the Moral Life of Medicine.* Durham, N.C.: Duke University Press, 1999.

Feibleman, James, and Julius W. Friend. *The Unlimited Community: A Study in the Possibility of Social Science.* London: G. Allen and Unwin, 1936.

Fisch, Max H. *Peirce, Semiotic, and Pragmatism.* Edited by Kenneth Laine Ketner and Christian J. W. Kloesel. Bloomington: Indiana University Press, 1986.

Futtrell, Ann Mace. *The Signs of Christianity in the Work of Walker Percy.* San Francisco: Catholic Scholars Press, 1994.

Girard, Rene. *I See Satan Fall Like Lightning.* Maryknoll, N.Y.: Orbis Press, 2001.

Gretlund, Jan Norby, and Karl-Heinz Westarp. *Walker Percy: Novelist and Philosopher.* Jackson: University Press of Mississippi, 1991.

Guardini, Romano. *The End of the Modern World.* Chicago: Henry Regnery Company, 1956.

Hardy, John Edward. *The Fiction of Walker Percy.* Urbana and Chicago: University of Illinois Press, 1987.

Hartshorne, Charles, and Paul Weiss. *Collected Papers of Charles Sanders Peirce.* Vols. 1 and 2. Cambridge: Harvard University Press, 1960.

———. *Collected Papers of Charles Sanders Peirce.* Vols. 5 and 6. Cambridge: Harvard University Press, 1963.

Hoopes, James, ed. *Peirce on Signs.* Chapel Hill: University of North Carolina Press, 1991.

Houser, Nathan, and Christian Kloesel, eds. *The Essential Peirce: Selected Philosophi-*

cal Writings, Vol. I (1867–1893). Bloomington and Indianapolis: Indiana University Press, 1992.

Houser, Nathan, and the Peirce Edition Project. *The Essential Peirce: Selected Philosophical Writings, Vol. II (1893–1913)*. Bloomington and Indianapolis: Indiana University Press, 1998.

Howland, Mary Deems. *The Gift of the Other: Gabriel Marcel's Concept of Intersubjectivity in Walker Percy's Novels*. Pittsburgh: Dusquesne University Press, 1989.

Jones, Anne Goodwyn. *Tomorrow Is Another Day: The Woman Writer in the South*. Baton Rouge: Louisiana State University Press, 1981.

Ketner, Kenneth Laine. *His Glassy Essence: An Autobiography of Charles Sanders Peirce*. Nashville: Vanderbilt University Press, 1998.

Kierkegaard, Søren. *Stages on Life's Way*. Translated by Walter Lowrie. Princeton: Princeton University Press, 1940.

Kilmartin, Edward J., S.J. *The Eucharist in the West*. Edited by Robert J. Daly, S.J. Collegeville, Minn.: The Liturgical Press, 1998.

Kobre, Michael. *Walker Percy's Voices*. Athens: University of Georgia Press, 2000.

Lawson, Lewis A. *Following Percy*. Troy, N.Y.: Whitston Publishing Company, 1988.

———. *Still Following Percy*. Jackson: University Press of Mississippi, 1996.

Lawson, Lewis A., and Victor A. Kramer. *Conversations with Walker Percy*. Jackson: University Press of Mississippi, 1985.

———. *More Conversations with Walker Percy*. Jackson: University Press of Mississippi, 1993.

Lawson, Lewis A., and Elzbieta Oleksy. *Walker Percy's Feminine Characters*. Troy, N.Y.: Whitston Publishing Company, 1995.

Levi, Primo. *The Drowned and the Saved*. Translated by Raymond Rosenthal. New York: Vintage International, 1989.

Luschei, Martin. *The Sovereign Wayfarer: Walker Percy's Diagnosis of the Malaise*. Baton Rouge: Louisiana University Press, 1972.

Lynch, William F. *Christ and Apollo: The Dimensions of the Literary Imagination*. New York: The New American Library, 1960.

Madden, David. *Rediscoveries*. New York: Crown Publishers, 1971.

Murphey, Murray G. *The Development of Peirce's Philosophy*. Indianapolis: The Hackett Publishing Co., 1993.

O'Connor, Flannery. *Mystery and Manners*. Selected and edited by Sally and Robert Fitzgerald. New York: Farrar, Straus, and Giroux, 1969.

Oleksy, Elzbieta. *Plight in Common: Hawthorne and Percy*. New York: Peter Lang, 1993.

Peirce, Charles Sanders. *Essays in the Philosophy of Science*. Edited by Vincent Tomas. New York: The Liberty Arts Press, 1957.

Potter, Vincent G. *Peirce's Philosophical Perspectives*. New York: Fordham University Press, 1996.

Powers, Joseph M. *Eucharistic Theology*. New York: Herder and Herder, 1967.

Pridgen, Allen. *Walker Percy's Sacramental Landscapes*. Selinsgrove, Pa.: Susquehanna University Press, 2000.

Prochaska, Bernadette. *The Myth of the Fall and Walker Percy's* The Last Gentleman. New York: Peter Lang, 1992.

Quinlan, Kieran. *Walker Percy: The Last Catholic Novelist*. Baton Rouge: Louisiana State University Press, 1996.

Rahner, Karl. *Theological Investigations*. Vol. 4. Translated by Kevin Smith. New York: Crossroads Publishing, 1982.

Raposa, Michael L. *Peirce's Philosophy of Religion*. Bloomington and Indianapolis: Indiana University Press, 1989.

Rudnicki, Robert N. *Percyscapes: The Fugue State in Twentieth Century Southern Fiction*. Baton Rouge: Louisiana State University Press, 1999.

Samway, Patrick, S.J. *A Thief of Peirce: The Letters of Kenneth Laine Ketner and Walker Percy*. Jackson: University Press of Mississippi, 1995.

————. *Walker Percy: A Life*. New York: Farrar, Straus, and Giroux, 1997.

Schillebeekx, E. *Christ the Sacrament of the Encounter with God*. New York: Sheed and Ward, 1963.

Sebeok, Thomas. *A Sign Is Just a Sign*. Bloomington: Indiana University Press, 1991.

Singer, Milton. *Man's Glassy Essence: Explorations in Semiotic Anthropology*. Bloomington: Indiana University Press, 1984.

Steiner, George. *Grammars of Creation*. New Haven: Yale University Press, 2001.

————. *Real Presences*. Chicago: University of Chicago Press, 1988.

Stern, Karl. *The Flight from Woman*. New York: Farrar, Straus, and Giroux, 1965.

Stuhr, John J., ed. *Classical American Philosophy: Essential Readings and Interpretive Essays*. New York: Oxford University Press, 1987.

Tate, Allen. *Collected Essays*. Denver: Allen Swallow Press, 1959.

Taylor, Jerome. *In Search of Self: Life, Death, and Walker Percy*. Cambridge, Mass.: Cowley Publications, 1986.

Tharpe, Jac. *Walker Percy*. New York: G.K. Hall and Co., 1983.

Tocqueville, Alexis de. *Democracy in America*. Vols. 1 and 2. Translated by Henry Reeve. New York: The Colonial Press, 1900.

Tolson, Jay. *Pilgrim in the Ruins: A Life of Walker Percy*. New York: Simon and Schuster, 1992.

————, ed. *The Correspondence of Shelby Foote and Walker Percy*. New York: W.W. Norton and Co., 1997.

Wiener, Philip P., ed. *Charles Sanders Peirce: Selected Writings*. New York: Dover Publications, 1958.

Wyatt-Brown, Bertram. *The House of Percy*. New York: Oxford University Press, 1994.

INDEX

Abstraction, 44
Agapism, 23, 253
Alienation, 3, 42, 44–45, 59, 182
Allen, William Rodney, 71
Amnesia, 111–12
Angelism/bestialism, 125, 128, 136, 138–39
Arnold, Matthew, 107
Augustine, Saint, 42, 44, 57, 64, 82, 125
Authority, 84, 100, 115, 163, 177, 224
Autonomous self, 166

Bacon, Francis, 123, 251
Baptism, 114
Barfield, Owen, 53, 186, 256–57
Barzun, Jacques, 151
Battle of Verdun, 190
Behaviorism, 43, 119, 129, 250
Blake, William, 199
Brooks, Cleanth, 162

Citizen Kane (Welles), 206
Ciuba, Gary, 193
Community, 1–2, 20; of charity, 99,
   104–6, 176, 180, 213, 219, 247; with
   God, 31, 33; in history, 29; of knowers,
   38; mystical, 5, 17, 23, 33, 48, 50,
   53, 55, 66, 75, 81, 89, 102, 107, 114,
   117–20, 144, 181, 185; of saints, 3, 56;
   scientific, 4, 7–8, 49; semiotic, 20, 27,
   29, 43, 51–53, 88, 121, 128, 144, 147, 149;
   utopian, 3

Corrington, Robert S., 19–20, 21–22, 24,
   180
Coupler, 19, 21, 25–26, 33–34

"Decline of the Western" (Percy), 14
Deconstruction, 36
"Delta Factor, The" (Percy), 18, 136
Demoniac self, 165–66
Derrida, Jacques, 224
Descartes, René, 13–14, 24–25, 42–43;
   victims of, 51, 65, 95, 154; women and,
   156–57
Desire, 82, 84
Despair, 54, 189–90
Donne, John, 88
Dualism, 42, 52, 147, 154

Eliot, T. S., 141, 199
Eucharist, 5, 11, 27, 53–56, 84–85; community and, 29–33; dispossession and, 87,
   125, 130–31, 138–39; real presence and,
   224–25; transubstantiation and, 142
Everydayness, 44, 50, 57
Evolution, 23, 250, 253

"Fateful Rift: The San Andreas Fault in
   the Modern Mind, The" (Percy), 13, 17
Faulkner, William, 127
"Fixation of Belief, The" (Peirce), 19
Foote, Shelby, 43
Freud, Sigmund, 220

Gift giving, 29–31
Girard, Rene, 14, 49, 133–34, 222
Gnosticism, 126
God, 22, 26–27, 44, 51, 57, 188
Good news, 23, 34–35, 37, 54, 57
Grace, 202
Grail quest, 159, 173, 176
Guardini, Romano, 6–7, 9, 118

Hardy, John Edward, 209–10
Hawthorne, Nathaniel, 69
Hemingway, Ernest, 206
Holy Spirit, 22, 25–26, 28, 32, 51
Humanism, 100–101, 188, 216

Idealism, 15, 24
Immanence, 111
Incarnation, 5, 8, 16; community and,
    104–6, 244; coupler and, 204–5; history
    and, 33, 37, 215; person and, 26–27;
    science and, 252
Individualism, 6, 13–14, 17, 42, 57, 71, 95,
    99, 252–53
Interpretant, 19, 21, 25–26, 33–34
Intersubjectivity, 9, 12, 18, 21, 25, 31

James, Henry, 206
Jaspers, Karl, 156
Jesus, 25, 27, 29, 31–32, 34, 46, 52–53
Jewish-Christian Event, 5, 8, 33–34, 37
Jews, 44, 53, 58, 73, 186, 213, 224, 226–27
John, Saint, 141

Keller, Helen, 136, 204–5, 213
Kennedy, John F., 82
Ketner, Kenneth L., 15, 23, 28, 37
Kierkegaard, Søren, 5, 34, 38, 61, 68, 165

Logos, 5, 46, 146, 215, 223; eucharist and,
    54; Holocaust and, 237; interpretant
    and, 22, 27–29; Jews and, 186; nominal-

ism and, 123–24, 132; signs and, 43–44,
    192, 244
"Loss of the Creature, The" (Percy), 8
Lost in the Cosmos (Percy), 49, 95, 152, 156
Love, agape, 23, 253

"Man on the Train, The" (Percy), 37–38,
    44
Marquand, John P., 39
Meredith, George, 174
"Message in the Bottle, The" (Percy),
    25–26, 28, 37, 112
Montaigne, Michel, 91
Moviegoing, 44
Musement, 43
Mystery, 10, 13, 185; everydayness and,
    41; Incarnation and, 27, 181–82;
    objectivism and, 151, 158; personhood
    and, 28; search and, 43–44, 48–52,
    198; sex and, 165; signs and, 78,
    109
Myth, 217, 227

New anthropology, 4, 15, 23
Nominalism, 6, 14, 16, 36, 121, 124, 133,
    249–50
"Notes for a Novel about the End of the
    World" (Percy), 120, 132, 227
"Novel: Dying Art or New Science?, The"
    (Percy), 154

O'Connor, Flannery, 11, 27, 29, 36, 218–19,
    222, 240, 242

Paul, Saint, 27, 32–33, 37, 41, 184–86, 226,
    257
Peirce, Charles S., 4–5, 12, 198, 220, 249;
    community of knowers and, 38; God
    and, 51, 78; nominalism and, 121;
    semiotic community and, 43, 146, 215,
    229; theosemiotic and, 180

Percy, Walker, novels by: *Lancelot*,
144–78; *The Last Gentleman*, 81–
117; *Love in the Ruins*, 118–43; *The
Moviegoer*, 41–80; *The Second Coming*,
179–214; *The Thanatos Syndrome*,
215–48
Poe, Edgar Allan, 206
Poinset, John, 249
Pornography, 86, 151
Possibility, 54, 88, 110, 180, 209

Raposa, Michael L., 11, 15, 51
Realism, 5–6, 9, 15, 17, 19, 249, 252
Real Presence, 5, 11, 29, 43, 46, 61
Repetition, 61–62
Role playing, 45–46
Rosenblum, Ethel, 186, 196

Sacrament, 11, 105, 198; of the dispos-
sessed, 85
Sartre, Jean Paul, 44
Satan, 132, 157, 204, 217, 222, 237, 244,
246–47
"Science, Religion, and the Tertium
Quid" (Percy), 27, 251
Scientific humanism, 6, 76–77, 79, 119,
188, 216
Scientism, 7–9, 23, 29, 35–36, 39, 41–43,
49, 54, 85, 90, 102, 110, 118–19, 122, 133,
150, 152, 181, 217, 255–56
Search, 4; for community, 6, 9, 13, 41, 145;
for God, 43–44, 46–47, 50; horizontal,
53; vertical, 49, 62–63
Sign, 9, 14, 21–22, 29–30, 42–43; Firstness,
Secondness, Thirdness, 21–22, 24;
triadic, 114–15
Sin, 21, 144–45, 161–62

Solitude à deux, 4, 55, 57–59, 82, 84, 88,
96, 116, 147, 175, 177–79
Steiner, George, 9–12, 32, 36, 121, 224, 227,
237
Stern, Karl, 154–55
Stoicism, 14, 46, 48, 88, 163, 166, 222
"Stoicism in the South" (Percy), 76
Structuralism, 36
Suicide, 185, 195, 212
Sullivan, Harry Stack, 220
Symbol, 22

Thanatos, 228, 241, 243
Theosemiotic, 22, 44, 146, 177, 179–80,
182, 224, 243, 251
Thomas Aquinas, Saint, 18, 35, 125, 133,
136
Tocqueville, Alexis de, 13, 42, 46, 71, 95,
126, 210
Transcendence, 111
Transsignification, 30, 224
Transubstantiation, 30
Triadicity, 4, 17, 179, 183, 249, 253;
triadic/dyadic, 18, 20–21, 25, 114–15,
148–50, 168, 173; triadic relations, 45,
233

Unlimited Community, The (Feibleman
and Friend), 17, 250, 252, 256
Utopia (More), 122

Voegelin, Eric, 89

Whitehead, Alfred North, 160
Winthrop, John, 127
Word, divine, 123–24, 132, 186, 192. *See
also* Logos
"Why Are You a Catholic?" (Percy), 10–11